10
Basic Steps
Toward
Christian
Maturity

LEADER'S GUIDE

Bill Bright

NewLife
PUBLICATIONS
A MINISTRY OF CAMPUS CRUSADE FOR CHRIST

Ten Basic Steps Toward Christian Maturity
Leader's Guide

for

Ten Basic Steps Toward Christian Maturity booklets and
A Handbook for Christian Maturity

Published by
New*Life* **Publications**
100 Sunport Lane
Orlando, FL 32809

Printed in the United States of America.

ISBN: 1-56399-028-8

Thomas Nelson, Inc., Nashville, Tennessee, is the exclusive distributor of this book to the trade markets in the United States and the District of Columbia.

Distributed in Canada by Campus Crusade for Christ of Canada, Surrey, B.C.

Unless otherwise indicated, all Scripture references are from the *New International Version,* © 1973, 1978, 1984 by the International Bible Society. Published by Zonder-van Bible Publishers, Grand Rapids, Michigan.

Scripture quotations designated TLB are from *The Living Bible,* © 1971 by Tyndale House Publishers, Wheaton, Illinois.

Scripture quotations designated Phillips are from *Letters to Young Churches, A Trans-lation of the New Testament Epistles,* by J. B. Phillips, © 1947, 1957 by the MacMillan Company, New York, New York.

Scripture quotations designated NKJ are from the *New King James Version,* © 1979, 1980, 1982 by Thomas Nelson Inc., Publishers, Nashville, Tennessee.

Scripture quotations designated NASB are from the *New American Standard Bible,* © 1960, 1962, 1963, 1968, 1971, 1972, 1973, 1975, 1977 by the Lockman Foundation, La Habra, California.

Any royalties from this book or the many other books by Bill Bright are dedicated to the glory of God and designated to the various ministries of Campus Crusade for Christ/NewLife Ministries.

For more information, write:

L.I.F.E.—P. O. Box 40, Flemmington Markets, 2129, Australia
Campus Crusade for Christ of Canada—Box 300, Vancouver, B.C., V6C 2X3, Canada
Campus Crusade for Christ—Fairgate House, King's Road, Tyseley, Birmingham, B11 2AA, England
Lay Institute for Evangelism—P. O. Box 8786, Auckland 3, New Zealand
Campus Crusade for Christ—Alexandra, P. O. Box 0205, Singapore 9115, Singapore
Great Commission Movement of Nigeria—P. O. Box 500, Jos, Plateau State Nigeria, West Africa
Campus Crusade for Christ International—100 Sunport Lane, Orlando, FL 32809, USA

Contents

Acknowledgments

The *Ten Basic Steps Toward Christian Maturity* series was a product of necessity. As the ministry of Campus Crusade for Christ expanded rapidly to scores of campuses across America, thousands of students committed their lives to Christ—several hundred on a single campus. Individual follow-up of all new believers soon became impossible. Who would help them grow in their new-found faith?

A Bible study series designed for new Christians was desperately needed—a study that would stimulate individuals and groups to explore the depths and the riches of God's Word. Although several excellent studies were available, we felt the particular need of new material for these college students.

In 1955, I asked several of my staff associates to assist me in preparing Bible studies that would stimulate both evangelism and Christian growth in a new believer. The contribution by campus staff members was especially significant because of their constant contact with students in introducing them to Christ and meeting regularly with them to disciple them. Thus, the *Ten Basic Steps Toward Christian Maturity* was the fruit of our combined labor.

The popularity of this Bible study series soon revealed an additional problem, the need for a leader's guide. The Leader's Guide for the *Ten Basic Steps* developed quickly, with many members of the staff contributing generously. On occasion, for example, I found myself involved in research and writing sessions with several of our staff—all seminary graduates, some with advanced degrees and one with his doctorate in theology. More important, all were actively engaged in "winning, building, and sending men" for Christ.

For this latest edition, I want to thank Don Tanner for his professional assistance in revising, expanding, and editing the contents. I also want to thank Joette Whims and Jean Bryant for their extensive help and for joining Don and me in the editorial process.

A Personal Word

Drew was a sharp, dedicated high school senior who provided leadership to the youth group in his church. Through the influence of his parents and the church, he received Christ as a young boy. But, like many young people who grow up in church, he experienced little spiritual growth.

One summer Drew rededicated his life to Christ, but he still felt something was missing . . .

Christine and Dale were both on their second marriage. Christine had met Dale soon after her divorce and married him because she was lonely. Then two children came along, and marital problems arose.

A friend introduced Dale to Jesus Christ and he became anxious to grow in his spiritual life. Christine, who had been a Christian for many years but had not been living a holy life, rededicated herself to serving the Lord. But Christine and Dale still had many issues they needed to re-solve between them. They needed biblical guidance and Christian fellowship . . .

How can people like Drew and Christine and Dale experience spiritual growth? How will they know how to tap into the great resources of an almighty God? One of the best ways I know is through a small group Bible study.

As a result of attending a Bible study like that, Drew came to realize that living the Christian life is not simply difficult—it is impossible. Only through the power of the Holy Spirit can we have the strength to resist temptation and make the right choices.

"The message had never reached me that I must let the Lord, in the form of the Holy Spirit, live the Christian life through me," Drew says. "I cannot express the joy I felt when I discovered that the 'burden' of living the Christian life is really no burden at all because the Holy Spirit will live it through me if I invite Him and trust Him to do so." His discovery of the person and power of God's Holy Spirit has transformed him into a joyful Christian and a vibrant witness for Christ.

Joining a group Bible study also gave Christine and Dale the resources to enrich their marriage and find the peace with God that they desired.

Leading Bible studies using the *Ten Basic Steps Toward Christian Maturity* will help you introduce others to this power source for their lives. These studies will take you on an exciting journey through many important scriptural concepts. You will deepen your understanding of vital truths and will help others experience the adventure of the Christian life. You and your group will learn how to apply what you learn in your daily lives. You also will help them develop leadership qualities that will enable them to influence others for Jesus Christ.

As I have seen many times over the years, leading a small group can benefit you even more than your group. The challenge of leadership will help you learn to delight in the Lord every day, even when circumstances are not so delightful. Boredom will become excitement. Hopelessness will become hope. Your walk with God will take on a new dimension of purpose and power because you are allowing the Holy Spirit to do His work in and through your life.

My prayer is that this series of studies will bless and enrich your life and the lives of your group members in a dramatic, supernatural way, that your leadership will help you toward full maturity in Jesus Christ as you become more like Him, and that you will become more effective in your personal witness for Him. I guarantee that leading this series of Bible studies will change your life forever. You will experience one of the deepest joys in life—seeing the Lord develop and mature others through you.

Bill Bright

What This Study Will Do for You

The *Ten Basic Steps* is a time-tested study series designed to provide you and your students with a sure foundation for your faith. It also will help your students discover how to enjoy what millions of other Christians around the world have experienced: the adventure of a full, purposeful, and fruitful life in Christ.

The Christian who has been living in spiritual defeat, powerless and fruitless, wondering if there is any validity to the Christian life, will find hope in these pages. The study will emphasize:

1) *The distinctiveness of Christianity.* No religion makes provision for the breach between God and man that the Bible calls sin. But Christianity does deal with it—not by what man can do for God, as taught in other religions, but through what God has done for man in sending His Son, Jesus Christ, to die on the cross for our sins.

2) *The distinctive claims of Christ.* Many people believe Christ was only a good moral teacher. This study will make it clear that He claimed to be God in human form. Those who study this series will decide whether He is the true God or a liar and imposter.

3) *The abundant life that God provides for every Christian through the power of the Holy Spirit.* The lives of many people have been utterly transformed through an understanding of the abundant life God has for them and of the doctrine of the filling of the Holy Spirit.

You are about to begin one of the most life-changing Bible studies ever developed.

4) *The importance of walking daily with God.* This study gives practical suggestions on how to walk daily with God. At the end of each lesson, students are challenged to apply the principles they learned. Because the studies build on each other, group members will find increasing commitment to live holy lives.

Certain basic spiritual truths, when understood and experienced by faith, bring revolutionary spiritual benefits. The proven principles in this study can help introduce non-Christians to the joyful adventure of a relationship with God.

In addition, this study is good for those who do not yet know Christ as Savior because it:

◆ Helps them understand the Bible

◆ Presents the claims and person of Christ

◆ Clearly shows them how to become Christians and gives them an opportunity to receive Christ

◆ Teaches them how to live the Christian life

The study will also benefit new Christians in the following ways:

◆ Aid them in their spiritual growth as they apply the principles they learn

◆ Increase their familiarity with the Bible

◆ Teach them the basic doctrines of the Christian faith

◆ Help them find scriptural solutions for the problems of their lives

◆ Inspire and equip them to share the gospel with others

Even the more mature Christians will benefit from this series. They will grow in their faith, and they will be challenged to affirm their commitment to our Lord. For them this study will do the following:

◆ Provide the tools needed to help another person find Christ or to help a younger Christian grow in his faith

◆ Help them establish a systematic devotional and study plan

A faithful study of the *Ten Basic Steps Toward Christian Maturity* and of the material in this Leader's Guide will prepare you for a more comprehensive ministry. It will focus and strengthen your own purpose, your desire to help change the world (your neighborhood, workplace, school, and other places to which God leads you) for Jesus Christ.

How to Start a Bible Study Group

Have you ever tried to follow a recipe or assemble a small appliance without reading the directions thoroughly? Possibly you got all the way through your work and discovered that you had left out an essential step, and the result was a disaster.

Personal preparation is a vital first step to starting your Bible study group. Be sure that Christ is Lord of your life, and that you are filled with the Holy Spirit.

I encourage you to read these booklets: the *Four Spiritual Laws* and *Have You Made the Wonderful Discovery of the Spirit-Filled Life?* They contain the basic principles you need to live that victorious Christian life and be an effective leader of your group. You can obtain the booklets from your local Christian bookstore, mail-order distributor, or NewLife Publications.

Next, pray for God's leading and blessing. If you are responsible for starting your own group, invite your friends or announce your plans for a Bible study to others at your job or in your school or neighborhood.

Often those to whom you have witnessed but who have not yet received Christ as Savior will be interested in participating in a Bible study group. You can also show the video *A Man Without Equal* to neighbors, friends, or relatives and encourage those who receive Christ or are interested in growing in their faith to participate in your

Personal preparation is a vital first step to starting your Bible study group.

group. The video presentation on page 22 will show you how to use the video.

New Christians and others who need follow-up are likely prospects for your group as well. Choose the ones you think would be most interested, pray about them individually, then visit each one personally. After you make the contacts, select a meeting place and time for your Bible study.

Keep your group small. With eight to twelve people, group members will feel freer to interact and discuss the lesson material. You will also be able to give them individual attention as they begin to apply biblical truths in their lives.

Be sure your meeting place is neat, attractive, and well-ventilated. Choose a place where you will be free from interruptions. If several days lapse between your initial contact and the first Bible study, remind those who have expressed interest. Make an announcement, speak to them personally, phone them, or send cards.

Avoid pressuring anyone to join your group. At the same time, do not have a negative or apologetic attitude. The best way to promote interest and enthusiasm is to be interested and enthusiastic yourself. Let me suggest a couple of approaches:

"John, you've expressed an interest in knowing more about Christianity and the Bible. (Show him Lesson 1 of the Introductory Step.) This has been a tremendous help to me in learning about the Bible in a short time. I think it could be a real help to both of us if we studied together."

Or, "Mary, several of us are getting together to study the Bible. We believe that if we do it as a group, we will all benefit. Why don't you join us?"

As you pray and wait on God, He will lead you to those He has chosen for your study.

Your Bible study group may be made up of Christians at different levels of spiritual maturity and possibly some who have not yet received Christ as Savior. A few may already be familiar with some of the content while for others it will be completely new.

The informal nature of the Bible study is ideal for helping students learn from each other as well as from the things you say. Your Leader's Guide is carefully designed to help you guide the group's discovery of scriptural principles and to show how these truths can be applied to their lives.

How to Lead a Bible Study Group

Carl Sharsmith, an 81-year-old tour guide in California's Yosemite Park, had a deep love for nature. He and his "Smokey Bear" hat with the cracked leather band had spent fifty years helping tourists discover the wonders of the spectacular park.

Today, his sunburned nose was dotted with flakes of white skin and his eyes were watery. He looked discouraged. He had heard once again the same old question he had heard repeatedly during his many years as a guide. A female tourist had rushed up to him and exclaimed, "I've got only an hour to spend at Yosemite. What should I do? Where should I go?"

The old naturalist replied with a sigh, "Ah, lady, only an hour." He paused and looked at the grandiose landscape all around them, then said, "I suppose that if I had only an hour to spend at Yosemite, I'd just walk over there by the river and sit down and cry."[1]

Maybe that's how you feel when you consider the content of the Bible and leading a Bible study. Perhaps you're thinking, *Leading a Bible study group scares me. How will I start the discussion? Will I have enough material? How can I help my group apply the biblical principles they are learning to*

❖

To be effective as a leader, you should work at putting into practice yourself the principles you will be teaching.

[1] Adapted from "Yosemite—Forever?" *National Geographic Magazine,* National Geographic Society, Washington, D. C., January 1985, vol. 167, no. 1, p. 55.

their lives? How can I pass on to others the joy and excitement I feel in my relationship with God?

The *Ten Basic Steps Toward Christian Maturity* Leader's Guide was designed to help you present basic biblical principles in a logical way and to give your students a broad survey of the Christian faith. They will learn how to tap into the supernatural power of God for those life situations that require more than will power.

As a leader, you will help your students grow and mature in Christ. To be more effective, you should work at putting into practice yourself the principles you will be teaching. It is not necessary to master each concept, or to feel that your performance in each area is perfect. It is essential, however, that you grow in your relationship with Christ, in your walk in the Spirit, in the study of God's Word, and in sharing your faith with others.

Remember, learning is accomplished only when lives are changed. Focus on the applications of the lessons, not just on memorizing the points. If your students are having problems in any particular area, concentrate on that, but let them discover for themselves how God works in their lives rather than relying on you for their learning.

Guidelines for Leading

Begin preparing for your group by thoroughly reading the following section of your Leader's Guide. When leading the sessions, follow these guidelines:

◆ Create an informal atmosphere so you and your group can get to know each other. Address each person by name. Introduce new members before the discussion begins. Contact visitors during the week following their visit and invite them to return for the next session.

◆ Pray daily for each person in your group.

◆ Keep your Bible open at all times. If your students are unfamiliar with the Bible, offer to help them find Scripture verses and allow time for them to locate the passages in their own Bibles. If a student does not have a Bible, help him obtain one. The lesson material uses the *New International Version*. Bring extra Bibles and pencils for students to use during the study time.

◆ Be yourself. Depend on the Holy Spirit to work through the person you are, not through an artificial "spiritual leader" image that you would like to project.

◆ Don't be bound to your notes. Maintain eye contact with your group.

◆ Do not leave your group once the discussion has started. If you need materials or extra chairs, ask someone else to get them.

◆ A group leader is a discussion guide, not a lecturer. Rather than dominating the discussion, draw out comments from your students. Be prepared to suggest ideas, give background material, and ask questions to keep the conversation lively and relevant. If a student is saying something productive and to the point, refrain from inserting your own thoughts. When he finishes, guide, clarify, and summarize. Keep the discussion centered on the principle passages of Scripture. Encourage silent members of the group to get involved in the discussion.

◆ When you ask a question, allow time for students to think before continuing. Then listen to their answers rather than mentally planning what you are going to say next. Remember, you are teaching people, not lessons.

◆ Make sure everyone understands the major points in the lesson.

◆ Get involved in the lives of your group members. Communicating the basic truths of the Christian life is more than passing on information; it is sharing life experiences. Help them put into practice the truths you are teaching. The way you model and mentor through your personal example will have a far greater impact on your group than any of the words you say in a meeting.

◆ Recognize that each group has its own personality. Some groups are active, others are more subdued. Adapt your leadership style to fit your group. Your most important quality as a leader is to be open to the Holy Spirit's guidance as you help your students apply the lessons they are learning.

How to Encourage Participation

The chief goal of your group is to help members mature in Christ. Your objective in all Bible studies is to encourage spiritual maturity that leads to evangelism—introducing non-Christians to Christ. Your main activity should be studying the Scriptures, and any discussion should follow the study outline in the lesson plan.

To encourage participation, sit in a circle. Ideally, no group should have more than twelve people to avoid losing a feeling of intimacy. When your group exceeds that number, you may want to divide into two Bible studies.

Here are some suggestions for encouraging members to participate and for making the discussion time interesting and practical:

◆ Ask the group to read the Bible passage to be discussed, with each person reading one verse aloud. Invite one member to summarize the passage in his own words before asking any questions about it.

◆ Break into teams of two or three to discuss certain parts of the lesson, then gather to share the answers with the entire group. This may be particularly helpful in areas that are more personal.

◆ When discussing the study questions, ask specific students to answer, but avoid embarrassing anyone. When you ask a question of a member, be sure he answers it aptly. If he stumbles, help him along and make him feel that he did answer the question, at least in part. Compliment him on his response.

◆ If you sense confusion about a question you ask, restate it in different words or from another point of view.

◆ If possible, have several parallel passages planned for each study Scripture and question. If students don't know how to answer a question, suggest that someone read one of the parallel passages. Ask the group, "What similarities do you see between this passage and the one we have been studying?" Then ask, "What light does this new passage throw upon the original question?"

◆ After one person has made a point, ask others if they agree. Invite them to state their reasons. Often a great deal can be learned by disagreeing over a passage. To keep the discussion from turning into an argument, remind everyone that you are studying what the Bible says about a specific subject.

◆ Keep the discussion relevant and personal. Don't let one person dominate the discussion. To redirect the discussion, restate the question or move on to the next question.

◆ If a person asks a question that is off the topic, tactfully explain that it would be best not to take class time to discuss it. Offer to help answer the question after the study is over.

◆ Define all unusual words.

◆ To stimulate discussion, ask such questions as, "What do you think this passage means?" "What can this passage teach us about God, Christ, ourselves, our responsibilities, our relationship with others?"

◆ Help the students apply the passage personally. Ask, "What significance does this have for us today?" "What does this mean to you?" "How does this verse make you feel?" "How does (or will) it affect your life?"

◆ Keep the discussion moving. If you go through the material too quickly, the study will be shallow; if you go too slowly, it will seem tedious and boring. Don't spend too much time on any one section, but be sure you cover each major point.

◆ At the end of the discussion, ask someone to summarize the points that have been made. It is usually wise for the leader to guide the final summary and application.

◆ Be punctual in beginning and ending the session.

◆ Make the group time enjoyaable. Allow extra time after the study for individual counseling, social interaction, and refreshments if appropriate.

Techniques of Asking Good Questions

Asking good questions can mean the difference between students really thinking or giving rote answers. Formulate extra questions that apply to your group. Learning how to ask the right questions can bring up problems that the students have been grappling with but have been reluctant to mention. Also, good questions will facilitate learning. Use the following suggestions as a guideline for developing your leadership in this area:

◆ Ask questions in an informal way, implying that the student is able to answer.

◆ Distribute questions so that all have an equal opportunity to respond, but avoid using a purely mechanical method such as going alphabetically or in seating order.

◆ Strike a balance between letting volunteers answer and encouraging shy people to respond.

◆ Plan your questions so you can lead your group through the material in an organized way.

◆ If the question is not understood, restate it or ask for someone in the group to explain what it means.

◆ When a person says he is not able to answer a question, assume this is true. Don't prod.

◆ Develop questions that apply to both the material and the group's immediate situation.

◆ Avoid asking one-answer questions or questions with obvious answers.

◆ If a question will be answered later in the lesson, don't respond or agree with the answer at that time.

Objectives of the Study

1. **Be sure that each person knows how to become a Christian.** Although you may have new believers in your group, you may also have worldly Christians (those who continually allow self rather than the Holy Spirit to control their lives) or non-Christians as well. In the Introductory Step, emphasize the difference between someone simply knowing about the material studied and experiencing the principles in his life.

2. **Be sure that each believer knows he is a Christian.** Many people are unsure of their relationship with God. At the end of the Introductory Step, each person in your class should be able to clearly explain his personal commitment to Christ and understand that his salvation is because of his trust in Christ and not in any works he may do (Ephesians 2:8,9).

3. **Help each person to grow in his Christian life.** While studying these lessons, the members of your group will learn who Jesus is, how to be sure of their salvation, how to experience God's love and forgiveness, how to be filled with the Holy Spirit and live a Spirit-filled life, and how to grow as a Christian.

4. **Help each person understand his role in helping to fulfill the Great Commission.** The main purpose of the Bible study is to encourage Christian growth and to challenge Christians to reach others for Christ and, in turn, help these new believers reach still others for our Lord. As one of its chief goals, each group should plan to produce leaders for other groups .

How to Teach the Lessons

To teach this series of studies most effectively, read "How to Use This Study" in the *Handbook for Christian Maturity* or in the individual *Ten Basic Steps* booklets. Study each part of the lesson before the group session. *There is no substitute for preparation.* Studying the lesson thoroughly will enable you to lead the discussion with confidence. If you take shortcuts in your preparation time, it will be obvious to your group.

Prepare yourself for each session by doing the following:

◆ Pray for the individuals in the group. Keep a list of each person's special needs and refer to your list during your personal prayer time.

◆ Thank God for what He will teach all of you.

◆ Read the objectives of the lesson.

◆ Study the verses and answers to the questions in each lesson. Since many of the answers are printed in your Leader's Guide, you may be tempted to skip this step. However, familiarity with the Scripture references and answers will help you during the group discussion.

Most of the student material in the *Handbook for Christian Maturity* and in the individual *Ten Basic Steps Toward Christian Maturity* booklets is reproduced in the lesson for your convenience. Suggested answers appear after many of the questions. Use them as a guide for your discussion.

Each lesson includes the following main parts:

Leader's Objective: This goal will help you keep the lesson on track. To help your students meet it, keep the goal in mind as you prepare the lesson and guide the discussion. A helpful technique is to jot the goal in your Leader's Guide where you want to emphasize it.

As you prepare your own objectives, also read the objectives appearing in the introduction of each lesson in the student's books. They will help you guide the students in establishing and reaching the desired goals. As you lead the study, encourage your students to memorize the verses listed in their manuals and review them regularly with your group to help them retain what they have learned. The suggested Bible reading should be done on the student's own time rather than in class.

Opening Prayer: The intent of the prayer is to focus on the truth being studied.

Discussion Starter: Your opening remarks and the resulting discussion should stimulate thinking but not necessarily supply answers. Guide the discussion by interjecting questions, but do not correct wrong answers at this time.

Lesson Development: This section gives directions for leading the Bible Study. The ideas will help you vary your presentation, involve each person, and help group members understand each principle studied. Adapt the teaching suggestions to your group size and personalities and to your leadership style.

When reading Scripture passages, use different methods. For example:

◆ Read the passage aloud while the group follows along.

◆ Have everyone read it silently.

◆ Ask a different person to read each paragraph or each verse.

◆ Ask one member to read while others follow along.

◆ Divide into groups of two or three and have each read the verses.

As you come to the questions from the students' books, discuss each of them. Encourage members to get their answers either from the Scripture or from their own thinking. Share the answers suggested in this Leader's Guide only if necessary.

Conclusion and Application: This section will challenge your group to apply what they have learned. Lead your students to make personal decisions. Many of the Life Application questions should be answered privately, silently, without discussion. Your role is to guide your students' thinking, then lead them into the prayer time. Plan frequent opportunities for group members to make definite commitments to the Lord.

Closing Prayer: These prayers should be worded to aid you in leading the students to a commitment to the Lord. Either you or one of the members may lead in prayer. Or give your students a moment to personally, silently communicate with God. Again, motivation and commitment to action are the main goals of this section.

A Man Without Equal Video Presentation

O ne of the most effective ways to introduce Jesus to others and to assist believers to grow and mature in their Christian faith is to show the thirty-minute video, *A Man Without Equal.* Showing this video in advance to different individuals and groups can help you begin your study group. Schedule several showings and challenge those who respond to the message in the video to join your Bible study. Here are some suggested ways you can use the video:

- ◆ Have a video party in your dorm room or student lounge.
- ◆ Plan a showing to your fraternity or sorority.
- ◆ Present the video to an athletic team.
- ◆ Show the video during your Sunday school class or an evening church service.
- ◆ Use it during a retreat.
- ◆ Invite friends and neighbors into your home for a special showing.
- ◆ Present the video during the lunch hour or another appropriate time at your job.
- ◆ Arrange showings to service men or women in your military unit.
- ◆ Use it as part of your prison ministry.
- ◆ Show the video to your civic group.
- ◆ Give a video to individuals whom you are seeking to introduce to Christ, and arrange a follow-up appointment.

Showing this video can help you begin your Bible study.

Prepare for your video showing by making a list of those you plan to invite. Pray for each one, asking God to prepare their hearts.

Choose the place for the meeting. You will need one to two hours, depending on whether you serve refreshments. Your home would be an excellent informal setting. For a larger group, consider renting a room in an apartment complex, piblic library, or other facility. Perhaps your employer has a meeting room you can reserve.

Then decide if you will provide refreshments. They should be simple and easy to serve so you can concentrate on the presentation. You could ask a Christian friend to be host and arrange for the food.

Begin inviting people two or three weeks before the presentation. If appropriate, send invitations. Those you contact are more likely to remember and respond to a written invitation than word-of-mouth or a telephone call. Mention in the invitation that you are showing a video about Jesus called *A Man Without Equal.* List the date, time, and place of the meeting. Include your phone number so people can let you know whether they will attend, ask questions about the meeting, or leave your number with a babysitter. If you are serving refreshments, mention that too.

The number of guests you invite will vary with your situation. If you know everyone on your prospective guest list quite well, send about twice as many invitations as you want guests at the presentation. If you do not know your potential guests, you may need to send six times as many invitations.

Two to three days before the meeting, call each person on your list. This will dramatically increase attendance, and allow you to answer any concerns or questions they may have about the event.

Prepare your materials in advance. You will need the following:

◆ A television set

◆ A VCR

◆ *A Man Without Equal* video

◆ The discussion card that comes with the video

◆ Blank 3×5 cards

◆ Pens or pencils

◆ A *Four Spiritual Laws* booklet for each person attending

The day of the video showing, arrange the meeting room so everyone will have a good view of the TV screen. Put your materials on the most centrally located table or chair so you can guide the discussion after the presentation. Greet your guests warmly as they arrive. Put them at ease and create a friendly atmosphere. Ask your guests about their families, jobs, schools, or other personal interests. Discuss current events from the newspaper, radio, or TV, or talk about a good book that you have read. Avoid discussing your church or Christian subjects that might make a non-Christian feel uncomfortable.

When it is time to begin the meeting, ask your guests to be seated a seat. Thank your host and state the reason for the showing. Keep your comments to just a couple of minutes. Then explain that you will be handing out cards for each of them to write down their comments after following the video.

Here is an example of what you could say:

Before we see the video, I want to thank Brian for providing refreshments. Both he and I are excited about what Jesus has been doing in our lives. That is why we have asked all of you to see this video. It shows who Jesus is and how He has changed the course of history.

After we have seen the video, we'll have a short discussion time. Then, I would like each of you to comment on the video and this evening's discussion. When we finish, we'll have something to eat and spend time getting to know each other.

I'm going to start the video now. I'm sure you will find it challenging.

Dim the lights and start the video. At the conclusion of the video, discuss questions 1 through 5 from the "Questions for Reflection and Discussion" that accompany the video. The following are sample responses to the questions:

1. What was Jesus' greatest teaching? (Mark 16:16; John 3:16-18) *That salvation is by faith, not works. According to Romans 3:23, all of us have sinned and do not measure up to God's standards. Sin is going our way independent of God. Jesus died on the cross to pay the penalty for our sins. He came to reconcile us to God.*

   Why was this teaching so unique? *All other major religions teach that we must work our way to God.*

   What does this teaching mean in your life? *It means that I can have a relationship with God without first having to make myself acceptable to Him.*

2. Give several examples of how Jesus' influence on people and nations has altered the course of history, your country, your

city, your neighborhood. *Allow guests to discuss each of these points freely.*

3. What are people in your circle of influence saying about Jesus? What are some of the doubts you have felt about Jesus either in the past or in the present? *Allow guests to give their opinions on both of these questions. Be sensitive to those who are still uncertain of what Jesus means to them.*

4. What personal feelings about Jesus were confirmed as you watched the video? *Begin the discussion by giving your feelings. Then let others respond.*

5. Jesus claimed to be the Son of God and the Savior of mankind. After viewing the video, who do you believe He is? *Jesus is the Son of God and my Savior.*

How would you explain this to others? *Let others give their ideas.*

Next, pass out the 3×5 cards and pencils. Ask the viewers to write their names, addresses, and telephone numbers on one side of the card. On the other side, ask them to:

1. Write brief answers to these questions:

◆ Have you received Jesus as your Savior and Lord? When?

◆ Are you interested in learning more about how Jesus can change your life?

Describe the Bible study that you will be starting. Explain that you will contact them later about the time and place for your group meeting.

2. Write specific comments about the video and the discussion.

If some in your group are Christians who are growing in their relationship to Christ, challenge them with question 6 from "Questions for Reflection and Discussion." If most are not believers or have just made a decision to follow Christ, skip this question and invite all those who have viewed the video to join your group.

Thank your guests for coming and explain that you will be available for any questions during the refreshment time. Then dismiss your group with a prayer similar to this one:

Dear Jesus,

Thank You for Your presence here in this meeting. Thank You for dying on the cross and paying for each of our sins. Help each person make a decision to receive You into his or her life. Help us serve You. Amen.

Collect the cards and serve the refreshments. While others are chatting and eating, be available to talk to anyone who may want to receive Christ as Savior or who has questions. If someone is unsure of how to receive Christ, go through the *Four Spiritual Laws* booklet with him.

After your guests leave, look over the 3×5 cards and plan when you can contact each person. Prayerfully do so over the next few days, if at all possible. Encourage each one to come to your group.

Through your obedience and the power of the Holy Spirit, you can help change your world for Christ through your study group. In the process, you will gain lifelong friendships and influence the lives of many people. And you will experience the joy and excitement that Christ gives to those who earnestly desire to serve others in His name.

The Uniqueness *of* Jesus

The Life & Teachings of Jesus

INTRODUCTION

Who Is Jesus Christ?

Opening Prayer

Discussion Starter

(In this opening session, introduce yourself, welcome everyone to the study, and be sure all the students have met each other. Then ask for brief responses to these questions:)

❓Who is Jesus Christ?

❓Explain your answer.

Lesson Development

(Ask the students to share insights about the paragraphs at the beginning of the lesson. When you get to the chart, you may use the following material to discuss the prophecies concerning Jesus:)

Following are some additional fulfilled prophecies:

◆ Zechariah 11:12; Matthew 27:9,10—The exact amount paid for Jesus' betrayal.

◆ Isaiah 50:6; Matthew 26:67—He would be scourged and spit upon.

Leader's Objective: To present Jesus Christ as the Son of God, to acquaint group members with His claims, and to enable them to recognize who He is

LESSON 1

Bible Study

Jesus' Claims Concerning Who He is

1. In your own words, write the claims Christ made concerning Himself in the following verses:

   Mark 14:61,62
   (I am the Christ.)

   John 6:38; 8:42
   (God the Father sent me.)

   John 5:17,18
   (I do whatever God the Father does.)

   John 10:30
   (I and the Father are one.)

   What did those who heard what Jesus said think He meant?

   John 14:7
   (We know God by knowing Jesus.)

   John 14:8,9
   (Anyone who has seen Jesus has seen the Father.)

2. What did Jesus claim to do in the following verses?

   John 5:22
   (Judge mankind.)

   Matthew 9:6
   (Forgive sins.)

   John 6:45–47
   (Anyone who comes to Jesus comes to the Father too.)

3. What did Jesus predict in the following verses?

   Mark 9:31
   (His betrayal and death.)

◆ Psalm 69:21; Matthew 27:34,48— He would be given gall and vinegar.

◆ Psalm 50:3–5; Ezekiel 21:27; Zechariah 14:1–7; Luke 1:31–33; Philippians 2:10,11 (all yet to be fulfilled)—He will come again in glory to judge the nations.

Jesus Christ exists eternally (John 8:56–58). To free men from condemnation for their sin, He took upon Himself the form of man, becoming totally human, yet totally divine (Philippians 2:6,7).

◆ His *humanity* is illustrated by His birth of a human mother, His natural human growth and development (Luke 2:40), His emotions, His need for sleep, His hunger, and His thirst.

◆ His *deity* is pointed out by the name Immanuel ("God with us") (Matthew 1:23), by the miracles He did (especially His resurrection), by His witness of Himself (John 5:17–19; 10:30–33), and by the witness of the New Testament writers.

Peter later states in Acts 4:12:

> Salvation is found in no one else, for there is no other name under heaven given to men by which we must be saved.

To prove His claims, Jesus preached sermons that have never been equaled (Matthew 5—7) and performed miracles such as feeding 5,000 people with five loaves of bread, walking on water, controlling the wind and other forces of nature, healing the desperately sick, giving life to a man who had been dead

Luke 18:31–33
(He would be handed over, mocked, spit on, flogged, and killed.)

John 14:1–3
(He would go to heaven to prepare a place for His followers, then come back again.)

4. What characteristics of Jesus are attributes of an omnipotent God?

John 2:24
(He knows all men.)

Matthew 8:26,27
(He controlled nature.)

John 11:43–45
(He raised the dead.)

According to the above passages, Jesus claimed to be God. He made the kinds of claims that only a person who presumed he was God would make. Both His friends and His enemies called Him God, and He never attempted to deny it. He even commended His followers for believing He was God.

The Importance of the Truth About His Identity

1. Suppose Jesus Christ were not God. If He knew He was not God and that none of those claims were true, what could we conclude about Him?
   (That He was a liar or an imposter.)

2. Suppose Jesus were sincerely wrong. Suppose He sincerely believed all these fantastic claims, four days, and finally rising from the dead Himself.

Following are some other conclusions about who Jesus is (note that at the time these statements were made, none of these men were disciples— they were independent observers):

◆ Philip: "We have found the one Moses wrote about in the Law, and about whom the prophets also wrote—Jesus of Nazareth, the son of Joseph" (John 1:45).

◆ Nathaniel: "You are the Son of God; you are the King of Israel" (John 1:49).

◆ The centurion: "Surely he was the Son of God" (Matthew 27:54).

(Refer to the Trilemma diagram in the student's book, and discuss it along with the questions.)

(Share your testimony about who Jesus is to you. Allow about two minutes. In presenting your testimony, talk about how you have examined the evidence regarding Christ and how you have invited Him into your life *and*

even though they were not true. What could we conclude about Him?
(He was crazy.)

3. Why is it important to investigate His claims?
(He claimed to be the only way to God. If that is true, His claims are essential for our future.)

What Others Said About Who He Was

1. His followers:

   John the Baptist (John 1:29)
   (The Lamb of God who takes away sin.)

   Peter (Matthew 16:16)
   (The Son of the living God.)

   How did Jesus respond to what Peter said (verse 17)?
   (God has revealed this to him.)

   Martha (John 11:27)
   (The Son of God.)

   Thomas (John 20:28)
   (My Lord and my God.)

   How does Christ's response to what Thomas said (verse 29) apply to you?
   (We are blessed because we believe even though we haven't seen Jesus.)

   Paul (2 Corinthians 5:21; Titus 2:13)
   (He was made sin for us; He is God and Savior.)

2. His enemies:

   The Jews (John 10:33)
   (He blasphemed because He claimed to be God.)

have made Him your Lord and Master. If you have never asked Him to be your Lord and Master, do so before class.)

It is vital to consider Jesus' claim to be God, to be the author of a new way of life. Wherever His message has gone, new life, new hope, and purpose for living have resulted. If His claims were false, a "lie" has accomplished more good than the "truth" ever has.

The Bible tells us "God so loved the world that he gave his one and only Son, that whoever believes in him shall not perish but have eternal life" (John 3:16). In other words, the great chasm between God and man cannot be bridged by man's effort but only by God's effort through His Son, Jesus Christ.

Religion and philosophy have been defined as man's attempts to find God.

Christianity has been defined as God's only means of reaching man.

Judas (Matthew 27:3,4)
(Innocent.)

Pilate (Matthew 27:22, 23)
(Hadn't committed any crime.)

The Roman soldier (Matthew 27:54)
(He was the Son of God.)

3. Who do *you* believe Jesus is and on what do you base that belief? List the facts that particularly help you know that He is God.

1. Why is it important that you personally recognize who Jesus Christ really is?

2. Have you invited Jesus Christ into your life? (See "Your Invitation to Life" on page 33.)

3. What changes do you expect to experience in your life as a result of receiving Christ as your Savior and Lord?

❖ ❖ ❖

Conclusion and Application

Our lives are filled with many activities —such as studies, finances, athletics, social life, business, and home life— with no real purpose or meaning.

Jesus wants to come into your life and give you that needed meaning and purpose. He wants to forgive your sins and bridge the chasm between you and God. He does not want to come into your life simply as a guest, but He wants to be in control. Regarding the Lordship of Christ, Romans 10:9 says, "If you confess with your mouth, 'Jesus is Lord,' and believe in your heart that God raised him from the dead, you will be saved."

Closing Prayer

(Give an opportunity for those present to silently invite Christ into their lives if they have not previously done so. Close in an audible prayer of thanksgiving, and then ask:)

If any of you have invited Christ into your life today, would you please let me know before you leave? Thank you.

❖ ❖ ❖

The Earthly Life of Jesus Christ

Opening Prayer

Discussion Starter

(Ask for responses to this statement, then discuss:)

Yes, Jesus was a great teacher, but there have been many other good teachers as well. I don't see why the teachings of Jesus are necessarily any more important than those of other great men.

Lesson Development

(Ask one of the group members to summarize the paragraphs appearing at the opening of this lesson in the student's book. Note the diagram and discuss it.)

Leader's Objective: To present Jesus Christ as the greatest person who has ever lived and to lead students to the conclusion that His moral character, teachings, and influence upon history demonstrate that He is God

LESSON 2

Bible Study

The Entrance of Jesus Christ Into the World

1. On the basis of His statement in John 17:5, where was Jesus Christ before He came into the world? *(With the Father.)*

2. Read Matthew 1:18–23. In your own words, summarize the circumstances that surrounded Jesus' physical birth.

The New Testament passes over the next thirty years of Jesus' life almost in silence. Apparently the gospel writers were more anxious to portray the character and ministry of Jesus than to give us a chronological biography.

The Character of Jesus

1. From these verses, describe the character of Jesus:

   Mark 1:40–42
   (Compassionate: "filled with compassion.")

   Luke 23:33,34
   (Forgiving.)

   John 2:13–17
   (Zealous.)

   John 13:1–17
   (Humble.)

   Romans 5:8–10
   (Loving and committed.)

2. How does Jesus' attitude contrast with the attitude

Consider the Old Testament prophecies about Jesus' birth.

❓Could Jesus have orchestrated the events of His birth to fulfill the prophecies of the Old Testament Messiah? What does this prove about His claim to be God?

❓Why do these characteristics make Jesus unique among men?

Jesus' traits drew people to Him. Yet it was only those who put their faith in Jesus who remained faithful to Him after His death and resurrection. The crowds abandoned Him when the tide of events turned against Him. That's why it is so important for our

of His contemporaries toward the following?

Adults (Matthew 14:15–21)
(Concerned for people's welfare even when His disciples urged Him to send them away.)

Children (Mark 10:13–16)
(Took time for children when others wanted to send them away.)

Those who offend (Luke 9:51–56)
(Did not want to pronounce judgment on the offenders when others did.)

3. Why did the following people love Christ?

The widow of Nain (Luke 7:11–15)
(He raised her son from the dead.)

The sinful woman (Luke 7:36–50)
(He forgave her when others condemned her.)

Mary and Martha (John 11:30–44)
(He wept with them and raised their brother from the dead.)

4. From the beginning of His life, Jesus demonstrated unfailing grace, amazing wisdom, and astounding understanding and knowledge. He consistently pleased God.

The crowds found His compassion constant, and He was humble and meek before His enemies. He treated the poor

relationship with Jesus to be built on faith rather than emotional reasons or physical needs.

Many of the people who followed Christ later played a part in His final days and became part of the early church. Nicodemus helped bury Jesus. Mary Magdalene was the first to see Jesus at the tomb. The disciples became the first preachers and teachers in the early church. They were convinced that Jesus was God and that He gave them eternal life.

with respect and the children with love and tenderness. His character was pure, selfless, and sinless.

Jesus also proved His divine character through His immeasurable love, an unconditional love unique in history. He willingly offered Himself as a sacrifice for all sin and evil, and He gave the free gift of everlasting life to every person who would accept it. Only God in the flesh could have embodied all these characteristics.

Read Hebrews 4:15. How can Jesus understand our feelings so completely?
(He was tempted like we are.)

According to Luke 2:42–47, when did Jesus first demonstrate His depth of knowledge and commitment?
(When He was 12 years old.)

What was the general reaction to Jesus' remarks?
(Everyone who heard Him was amazed at His understanding and wisdom.)

5. Read Matthew 7:28,29. What other reactions do you think the people had to His teachings besides amazement?
(Respect, love, attraction to Him.)

Imagine yourself in Jesus' day, listening to Him

❖ How does Jesus' character help you trust Him more?

(Describe a time when you were in a crisis or under emotional stress and turned to Jesus for comfort and consolation. Explain to your students what it is about Jesus that makes Him such a good friend to you.)

Jesus caused people to take notice. Not all the reactions to Jesus' character were positive. Many religious leaders despised Jesus for claiming to be God. Although they admitted that He taught with authority and that He did miracles with tremendous power, these religious leaders would not believe that He was God. That made what He did very offensive to them and led to His death at their hands.

People around Jesus had either one reaction or the other. No one remained neutral to Him.

teach and observing His behavior. What would your reaction be?

6. How do you feel about Jesus?

Why?

Jesus Christ as a Teacher

1. What did Christ teach about the new birth (John 3:1–8)?
   (It is absolutely necessary in order to see the kingdom of God.)

   Why did he describe salvation in this way?
   (He wanted to help people understand the complete transformation when we receive Christ.)

2. What did Christ teach regarding His claims about Himself?

   John 10:11
   (He is the Good Shepherd, laying down His life for the sheep.)

   John 13:13,14
   (He is both Teacher and Lord.)

   John 15:1,5
   (He is the vine; we are the branches.)

   Matthew 5:17
   (He came not to abolish the Old Testament, but to fulfill it.)

   John 11:25,26
   (He is the resurrection and the life.)

   Which of these claims do you think is most important? Why?

In His conversation with Nicodemus, a religious leader, Jesus clearly explains that just as one enters the world as a physical being through physical birth, one can become a spiritual being (child of God, John 1:12) only through a spiritual birth.

The ideas and morals Jesus taught have been proven to be effective for almost 2,000 years. But His teaching that salvation is by faith, not works, is the most transforming and revolutionary idea ever taught. It was directly the opposite of what the religious leaders of His day were teaching. They were embroiled in traditions and ritual.

Today the same pattern is happening. Many religious people believe they have to earn the right to fellowship with God. But that is not possible. Only by listening to what Jesus teaches and receiving His offer for pardon from sin can we approach a holy and righteous God.

Jesus refers in Matthew 5:17 to prophecy and the Old Testament. At another time when He was in the synagogue, He read from Isaiah 61, the great prophecy of the Messiah. He laid the scroll down with the statement, "Today this Scripture is fulfilled in your hearing" (Luke 4:21).

Which has meant the most to you personally? Why?

3. What did Christ teach about His demands of His followers?

Mark 8:38
(They were not to be ashamed of Him.)

Mark 10:29,30
(Their faithfulness will be generously rewarded.)

Matthew 9:9
(He calls for immediate obedience.)

Matthew 11:29
(He wants us to work with Him and learn from Him.)

Luke 9:23
(His followers are to deny themselves and take up His cross and follow Him.)

John 13:34,35
(Those who would be His followers are to love one another.)

Which of these demands do you find easiest to follow?

How do you think Jesus wants you to deal with the difficult ones?

4. Many view Jesus as the greatest teacher in history. No other man has been quoted as often or has inspired as many books and articles. His teachings have given us clear, profound insights into the deepest questions of life. People flocked to hear Him speak. The dis-

Jesus' demands are not simply for ethical obedience; they are for completely committing yourself to Him. They represent the "totalitarian" claim of Jesus.

◆ Jesus demands public confession of Him (Matthew 1:32; Luke 12:8; Mark 8:38).

◆ He demands that we honor and care for others (Matthew 10:40; Luke 10:16; Mark 9:37).

◆ He demands first priority in our lives (Matthew 10:37; Luke 14:26; Mark 8:34).

◆ He demands that we believe only in Him (Acts 16:31).

In *The Impact of Jesus Christ on History,* the British scholar W. H. Griffith Thomas said:

In the case of all the other great names of the world's history ... experience has been that the particular man is first a power, then only a name, and last of all a mere memory. Of Jesus Christ the exact opposite is true. He died on a cross of shame,

ciples left everything to follow Him.

What kind of teacher could inspire such loyalty? (See John 6:66–69 for help in formulating your answer.)
(A person who is self-sacrificing, has unconditional love, and is God in the flesh.)

From the following verses, list characteristics of Jesus that made Him such an excellent teacher:

Mark 6:34
(Compassionate.)

Luke 21:29–38
(Wise, knows the future.)

Luke 4:14–30
(Knew the Scriptures, spoke the truth regardless of the consequences.)

John 3:1–8; 7:50,51; 19:38–42
(Understood the heart and needs of a person, took time with individuals.)

5. Carefully read Matthew 7:7–12 from the Sermon on the Mount. How did Jesus use the following teaching methods to emphasize His lessons?

Repetition of ideas
(Repeats ask, seek, and find.)

Practical application
(Relates the point to a father/son relationship— something common to His listeners.)

His name gradually became more and more powerful, and He is the greatest influence in the world today.

The present social status of men, women, and children is so familiar to us that we sometimes fail to realize what it was before Christ came. In the Roman world the father had absolute right over his children to sell, to enslave, to kill them. It is Christianity that has made these atrocities impossible. Woman was the living chattel of her husband, as she is still in some parts of the world. It is through Christianity that she has obtained a new status, and now in Christian countries, 'Home' receives its true and full meaning. The slavery of the Roman Empire was absolute . . . often exercised with cruelty and ferocity. But Christianity proclaimed the universality and brotherhood of all men in Christ, and thereby struck at the root of slavery, and wherever the Gospel of Christ has had its way, slavery has been compelled to disappear.

Caleb Cushing, statesman and former Attorney General of the United States, suggests:

The Christian religion levels upward, elevating all men to the same high standard of sanctity, faith and spiritual promise on earth as in heaven.

Clear summarization
(Is concise and focused on the important points.)

6. What was even more important than Christ's effective teaching methods (Matthew 7:29)?
(His authority.)

Where did He get this authority (John 12:49, 50)?
(From His Father.)

Summarize how Jesus' earthly life confirmed His deity.
(Jesus had a unique birth; had a sinless, loving character; taught with authority; was an example to His followers.)

LIFE APPLICATION

1. Give at least three reasons you can trust Jesus' teachings:
   1) *(He is God.)*
   2) *(He knows the future.)*
   3) *(He loves me.)*

2. List three ways these teachings can change your life:
   1)
   2)
   3)

3. Plan how you will implement these changes.

Christ's authority is a central issue. If He is God, He has all authority. If He is an impostor or a liar, He cannot back up what He says. Jesus proved His authority by the miracles He did and by raising from the dead on the third day.

Throughout history, Jesus Christ has transformed lives. Today He is continuing to change lives by providing fellowship with God to those who receive Him as Savior and Lord.

Conclusion and Application

We have seen how Jesus' character, His teachings, and His influence upon history prove that He is the Son of God. If you have never asked Him to come into your life, to take the throne of your heart, I urge you to do it now. In Revelation 3:20, Jesus says:

> Behold, I stand at the door [of your heart and life] and knock; if anyone hears my voice and opens the door [inviting Him to enter], I will come in.

Ask Him to come in—to forgive your sins, to empower you to have the kind of life He wants you to live, to enrich your life with His presence, pardon, power, and peace. Let's take a few minutes for prayer.

Closing Prayer

You may wish to pray the following or a similar prayer:

Lord Jesus, I need You. Thank You for dying on the cross for my sins. I open the door of my life and receive You as my Savior and Lord. Thank You for forgiving my sins and giving me eternal life. Take control of the throne of my life. Make me the kind of person You want me to be.

Jesus will answer our prayer. First John 5:14,15 tells us that if we ask anything according to His will, He hears and answers. Verses 11 and 12 tell us that when Christ comes into our lives, we have eternal life and our sin is forgiven. We become children of God and have peace with God. Jesus provides power to live and experience the "abundant life" He promises (John 10:10). He can now direct us in lives of purpose and fulfillment.

The Death of Jesus Christ

Opening Prayer

Discussion Starter

 Have you ever heard this: "I believe that Jesus was a great teacher and spiritual model, but not God. He may have died for His cause, whatever that was, but I don't see what His death has to do with me 2,000 years later."

 What do you think would be a good response?

Lesson Development

(Ask one of the group members to summarize the paragraphs appearing at the opening of this lesson in the student's book.)

❖

Leader's Objective: To demonstrate the significance of Christ's death and the importance of receiving Him as Savior and Lord, and to give group members another opportunity to invite Him into their lives

LESSON 3

Bible Study

The Need for the Death of Jesus Christ

1. Carefully read Romans 3:10–12 and 3:23.

   How many times does the writer, Paul, use terms like *all, none,* or their equivalents?
   (Eight times.)

   Why do you think he repeats these terms?
   (To emphasize that there was no exception.)

   What does this tell you about moral, respectable people?
   (They are not acceptable to God without Christ.)

2. What is the result of sin (Romans 6:23)?
   (Spiritual and physical death.)

The Result of the Death of Christ

1. Read 2 Corinthians 5:21 carefully.

   How good does it say Christ was?
   (He had no sin.)

   But what happened to Him when He died on the cross to pay the penalty of our sins?
   (He became sin on our behalf.)

   What was the result for you?
   (We can become the righteousness of God in Him.)

Read Romans 1:13–20. Notice especially verse 20:

> God's invisible qualities—his eternal power and divine nature— have been clearly seen, being understood from what has been made, so that men are without excuse.

❓Why can God rightfully punish anyone who does not glorify Him?

Read Romans 1:22–32.

❓What mental, physical, and social problems have resulted from man's choice to go his own independent way?

The apostle Paul emphasizes many times in his writings that Jesus Christ is the only mediator between God and man because He removed the sin barrier between God and man (Colossians 1:20; 1 Corinthians 2:2).

(Ask students to turn to a partner. Give pairs one or more of these passages to look up: Acts 4:12; 1 Peter

2. What did Christ teach concerning His death (Mark 8:31,32)?
(He would suffer, be rejected, and killed, and He would rise again.)

3. How did Christ feel about such a death (Hebrews 12:2)?
(He submitted voluntarily; knowing it would bring joy, He endured the cross but despised the shame.)

4. Describe the effect of Christ's death with respect to God's holiness (Romans 3:25; John 4:10).
(God demands justice, and Jesus' death provides justice freely to anyone who will receive it.)

5. Why did He die for us (1 Peter 3:18)?
(So He could bring us to God.)

6. How did Christ's death affect your relationship with God (Colossians 1:21,22; Romans 5:10, 11)?
(We were reconciled to God; we are holy and blameless in His sight.)

Significance of the Death of Christ

1. What is the only thing we can do to make sure that the death of Christ applies to us so we can be saved (Acts 16:31)?
(Believe on the Lord Jesus Christ, personally accepting His death as payment for our own sins.)

1:18,19; 2:21,24; 3:18; Ephesians 2:16,18; and 1 Timothy 2:5. Instruct pairs to write down phrases that show that Jesus is the only way to God.)

Imagine getting a traffic ticket for speeding. When you show up in court, your own father is the judge. Would it be fair for him to fine everyone else who has a ticket, but excuse you because you are his child? Of course not.

Suppose then, he fines you one hundred dollars. Since you do not have the money, you must spend thirty days in jail. But because he loves you, your father steps down from the judge's bench and pays the fine for you. Justice is satisfied; you go free. The only condition is that you accept your father's payment.

Similarly, we cannot redeem ourselves. Only one without sin could satisfy the justice of God. The substitute had to be a man to take the place of man. He had to be sinless to die for the sinner.

To this purpose God sent Jesus Christ, who offered Himself as the required substitute. Coming to this world and taking man's place, He accepted the full penalty for man's sin.

(Ask pairs to read the phrases they wrote down.)

2. Can we work for salvation (Ephesians 2:8,9)?
(No.)

Why not?
(We receive it because of God's grace, not our works, so no one can boast.)

LIFE APPLICATION

1. Read John 3:18 carefully. What two kinds of people are described here?
(Believers and non-believers.)

2. What is the only reason any person will be condemned?
(Because he does not believe in the Son of God.)

3. According to what the Bible says here, are you condemned?

4. According to 1 John 5:11, 12, do you have eternal life? (Do not confuse 1 John, the Epistle, near the end of the New Testament, with the Gospel of John.)

5. According to that same passage, how can you know?

6. Have you made the decision to accept Christ's death on the cross for you, and have you received Him into your life as Savior and Lord?

If you would like to receive Him as your Savior right now, pray a prayer like this one from your heart:

Lord Jesus, I want to know you personally. Thank

Conclusion and Application

(Answer questions 1 and 2 as a group. Then go over questions 3 through 6, having the students answer silently.)

Apart from Jesus Christ, it is impossible for man to know God. By His death on the cross, Christ became your substitute, taking upon Himself the penalty for your sin. This can become effective for you right now, if you receive Him as your personal Savior. Ask Him to forgive your sin, come into your life, and guide you to live for Him. If you already know Christ as your personal Savior, pause now to ask guidance in sharing these truths with someone who does not know Him.

Closing Prayer

If you would like to receive Christ as your Savior right now, silently pray the prayer in your book.

(Observe a time of silent prayer to give opportunity for those who either wish to receive Christ as Savior or to pray for guidance. Then say:)

If you have prayed to receive Jesus as your Savior, please talk to me after the session.

(Close with a prayer of thanksgiving. If someone does meet with you

You for dying on the cross for my sins. I open the door of my life and receive You as my Savior and Lord. Thank You for forgiving my sins and giving me eternal life. Make me the kind of person You want me to be. Amen.

after the session and tells you that he has received Christ, say:)

If you have invited Christ into your life, you can now have confidence that He is in your life as He promised. Jesus would not deceive you. You can be sure, if you asked Him into your life, that He now lives within you and will give you abundant life. Remember this promise in Hebrews 13:5: "I will never leave you nor forsake you" (NKJ).

The Resurrection of Jesus Christ

Opening Prayer

Discussion Starter

Each spring, we celebrate Easter as a reminder of the resurrection of Jesus Christ three days after His death.

❓How do we know that Jesus actually did rise from the dead?

❓How many items of evidence can you think of?

Lesson Development

(Ask one of the group members to summarize the paragraphs appearing at the opening of this lesson in the student's book.)

(Read aloud the account of the resurrection found in Mark 16:1–8. Emphasize verse 6. Ask:)

❓What difference does it make whether or not Christ truly rose from the dead?

❓What does His resurrection prove?

Leader's Objective: To present historical, factual evidence regarding Christ's resurrection, to consider the importance of this event to us, and to lead students to build their Christian experience upon this basis

Bible Study

Five Proofs That Jesus Actually Rose From the Dead

1. *The resurrection was foretold by Jesus Christ, the Son of God.*

   What did Jesus tell His disciples in Luke 18:31–33?
   (He would be killed and rise again the third day.)

   If Jesus had clearly predicted that He would rise from the dead, then failed to do so, what would this say about Him?
   (He was a liar and not God.)

2. *The resurrection of Christ is the only reasonable explanation for the empty tomb.*

   What did Jesus' friends do to make certain His body would not be taken from the tomb (Mark 15:46)?
   (A stone was rolled against the entrance to the tomb.)

   What did Jesus' enemies do to make sure His body would not be taken (Matthew 27:62–66)?
   (They assigned guards to make the grave secure, and they set an official seal on the stone.)

   But on Sunday morning the tomb was *empty!*

   Note: If Jesus had not been killed, but only

(After discussing each proof that Jesus rose from the dead, ask:)

❷ If someone you know were to question the authenticity of Christ's resurrection, how could you answer him?

(Guide students in formulating short, insightful responses to each proof.)

Philip Schaff, one of the leading church historians, recorded in his book *History of Christianity:*

> The Christian church rests on the resurrection of its Founder. Without this fact the church could never have been born, or if born, it would soon have died a natural death. The miracle of the resurrection and the existence of Christianity are so closely connected that they must stand or fall together.

The disciples had seen Jesus do many miracles, including raising people from the dead. Many times Jesus explained to His disciples of His coming death and resurrection.

❷ Why do you think they were so surprised when it all happened?

❷ What physical things were done to prevent Jesus' resurrection?

❷ Why do you think God allowed these to be put into place?

Jesus' claim to raise from the dead in three days was so well-known that His enemies were well aware of it. What do you think motivated the chief priests and Pharisees to go to Pilate?

weakened and wounded by the crucifixion, the stone and the soldiers would have prevented His escape from the tomb. If Jesus' friends had tried to steal His body, the stone and the soldiers would likewise have prevented them. Jesus' enemies would never have taken the body since its absence from the tomb would only serve to encourage belief in His resurrection. *Only His resurrection can account for the empty tomb!*

3. *The resurrection is the only reasonable explanation for the appearance of Jesus Christ to His disciples.*

List all the individuals or groups who actually saw the risen Christ, according to 1 Corinthians 15:4–8.
(Peter, the twelve, 500 followers of Jesus, James, all the apostles, Paul.)

If Christ had not risen from the dead, what could we then conclude about all these witnesses (1 Corinthians 15:15)?
(They would all have been false witnesses.)

What else would be true if Christ had not risen from the dead (1 Corinthians 15:17)?
(Your faith is worthless; you are still in your sins.)

When Christ appeared to His followers, what

Each of the gospel writers—Matthew, Mark, Luke, and John—describe Jesus' friends' initial reactions when they learned of the resurrection.

(Look up several of these accounts and discuss how authentic the reactions were:)

◆ Matthew 27:16,17

◆ Mark 16:9–11,13,14

◆ Luke 24:9–11,36,37

◆ John 20:1,2,24,25

❓From the accounts of Jesus' appearance to His friends, how did He treat them?

❓How does this prove that He was the same person who was crucified?

things did He do to prove He was not a hallucination (Luke 24:36–43)?
(He asked them to touch Him and see that He had flesh and bones, and He ate a piece of broiled fish.)

4. *The dramatic change in the lives of His followers.*

Look up these verses and describe the differences in these people:

Peter (Luke 22:54–62; Acts 4:1–22)
(From a coward and a liar to a bold witness for Christ.)

Thomas (John 20:24–28; Acts 1:12–14)
(From a disbeliever to a believing pray-er.)

Paul (Acts 7:54–8:3; Acts 16:16–40)
(From a persecutor of Christ's followers to a missionary for the gospel.)

5. *The resurrection is the only reasonable explanation for the beginning of the Christian church.*

Within a few weeks after Jesus' resurrection, Peter preached at Pentecost, and the Christian church began. What was the subject of his sermon (Acts 2:14–36)?
(The resurrection of Christ.)

If Jesus' body were still in the tomb, how do you think Peter's audience would have responded to this sermon?

❓What changes have you seen in your life or in the lives of others that proves Jesus is alive?

❓If you were to point to one thing in your church that proves Jesus is alive, what would it be?

Why?

Christ's resurrection shows:

◆ That Jesus is God (Romans 1:4)

◆ That Jesus' death was accepted by God the Father as payment for our sin (Romans 4:25)

◆ That Christ is our High Priest and intercedes for us (1 Timothy 2:5,6; Romans 8:34)

(They would have turned away and even mocked it.)

But how did they respond (Acts 2:37,38, 41,42)?
(They repented, were baptized, added to the church, and continued in their Christian lives.)

The Results of the Resurrection

1. What does the resurrection tell us about the following:

   Jesus Christ (Romans 1:4)?
   (He "was declared with power to be the Son of God.")

   The power God can now exercise in our lives (Ephesians 1:19,20)?
   (God gives us the same incomparable power He used to raise Jesus.)

   What will eventually happen to our bodies (Philippians 3:21)?
   (They will be transformed so that they will be like Jesus' glorious body.)

2. How would your life be affected if Christ had not risen from the dead (1 Corinthians 15:12–26)?
   (My faith would be useless; my sins would not be forgiven; I would have no hope; I could not look forward to Christ's return.)

3. If we can believe the resurrection, why is it then logical to believe all the

◆ That we receive many blessings because of His resurrection (1 Peter 1:3–5)

The ascension of Christ means that He went back to heaven in His resurrection body.

The exaltation of Christ means that God the Father gave Jesus the position of honor and power at the Father's right hand.

miracles that Jesus performed?
(The resurrection of His own body is a greater miracle than all the others.)

The Visible Return of Christ

1. Describe the way in which Christ will return to earth (Matthew 24:30; Acts 1:11).
   (Visibly in the sky, the same way He ascended to heaven.)

2. How does this compare to the first time Christ came to earth?
   (The first time He came as a lowly baby with no glory or power; when He returns, He will have all glory and power.)

3. What will happen to the Christian when Christ comes for him (1 Corinthians 15:51,52; Philippians 3:20,21)?
   (We will receive imperishable bodies like Christ's.)

4. What will be the condition of the earth when Christ returns (Matthew 24:6–8)?
   (There will be wars, famines, and earthquakes.)

5. What will happen to those who are not Christians when He returns (2 Thessalonians 1:7–9)?
   (They will be eternally punished.)

6. What is our present hope (1 John 2:2,3)?
   (Jesus has atoned [paid for] our sins.)

The second coming of Christ is mentioned more than three hundred times in the New Testament. Whole chapters are devoted to the subject (Matthew 24,25; Mark 13; Luke 21; 1 Corinthians 15) and some books (1 Thessalonians; 2 Thessalonians; Revelation) have Christ's return as their main subject.

❓How does an understanding of Christ as Prophet, Priest, and King hinge on His return to earth?

As Prophet, Jesus predicted His return to earth. As Priest, Jesus conquered sin and death, which allows Him to be the Messiah. As Messiah, He is the promised King who will rule when He returns to earth.

❓How does the church's observance of the Lord's Supper refer to Jesus' return?

In Mark 14:25, Jesus says, "I will not drink again of the fruit of the vine until that day when I drink it anew in the kingdom of God." The Kingdom of God refers to the kingdom that Christ will set up when He returns to earth. (See Revelation 20:4–6.) Whenever we observe the Lord's Supper, we can also remember that Jesus will return to reign as King of kings. Then He will drink with us.

Conclusion and Application

(Have students give brief statements about what the resurrection means to them. Then read this quote:)

Hebrews 13:8 says Jesus is the same today, and He can transform your life.

1. How would your life be different from what it is if Jesus had not risen from the dead?

2. How do you think His "resurrection life" can be seen in you on a daily basis?

3. How can your life be different if you allow Jesus to transform it?

The *Encyclopaedia Britannica* records:

> We have evidence that a very few weeks after the event, Jesus Christ's followers, who had scattered in dismay, were reunited at Jerusalem . . . bound together in a religious society through a common conviction . . . They were fully persuaded that He was alive, and that he had been seen by individuals and by groups of his followers. They were eagerly expecting that He would quite shortly return as the Messiah of their race. The strength and the sincerity of their conviction were tested by persecution and proved by their steadfastness. The religious quality of their attitude to Jesus was evidenced by devotion, self-sacrifice and a sense of obligation to Him and they had a message concerning this same Jesus which they proceeded to proclaim with enthusiasm and amazing success (*Encyclopaedia Britannica,* 1956, p.15).

The reaction of Christ's followers after the resurrection is powerful proof that Jesus did, in fact, raise from the dead.

Closing Prayer

(Give opportunity for those present to pray silently, asking Christ to become their personal Savior. Encourage those who already know Him as Savior to give Him preeminence in their lives, asking Him—in silent prayer—to take control. Close with an audible prayer of thanksgiving for the resurrection of Jesus.)

Jesus Christ Living in the Christian

Opening Prayer

Discussion Starter

Name at least one person whom you believe is living "the Christian life," and tell what makes his life different.

Lesson Development

(Ask one of the group members to summarize the paragraphs appearing at the opening of this lesson in the student's book. Note the diagram and discuss it.)

Leader's Objective: To demonstrate that a person cannot live the Christian life by his own power and resources, that Christ alone can make a life of victory and power a reality, and to motivate students toward absolute surrender to the Lordship of Christ

Bible Study

The Need for Jesus Christ to Live in the Christian

1. What was Jesus unwilling to entrust to men (John 2:24,25)?
   (Who and what He was.)

   Why?
   (He knew people were evil and would not understand.)

2. What kinds of things are in our hearts (Mark 7:21–23)?
   (Evil thoughts and wicked deeds.)

3. How did the apostle Paul, one of the world's greatest Christians, evaluate his human nature (Romans 7:18)?
   (He knew his sinful nature was completely bad.)

4. What is our condition apart from Jesus Christ (John 15:4,5)?
   (We can't do anything good apart from Jesus.)

The Fact That Jesus Christ Lives in the Christian

1. Restate Revelation 3:20 in your own words.

   Note: The word *sup* that appears in some translations is Old English for "eat" or "dine," and it describes the idea of fellowship in its original meaning.

Without Jesus, we cannot live the Christian live. He is our life. He is our strength and power.

Charles Trumbull said:

> Jesus Christ does not want to be our helper; He wants to be our life. He does not want us to work for Him—He wants us to let Him do His work through us, using us as we use a pencil to write with—better still, using us as one of the fingers on His hand.

> When our life is not only Christ's, but Christ, our life will be a winning life; for He cannot fail. And a winning life *is* a fruit-bearing life, a serving life. This fruit-bearing and service, habitual and constant, must all be by faith in Him; our works are the *result* of His life in us: not the condition or the secret or the cause of the Life.

Christ must be truly at home in your heart.

When you invited Jesus Christ to come into your life as Savior, He heard and answered your prayer. When He came in, you were then born spiritually (John 3:3,6), becoming a child of God (John 1:12). However, the New Testament teaches that now Christ must be

2. What guarantee does Jesus Christ give in this verse, and how can we believe Him?
(He will come in; He does not lie.)

3. How do you know that Jesus Christ has entered your life?
(I asked Him to come in.)

4. How do you know that Jesus will never leave you even when you sin (Hebrews 13:5)?
(He promised He won't leave us.)

5. If you do sin, how can you renew your fellowship with Him (1 John 1:9)?
(If we confess our sins, He will forgive and restore us to His fellowship.)

Note: *Salvation* differs from *fellowship*. Salvation is having our sins forgiven and receiving eternal life. Fellowship is our daily relationship, or communion, with Christ. Through sin we may often lose our fellowship in the same way a child loses fellowship with his father through disobedience. However, the child does not lose his relationship as a son, nor do we lose our relationship with God. He is still our heavenly Father. (See John 10:27–29.)

Jesus Christ at Home Within the Christian

When Jesus Christ lives within us, what can He do for

allowed to direct and guide your life. Ephesians 3:17 expresses the prayer that "Christ may dwell in your hearts through faith."

In the *Amplified New Testament* this Scripture is translated: "May Christ through your faith (actually) dwell—settle down, abide, make His permanent home—in your hearts."

(Discuss the diagram in the student's book.)

❓How does knowing that you have a permanent place in God's family make you feel?

❓How does knowing this make your fellowship with God better?

After we receive Christ as Savior, fulfilling two conditions will help us find fullness of life.

us as we face the following problems?

1. Emptiness (John 6:35)
   (He will fill us—we will not hunger or thirst.)
2. Anxiety (John 14:27)
   (He gives us peace.)
3. Unhappiness (John 15:11)
   (He will give us His joy if we abide in Him.)
4. Lack of power (Philippians 4:13)
   (He gives us strength.)

LIFE APPLICATION

1. What must we do so that Jesus Christ can live His victorious life through us (Romans 6:13; 12:1,2)?
   (We must present our bodies to God as instruments of righteousness.)
2. Read and meditate on John 3:16. On the basis of this verse, why do you think we should give control of our lives to God?
   (God offered His Son for us first; He loves us so much we never have to be afraid of giving our lives to Him.)
3. Right now, surrender control of your life to God. Be willing to give Him every area—your family, job, finances, even your health. Pray this simple prayer:

   Dear Father, I need You. I acknowledge that I have been directing my own life, and that, as a result, I have sinned against You. I thank You for forgiving

◆ Surrender totally to Christ as Master

◆ Believe that God has completely set us free from sin

These two conditions are not dependent on how we feel, but on our faith. We can say, "I know God is meeting all my needs now."

Conclusion and Application

Have you ever surrendered your life completely to Him? Let's take a few moments of silent prayer to do just that. The prayer printed in your book will help you. If you have never asked Jesus to be your Savior, I invite you to do that during this time.

my sins through Christ's death on the cross for me. I now invite Christ to again take His place on the throne of my life. Fill me with the Holy Spirit as You commanded me to be filled in Ephesians 5:18, and as You promised in Your Word that You would if I ask in faith. I now thank You for directing my life and for filling me with the Holy Spirit. Amen.

Closing Prayer

(Spend a few moments in silent prayer, then close in verbal prayer.)

The Church of Jesus Christ

Opening Prayer

Discussion Starter

❓ How do you think the world would be different without the influence of Jesus Christ?

❓ How does the local church fit into this influence?

Lesson Development

(Ask one of the group members to summarize the paragraphs appearing at the opening of this lesson in the student's book.)

❖

Leader's Objective: To teach students about the church (universal and local) and help them appreciate its purpose and importance; to lead them to commitment of service in a local church

LESSON 6

Bible Study

The Universal Church

1. Paul frequently compares the church to a body. Who is the only head (Ephesians 5:23)?
   (Christ.)

   Who are the members (1 Corinthians 12:27)?
   (Individual Christians.)

2. How does Christ see the church (1 Corinthians 12:12,13)?
   (As many members united in one body.)

3. As members of His body, how should we feel toward each other (1 Corinthians 12:25,26)?
   (We should care sincerely for one another, suffering and rejoicing together.)

   Name some specific ways we can express these feelings.

4. Read Acts 1:6–11 carefully.

   According to verse 8, what is to be the church's great concern?
   (To be Christ's witnesses locally and worldwide.)

   Where does the Bible say Jesus went physically (verse 9)?
   (He was lifted up and a cloud received Him.)

   Describe in your own words how Jesus will come again for His church (verse 11).

The New Testament word used for the church appears at least 135 times. The word is *soma.*

The word refers to a small or large number of people closely united into one group. That is the New Testament view of the church.

(Read Ephesians 4:4–6.)

To list the "one body" together with these other great truths emphasizes the importance of viewing the church as one united body.

In Romans 12:4,5 Paul makes the reader clearly aware of the unity that exists among the members of the Body of Christ.

Scripture expressly states that there should be no division or jealousy in the body—if one member suffers, all the other members suffer also, and if one member is honored, all the other members rejoice with the honored member.

No member of the body can say to another, "I do not need you," for God has arranged the body so that all the members are interdependent.

Who knows when that will be (verse 7)? (See also Mark 13:32,33.)
(Only the Father.)

Although Jesus is spiritually present in our hearts, He is also with God the Father in heaven. In the future, He will return to judge the world and rule the nations (Matthew 25:31,32). In the meantime, the church is to be His witness on earth and bring as many people as possible into a personal relationship with Him.

5. In light of this, what should be one of your main purposes while here on earth?
(To tell everyone who will listen about God's love and forgiveness.)

The Local Church

1. What are Christians *not* to do (Hebrews 10:25)?
(We are not to forsake our own assembling together.)

Note: The "meeting together" refers to the regular assembling of the local church.

2. We are saved by faith. But the church has two simple, yet meaningful,

Within the great company of believers known as the universal church are included a great number of local churches—individual groups of believers. Paul made many references to churches in particular geographic locations (Romans 16:1; 1 Corinthians 1:2; Galatians 1:2,22; 1 Thessalonians 1:1; and others). The book of Revelation speaks specifically to seven churches in Asia (chapters 2 and 3).

The term *church* means "an assembly of called-out ones"—not a building, but people. Believers are the "called-out ones" who gather together for instruction and worship. The significance of the local church is made obvious throughout the book of Acts—everywhere Paul went, local assemblies of believers were established.

❷Why should we not neglect church attendance?

Hebrews 10:25 was written to show the need for Christian fellowship and exhortation. It is a command of God.

Baptism was instituted by the Lord, by example as well as by commandment (Mark 1:9).

ordinances that we are to observe: baptism and communion.

According to Matthew 28:18,19, why should we be baptized?
(It is a testimony, or confession of faith, and a step of obedience to Christ.)

What is the purpose of the communion service (1 Corinthians 11:23–26)?
(It is a commemoration— we look back to Christ's death on Calvary, and ahead to His return.)

3. Write your own one-sentence description of each of the following local churches:

The church in Jerusalem (Acts 4:32,33)
(The people were of one heart and mind and shared everything.)

The church in Thessalonica (1 Thessalonians 1:6–10)
(The believers were joyful in suffering and were known for their faith.)

The church in Laodicea (Revelation 3:14–17)
(The believers were lukewarm in their faith and

The significance of baptism is correctly interpreted only when we keep in mind that one must be a regenerated believer before he can truly partake of the ordinance. Baptism then symbolizes the cleansing from sin that has taken place. By picturing Christ's death, burial, and resurrection, baptism also pictures our spiritual death to sin, the burial of our old nature, and our resurrection into newness of life (Romans 6:3–8; Galatians 3:27).

The *Lord's Supper* was instituted by our Lord Jesus Christ at the feast of the Passover, on the night preceding His arrest and trial (Matthew 26:19–29). The *bread* symbolized the body of the Lord, given in death, the sacrifice for all sin. The *wine* symbolized the blood of Christ, shed "for many for the forgiveness of sins" (Matthew 26:28).

Some people say they can be Christians and not attend church. That is true, but one cannot be a *dedicated* Christian and not take time to worship God with others and to participate in the ordinances. Not to fellowship with other members of the body of Christ is to disobey the command of our Lord.

❓What would a community be like without a church?

❓Would you like to live there?

❓What would the implications be if we violate this command?

Purposes of the Local Church

The purposes for which the local church was established include:

were rich in material possessions.)

Just as some New Testament churches were dynamic and others were powerless, so it is today. Not all churches are vital, and great variety exists even within a single denomination. To stimulate your Christian growth, you should attend a church that exalts Christ, teaches the Bible, explains clearly what a Christian is and how to become one, and provides loving fellowship.

4. What could happen to your spiritual growth if you:

Do not attend church regularly?

Attend a church that is powerless?

◆ To *glorify Christ* (Ephesians 3:20,21)

◆ To *instruct believers* so that they are equipped to minister to other believers and to non-believers (2 Timothy 4:2)

◆ To *witness for Christ* (Acts 1:8; 13:1–4; Revelation 1:20; John 15:16)

◆ To *draw near to God* (Hebrews 10:22)

◆ To *strengthen our faith* (Hebrews 10:23)

◆ To *help others* (Hebrews 10:24)

◆ To *encourage each other* (Hebrews 10:25)

Reasons for Church Membership

It is important for us to realize the real reason for joining a church. Joining a church does not make one a Christian, but when we are true believers and Christ is our Savior and Lord, we need the church for a number of reasons.

❓What would you say they are?

◆ For fellowship with God's children

◆ For our own spiritual help and growth

◆ In remembrance of the Savior and His death, resurrection, and ascension

◆ To follow Christ's command to reach the world with His message of love and forgiveness

The church is not an organization of perfect individuals, but a group of people who desire to experience growth in their Christian lives. The church is somewhat like a hospital, where repairs can be made when we break down spiritually. Members meet there to learn more about God and to encourage each other.

Conclusion and Application

Following are some suggestions to make your church worship more meaningful:

◆ Bow for silent prayer before the service begins. Pray for yourself, the minister, those taking part, and those worshiping. Ask that Christ be real to them and that those who do not know Christ may come to know, trust, and obey Him.

◆ Meditate on the words of the hymns.

◆ Take your Bible to church with you. Underline portions that are especially meaningful.

◆ Take notes on the sermon. Review them later in the day and apply what you learned to your daily living.

(Conclude the session by doing the following:

◆ Encourage students to participate in the ministry of a local church.

◆ Recommend that those who recently received Christ become members of a local church.

◆ Caution students to avoid criticizing other Christians, churches, and pastors who seem to be less zealous.)

(Say the following:)

Because a person received Christ does not mean he is perfect, although he is changed. When a caterpillar becomes a butterfly it

1. Give at least two reasons it is important for us to be a part of a local church.
   1)
   2)

2. If you are not active in a local church, plan right now to get involved.
   ◆ Ask your Christian friends to recommend dynamic churches. Write those church names here:
   ◆ Pray over the list.
   ◆ Ask God to help you select the best one for you.
   ◆ Visit each until you prayerfully decide on one.
   ◆ Then look for ways to serve the Lord in your church.

no longer crawls in the dust. It may light there for a time but it does not stay. For the one who truly knows Christ as his personal Savior, the "old life" does not satisfy. He may slip for a time but as soon as he confesses he "soars in the heavens" again.

Closing Prayer

Recap

Opening Prayer

Discussion Starter

How has what you have learned about Jesus changed your daily life?

How have your views of the church changed?

Lesson Development

(Any appropriate material from previous lessons that was not sufficiently covered could be used at this time, and you also may deal with any point that the group members may not understand as well as they could.)

(Then go over the remaining Recap questions and answers. This material will benefit both the students and you by giving you a deeper appreciation of God's Word.)

Leader's Objective: To be sure students have a full and well-grounded understanding of the person of Jesus Christ; to lead them into any commitments appropriate at this point

LESSON 7

The following questions will help you review this Step. If necessary, reread the appropriate lesson(s).

1. List ways the memory verses have helped you in your daily life during the weeks of this study.

2. What do you think is the most important way in which Jesus Christ is different from other people?

   What does that mean to you?

   How does it affect your life?

3. Who is Jesus Christ to you?

   What has He given you?

4. Why do you suppose Jesus' enemies did not want to believe His claims about who He was?

5. Why did Jesus' friends, who had watched Him die, believe in the resurrection?

LIFE APPLICATION

1. What does it mean to you now to have Jesus living within you?

2. How does your present relationship with Christ help you develop a rich fellowship with your local church?

3. How can you improve your relationship with other Christians?

4. How does your fellowship in your church help

(Use this lesson to encourage students who have not received Christ to do so and to encourage Christians to commit themselves totally to God's control. Also, explain that this study is the first in a series.)

(Bring a student's book for *Step One: the Christian and the Abundant Life* to show group members, and invite them to attend the next study in the series. Read through the Contents page to give students an idea of what they will learn.)

Conclusion and Application

God offers a wonderful plan for our lives. He did not intend for man to experience a negative, miserable, defeated existence. The Bible tells us that God meant for man to live life to the fullest. Jesus said, "I have come that they may have life, and that they may have it more abundantly" (John 10:10, NKJ).

Every man is seeking happiness. The Bible says there is only one way to know true happiness and this is

your relationship with God?

5. Write down ways you could make the relationship more vital.

through God's plan in a personal relationship with Jesus Christ.

❓Do you know Him as your Savior?

❓Would you like to know Him?

As we close in prayer, if you are not sure that Christ is in your heart, ask Him to come in.

Closing Prayer

Let me first read for you the prayer I will pray. (Read it.) Now, as I pray this prayer, you may want to make it your personal prayer. If so, just repeat it, in your heart, after me.

> Lord Jesus, I need You. Thank You for dying on the cross for my sins. I open the door of my life to You and receive You as my Savior and Lord. Thank You for forgiving my sins and giving me eternal life. Take control of the throne of my life. Make me the kind of person You want me to be.

❓If you have done this, where is He right now?

❓As you leave today, won't you come and tell me if you have made this decision?

The Christian *Adventure*

Beginning the Exciting Journey of Faith

STEP 1

The Christian's Certainty

Opening Prayer

Discussion Starter

Encourage students to read on their own the article located at the beginning of their Study Guide.

❓ If someone told you he thought he had received Christ and had become a Christian, but was not really sure of it, what would you tell him? (Try to get some different answers and allow a few minutes of discussion. *Do not* give any answers yourself at this time.)

Lesson Development

(Ask one of the group members to summarize the paragraphs appearing at the opening of the lesson in the student's book. Note the diagram and discuss it.)

(For the Bible Study, assign each question of the lesson to someone in the class. After each answer, promote discussion with further questions, insights, and illustrations given.)

Leader's Objective: To lead Christians, both new and older, to assurance of their eternal salvation and to an awareness of the presence of Jesus Christ in their lives

LESSON 1

Bible Study

Christian Certainty

1. What must one do to become a Christian (John 1:12)?
   (Receive Jesus Christ as Savior and Lord.)

2. To be a son of God is to be born of whom (John 1:13)?
   (God.)

3. To believe in Jesus Christ is to possess and to be free from what (John 5:24)?
   (To possess eternal life and be free from judgment.)

❓What does it mean to receive Christ?

It means the same thing as "to receive a gift someone offers—we put forth our hand and take the proffered gift" (Donald Gray Barnhouse). Notice Romans 6:23:

> The *gift* of God is eternal life in Christ Jesus our Lord.

"To believe on His name" is an expression that means "to have faith in all that He is."

By receiving Jesus Christ by faith we become Christians.

John 1:13 talks about the family of God.

❓Isn't everyone God's child?

The answer is no. Everyone is a creation of God, but only those who have received His Son are members of His family.

A carpenter once said to a minister, "I believe that God created all men, therefore all men must be His children."

The minister replied, "Have you ever made a table?"

"Why, of course," said the carpenter, "scores of them."

"Are the tables your children because you made them?"

"Oh, no," said the carpenter.

"Why not?" asked the minister.

"Well, because they don't have my life in them."

"Exactly," said the minister. "Do you have God's life in you?"

4. What did Christ do with our sins (1 Peter 2:24, 25)?
(He bore them in His own body on the cross.)

How should this affect our lives?

5. What three things characterize Jesus' sheep (John 10:27)?
(They listen to my voice; I know them; They follow me.)

This is what it means to be God's child—you must have God's life in you, and this comes only by receiving Christ.

J. B. Phillips translates this Scripture:

> I solemnly assure you that the man who hears what I have to say and believes in the one who has sent Me, has eternal life. He does not have to face judgment; he has already passed from death into life (John 5:24).

❓When do you get eternal (everlasting) life?

According to this verse, we receive eternal life when we believe.

Christianity is not "pie in the sky when I die"; it is new life here and now. Alexander Maclaren says, "Eternal life is not reserved to be entered on in the blessed future, but is a present possession . . . heaven is not different in kind and circumstance from the Christian life on earth, but differs mainly in degree and circumstance."

❓But what is eternal life?

It is not endless existence, since all men—Christian and non-Christian—have this according to Matthew 25:46. Rather, it is a rich, abundant, full life, centered around our Lord Jesus Christ and in vital contact with Him here on earth and for all eternity, which no non-Christian has. (See John 10:10.)

Phillips again has a good translation of these verses:

> And He personally bore our sins in His own body on the cross so that we might be dead to sin and be alive

6. What is your relationship with Christ, as He Himself states in John 10:28–30?
   (You have eternal life; you shall never perish; and no one can snatch you out of the Father's hand.)

7. What are the implications of failing to believe the testimony that God has given regarding His Son (1 John 5:10,11)?
   (We make God a liar.)

8. The resurrection of Jesus is history's most revolutionary event. How does it prove Christ's claim to be God (Romans 1:4)?
   (Only the Son of God has the power and holiness to rise from the dead.)

Why is the resurrection so essential to our faith (1 Corinthians 15:17; Ephesians 2:4–10)?
   (We would still be in our sins; we have life because Christ lives.)

to all that is good. It was the suffering that He bore which has healed you. You had wandered away like so many sheep, but now you have returned to the shepherd and guardian of your soul (1 Peter 2:24,25).

Suppose you get a traffic ticket for speeding, but when you show up in court, you discover that your own father is the judge.

Because you are his son, would it be fair for him to fine everyone else who has a ticket but excuse you? Of course not.

Suppose, then, he fines you eighty dollars or thirty days in jail. Since you do not have the eighty dollars, you must spend thirty days in jail. But because he loves you, your father steps down off the judge's bench, and holds out eighty dollars. Justice is satisfied, yet you go free. The only condition is that you accept your father's payment.

Similarly, we have violated God's laws, and justice demands the penalty be paid. But because of His love for us, God has paid the penalty for us in the person of His Son. We must accept this payment to be forgiven.

The life of a shepherd in biblical countries forms the background for these verses. After watering and resting his sheep, the shepherd calls them to go to another feeding ground. At the first sound of his call, which is usually a peculiar guttural sound hard to imitate, the flock follow off . . . Even should two shepherds call their flocks at the same time and the sheep be intermingled, they never mistake their own master's voice.

Note that John 10:28–30 teaches that a Christian can *never* be lost. He may sin and lose his fellowship, or communication with God, but he can never lose his salvation.

New Life

1. In John 3:3–7, what did Jesus tell Nicodemus about seeing and entering the kingdom of God? *(A person must be born again to see or enter the kingdom of God.)*

❓What does it mean to be born again?

◆ It does not mean that we "turn over a new leaf." It is a far more radical change than that.

◆ It applies to good as well as bad people. Nicodemus, to whom Jesus spoke these words, was a Pharisee, a ruler of the Jews, one of the great religious leaders of his day. He was moral and ethical, prayed seven times a day, and worshipped at the synagogue faithfully—a good man. Yet, Jesus said to Nicodemus, "You must be born again" (John 3:7).

2. At physical birth one receives many things he is not aware of: family name, privileges, wealth, love, care, and protection. At spiritual birth one becomes a son of God and receives forgiveness of sin; eternal life, a divine inheritance, and God's love, care, and protection.

God has given us these because of His great love. God's gifts are never based on man's changing emotions, but on His own unchanging Word.

Birth gives life. A new birth means that a new life must be given to us. This new life is the eternal life that comes when we receive Christ.

A caterpillar crawling in the dust is an ugly, hairy worm. But one day this worm weaves around its body a cocoon. Out of this cocoon emerges a beautiful butterfly.

We do not understand fully what has taken place. We realize only that where once a worm crawled in the dust, now a butterfly soars through the air. So it is in the life of a Christian. Where once we lived on the lowest level as sinful, egocentric individuals, we now dwell on the highest plane, experiencing a full and abundant life as children of God. An individual becomes a Christian through spiritual birth.

In your own words, describe what you have according to these verses:

Ephesians 1:7
(Redemption, forgiveness.)

Romans 5:1
(Peace with God.)

The four verses listed here describe some of the results of receiving Christ. According to these passages we have:

Forgiveness. All of our disobedience to God is eternally forgiven. Christ alone offers the solution to the universal guilt problem.

Peace. According to the Bible, even the very best non-Christians are at war with God. When the United States was at war with Japan, only active hostility existed between the two. This did not change until they signed the peace treaty in Tokyo Bay.

Similarly, all non-Christians, whether they know it or not, are at war with God and have no hope for communication or friendship with Him until they make peace through Christ.

Romans 3:22
(Righteousness from God.)

Righteousness. This is not a personal righteousness of everyday life, but the righteousness of God given to us when we receive Christ. God has assigned Christ's righteousness to us and He assigned our sins to Christ as He suffered on the cross.

Colossians 1:27
("Christ in you, the hope of glory.")

Christ in you. Although God forgives us, makes peace with us, and clothes us with Christ's righteousness, this would do us little good in this life unless Christ came to live in our hearts. Because He is in our hearts, we have a new strength from Him and are able to keep His commandments.

3. As you begin to live the Christian life, what three evidences in your life will assure you that you know Jesus Christ?

1 John 2:3
(If we obey His com-mands.)

1 John 3:14
(If we love our brothers and sisters in Christ.)

Romans 8:16
(The Spirit bears witness to us.)

LIFE APPLICATION

1. Who is Jesus Christ to you?

2. What is your relationship with God?

3. What kind of life do you now possess?

4. What about your sins?

5. Why are you sure (or doubtful) of your salvation?

6. What changes do you believe have taken place because Christ is in your life?

You are always the son or daughter of your mother and father. This never changes. You may argue with your parents and even not be on speaking terms, but you would still be their child. You simply would have no fellowship with them. We are *always* God's children if we are Christians, even if we lose our fellowship with Him through sin.

Conclusion and Application

(Allow students private time to answer the questions in the "Life Application" section of the lesson, and give them an opportunity to share their answers if they desire.)

❓What is the result of being sure we have received Christ and knowing He has given us eternal life?

Basically, it is that we are now set free from fear and doubt, and we can begin to enjoy God and the life of purpose and meaning that He has for us.

The Christian who does not have assurance looks at God fearfully, never knowing whether the Father has received him or not. He usually is defeated and miserable. But the Christian who has assurance can live joyfully because he belongs to God. And instead of always regarding Him with fear, the Christian will learn to love Him and serve Him.

Closing Prayer

The Christ-Controlled Life

Opening Prayer

Discussion Starter

❓What do we mean when we talk about Jesus Christ controlling our lives?

❓Is the Christ-controlled life a perfect one?

❓If Christ controlled every area of your life, what would happen to your individual personality? Would you lose it?

Lesson Development

(Ask one of the students to summarize the opening paragraphs in the student's Study Guide. Give students time to look up the Scriptures in the lesson and record their answers. Then discuss the Scripture and diagram at the beginning of the Bible Study section.)

❓What does the Scripture in question 1 mean when it says the natural man does not accept the things of the Spirit of God?

A person without God's Holy Spirit naturally rejects God's wisdom and

Leader's Objective: To show the difference between the worldly Christian and the Christ-controlled Christian; to motivate students to yield their lives to Christ's control

80

LESSON 2

Bible Study

The Non-Christian or Natural Man

1. What adjective do you think best describes the man who does not understand the things of the Spirit of God (1 Corinthians 2:14)?
   (Students should use their own terminology.)

2. What terms describe self in the following verses?

   Romans 6:6
   (Body of sin.)

   Galatians 5:16,17
   (The sinful nature.)

3. List at least three characteristics of the man without Christ, as described in Ephesians 2:1–3.
   (Dead in transgressions and sins; follows the way of the world; object of wrath.)

4. What is the condition of the heart of the natural man (Jeremiah 17:9)?
   (His heart is wicked and he cannot change it. Sometimes he himself doesn't even know how bad he is.)

commands because he cannot understand them.

❓Can you give us a good illustration?

(If students don't have illustrations, you might supply some from your own witnessing experiences.)

Note that the non-Christian can understand the Bible intellectually, but until he is converted he cannot respond to its truth.

Bertrand Russell, a great philosopher who won the 1950 Nobel Prize for Literature, was consistently antagonistic toward Christianity. One of his works was entitled *Why I Am Not a Christian.* He obviously was brilliant and capable of understanding the Bible intellectually, but he could not accept its truth. God is a Spirit, and His truth is spiritually discerned.

Every man without Christ is under Satan's dominion. The phrase "prince of the power of the air" is a description of Satan. The Greek word for *air* here means "the lower, denser atmosphere."

Kenneth Wuest said, "The kingdom of Satan is in this lower atmosphere where we human beings are . . . The unsaved order their behavior according to his dictates and those of his demons."

❓How can we explain that some non-Christians have much higher standards than others, if all are under Satan's control?

John Calvin said:

   For in all ages there have been some persons who . . . have devoted their whole lives to the pursuit of

5. List the thirteen sins that Jesus said come from the heart of man (Mark 7:20–23).
   (Evil thoughts, sexual immorality, theft, murder, adultery, greed, malice, deceit, lewdness, envy, slander, arrogance, and folly.)

6. Summarize the relationship between God and the non-Christian (John 3:36).
   (Students should answer in their own words.)

7. How, then, does one become a Christian (John 1:12; Revelation 3:20)?
   (Receive Jesus, open the door, invite Him into one's heart and life.)

The Spiritual or Christ-Controlled Christian

1. What are some other characteristics of a life controlled by God's Spirit (Galatians 5:22,23)?
   (Love, joy, peace, patience, kindness, goodness, faithfulness, gentleness, self control.)

2. In what sense could the Spirit-controlled life be called the exchanged life (Galatians 2:20)?
   (It is not really me living, but Christ living in me.)

3. Where does the Christian receive the power to live this otherwise impossible life (Philippians 4:13)?
   (From Christ.)

virtue . . . Amidst this corruption of nature there is some room for divine grace . . . For should the Lord permit the minds of all men to give up the reins to every lawless passion, there certainly would not be an individual in the world whose actions would not evince all the crimes for which Paul condemns human nature in general.

Matthew Henry comments on John 3:36, "He that believeth not on the Son is undone . . . [He] cannot be happy in this world nor that to come."

(Discuss the diagram in the student's Study Guide.)

Galatians 2:20 clearly explains that the Christ-controlled life is Christ living through the Christian. Kenneth Wuest notes, "Instead of attempting to live his life in obedience to . . . the Mosaic law, Paul now yields to the indwelling Holy Spirit and cooperates with Him in the production of a life pleasing to God."

Alexander Maclaren comments on Philippians 4:13:

A godless life has a weakness at the heart of its loneliness, but Christ and I are always in the majority.

"The man whose mind . . . shares the thoughts of Christ . . . is beyond natural man's assessment. The mere humanist is no more competent in the spiritual sphere than one who is tone-deaf is capable of criticizing music, or a man who is color-blind is qualified to discuss a painting" (*Abingdon Bible Commentary*).

4. What does the spiritual Christian have that will enable him to understand the things of God (1 Corinthians 2:14–16)? *(The mind of Christ.)*

"Men of intellectual gifts who are ignorant of the things of Christ talk learnedly and patronizingly about things of which they are grossly ignorant. The spiritual man is superior to all this false knowledge" (A. T. Robertson).

This is one of the differences the indwelling Holy Spirit can make in one's life. The Christ-controlled life does not mean our individual personality is abolished. Rather, Christ expresses Himself through each of us, using our differences.

For example, Paul was a logical thinker before conversion, and God used this element when He inspired Paul to write logical treatises like the Epistle to the Romans. John, on the other hand, thought more mystically, and God used this element in his personality to write the Gospel of John. God did not change their personalities —He used them as His instruments.

The Worldly Christian and the Solution

1. Describe the worldly Christian as presented in 1 Corinthians 3:1–3. *(A man of flesh, an infant in Christ, still worldly, jealous, quarrelsome, and acting like mere men.)*

Name five or six practices that result from worldliness (Galatians 5:19–21). *(Immorality, impurity, debauchery, idolatry, witchcraft, hatred, discord, jealousy, fits of rage, selfish ambition, dissen-*

❓What does worldly or "carnal" mean?

(The dictionary says of carnal: worldly or earthly; not spiritual; not holy or sanctified.)

The worldly or "carnal mind," our self-centered ego, is opposed to God and could not be subject to Him even if it wanted to. Our own ego naturally

sions, factions, envy, drunkenness, orgies.)

Summarize in your own words the relationship between the worldly mind and God, as described in Romans 8:7.
(Hostile to God, does not submit to the law of God, not even able to.)

2. The solution to worldliness (the self-controlled life) is threefold:

1) We must *confess* our sins, recognizing that we have been rulers of our own lives. When we confess them, what will God do (1 John 1:9)?
(Forgive our sins and cleanse us from all unrighteousness.)

Read Proverbs 28:13. What is the result of not admitting sin?
(The person will not prosper.)

What is the result of admitting sin (Proverbs 28:13; Psalm 32:1)?
(The person will find mercy and blessing.)

2) We must *surrender,* or yield, the throne to Christ. State in your own words how Paul describes the act of presenting ourselves to God in Romans 12:1,2.
(Let several students give their answers.)

3) By *faith* we must *recognize* that Christ assumed control of our lives upon

"rebels against His authority, thwarts His design, opposes His interest, spits in His face" (Matthew Henry).

Ruth Paxson says of the worldly (carnal) man, "Christ has a place in his heart but not *the* place of supremacy and pre-eminence . . . He, the carnal man, attempts to live in two spheres, the heavenly and the earthly—and he fails in both."

The first part of 1 John 1:9 should never be read without looking at the last part. God openly and freely forgives us because Christ has died for us.

We must confess all *known* sins. "The word *confess* is *homologeo,* from *homos,* 'the same,' and *lego,* 'to say,' thus 'to say the same thing as another,' or to 'agree with another' . . . means therefore to say the same thing that God does about that sin, to agree with God as to all the implications of that sin" (Kenneth Wuest).

❓What is "surrender"?

Surrender is the "deliberate, voluntary transference of the . . . whole being, spirit soul and body from self to Christ, to whom it rightfully belongs by creation and by purchase . . . The question is not, 'Do I belong to God? but 'Have I yielded to God that which already belongs to Him?' " (James McConkey).

our invitation. How can you be sure that if you ask Jesus Christ to assume His rightful place on the throne of your life, He will do so (1 John 5:14,15)?
(God promises to give us what we ask for when we ask according to His will.)

We receive the Lord Jesus Christ by faith. How then do we allow Him to control our lives moment by moment (Colossians 2:6)?
(We live in Christ by faith.)

Give three reasons faith is so important (Hebrews 11:6; Romans 14:23; Romans 1:17).

1) *(Without faith it is impossible to please Him.)*

2) *(Whatever is not from faith is sin.)*

3) *(The righteous shall live by faith; faith becomes our way of life.)*

The secret of the abundant life is to allow Jesus Christ to control your life moment by moment through His Holy

❓Why do some Christians surrender to Christ but fail to experience victory?

They fail because of a lack of faith.

Someone has said, "Surrender opens the door; faith believes that Christ enters, fills, abides."

The two elements of faith are:

◆ *Knowledge*
"Faith is not ignorance; it is not closing one's eyes to the facts. Faith is never afraid to look truth squarely in the face. Man is not saved by knowledge, but he cannot be saved without it" (Lindsell and Woodbridge).

We have a knowledge that God will take control of our lives because it is His will (1 John 5:14,15), and we must give a rational assent to the truth to be believed.

◆ *Personal Appropriation*
"Mental assent is not enough. The will must be exercised and a decision must be made" (Lindsell and Woodbridge).

As we must have sufficient trust in another person to commit ourselves in a marriage, it is only after we commit ourselves to Christ in faith, believing He will control our lives, that His control becomes a reality.

Conclusion and Application

(Give each group member a sheet of paper and briefly go over the suggestions in the "Life Application" with them. Then allow a quiet time for the

Spirit living within you. When you realize that you have sinned, confess your sin immediately; thank God for forgiving you and continue to walk in fellowship with God.

1. In prayer, examine your attitude. Do you honestly want Christ to control your life? If not, ask God to change your heart. Thank Him, by faith, that He has begun to do so.

2. List areas of your life that you believe should be brought under the control of Jesus Christ.

3. Ask God to show you ways to bring these areas under His control.

4. To make 1 John 1:9 meaningful in your life:

   ◆ List your sins and failures on a separate sheet of paper.

   ◆ Claim 1 John 1:9 for your own life by writing the words of the verse over the list.

   ◆ Thank God for His forgiveness and cleansing.

   ◆ Destroy the list.

   ◆ Make restitution wherever appropriate and possible.

students to think through this material and do the writing.)

(After 5 or 10 minutes, have them write the words of 1 John 1:9 over their lists, and then lead them in a closing prayer of thanksgiving for forgiveness and cleansing. As a leader, you will benefit by taking part in this exercise, too.)

Closing Prayer

Five Principles of Growth

Opening Prayer

Discussion Starter

(Read the following excerpt to the class.)

"I do not consider myself to have 'arrived' spiritually, nor do I consider myself already perfect. But I keep on, grasping ever more firmly that purpose for which Christ grasped me ... But I do concentrate on this: I leave the past behind and ... go straight for the goal—my reward the honor of being called by God in Christ."

❷ Who wrote this?

❷ Do you have any idea how long he had been a Christian when he wrote it?

The excerpt is from Philippians 3:12,13 in the Phillips translation. These verses were written by Paul, probably the greatest Christian of all time, *at least 25 years* after his conversion! If he still needed to grow, we certainly need to even more, don't we? The way we grow is by practicing what is learned in this lesson.

Leader's Objective: To teach the students principles essential to spiritual growth and to motivate them to begin to practice those principles in their everyday lives

LESSON 3

Bible Study

Principle One:
We Must Study God's Word

Read James 1:18–27.

You would not think of going without physical food for a week or even a day, would you? It is necessary for physical life. Without food, we become weakened and eventually may become ill. Lack of spiritual food produces the same results in our spiritual lives.

1. What is the food of the young Christian (1 Peter 2:2)?
   (The Word of God.)

   In what ways have you made it a consistent spiritual diet?

   Read Psalm 119. Write down several ways that God's Word can help you in your daily life.

2. Jesus said, "Man shall not live by bread alone." How did He say we should live and be nourished (Matthew 4:4)?
   ("On every word that comes from the mouth of God.")

   How have you applied this to your life? Describe how it has nourished your spiritual life.

3. List the two characteristics of the workman

Lesson Development

(Ask one of the group members to summarize the paragraphs appearing at the opening of this lesson in the student's book. Note the diagram and discuss it.)

These verses compare the Bible to physical food.

Matthew Henry remarks, "A new life requires suitable food. They, being newly born (spiritually), must desire the milk of the word. Infants desire common milk, and their desires toward it are fervent and frequent."

Phillips translates 2 Timothy 2:15: "For yourself, concentrate on winning God's approval, being a workman with nothing to be ashamed of, and who knows how to use the Word to best advantage."

God approves, according to 2 Timothy 2:15.

1) *(Does not need to be ashamed.)*

2) *(Correctly handles the Word of truth.)*

What steps have you taken to make these characteristics true in your life?

4. What did Jesus say about those who read and believe God's Word (John 8:31,32)?
("You are really my disciples.")

What does this mean to your way of life?

5. When does the man who is spiritually mature meditate on the Word of God (Psalm 1:2,3)?
(Day and night.)

How can you do this in our hectic, pull-apart world?

6. In what specific ways do you expect God's Word to affect you?

Principle Two: We Must Pray

Read Matthew 26:31–75.

Study the above passage and answer the following questions:

1. What was Jesus' command in Matthew 26:41?
("Watch and pray.")

Matthew Henry comments on this verse: "Workmen that are unskillful or unfaithful, or lazy, have need to be ashamed; but those who mind their business, and keep to their work, are workmen that need not be ashamed. And what is their work? . . . Not to invent a new gospel, but rightly to divide the gospel that is committed to their trust."

Here are some notable sayings about the Bible:

"It is impossible rightly to govern the world without God and the Bible" (George Washington).

"I am profitably engaged in reading the Bible. Take all of this book . . . and you will live and die a better man" (Abraham Lincoln).

"The vigor of our spiritual life will be in exact proportion to the place held by the Bible in our life and thoughts" (George Mueller).

"I prayed for faith . . . But faith did not seem to come. One day I read in the tenth chapter of Romans, 'Now faith cometh by hearing, and hearing by the Word of God.' I had closed my Bible and prayed for faith. I now opened my Bible and began to study, and faith has been growing ever since" (Dwight L. Moody).

(Ask one of the group members to summarize the opening paragraphs in this section in the student's book. Then discuss the diagram and the questions.)

Why did He command it?
(So that you will not fall into temptation.)

Jesus commanded His disciples to "watch and pray." The word *watch* means to "be wide awake, alert."

Alexander Maclaren said, "Watchfulness and prayer are inseparable. The one discerns dangers; the other arms against them."

A major cause of Peter's failure was prayerlessness.

2. Why did Peter fail to resist temptation?
   (His flesh was weak because of his prayerlessness.)

3. What was the most serious result of Peter's prayerlessness?
   (He denied Jesus three times.)

   Think about your own prayer life. What has been the result of prayerlessness in your life?

❓Why do you think Peter failed to pray?

Apparently he did not feel sufficient need of it. He would rather sleep. When physically exhausted, sleep is undoubtedly more important than prayer, but at this crisis moment Peter should have prayed. A further look at the chapter reveals why Peter felt so little need of prayer and why he failed so tragically. Matthew 26:33,35 shows that Peter had too much confidence in himself.

On these verses Matthew Henry says, "He fancied himself better armed against temptation than anyone else, and this was his weakness and folly."

4. How did Christ experience inner power to face the severest test of His life?
   (By spending so much time in concentrated prayer.)

5. How often are we to pray (1 Thessalonians 5:17)?
   (Continually.)

Prayer without ceasing involves conversing with our heavenly Father in a simple and free way throughout the day. Our prayer life should be such that we come to know the Lord Jesus in an intimate, personal way. Our

Here are some notable sayings about prayer:

"Prayer took much of the time and strength of Jesus. One who does not spend much time in prayer cannot properly be called a follower of Jesus Christ" (R. A. Torrey).

"I never prayed sincerely for anything but [that] it came, at some time . . . somehow, in some shape" (Adoniram Judson).

prayer life becomes effective as our relationship with Christ becomes more intimate.

I will do whatever you ask in my name, so that the Son may bring glory to the Father. You may ask me for anything in my name, and I will do it (John 14:13,14).

List ways you can increase the amount of time you spend in prayer.

Principle Three: We Must Fellowship With Other Christians

Read 1 Corinthians 12:12–27.

1. As God's children, what should we not neglect (Hebrews 10:23–25)? *(Our own assembling together.)*

2. According to the above verses, what should we do for one another? *(Stimulate each other to love and good deeds, encourage one another.)*

In what ways have you done them recently and for whom?

(Ask a group member to read the paragraph in the student's Study Guide under principle three, and discuss the diagram.)

Here are some notable sayings about the church:

"It is the will of Christ that his followers should assemble together . . . The communion of the saints is a great help and privilege, and a good means of steadiness and perseverance" (Matthew Henry).

"Every true follower of Christ should be identified in some way with the Christian community. The church needs men, but more than this, men need the church" (Lindsell and Woodbridge).

Think of a group you may belong to—a fraternity or sorority, a political group, or a social club. Now suppose the members of this group never came together and most of them did not even know each other. All business was transacted by mail.

❷ How much would this group mean to its members?

❓How much enthusiasm would they have for it?

❓How much good would the group do them?

Likewise, Christians who have little to do with each other and never come together in a group, can accomplish nothing. If the early Christians had not assembled for mutual encouragement and common worship, Christianity never could have survived and we would not know Christ today!

3. The new believers in Acts 2:42 continued stead-fastly in what four things?

This Scripture pictures the Christian church right after it came into being, with these four characteristics:

1) *(The apostles' teaching.)*

Adherence to the apostles' doctrines, which are now contained for us in the New Testament. We should select a church where the Bible is explained and preached.

2) *(Fellowship.)*

Fellowship. The Christians regularly met together for fellowship and mutual encouragement.

3) *(Breaking of bread.)*

Breaking of bread, which was the communion service. Since Christians had no church buildings then, this was done in homes. Usually they ate a meal also, which was known as a "love feast." It was a time of very close fellowship.

4) *(Prayer.)*

Prayers. Systematic, definite, positive praying, not as individuals only, but in connection with one another.

Why is each one so vital to spiritual growth?

Verse 43 describes the effect this new society had upon the outside world. These early Christians had a closeness, a fellowship, and a vitality that many churches lack today.

4. In what ways do you profit from Christian fellowship? Be specific.
(We can profit from others' experiences.
We receive mutual encouragement.
We have the opportunity for group prayer; God especially honors united prayer (Matthew 18:19).
We can learn what others have discovered in the Bible.
We can be involved in the planning and teamwork for reaching others with the message of Christ.)

5. Why is it important that a Christian be part of a small group with other Christians sharing the Word of God?
(To receive support and encouragement, and to build each other up in the faith.)

Why is it so necessary to work out conflicts with members of your Christian circle?
(So our fellowship is unbroken and we can function as members of Christ's body.)

What can happen if you don't?

What steps can you take to resolve conflict with others? (Read 1 Peter 3:8–11.)
(Don't repay evil with evil; keep your words and attitude loving; seek peace.)

❖How do you think the practices of the church described in verse 42 related to its effectiveness?

In contrast to the closeness of the early Christians, A. B. Bruce has compared many churches today to a restaurant "where all kinds of people meet for a short space, sit down together ... then part, neither knowing nor caring anything about each other."

Fellowship means more than mere friendship. The Greek word for fellowship is *koinonia,* which means "sharing in common." We desperately need to share our Christian experiences with other believers and likewise allow them to share with us. The church, where we gather together to worship God and to hear His Word preached, is His appointed place for Christians to meet in fellowship. In addition to church gatherings, other meetings— on campus, at work, in homes, or at other places—can also be extremely helpful. Those meetings, however, should never take the place of regular church attendance.

Principle Four:
We Must Witness for Christ

Read Acts 26:12–29.

1. In Romans 1:14–16, Paul tells us his own attitude about sharing the gospel with others. Using his three "I am's" as the keys to the passage, describe his attitude in your own words.
   ("I am obligated both to Greeks and non-Greeks ... I am so eager to preach the gospel...I am not ashamed of the gospel.")

2. Compare your own attitude concerning witnessing with that of Paul (Colossians 1:28).

3. What did Peter tell us we should always be ready to do (1 Peter 3:15)?
   ("To give an answer... for the hope that you have.")

   Where and when can you do this?

4. What was Jesus' promise in Acts 1:8?
   ("[You] will receive power ... be my witnesses.")

   How is His promise shown in your life today?

5. Name at least three people to whom you are impressed to witness in the power of the Holy Spirit.
   1)
   2)
   3)

(Have someone read the paragraph under principle four in the student's book, and discuss it and the diagram.)

Paul's three great "I am's":

♦ *"I am obligated"*—The Greeks Paul refers to here were those versed in Greek language and culture. The non-Greeks were people not associated with Greek culture, generally the less educated. The wise were the morally wise; the foolish were those of low morals. So in this verse Paul makes clear that our obligation is to all kinds of people, cultured and crude, good and bad. We have a universal debt.

♦ *"I am eager"*—The Greek word for eager means "of a forward mind," hence, willing and ready. Paul did not witness out of sheer duty; he was eager to so serve His Lord. God should not have to force us to witness. Compare 2 Corinthians 5:14.

♦ *"I am not ashamed"*—There was a great deal in the gospel that might tempt Paul to be ashamed, for it centered around a man who was crucified. It had little appeal to the scholars of the day, and its followers were persecuted and despised. But Paul was not ashamed. James Denney notes, "The conception of the gospel as a force ... is demonstrated, not by argument, but by what it does; and looking to what it can do, Paul is proud to preach it anywhere."

Prayerfully ask God to show you ways to share your faith in Christ with each one.

It is the privilege and responsibility of every Christian to reach his world with the message of Christ. If you would like to receive more information on how to witness effectively for Christ, write to Campus Crusade for Christ, 100 Sunport Lane, Dept. 21-00, Orlando, FL 32809. Ask for specially prepared materials to help you witness for Christ.

Here are some helpful suggestions for witnessing:

Combine aggressiveness with tact. People will not generally come to you. Often you must go to them and make your own openings for presenting the gospel. But *always* demonstrate love and tact. Irreparable damage can be done by those who witness in an offensive manner. If you are driving people away rather than winning them, you need to change your methods.

Use a good plan of presentation, such as the *Four Spiritual Laws,* which can be obtained from Campus Crusade. This will make your witnessing more organized, concise, and effective.

Avoid arguing. Arguments never win people and usually drive them away. If the person wants to argue, don't feel obliged to continue witnessing.

Expect people to trust Christ. In John 15:5,8, Jesus promises us much fruit if we follow Him. In Matthew 9:37,38, He says the harvest is great and the laborers are few. Multitudes are waiting to hear the gospel, so you need have no fear in approaching people. If some do not accept, do not be discouraged. Sooner or later, others will.

(Share with the class one of your own witnessing experiences.)

Principle Five:
We Must Obey God

Read Romans 6:14–23.

1. What did Christ teach concerning the possibility of serving more than

(Ask a student to read aloud the paragraph in the student's Study Guide under principle five, and discuss the diagram.)

Here are some reasons we should obey God:

one master (Matthew 6:24)?
(It is impossible to serve or love or hold to two masters.)

2. How much should you love the Lord (Matthew 22:37)?
(Completely, with all your heart, soul and mind.)

3. How can you prove that you love Him (John 14:21)?
(By keeping His commands.)

How have you done this today?

This week?

4. What will be the result of keeping Christ's commandments (John 15:10, 11)?
(You will remain in His love and your joy will be complete.)

5. What is God's standard of life for those who say they are abiding in Christ (1 John 2:6)?
(They are to be walking as Christ walked.)

6. Where do we get the power to obey God (Philippians 2:13)?
(God is at work in us.)

What happens if we try to obey God's commands in our own effort?

7. In light of Luke 6:46–49, why do you think obedience to Christ is imperative for your life?

◆ Because we love Him (John 14:21).

◆ Because we cannot possibly benefit by disobedience (Job 9:4; Galatians 6:7,8).

Before his conversion, Paul was convinced that Christianity was a fraud and a heresy, so he took extreme measures to stamp it out.

After his conversion, when he realized his mistake, he began to serve God with all of his heart. He was always either for or against Christianity, but he never made the mistake of trying to be neutral.

Revelation 3:16 says that God counts lukewarmness and neutrality a greater sin toward Christ than active opposition to Him!

Matthew Henry comments on Matthew 6:24:

Our Lord Jesus here exposes . . . those . . . who think to divide between God and the world, to have a treasure on earth and a treasure in heaven too . . . He does not say we must not or we should not, but we cannot serve God and mammon.

Matthew Henry also said, "Our love of God must be a sincere love, and not in word and tongue only, as theirs is who say they love Him, but their hearts are not with Him . . . All the powers of the soul must be engaged for Him, and carried out toward Him. This is the first and great commandment."

On this chart, list the five key principles of Christian growth, a key verse relating to each one, why it is essential to spiritual maturity, and at least one way you can apply each principle to your own life.

❖   ❖   ❖

Conclusion and Application

C. T. Studd—a missionary to Africa who gave up fame, fortune, and family to be spent for God on a primitive continent—wrote, "If Christ be God, and died for me, there is nothing too great that I can do for Him."

(See the student's Study Guide for the chart referred to in the "Life Application.")

Closing Prayer

❖   ❖   ❖

The Christian's Authority

Opening Prayer

Discussion Starter

A biographer of General Douglas MacArthur recorded that one evening before a major battle in the Pacific, feeling uneasy, the general picked up his Bible and read until he felt at peace. Then he went to bed and slept soundly, even though the battle the next day would play a decisive role in the course of World War II.

Why do you suppose he read the Bible?

Why not Shakespeare, or some great novel, or some discourse on philosophy?

Because of its authority as God's Word to man, the Bible has the power to bring peace, happiness, and comfort as no other book can do.

Lesson Development

(Ask one of the group members to summarize the paragraphs at the opening of this lesson in the student's book. Note the diagram and discuss it.)

Leader's Objective: To demonstrate the dependability and authority of the Bible, and to motivate students to study it and apply its truths to their lives

Bible Study

Biblical Claims of Authority

1. What were the attitudes of the following prophets concerning their writings?

   Isaiah 43:1–12
   (This is what the Lord says.)

   Jeremiah 23:1–8
   (Declares the Lord.)

   Ezekiel 36:32–38
   (Declares the sovereign Lord.)

2. What were the attitudes of the following authors toward other writers of Scripture?

   Paul (Romans 3:1,2)
   ("They have been entrusted with the very words of God.")

   Peter (2 Peter 1:19–21)
   ("These men were carried along by the Holy Spirit.")

   The writer of Hebrews (1:1)
   ("God spoke...to our forefathers.")

3. If these writers had this high regard for Scripture, how should we view the Bible?

   What part should God's Word have in our lives and in the way we evaluate and react to circumstances and events?

❷Why has the Bible met man's basic need?

It is an authoritative message from God, who knows the human heart as no one else can, so it naturally meets the needs of the human heart as nothing else can.

Carl F. H. Henry writes concerning the Old Testament prophets:

> Both in speech and writing they are marked off by their unswerving assurance that they were spokesmen for the living God ... The constantly repeated formula, 'thus saith the Lord,' is so characteristic of the prophets as to leave no doubt that they considered themselves chosen agents of the divine self-communication.

New Testament writers likewise viewed Old Testament Scripture as being inspired of God. Carl F. H. Henry wrote that toward their own writings:

> ...they extended the traditional claims of divine inspiration. Jesus ...spoke of a further ministry of teaching by the Spirit (John 14:26; 16:13). The apostles assert confidently that they thus speak by the Spirit (1 Peter 1:12).

> ...They not only assume a divine authority (1 Thessalonians 4:2,15; 2 Thessalonians 3:6,12), but they make acceptance of their written commands a test of spiritual obedience (1 Corinthians 14:37).

Either writers of the Bible were deluded, or the Bible is from God. But this greatest and most influential book of all time does not give evidence of being the product of deluded men. Rather, the power of the Bible demon-

Purpose of Personal Bible Study

1. Name some practical results of a thorough study of the Word of God (2 Timothy 3:15–17).
   (Gives wisdom, knowledge of salvation, is useful for teaching, rebuking, correcting, training in righteousness; equips men of God for every good work.)

   What changes have you seen in your life from your study of the Bible?

2. In Acts 20:32, Paul says that the Word of God is able to do what two things?
   (Build you up;
   Give you inheritance among all those who are sanctified.)

3. What should be the effect of reading the Bible on your own life (James 1:22–25)?
   (It reveals who you really are; it helps you remember how to be obedient; and it promises blessings when you do obey God's Word.)

   Think of a difficult circumstance in your life. In what ways is reading and meditating on God's Word helping you cope with the situation?

   How are you applying God's Word to your problem?

strates that it does indeed come from God.

Additional results of Bible study are found in John 15:3,7; Romans 15:4; and 1 Peter 2:2,3.

One who hears and studies God's Word without doing anything about it is like a man who looks in a mirror, sees that his face is dirty and unshaven, yet goes away without washing or shaving.

Herbert Spencer said, "The great aim of education is not knowledge but action."

Phillips translates 1 John 2:4–6 this way:

> It is only when we obey God's laws that we can be quite sure that we really know Him. The man who claims to know God but does not obey His laws is not only a liar but lives in self-delusion. In practice, the more a man learns to obey God's laws, the more truly and fully does he express his love for Him. Obedience is the test of whether we really live 'in God' or not.

Bible Study Exercise

(If time permits, go over the sections on preparation and procedure for personal Bible study in the student's book. Then give each group member two 8½ x 11 sheets of paper. Have them make two columns on one sheet. Over the first column they are to write "OBSERVATION"; over the second, "INTERPRETATION." Then at the top of the second sheet have them write "APPLICATION."

Preparations for Personal Bible Study

1. Set aside a definite time. When did Moses meet with God (Exodus 34:2–4)?
   (Early in the morning.)

   When did Christ meet with God (Mark 1:35)?
   (In the early morning before dawn.)

   When is the best time for you?

2. Find a definite place. Where did Christ pray (Mark 1:35)?
   (Where he could be alone.)

   What is the value of being alone?
   (You have no distractions.)

3. Employ these tools:
   ◆ Modern translation of the Bible
   ◆ Notebook and pen
   ◆ Dictionary

   How can you use these tools in your Bible study?

Procedure for Personal Bible Study

Using Psalm 119:57–104, go through these three major steps of methodical Bible study:

1. *Observation:* What does the passage say?

Have the class divide into small groups and spend about twenty minutes studying Luke 19:1–10, recording their findings on their papers and answering the questions in the "Life Application."

Afterward, have them come back together and share their results.

This is inductive Bible study, and a sample might look like the following.)

OBSERVATION	INTERPRETATION
Verses 1,2—Zacchaeus was a *chief* tax collector and *very* rich.	Tax collectors were often cruel and dishonest. Zacchaeus had probably been unscrupulous in acquiring his riches.
Verses 3,4—Zacchaeus *ran* ahead of the crowd and climbed a sycamore tree to see Jesus.	He must have been extremely anxious to see Jesus to go to so much trouble. His behavior was even more remarkable considering his wealth and high position.
Verses 5,6—Jesus saw Zacchaeus and invited Himself to stay at his house. Zacchaeus responded by receiving Jesus *joyfully.*	Jesus evidently had observed Zacchaeus' behavior and detected a hungry soul, thus He had no reservations about His boldness.
Verse 7—The crowd murmured against Jesus because He stayed with a man of bad reputation rather than with one of the religious rulers.	The crowd must have been very self-righteous. They should have been overjoyed that such a man as Zacchaeus would be interested in Jesus.

Read quickly for content. Read again carefully, underlining key words and phrases.

2. *Interpretation:* What does the passage mean?

Ask God to give you understanding of the passage. Consult a dictionary or modern translation for the precise meaning of words.

Ask: Who? What? When? Where? Why? How?

3. *Application:* Ask yourself, *What does the passage mean to me and how can I apply it to my life?*

Make a list of the following:

♦ Attitudes to be changed

♦ Actions to take or avoid

♦ Promises to claim

♦ Sins to confess and forsake

♦ Examples to follow

♦ Other personal applications

Verse 8,9—Zacchaeus publicly announced that he would give half of his fortune to the poor, and offered to restore *four* times as much as he may have cheated any individual. Jesus responded by announcing that *this day* Zacchaeus had acquired salvation, and that he was a true descendant of Abraham.	Zacchaeus offered proof of a conversion experience. Before this time money had probably been his god, but he gave up what he had considered most dear for something worth much more. Jesus' response showed how willing God is to forget past sins when we give evidence of true repentance.
Verse 10—Jesus said He came specifically to save the lost.	This is apparently the whole point of the story. Zacchaeus was lost, and now was found. The crowd also was lost, but did not know it, hence remained lost.

APPLICATION
(Through first 7 verses)

Verses 1–4: (1) Among even the least likely people there are those ready to receive God. Do I have friends who are outwardly sinful and godless, but *inwardly* as anxious as Zacchaeus to know Christ? (2) God responds immediately to a seeking heart. Zacchaeus did not have to wait to find salvation. I do not have to wait to find God in my daily experience either. I can know Him *now.*

Verses 5,6: (1) Jesus knows who will respond to Him and who will not—if I am led by Him, I will come into contact with hungry souls just as He did.

LIFE APPLICATION

1. Study Luke 19:1–10 and apply the Bible study method you have just learned.

   What does the passage say?

   What does it mean?

   How does this apply to you?

   How effective will this method of Bible study be for you now with other Scripture passages?

2. What changes in your life do you expect as you proceed with more in-depth Bible study?

3. Plan your Bible study time for the next four weeks.

   Write down the time, the place, and the passages to be studied.

(2) Jesus was bold in inviting Himself to stay with Zacchaeus. If I meet one who is hungry for God, can I be bold with him, too?

Verse 7: (1) How easy it is to be snobbish. Do I purposely steer clear of others just because they don't measure up to my standards?
(2) How easy it is to be self-righteous. Zacchaeus *knew* he needed Jesus—the crowd did not. Do I feel I am pretty good, and do not need Jesus as much as others?

(Have students continue application of other verses on their own.)

Conclusion and Application

(Use the Bible study exercise in the "Life Application" section as your conclusion.)

(If you didn't have time to finish in class, encourage the students to complete it at home.)

Closing Prayer

Learning to Pray

Opening Prayer

Discussion Starter

❷ What do you think are the main ingredients in a meaningful dialogue between two people? Name at least five things.

❷ How does each of these ingredients relate to your communication with God?

❷ How is communicating with God different from communicating with another person?

❷ In your opinion, does this make communicating with God harder or easier?

❷ What things keep you from having a more effective prayer life?

Leader's Objective: To help students discover what prayer is, to give them the basic elements of how to pray, and to encourage them to begin a consistent, effective prayer life

Lesson Development

(Ask a volunteer to summarize the material in the opening paragraphs of this lesson in the student's book. Then discuss the questions and answers.)

LESSON 5

Bible Study

What Is Prayer?

Since prayer is communication between two persons, it can also be described as a dialogue. Write a sentence about the part each of the following statements have in the dialogue between the believer and God:

1. Prayer is the privilege of believers (1 John 3:22, 23).
   (We pray and receive what we ask for because we keep God's commandments. His greatest commandments are that we believe in Jesus and love one another.)

2. We relate to God as children to a father (Ephesians 2:4,5,8; 1 Peter 5:7).
   (God loves us so much that we were made alive in Christ, and we can put all of our cares on Him.)

3. God wants to hear what we say (Psalms 62:8; 65:2; Proverbs 15:8).
   (God wants to be our refuge; He promises to listen to us; He delights in our prayers.)

4. God delights in and longs for our fellowship (Psalm 27:8; John 4:23; Proverbs 15:8).
   (God wants us to seek Him; He delights in talking to us. He wants to hear

Some essentials for true communication are listening, having an open heart, and enjoying a unity of thought and spirit. Dialogue does not depend on how much you know but on how much of yourself you bring to the conversation.

A dialogue is not a "have-to" on anyone's part. Dialogue happens when both parties participate willingly. In prayer, God willingly agrees to listen to us.

❓What are the qualities of a loving father-son dialogue?

❓How is it like our communication with God?

Listening is an essential ingredient in dialogue, and God has promised to listen to us.

God's communication with us goes beyond mere dialogue, all the way to close friendship and unconditional love. These things make our dialogue with Him meaningful, safe, and enjoyable.

us and answer our prayers; He wants us to share His Spirit.)

5. We can talk to God about anything (Matthew 7:7; John 16:24).
   (God promises to give us what we ask for when we seek Him; when we receive what He gives us, we will also have joy.)

6. Prayer can keep us from sin (Matthew 26:41).
   (Because our spirit is weak, we need to communicate moment by moment with God to stay away from sin.)

How to Pray

1. What part does the Holy Spirit play in prayer (Romans 8:26,27)?
   (He intercedes for us when we do not know how to pray.)

2. What do these verses teach about how to pray?
   Psalm 145:18
   (The Lord is near to us when we pray in truth.)
   Matthew 6:5–7
   (We should pray in secret, humbly, and avoid meaningless words.)
   Matthew 21:22
   (Believe God will give you what you ask for.)
   Philippians 4:6
   (Bring all your requests to God, and be thankful.)

3. What vital elements of prayer are found in Acts 4:24–30?
   (Unity between Chris-

Dialogue implies an openness with each other. Since God knows all about us, we do not need to fear talking to Him about anything.

When we talk with someone, we are constantly being influenced by that person. When we continually talk with God, we will be influenced by Him rather than by temptations or worldly desires.

Many Christians get caught up in the "how" of prayer and make communication with God a difficult and cumbersome experience. But God wants us to come to Him wherever we are and at all times. He does not require special words, only a clean heart.

The story is told of a saintly man who was known for his prayer life. One day his friends decided to secretly find out how long he prayed before going to bed. They hid themselves outside his window and waited.

To their surprise, he just got into bed, arranged his covers, and prayed, "Good night, Lord Jesus. I have had a wonderful time with You today, and look forward to spending another day with You tomorrow, if You see fit to spare me."

To this man, prayer was walking and talking with God throughout his day.

tians, praise to God, petitions for ministry.)

4. What vital elements of prayer did Christ include in His prayer in John 17? *(Praise, submission to God's will, prayer for Himself and His work, prayer for others, prayer that others would know about Himself, prayer for spiritual unity and growth for His friends.)*

5. What are some of the promises Christ makes to you when you pray?

   Matthew 6:6
   (The Father will reward our prayers.)

   Matthew 18:20
   (When we pray with others, God will be there.)

   Luke 11:9–13
   (The Father will give us good things when we ask.)

   John 14:13,14
   (When we ask in Jesus' name, He will answer.)

First Thessalonians 5:17 tells us to pray continually. If we are always conversing with God, we will find our Christian life truly an adventure with Him.

God has given us many more promises concerning prayer. You may want to look them up in your Bible. (Show your students how to use a Bible concordance to look up more references to prayer on their own. Suggest that they list these promises and tuck them into their Bibles or prayer notebooks so they can review the promises periodically.)

Steps to Having an Effective Prayer Life

Read the following verses and explain why each step is necessary to pray effectively.

1. Abide (John 15:7)
   (This is the key to successful prayer. Christ commands us to abide in Him.)

Abiding is:

◆ Living a life of faith and obedience

◆ In the fullness of the Holy Spirit

◆ Surrendered to the Lordship of Christ

◆ With no unconfessed sin

◆ Being totally available to God

❓If you abide in Christ, how will your life change?

2. Ask (James 4:2,3)
   (If we expect answers to our prayers, we must first ask.)

3. Believe (Matthew 21:22)
   (Believing is at the heart of answered prayer.)

Asking is such a simple direction. Yet when we ask, we are showing our dependence and faith in God.

❓What does not asking imply?

Faith (or believing) comes from God. It is not something we try to muster on our own. A life of faith is experienced by those who walk in obedience. Only when we let God control our lives can we pray in faith. (Give an example from your life of a time when you prayed in faith and the results you saw.)

In 1954, Roger Bannister broke the four-minute mile. It had never been broken before in all the centuries of recorded history, but Bannister believed it could be done. He developed a mental picture of himself breaking the four-minute mile record, and he did it. Since 1954, several hundred other athletes have broken the four-minute mile, simply because Roger Bannister proved it could be done.

If an individual with only human resources is able to accomplish outstanding success, how much more can you accomplish when you place your faith in the omnipotent God and draw upon His supernatural, inexhaustible resources? Certainly, you can do all that God wants you to and see His blessings on your life for your obedience in prayer.

4. Receive (1 John 5:14,15)
   (By faith, claim the answer to your request.)

If you know you are abiding in Christ and are controlled by the Holy Spirit and are praying according to the Word and will of God, you can expect God to answer your prayer (1 John

1. Set a time and place for your daily prayer time.

   Time _____

   Place _____

2. Use a small notebook to help you pray effectively.

   ◆ On page one, make a list of people whom you want to remember daily in prayer.

   ◆ On page two, write a list of things for which you will praise and thank God. Update this list daily.

   ◆ On page three, write the date, prayer requests, and Scripture verses relating to your requests. Leave room to write down the answer and date for each request.

   ◆ Each day, repeat the first two points, checking for answered prayers to record on earlier days.

   ◆ Keep this notebook with your Bible so you can refer to it during the day to pray for and record concerns, needs, praises, or thanks that come to mind.

5:14,15). So be prepared to receive the answer. Imagine right now that you are receiving the answer to your request, and begin to thank God for it.

Conclusion and Application

Remember that, as you bow in prayer, you are tapping a source of power that can change the course of history. God's mighty power, His love, His wisdom, and His grace are available to you if you will but believe Him and claim them. Jesus promised in John 14:12 that you would do the same miracles He did, and even greater ones.

One way to ensure that we have a consistent prayer life is to begin a prayer notebook. First, would a few of you share some of your creative ideas for personal prayer times? (Have some of the students share.)

Prayer changes things—and people. By way of encouragement, turn to the person next to you and share an answer to prayer you experienced that changed a person or situation. (Wait a few moments for partners to share.)

(If you have time, help your group members begin their prayer notebook. Have pieces of paper available; show them how to set up their notebooks; then go through a sample prayer time.)

Closing Prayer

The Importance of the Church

Opening Prayer

Discussion Starter

❷ Why do you think Jesus Christ founded the local church?

(Have students list as many reasons as possible.)

Lesson Development

(Ask one of the group members to summarize the paragraphs appearing at the opening of this lesson in the student's book; note the diagram and discuss it.)

The early Christians also studied the Bible, had fellowship with each other, celebrated the communion service, and witnessed fearlessly in every place possible.

Leader's Objective: To demonstrate to the students the importance of the church and to encourage them to be active in it

LESSON 6

Bible Study

Composition of the Church

1. What did the early Christians do that we should do also?

   Acts 2:41,42
   (They were baptized and added to the church; were taught, fellowshipped, shared in the Lord's Supper, and prayed.)

   Acts 4:31
   (They prayed, were filled with the Holy Spirit, and preached the Word.)

   Acts 5:41,42; 8:4
   (They rejoiced, taught, and preached Jesus as Christ.)

   List several ways you can apply these in your Christian walk.

2. As God's children, how do we obey the instruction given in Hebrews 10:25?
   (Assemble together, share in worship, fellowship, church activities, and witnessing.)

3. The entire church is compared to a __(body)__ of which Christ is the __(head)__ and the individual believers are the __(members)__ (Colossians 1:18; 1 Corinthians 12:27).

4. Read 1 Thessalonians 1:1–10, then list here

Concerning the early church, which we read about in the Book of Acts and the New Testament Epistles, J. B. Phillips says:

> The great difference between present-day Christianity and that of which we read in these letters is that to us it is primarily a performance, to them it was a real experience . . . the invasion of their lives by a new quality of life altogether.

The Bible *commands* Christians to assemble regularly.

> The Christian life is not just our own private affair. If we have been born again into God's family, not only has He become our Father but every other Christian believer in the world . . . has become our brother or sister in Christ . . . Every Christian's place is in a local church (John R. Stott).

Matthew Henry says about the church as the body of Christ:

> Each [Christian] stands related to the body as a part of it . . . Mutual indifference, . . . contempt, and hatred, and envy, and strife, are very unnatural in Christians. It is like the members of the same body being destitute of all concern for one another.

some qualities God desires in members of any church.
(Work of faith, labor of love, endurance inspired by hope, imitators of Paul and Lord, model to all believers, good reputation, turn to God from idols, wait for Jesus' return.)

In what ways do you demonstrate these qualities?

Ordinances of the Church

1. What do you believe baptism accomplishes (Matthew 28:19)?
   (It is an act of obedience, public proclamation of faith, announcement to world of identification with Christ and His cause.)

   Who is eligible for baptism?
   (Those who are discipled.)

   What was the significance of your baptism?

   Baptism was an initiatory rite practiced by the Jews in the time of Jesus to signify that an individual was identifying himself with Judaism as a convert, or with a particular movement within Judaism, such as that led by John the Baptist.

   The early church took over this rite so that Christians could make a public proclamation of their faith and announce to the world that they had identified themselves with Christ and His cause.

   To all churches, baptism is essential to an obedient walk with the Lord.

2. What is the meaning of the communion service (1 Corinthians 11:23–26)?
   (It is an act of obedience, a time of facing Jesus' death, and a time to examine our lives.)

   How do you prepare yourself to observe the Lord's Supper?

   (Ask the group members to share their understanding of the meaning of the communion service.)

   Celebration of the Lord's Supper was given to the disciples to be incorporated into their remembrance of Him. Participation in this act also is essential to the obedient walk of the believer.

Purposes of the Church

1. What should be one of the basic purposes of a church (2 Timothy 4:2)? *(Preach the Word of God.)*

   How does the church you attend fulfill the purposes given in this verse?

2. List several of your own reasons for joining a church.

3. What should the church believe about Christ's:

   Birth (Matthew 1:23) *(He was virgin-born.)*

   Deity (John 1:14) *(The Word [God] became flesh.)*

   Death (1 Peter 2:24) *(Jesus died for our sins.)*

Kenneth Wuest says:

> The preacher must present, not book reviews, not politics, not economics, not current topics of the day, not a philosophy of life denying the Bible and based upon unproven theories of science, but the Word. The preacher . . . cannot choose his message. He is given a message to proclaim by his Sovereign. If he will not proclaim that, let him step down from his exalted position.

A church should believe five basic things (among others):

◆ *The virgin birth*—"Practically every person who denies the doctrine rejects the supernatural as such . . . (and that denial) deprives us of knowledge as to the manner in which He entered the world. It seriously weakens, if it does not destroy, the doctrine of the incarnation (God manifest in the flesh) upon which our confidence rests and without which the Christian faith cannot survive" (Lindsell and Woodbridge).

◆ *The deity of Christ*—"Unfortunately some believe that His deity is of little importance and . . . that the Christian faith is coherent, sufficient, and satisfactory even if Jesus is not God . . . If Jesus is not God, then He bore false witness. He was a liar and thus a sinner Himself . . . The Bible itself would be an unreliable witness . . . founded on error" (Lindsell and Woodbridge).

◆ *The death of Christ*—"Man separates himself from God by sin, and death is the natural result . . . But it was not that way that Jesus became subject to death since He had no personal sin ... Death is ... the judicially imposed and inflicted punishment of sin ... It is from this ... point of view that the death of Christ must be considered" (Louis Berkhof).

When Christ died, *He* bore the punishment for *our* sins.

Resurrection (1 Corinthians 15:3,4)
(It is a fact.)

◆ *The resurrection of Christ*—According to A. H. Strong, "The resurrection of our Lord teaches three important lessons:

1) It showed that His work of atonement was completed and was stamped with divine approval.

2) It showed Him to be Lord of all and gave the one sufficient external proof of Christianity.

3) It furnished the ground and pledge of our own resurrection, and thus 'brought life and immortality to light' (2 Timothy 1:10)."

Second coming (1 Thessalonians 4:16,17)?
(It will occur.)

◆ *Second coming of Christ*—"The faith in a second coming of Christ has lost its hold upon many Christians in our day. But it still serves to stimulate and admonish the great body, and we can never dispense with its solemn and mighty influence" (A. H. Strong).

Where does your church stand on these truths? It may be helpful to obtain a doctrinal statement from your church and research these areas.

God has given the following to the church:

◆ *Evangelists*—Evangelists are those who present the gospel to the lost. Billy Graham, foreign missionaries, and many laymen effective in win-

4. What abilities does God give (besides those of serving as a prophet or apostle) to strengthen the church members (Ephesians 4:11–13)?
(To be effective as evangelists, pastors, and teachers.)

Which of these roles do you fill?

Which would you like to be involved in?

Why?

How are you preparing yourself for that ministry?

ning others to Christ have been given the gift of evangelism. We are all to witness, but it seems, since certain people are so effective in this area, that God has given this special gift to them.

◆ *Pastors and teachers*—The original Greek makes clear that these are one and the same (pastor-teacher). The term "pastor" originally meant "a feeder of sheep," and it came to be applied to Christians who teach. Ministers are, of course, teachers, but many who never enter the ministry also have this gift and are expected to exercise it.

Many gifts given to the church are not listed here. But God has gifted each of us in some special area.

He expects you to develop your gifts and use them for His glory. The following are examples of some gifts God can bestow on us that we can use for Him:

Superior intellect—You can use this to gain a deeper understanding of the Scriptures and teach others.

Leadership and administrative abilities—You could help organize and oversee some of the Christian activities on your campus, in your community, or in your church.

The ability to help others—You could look for ways God can use you to aid other Christians and to help your church in its ministries.

Maybe, as you evaluate yourself, you feel you are only average. Do not be discouraged. You undoubtedly have

LIFE APPLICATION

1. If you are not already active in a local church, prayerfully list two or three that you will visit in the next month, with the purpose of attending one regularly.

Before you attend the first service, list the qualities you feel are essential for spiritual growth and fellowship. Ask God to show you which church He is leading you to join.

2. The following are suggestions for making your church worship more meaningful:

   ◆ Bow for silent prayer before the service begins. Pray for yourself, for the minister, for those taking part in the service and for those worshiping, that Christ will be very real to all, and that those who do not know Christ may come to know Him.

   ◆ Always take your Bible. Underline portions that are made especially meaningful by the sermons.

   ◆ Take notes on the sermon and apply them to your life.

   Can you list some other ways?

3. If you are a part of a local church, ask God to show you ways you can be more used by Him in the church. List the ways of service that He reveals to you.

hidden talents that God will develop as you follow His will. You must never forget that many average people in the Bible accomplished great feats because they trusted in a great God. Study Hebrews 11.

Conclusion and Application

Writing for the *Ladies' Home Journal,* in an article called, "Shall We Do Away With the Church?" President Theodore Roosevelt once said, "In the pioneer days of the West, we found it an unfailing rule that after a community had existed for a certain length of time, either a church was built or else the community began to go downhill."

Closing Prayer

(Observe a few moments of silence and instruct group members to listen to the inner voice of God as He instructs each one in his relationship with his own church, and give that person an opportunity to make a commitment. Then continue in spoken prayer.)

Recap

Opening Prayer

Discussion Starter

(The first question in the student's Study Guide may be used to start the discussion of this lesson.)

Lesson Development

(Any appropriate material from previous lessons that was not sufficiently covered could be used at this time, and you also may deal with any point that the group members may not understand as well as they could.)

(Then go over the remaining Recap questions and answers. This material will benefit both the students and you by giving you a deeper appreciation of God's Word.)

Leader's Objective: To impress more deeply upon the hearts of the group members the Christian principles and truths presented in the six previous lessons, and to lead the members to any further commitments needed

LESSON 7

The following questions will help you review this Step. If necessary, reread the appropriate lesson(s).

1. Assurance of salvation: Suppose you have just made the great discovery of knowing Jesus Christ personally. In your enthusiasm, you tell someone close to you that you have become a Christian and have eternal life. He replies, "That's mere presumption on your part. No one can be sure that he has eternal life."

   How would you answer him?

   What verse(s) would you use as your authority? *(Possible: John 1:12; 3:16,36; 10:28–30; 1 John 5:12; and others.)*

   (Use question 1 as a way to make sure your students understand how to become a Christian and to be sure they are Christians. You may want to have your group divide into pairs and have each person explain to his partner how he knows for sure that he is a Christian.)

2. Name some of the qualities of a Christ-controlled life.
   (Love, joy, peace, patience, kindness, goodness, faithfulness, gentleness, self-control, Christ-centered, empowered by the Holy Spirit, witnessing, effective prayer life, trusting and obeying God.)

   How are they evident in your life?

3. List the five principles of growth.
   (Bible study; prayer; fellowship; witnessing; obedience.)

   (For question 3, refer to the diagram in Lesson 4.)

Summarize briefly how each of these principles is helping you grow spiritually. How do they interact in your life?

4. What are the three major steps in methodical Bible study?
(Observation: What does it say?
Interpretation: What does it mean?
Application: How does it apply to my life?)

How have these helped you in your study?

List at least three ways Scripture can be applied to your life.
(Change attitudes; confess sins; avoid sinful actions; follow examples; claim promises.)

5. Describe the role that the Bible has played in your life in the past week.

How can you rely more fully on its power next week?

How has using the steps to an effective prayer life changed the way you pray?

How has having a daily prayer time helped your attitudes and actions?

6. Name some characteristics of a New Testament church.
(Preaches the Word of God; believes in the virgin birth and the deity of Jesus, in His atoning death and resurrection, and in His second coming.)

(Use questions 4 and 5 to challenge your students to make the Bible an integral part of their lives. Offer examples of how God used His Word in your life and mention the practical ways you use the Bible to make decisions, to find comfort, to avoid temptation, and to guide you. Do the same for your prayer life. Also give students an opportunity the share their practical examples.)

How does your church compare?

7. What are the two ordinances of the local church?
(Baptism and the Lord's supper.)

8. Whom does God give to the church to strengthen its members?
(Evangelists, pastors, and teachers.)

Which of these roles would you like to fill?

How are you preparing yourself for ministry?

LIFE APPLICATION

1. In what specific ways is your life different now than when you began this study about the Christian adventure?

2. In what areas do you need to obey the Scripture more?

3. Explain to several Christian friends the excitement you feel about Jesus and how your Christian life is an adventure. Use examples of how God has worked in your life and how He has answered your prayers.

(Challenge your students to get involved in a ministry in their local church. Discuss how having a ministry will enrich your life and help you grow in Christ.)

Conclusion and Application

(Give group members a few minutes to think about the "Life Application" questions and then discuss their answers.)

Closing Prayer

(Start with a short time of silent prayer for personal, private commitments to be made. Then conclude by praying aloud.)

❖   ❖   ❖

The Christian and the Abundant Life

Focusing on New Priorities

STEP 2

What Is the Christian Life?

Opening Prayer

Discussion Starter

❓What would you expect in the life of a person who has been made a new creation?

Lesson Development

(Ask one of the group members to summarize the paragraphs appearing at the opening of this lesson in the student's book. Note the diagram and discuss it.)

(One suggested method for studying this lesson is to divide the class into four groups and assign each group a section of the lesson.)

Group 1—A New Creation
Group 2—A New Relationship
          With God
Group 3—A New Motivation
Group 4—A New Relationship
          With Mankind

(Ask each group to discuss and review one or two verses under its topic. The small groups should then reconvene and summarize their conclusions to the entire group.)

❖

Leader's Objective: To explain to the new Christian the difference between his new life in Christ and his old life; to lead the student to whichever commitment is necessary —new birth, or deeper awareness of his new life

LESSON 1

Bible Study

A New Creation

1. On the basis of 2 Corinthians 5:17, what has happened to you?
   (You have become a new creature, or creation.)

   What are some evidences in your life of new things having come, and old things having passed away?

2. To what does the Bible compare this experience of newness (John 3:3)?
   (A new birth.)

   Compare the experience of physical birth with spiritual birth. What are the similarities?

3. How was your new birth accomplished (John 3:16; 1:12,13)?
   (You believe in the Son, receive Him, and thus are born of the will of God.)

4. According to Ephesians 2:8,9, what did you do to merit this gift?
   (Nothing except receive it as a gift.)

   Why is this so important to our spiritual well-being?

5. Colossians 1:13,14 speaks of two kingdoms. Describe the nature of each kingdom in relation to your life before and after you received Christ.

As a result of the new birth, you will experience "Christ living in you."

Physically, life requires birth at a particular time and place. Similarly in the Christian life, you personally receive Christ at a definite time and place.

Many genuine Christians, however, cannot identify the time or place of their conversion yet know with certainty that Jesus Christ lives within them.

(Ask someone in the group to describe a time when they held a new baby. Then say:)

Mankind's attempt to reach God is the opposite of God's way of reaching down to man. Mere religion is like taking a corpse, washing and dressing it, then claiming it is acceptable. The result is that the corpse goes right on decaying. There is no sign of life.

But God doesn't "make over" our sinful natures. He gives us a new birth. We're like that new baby—clean and full of promise for growth and learning. Our future is ahead of us—not behind us.

A New Relationship With God

1. What are you called (1 Peter 2:2)?
   (Newborn baby.)

   What should be your desire?
   (To crave the pure milk of the Word.)

   God's Word tells us that we have the *right* (Greek word means "authority") to call ourselves members of His family. As newborn Christians, we are called "babies" and as such we must immediately receive nourishment. Therefore, as soon as we receive Christ, it is essential that we immediately begin studying the Word of God and fellowship with other members of God's family in church and in other Christian groups.

2. What is your new relationship with God (John 1:12)?
   (You are His child.)

3. What does it mean to you to be a partaker of the divine nature (2 Peter 1:4)?
   (To become more godly.)

   God imparts His nature to us immediately at our spiritual birth. The evidence of His nature is more apparent in some people than in others. *If we give Him our all, He can accomplish more quickly what He wills for us.* This means a total surrender of our lives to God.

4. How do you know that you are God's child (Galatians 4:6; Romans 8:16)?
   (His Holy Spirit dwells within you and witnesses with your spirit.)

   God reveals Himself in each life, assuring us of our salvation. The way He reveals Himself may be completely different in each case. The important thing is that you *know.* See 1 John 5:11–13 for further assurance of what God gives us.

A New Motivation

1. How does the love of Christ motivate you (2 Corinthians 5:14,15)?
   (When you see how much He has sacrificed for you, you want to live for Him.)

   Christ lives in you. He loves, acts, talks through you. Your entire life becomes different because you are no longer living your life, but Christ is living it in you (Galatians 2:20)! His motives are yours. As you study the

2. What has replaced self as the most important factor (verse 15)?
   (Our love for Jesus.)

3. What two things have happened in your life to give you new motivation, according to Colossians 3:1–4?

   (My life is hidden in God; Christ is my life.)

   What has happened to your old life according to verse 3?
   (It is dead.)

   What will motivate you to seek those things that are above, according to verse 1?
   (I have been raised with Christ and given new life.)

   What is the promise we are given (verse 4)?
   (When Christ appears we will appear with Him in glory.)

   How does it affect your motivation?

A New Relationship With Mankind

1. What is new about your relationship with people (1 John 3:11,14)?
   (We are to love one another.)

2. How can you show that you are a follower of Christ (John 13:35)?
   (By having love for each other.)

Bible you will see how He moved among men and had a heart for those around Him. As you "let Jesus live" through you, you will be amazed at your reason for doing things—"for the glory of God."

(Encourage your students to read Matthew 6:19–34 at their first opportunity to become acquainted with the mind of God regarding how to live.)

Through Christians, Christ comforts lonely hearts, instructs and teaches, seeks and saves the lost, and can again walk among men and tell them of His love and sacrifice for their sins.

In what ways are you doing this in your everyday life?

3. Read 2 Corinthians 5:18–21. Describe the ministry that has been given to you.
   (It is a ministry of reconciliation.)

   We are called *(ambassadors)* for Christ (verse 20). In what ways are you fulfilling your call?

4. As a follower of Christ, what is the greatest thing you can do (Matthew 4:19)?
   (Be a fisher of men.)

   Name at least three ways you can do that in your own life.
   1)
   2)
   3)

5. How can your friends benefit from the message you deliver to them (1 John 1:3,4)?
   (They will have fellowship with other Christians and with God, and our joy will be complete.)

LIFE APPLICATION

1. What is the greatest change you have seen in your life since you became a new creation in Christ Jesus?

2. In your new relationship with God, what now can be your response toward problems, disappoint-

As a child of God, your concern is for the whole world. You want others to know the Lord as you do because Jesus Christ died for the world. Your relationship with man is now worldwide and your responsibility is to let Jesus Christ live in you to reconcile the world to Himself.

Conclusion and Application

The Christian life begins with a new birth. It is a personal daily relationship with Christ. It is simply Christ living in you!

ments, and frustrations (1 Peter 5:7; Romans 8:28)?

3. How will you change your goals as a result of your new motivation?

4. What is your responsibility now to other men and women?

   How will you carry it out?

5. List two changes you would like to see in your life now that you are a Christian. Ask God to bring about those changes.

   1)

   2)

Closing Prayer

(Read the following prayers and give those representing each group an opportunity to pray a similar prayer.)

(Salvation:) Lord Jesus, come into my life; forgive me of my sins and change me. Give me a new life, Your life. I exchange my life for Yours.

(Changed life:) Thank You, Lord, for giving me a new life. Make me more conscious of Your presence in my life. I pray that others will see the change in me and want to come to know You, too.

(After a period of silence, close with a brief prayer.)

Appraising Your Spiritual Life

Opening Prayer

(Say to students:)
This study is a very personal one because God and you are the only ones who know your heart. As we work through the study, imagine that you were alone with Christ the day He told this parable. Ask Him to show you on which ground you stand, and be willing to act on what He reveals to you. (After a minute or two of silent prayer, close with a brief prayer aloud.)

Discussion Starter

(As you read these true-false statements, have the students record their answers on a piece of paper.)

1. All good soil produces the same amount of fruit. *(F)*

2. Rocky ground refers to an unreceptive heart. *(F)*

3. Thorny soil includes the deceitfulness of riches. *(T)*

4. Every Christian should be fruitful. *(T)*

5. This parable refers only to people in college. *(F)*

Leader's Objective: To help each student evaluate his or her personal relationship with Christ

LESSON 2

Bible Study

Types of Soil

Read the parable of the sower in Matthew 13:1–23; Mark 4:3–20; Luke 8:4–15.

1. To what does the seed refer (Mark 4:14)?
   (The Word.)

2. What are the four kinds of soil referred to in Matthew 13:4–8?
   (Roadside; rocky; thorny; good.)

Making Soil Productive

1. What does each kind of soil represent?

   Compare Matthew 13:4 with 18,19.
   (Roadside: hard, unreceptive heart, no germination, Satan takes seed.)

   Compare verses 5,6 with 20,21.
   (Rocky: receives with joy, falls in persecution, weak roots.)

   Compare verse 7 with 22.
   (Thorny: worries of world, deceitfulness of riches choke the Word.)

   Compare verse 8 with 23.
   (Good: hears Word, understands, bears fruit to varying degrees.)

6. Patience comes through the trying of our faith. *(T)*

7. God's Word offers the solution to every "care" in life. *(T)*

8. My life would be different if I learned God's solutions and applied them. *(T)*

(Read the answers and have each person correct his own paper. Stress the need to know these truths.)

Lesson Development

(Choose one of the references of the parable of the sower—Matthew 13:1–23, Mark 4:3–20, or Luke 8:4–15—and either ask your group to read aloud in unison or go around the group with each person reading one verse until the passage is completed. Then discuss answers to the questions.)

Roadside soil: A life on which the Word of God has fallen but where Satan, by creating a hard heart or a lack of receptiveness, has snatched away the seed.

Rocky soil: Those who, when they have heard the Word, immediately receive it with gladness and follow Christ for a time, but when difficulty or persecution arises are not rooted enough to stand.

Thorny soil: Cares of the world can be any burden, problem, or decision that is carried by self instead of being cast on the Lord: grades, dating, spouse, job, future, health, etc. Deceitfulness of riches refers to allowing things to give you a false sense of security—believing that this is what brings

2. What must happen for the roadside soil to be changed (Hebrews 3:15)? *(Hearts must not be hardened, but must be made receptive. See also Romans 10:17.)*

3. How can unproductive, rocky ground be made productive (1 Corinthians 10:13 and Proverbs 29:25)?
   (Look for God's provision for endurance/escape; trust Him.)

fulfillment and happiness—for instance, a rich, successful man who ends his life in suicide. Lusts are great, driving, fleshly desires, and they apply to all of life including possessions and ambitions.

We are promised that persecution will come so that:

> . . . no one would be unsettled by these trials. You know quite well that we were destined for them (1 Thessalonians 3:3).

> To this you were called, because Christ suffered for you, leaving you an example, that you should follow in his steps (1 Peter 2:21).

Yet 1 Corinthians 10:13 tells us God has promised us nothing too great to bear:

> No temptation has seized you except what is common to man. And God is faithful; he will not let you be tempted beyond what you can bear. But when you are tempted, he will also provide a way out so that you can stand up under it.

(Encourage students to memorize this important verse.)

And Romans 8:28 reminds us that:

> God works for the good of those who love him, who have been called according to his purpose.

For God's answers to:

◆ Ridicule from the world—see John 15:18–21

◆ Persecution from Satan—see Revelation 2:10

◆ Strife from within—see Romans 7:15–25

4. How can individuals described as thorny soil become vital and effective Christians (1 Peter 5:7; Matthew 6:19–21)?
(By casting all anxiety on Him.)

In the Amplified Version of the Bible, 1 Peter 5:7 says,

> Casting the whole of your care—all your anxieties, all your worries, all your concerns, once and for all—on Him; for He cares for you affectionately, and cares about you watchfully.

See also Psalm 37:1–7.

For further information about the deceitfulness of riches and the dangers of lust, see Matthew 6:19–21; 1 John 2:15–17; and 1 Corinthians 6:18.

Determine to be a single-minded person. James 1:8 refers to "a double-minded man, unstable in all he does." James 4:8 says,

> Come near to God and he will come near to you. Wash your hands, you sinners, and purify your hearts, you double-minded.

Result of Dwelling in Good Soil

1. What condition in a Christian results in abundance of fruit (Mark 4:20; Luke 8:15)?
(He must hear the Word and accept it.)

To live the victorious life is to live on *good ground* and to *abide* in Christ.

> I am the vine; you are the branches. If a man remains in me and I in him, he will bear much fruit; apart from me you can do nothing (John 15:5).

In the Amplified Version, Galatians 5:22,23 gives us the fruit of the Spirit this way:

> The fruit of the (Holy) Spirit, (the work which His presence within accomplishes) is love, joy (gladness), peace, patience (an even temper, forbearance), kindness, goodness (benevolence), faithfulness, meekness (humility), gentleness, self-control (self-restraint, continence). Against such things there is no law (that can bring a charge).

2. What type of soil do most of the professing Christians you know represent?

3. What type of soil would you say your life now represents?

4. What type of soil do you want your life to represent?

1. How must the soil of your life be changed to become good ground or to increase in its fruitfulness?

2. List several problem areas that need changing.

3. What must you trust Christ to do?

❖ ❖ ❖

We are instructed in 2 Peter 1:5–7 to have faith, moral excellence, knowledge, self-control, perseverance, godliness, brotherly kindness, and love in order to be fruitful. In John 15:16, Jesus says we should bear much fruit and that our fruit should last.

Conclusion and Application

Only good soil brings forth fruit: some thirty times, some sixty, some one hundred. This is referred to in John 15:1–5 as fruit, more fruit, much fruit:

On the one hand	*On the other hand*
Neglect the Word	Hear the Word
Fear of man	Trust in the Lord
Satan's snares	God's victory
Flesh pleased	Spirit fed
Burdened	Carefree
Materialistic	Spiritual
Worldly	Godly
Fruitless	Fruitful

Closing Prayer

❖ ❖ ❖

Living Abundantly

Opening Prayer

Discussion Starter

(Ask each person in the group to write his definition of what abundant life really is. Then invite volunteers to share their ideas.)

Lesson Development

(Ask one of the group members to summarize the paragraphs appearing at the opening of this lesson in the student's book.)

At the moment you became a Christian, God not only forgave you of all your sins, but also gave you all you need to live a victorious Christian life. *God does not need to do something new—He has already done all that needs to be done.* You need only receive this provision by faith, just as you received forgiveness of sins for salvation by faith.

(Note the diagram that appears in the student's book and discuss it.)

Romans 6:3 says that all who have received Jesus Christ were "baptized into His death." Although baptism pri-

Leader's Objective: To show that the abundant life is possible in practical, everyday life and to provide guidance in how students can live the abundant life

L E S S O N   3

Bible Study

The Basis of Abundant Living

Read Romans 6:1–23.

1. What do you know happened to you when you became a Christian (verse 6)?
   (My old self was crucified with Christ and I am no longer in bondage to sin.)

2. According to verse 11, what must you do?
   (Count myself dead to sin but alive to God in Christ.)

marily means to dip, immerse, or sink, this passage does not refer to water baptism.

Rather, the verse teaches that as a result of our new birth, we are immersed in Christ, indissolubly joined to Him. In John 15:1–6, Jesus pictures this union as a vine and its branches. In 1 Corinthians 12, Paul refers to it as the union of a body with its members.

❯What does this spiritual union with Jesus Christ mean?

It means that when Christ died, we took part in His death. He paid the penalty for our sin and satisfied all of God's demands. Sin has no claim on Him whatsoever. Since we are in Him, this now becomes true of us. Sin can make no demands on us. We are free from it just as Christ is.

Since Christ rose from the dead and lives a resurrected life, this is also true of all who are in Him. We have risen and can now live a resurrected life, a life of victory over sin.

> If we have been united with him in his death, we will certainly also be united with him in his resurrection (Romans 6:5).

All who are in Christ should live the life that overcomes sin. Christ has paid for your sins; you are free from them. You can live in victory over them through His power. Know these facts from God's Word!

Consider yourself dead to sin. Count on that fact. You are dead to sin and its control. But you may say, "I do not *feel* dead to sin. Sin seems as strong as ever in me."

Paul does not say *feel,* he says *count.* Count upon it in spite of feelings because *you actually are!* Even if you never count on it, you are still dead to sin. You are like a man who has a bank account of thousands of dollars and never uses it. It is still his whether he uses it or not.

Victory is not fighting off your wrong desires or concealing your wrong feelings—that is counterfeit. Victorious living is a gift of God. Acknowledge it and thank Him for it.

Consider yourself to be alive in Jesus Christ. A dead man is no good to anyone. Take hold by faith of the fact that you are now alive in Jesus Christ and do not fool yourself into thinking that you must help Him accomplish His will in your life.

3. According to verse 13, what is your responsibility?
   (Offer—yield—my body not to sin, but to God for righteousness.)

❓Have you ever considered why God asks for the parts of your physical body?

In Romans 12:1,2 you will find an exhortation similar to the one in verse 13. *The Lord Jesus needs a body prepared for Him now, just as He did while He was on earth.* Our bodies are the ones He has chosen to use. Galatians 2:20 becomes true in your life:

> I have been crucified with Christ and I no longer live, but Christ lives in me.

The only thing that keeps the Lord from operating in your life at 100 percent potential is you. The Lord does not want you to try to live the Christian life. He wants to live it by faith through and for you.

We need a proper perspective on life. We must not forfeit the lasting good for the immediate pleasure that passes so quickly. We must count the cost! The Bible says:

> A man reaps what he sows (Galatians 6:7).

4. According to verse 16, man is a servant either of sin or of righteousness. What determines his allegiance?
(Whatever he yields himself to: sin or obedience.)

There are two competing powers in the world: God and Satan. Many times we fool ourselves into thinking that we are our own rulers when actually we are controlled by Satan. He tries to blind our eyes to the truth, as he has been doing since creation, and we often are not smart enough to recognize him.

Review Romans 6:6,11, 13,16 and note the progression:

◆ *Know* that you have been crucified with Christ.

◆ *Count* yourself dead to sin and alive to Jesus Christ.

◆ *Offer* yourself unto God.

◆ *Obey* God.

We are to obey God from the heart. You may say, "But my heart is deceitful."

When you yield yourself to God, He says He will "give you a new heart . . . and move you to follow my decrees" (Ezekiel 36:26,27). Obeying God will become a natural thing, resulting in the abundant life for which you were created. If you do these things, "sin shall not be your master" (Romans 6:14).

Using these four steps, dedicate yourself to serving God rather than sin.

5. Describe the benefits you have already seen from righteous living.

The Practice of Abundant Living

Read Psalm 37:1–7,34.

1. What wrong attitudes are given in verse 1?
(Worry and envy.)

God wants us to trust Him in all things. When we worry, we show that we do not believe He really causes all things to work together for good to those who love Him (see Romans 8:28). The saying, "Why pray when you can worry?" may be true in many lives, but it is not pleasing to God.

Try thanking the Lord instead of worrying. Your whole attitude will be changed.

> Give thanks in all circumstances, for this is God's will for you in Christ Jesus (1 Thessalonians 5:18).

2. What is to be your attitude toward the Lord (verse 3)?
(Trust in the Lord.)

❓What does it mean to trust?

Trust.

The Amplified New Testament defines it as, "confidence in His power, wisdom, and goodness." If you have confidence in God, you know that His way is best and that He is in control of your life.

In the Lord.

It is one thing to trust someone who is not trustworthy, but quite another to trust a God who has never, ever failed or let one of His children down. We can trust because the One in whom we trust is worthy of it. See also Hebrews 13:5.

3. What must you do to receive the desires of your heart (verse 4)?
(Delight myself in the Lord.)

Most Christians think that if they just serve God, they'll get all they want. But this verse puts first things first. Delight in the Lord *first, then* He will give you the desires of your heart. You cannot fool God. He "looks upon the heart" and He knows whether you are "delighting" yourself in Him for Himself, or for what you can get from Him.

This goes back to "obeying from the heart." When you yield or present yourself to Him, God makes it possible to delight yourself in Him, making His every wish your command.

4. Why is it necessary to consider verse 5 when you plan your future?
(God knows beginning and end and what's best for us.)

5. How can you apply the instruction in verse 7? Be specific.
(Rest in the Lord; wait patiently for Him; don't fret because of evil-doers.)

6. What does verse 34 mean to you?

Now, review each of the above references and note the progression:

◆ Do not *fret*.

◆ *Trust* in the Lord.

◆ *Delight* yourself in the Lord.

◆ *Commit* your way to the Lord.

◆ *Be still* before the Lord.

◆ *Wait* on the Lord.

(See Directory of Terms below.)

The secret of the abundant life is contained in these key words: *know, count, offer, obey, fret not, trust, delight, commit, be still,* and *wait.* (Underline these words in Romans 6 and Psalm 37 in your Bible.)

Jesus Christ came to do the Father's will. When we let Jesus Christ live in and through us, He does His will in and through us, and God is glorified in us. This is the greatest privilege we can have in life.

❷ What can you do when you do not know God's will in a certain matter?

Rest in the Lord and wait patiently for Him.

Rest in Him. Take advantage of the time of indecision by being with Him. Learn His ways. Memorize His promises. Do not waste this precious time when you could be learning so much from Him. Leave the situation in His hands and He will work it out and will always tell you the answer in time for you to do what He wants you to do.

> Do not be anxious about anything, but in everything, by prayer and petition, with thanksgiving, present your requests to God (Philippians 4:6).

Lack of patience is lack of trust, and God often will not let you know His will until you trust His judgment of time as well.

(See the Directory of Terms in the student's book, and discuss each term.)

1. In the chart below, indicate which key words of the abundant life you are now applying, and which you need to begin to apply, through the power of Christ.

2. How do you plan to apply these? Be specific.

❖ ❖ ❖

Conclusion and Application

God does not call us to a life of victory and abundance and then leave us to find it on our own. He has provided everything we need in His Son, Jesus Christ.

(See the chart in the student's book and discuss it.)

Closing Prayer

❖ ❖ ❖

The Abiding Life

Opening Prayer

Discussion Starter

❓In thinking about your life, have you ever wondered why there are times you are not happy and the Lord seems far away?

❓Why do you think that is?

There are many keys in Scripture that unlock great experiences. Today we will discuss the key that unlocks joy—*real* joy, which is full and which remains.

Lesson Development

(Ask one of the group members to summarize the paragraphs appearing at the opening of this lesson in the student's book. Note the diagram and discuss it.)

(Ask another student to read the paragraph at the beginning of the Bible Study, and then proceed to the questions and answers.)

Leader's Objective: To bring group members to an understanding of the principle of abiding in Christ and of how they can abide in Him more consistently

LESSON 4

Bible Study

The Abiding Life

"Abiding is the key to Christian experience by which the divine attributes are transplanted into human soil, to the transforming of character and conduct."
—Norman B. Harrison

1. In John 15:5, Jesus referred to Himself as the *(vine)* and Christians as the *(branches)*.

   What is the relationship between Christ and you, as illustrated in that verse?

2. Why does Jesus prune every branch that bears fruit (John 15:2)?
   (So it will bear more fruit.)

   What are some experiences you can identify as "pruning" in your life as a Christian? (See Hebrews 12:6; Romans 5:3–5.)

   What were the results?

   What did you learn through these situations?

Results of Abiding in Christ

1. Read John 15:7–11. List two necessary qualifications for effective prayer according to verse 7.
   (We must abide in Christ; His words must abide in us.)

When we abide in the vine, we bear fruit. A branch never worries about fruit bearing. The only thing that can prevent the branch from bearing fruit is an obstruction that keeps the sap from flowing through the branch.

Sin obstructs the flow of life through us from the Lord Jesus. God has to prune our lives to keep us free from obstruction.

The branch does nothing of its own will, but only what the vine does through it. We as Christians cannot produce in our own strength, but only as we let the life of the "Vine" accomplish His purpose through us.

We must abide in Christ to have our prayers answered. This is how we know the Father's will (John 15:7).

His words must abide in us so that we might know what His will is when we pray. He cannot answer any prayer that is contrary to His Word.

2. Jesus glorified God. How can you glorify God (verse 8)?
(By bearing much fruit.)

3. Christ commands us to continue in His love. How great do you believe this love to be (verse 9)?
(As great as the Father's love for Christ.)

How are we to abide in Christ's love (verse 10)?
(By obeying His commandments.)

How do you think the result promised in verse 11 will be revealed in your life today?

4. What has Christ chosen us to do (John 15:16)?
(Go and bear fruit.)

What is meant by "fruit"? (See Matthew 4:19; Galatians 5:22,23; Ephesians 5:9; Philippians 1:11.)
(A godly life and the souls of men and women.)

5. Why do you think Jesus chose this particular way

Andrew Murray says, "The most heavily laden branches bow the lowest."

Faith in His love will enable us to continue in His love. Let His love permeate your being. It is with this same infinite, eternal love that Christ invites you to abide in Him.

> I have loved you with an everlasting love (Jeremiah 31:3).

It is a perfect love. It gives all, and holds nothing back. He sacrificed His throne and crown for you. It is an unchangeable love.

> Jesus Christ is the same yesterday and today and forever (Hebrews 13:8).

By abiding in His love you will learn to trust Him in all circumstances. Meditate upon His love and His care for you as an individual.

Many Christians are not joyful because they are not abiding. Those who yield themselves unreservedly to abiding in Christ have a bright and blessed life; their faith comes true—the joy of the Lord is theirs.

Jesus Christ commanded Peter:

> Follow me and I will make you fishers of men (Matthew 4:19).

Those who abide in Christ are given the great blessing of offering to others what will bless and transform their lives. We need to have only one care: to abide closely, fully, wholly. God will give the fruit.

As you grow closer to Christ, the passion for souls that urged Him to

to illustrate our abiding in Him?

6. Will you be able to do what Christ expects of you?

How do you know?

1. Write briefly what you need to do to begin abiding in Christ more consistently.

2. What do you think He will do as a result?

3. How do you think that will affect your life?

❖ ❖ ❖

Calvary will compel you more and more to devote your life to introducing others to Christ.

Conclusion and Application

It takes time to grow into maturity. Do not expect to abide in Christ unless you spend adequate time with Him. You need to meet with Him day by day—to put yourself into contact with the living Jesus. Fill your heart with His Word; pray at every spare moment, acknowledging His presence with you and in you.

Confide in Him; live and dwell in Him. Rely only upon Him in all circumstances of your life. Learn the secret of the abiding life, then share it with others that they may know the joy of the Christian life.

Closing Prayer

(Give opportunity for those who have never trusted Christ to pray, placing their faith in Him to come into their lives and forgive them of their sins and live through them from this moment on.)

(Then pray also for Christians to grow in their faith and in their desire to witness.)

The Cleansed Life

Opening Prayer

Discussion Starter

The Christian life on earth is a victorious one, but we are not perfect. When we became Christians, God united us with Christ, made us new creatures, and gave us His Holy Spirit, but He also left us with the sin nature we had before we received Christ. When Christ comes again, we will receive a new body and at last lose our sin nature, but until then it will be constantly with us. We see in 1 John 1:8:

> If we claim to be without sin, we deceive ourselves and the truth is not in us.

Why do you think God has not taken away our sin nature?

Let's look at 2 Corinthians 4:7. It tells us:

> We have this treasure in jars of clay to show that this all-surpassing power is from God and not from us.

God has left us with these "jars of clay" for a short while that we might live and walk by faith and demonstrate His power. It would be nothing for

Leader's Objective: To teach the reality of moment-by-moment cleansing from sin (forgiveness) through immediate confession

LESSON 5

Bible Study

Living "Out of Fellowship" With God

1. What characterizes a person who is not in fellowship with God (James 1:8)?
   (He is double-minded and unstable.)

   Think back on your life. How has this verse characterized you?

   In what way(s) has this changed since you came to know Jesus Christ?

2. Read Isaiah 59:2. What is the result of sin in one's life?
   (Separation from God, God's face hidden, God does not hear your prayers.)

3. Do you think sin in your life has affected your relationship with God?
   How?

Him to use strong, well-equipped vessels to do great tasks. But to use weak, sinful vessels like us to accomplish great works is more to His glory, and the "power is from God and not from us."

Lesson Development

(Ask one of the group members to summarize the paragraphs appearing at the opening of this lesson in the student's book. Note the diagram and discuss it.)

Instability is a result of being double-minded. A person who is trying to serve two gods, who sits on the fence, and who compromises to fit each situation in which he finds himself, is unstable.

In 1 Kings 18:21, Elijah said:

> How long will you waver between two opinions? If the Lord is God, follow him; but if Baal is God, follow him.

Don't be double-minded!

Even the smallest sin denies us the joy of fellowship with our Lord.

As an illustration, suppose you are dating someone and a minor problem comes up. You know how it goes—if a little thing comes between you and it's not dealt with, it soon builds a big wall and you can't get through to each other. There is no fellowship, no communication.

The Lord does not answer our prayers when we have sin in our lives.

If I had cherished sin in my heart, the Lord would not have listened (Psalm 66:18).

The more sin we allow in our lives, the more miserable we feel. God feels all of this with us and longs for us to come immediately for cleansing so we can walk together as before.

How to Be Cleansed

1. What is the condition for cleansing and forgiveness (1 John 1:9)?
   (We must confess our sin.)

The word confess means "to say the same thing as another—to agree with God."

Confession involves three things:

◆ Agreeing that you have sinned (be specific)

◆ Agreeing that Christ's death on the cross paid the penalty for that sin

◆ Repentance—changing your attitude toward that sin, which will result in a change of action toward that sin

When God brings to your attention the fact that something you have done is sin, you are to confess—say the same thing God says about that specific sin. Do not just say, "I have sinned," but state what the sin was and agree with God, looking at it from His viewpoint. Then determine to

A man who had been a wonderful Christian for many years was telling another man that he had never known an hour of defeat in his fifty years of Christian life.

"What?" asked the other man in astonishment. "You have never known any defeat in your Christian life?"

"No, I didn't put it that way," said the first man. "I've known moments of defeat, but never an hour. I always get back into fellowship immediately by confessing my sin and claiming the promise from God's Word—1 John 1:9."

It is impossible to hide our sin from God. He is aware of all that we do. Someone may ask, "Then why do we have to confess to Him, if He already knows?" Confession is agreeing with God that what we did was displeasing to Him.

Because of God's mercy, He provided for our forgiveness because we

put it out of your life and not do it again.

2. What two things did the psalmist do about his sin in Psalm 32:5?
(He acknowledged his sin; he confessed his sin.)

Read Proverbs 28:13. What is the result of not admitting sin?
(We will not prosper.)

Of admitting sin?
(We will find mercy.)

3. In what situations has each of these results been true in your life?

Living "In Fellowship" With God

1. Notice in the diagram on page 43 that, when we confess our sins, God restores us to fellowship. Walking in fellowship with the Father and the Son is referred to as "walking in the light."

Read 1 John 1:7 and list two results promised.
(Fellowship with one another; cleansing from sin.)

Give an example of how you have experienced each in your life.

2. When we are in fellowship with God, specific things are happening within us. According to Philippians 2:13 and 4:13, what are they?
(God is at work in us; He wills and works for His good purpose; we can do all things because He strengthens us.)

could never make up for the sins we commit. It takes faith in His provision to believe that He cleanses us, completely apart from anything we can do. God is glorified when we acknowledge His forgiveness.

We in our own strength cannot "forsake" our sins. By faith we must accept from Christ our victory over temptation. Christ is faithful, and it is His responsibility to accomplish this miracle in our lives as we confess our sins and abide in Him. He is always true to His promises and responsibility toward us.

Pardon from sin, purpose, peace, power, and joy are the results of being in fellowship with God. Inner stability and all the qualities of Christ become ours because we are in Him.

Almighty God Himself lives, moves, and has His being in and through us.

All power in heaven and on earth is ours. We have a life that has power because it is cleansed, and it is filled with the Holy Spirit of God.

Describe how the verses can help you overcome specific temptations or weaknesses you face.

3. What is this power within us and what is its result (Romans 8:9; Galatians 5:22,23)?
(The Spirit of God—Spirit of Christ; spiritual fruit.)

List several ways the qualities found in Galatians 5:22,23 are at work in your life.

4. What should be our attitude when tempted (Romans 6:11–14)?
(We should consider ourselves dead to sin and alive in Jesus, and refuse to let sin master us.)

Why (Colossians 3:3)?
(Because our life is not our own.)

Identify ways you can obey the instructions given in Romans 6:11–14.

LIFE APPLICATION

1. In your own words, write what you will do when you find anything that breaks your fellowship with the Lord.

2. Summarize the reasons it is so important to confess sin as soon as you are aware of it.

3. Use these steps to confess your sin:

   1) Ask the Holy Spirit to reveal the sins in your life.

Jesus manifests Himself to those who are obedient to His commands (John 14:21).

In Charles Dickens' story, *A Christmas Carol*, Ebenezer Scrooge was visited by the spirit of his former business partner, Jacob Marley. Marley drug behind him a long, heavy chain of metal links that was formed in his life by the thoughtless, selfish deeds he had done.

This is a picture of how sin enslaves us. But, as Christians, we do not need to be bound by temptation and sin. Jesus has broken the chains of sin for us. Paul says we are dead to sin and alive to Christ. We do not live under law but under grace.

That is why it is so important to live a cleansed life. As we yield ourselves to God and confess our sin immediately, we will experience a free, joyful fellowship with God and our lives will be abundant and righteous.

Conclusion and Application

Confession of sin means agreeing with God concerning our sin, naming our sin, and recognizing His opinion of it. Confession suggests a willingness to repent, to turn from going our way toward going God's way. We want to deal with sin now. As we continue to claim 1 John 1:9, we will do one of two things: either we will stop that sin, or we will stop praying.

2) List the sins on a piece of paper.

3) Confess the sins.

4) Write 1 John 1:9 across the sins.

5) Thank God for His complete forgiveness.

6) Destroy the paper to signify what happened to your sins.

❖　❖　❖

Closing Prayer

(Say to the class:) Perhaps you have never appropriated the cleansing power of the blood of Jesus Christ. Maybe you have never asked Him to forgive your sin, come into your life, and live in and through you.

Wouldn't you like to invite Him to come into your life now?

On the authority of Revelation 3:20, He promises to come into your life. Isaiah 1:18 says:

> Though your sins are like scarlet, they shall be as white as snow; though they are red as crimson, they shall be like wool.

Will you accept His forgiveness for your sin now? (Allow time for a brief silent prayer.)

Did you ask Christ to come into your heart and cleanse you of your sin?

If you were sincere, you can be sure He came in and you have been forgiven. Now, thank Him for what He has done for you. And come and tell me what you have done so I can rejoice with you and help you in your Christian growth.

❖　❖　❖

Victorious in Spiritual Warfare

Opening Prayer

Discussion Starter

(Ask students to read Ephesians 6:10–18. Then have them close their Bibles and study books. Ask them to write all the pieces of armor they can remember.)

Lesson Development

(Invite one of the group members to summarize the paragraphs appearing at the opening of this lesson in the student's book.)

The Bible teaches very clearly that the Christian life is not only a walk, but also a warfare. Many Christians do not realize this. They think living the Christian life means escaping all trials, difficulties, and temptations, and they expect to glide through their years on earth with scarcely a problem.

The truth is that we are strangers and pilgrims on this earth (1 Peter 2:11), living in a world ruled by Satan, and we repeatedly face opposition and difficulty. The Christian life should be a victorious one, but it is not always

❖

Leader's Objective: To bring students to an awareness of spiritual warfare, and to teach them how to use the armor God has provided

LESSON 6

Bible Study

Describe in your own words the picture depicted in Paul's command given in Ephesians 6:10–18.

We Are On the Battlefield

1. What two things will putting on the whole armor of God help you to do (verses 10,11)?
   (Be strong in the Lord; stand firm against the schemes of the devil.)

   How are we to defend ourselves against our enemies (verses 10–13)?
   (Put on the armor of God; stand your ground.)

2. Who are the enemies?

   James 4:4
   (The world.)

   Galatians 5:16,17
   (Our sinful nature.)

easy. We must be strengthened continually "in the Lord and in his mighty power" (Ephesians 6:10).

(Assign each student one statement about spiritual warfare on page 50 in the student's book, and ask him to write one practical example of how that action can help deal with the spiritual guerillas in the life of a Christian.)

(Note the diagram at the beginning of this lesson in the student's Study Guide and discuss it.)

There are so many philosophies and false doctrines that would mislead us. Our only defense is to put on the whole armor of God.

The *world* refers to our present world system, and it is ruled by Satan. Those who are of the world—non-Christian humanity—will ridicule us and try to get us to live by its standards. But the Bible says, "Set your minds on things above, not on earthly things" (Colossians 3:2). The Christian must not be conformed to this world (Romans 12:2), and he is not to love the world (1 John 2:15). The world, with all its temporary pleasures, will pass away. But the Christian lives with eternal values in mind.

Our old *sin nature* is our fleshly desires. God has left it with us and it is always hostile toward Him (Romans 8:7). Our sin nature will always tempt us, always assert itself, always try to entice us away from God. We can

153

never trust it, but we can have victory over it. Romans 6:11 says we must count upon the fact that we are dead to sin. When we realize that God judged the flesh on the cross, and that it no longer has control over us, we can overcome it. We can rest confidently in the victory God gave at the cross.

1 Peter 5:8
(The devil.)

Satan, or the *devil,* our third enemy, is the strongest power in the universe next to God. Satan is alive and active, but he is a defeated foe. John 12:31 tells us he was defeated at the cross, although he continually tries to frighten Christians.

We have no strength in ourselves to match Satan's power. If we trust in our own cunning or wisdom to outwit him, he will defeat us every time. But when we rely on God's strength and not our own, we have victory. No Christian need ever fear the devil.

Whenever Satan attacks, we are to resist him in God's strength, and he must flee (James 4:7). When we pray, we should claim God's victory over Satan at the cross, and he will be driven out. The Christian, in the name of Jesus Christ, has the authority to trample underfoot the devil with all his power. Our victory has already been assured by the resurrection of Jesus Christ from the dead. We need to act on these facts, and by faith claim our victory in the name of Christ.

3. Name the six protective pieces of armor that God provides and expects you to wear (Ephesians 6:14–17).

1) *(Belt of truth.)*

Belt of truth—In New Testament times, soldiers used a 6- to 8-inch belt to gather up their flowing garments and as a foundation upon which to hang their swords and other weapons.

The belt facilitated movement for the soldier in battle. Truth (Jesus Christ) is the belt that facilitates movement in the Christian's warfare. Knowing the truth frees us from sin and allows us to obey our new Captain, Jesus Christ, in the great battle in which we are engaged. See John 14:6; 8:32; 8:36.

2) *(Breastplate of right-eousness.)*

Breastplate of righteousness—Jesus frees us from the penalty of our sin. We can fight the good fight because He is our righteousness. See 2 Corinthians 5:21 and Romans 3:22.

3) *(Gospel of peace.)*

Feet fitted with the gospel of peace—We were at war with God, but now are reconciled to Him and at peace. We are free from condemnation. This is the message we take with us wherever we go. Every step you take should bear the news—the gospel of peace. See 1 Corinthians 15:1 and 3,4; Philippians 4:7; Romans 5:1.

4) *(Shield of faith.)*

Shield of faith—We take the faith of Jesus Christ which frees us from doubt. He is always faithful. We fight in His strength, knowing the battle is the Lord's (1 Chronicles 20:15). See also Galatians 2:20 and 2 Timothy 2:13.

5) *(Helmet of salvation.)*

Helmet of salvation—Jesus Christ Himself becomes our salvation. Being assured of our salvation gives us the confidence we need to fight the battle. See Acts 15:11 and 2 Peter 1:10.

6) *(Sword of the Spirit.)*

Sword of the Spirit—This is the weapon that the Holy Spirit uses to convict the hearts of men and women, not our brilliant oratory or our persuasiveness, but the Word of God. We can expect no conviction of sin or awareness of the need for the Savior apart

4. How can you employ the sword of God's Word (verse 17) for defense against temptation (Psalm 119:9,11)?

(By living according to the Word, and by hiding it in my heart.)

5. List some ways the sword of God's Word can be used in an offensive action (2 Timothy 3:16,17). *(Teaching, rebuking, correcting, training in righteousness.)*

6. How can you stay alert and always be prepared (Ephesians 6:18; Colossians 4:2)? *(By being in constant prayer.)*

We Are More Than Conquerors Through Christ!

1. How should you respond to these enemies?

from the Word. Learn it from cover to cover. Learn the answer to every problem you face by searching the Bible's pages. This is your only offense. Use it always!

Teaching—The sword of God's Word is the Christian's source of teaching or doctrine. The victorious Christian knows the Word of God and applies it to everyday experiences.

Rebuking—To rebuke is to reprove a person for wrong words or actions. We should always use the Word of God when showing someone that a part of his life is displeasing to the Lord. It should not be just our opinion.

Correcting—Through the Word of God we can correct errors of doctrine taught by others. If we give our own opinion, theirs is as good as ours. Always use the Word of God to correct error.

Training in Righteousness—The Bible is the *Holy* Bible. It alone has the perfect standard of righteousness. Someone has well said, "God's Word will keep you from sin, or sin will keep you from God's Word."

This does not mean we must be always on our knees, but we can be continually in an attitude of prayer. The battle is fought by the Lord Jesus Christ, but we allow Him to fight through us by yielding ourselves to Him in prayer.

Then we must watch for the enemy and the opportunities for offensive attack. We must "keep on keeping on."

Romans 12:2
(Renew my mind.)

Galatians 5:16
(Live by the Spirit.)

James 4:7
(Submit myself to God; resist the devil.)

2. When you consider the pieces of armor and weapons provided, who can you conclude is really fighting the battle (Ephesians 6:10)?
(The Lord.)

3. Why can you always expect God to be the winner (1 John 4:4)?
("The one who is in you is greater than the one in the world.")

4. How does Romans 8:31 affect your attitude toward adversity and temptation?
(If God is for us, no one can win against us.)

5. How do these principles help you to live a more abundant life?

LIFE APPLICATION

1. Describe a specific situation in your life right now in which you need to employ a spiritual "weapon."

2. Which weapon(s) will you use and how?

3. What results do you expect?

Be aware of the battle, and be constant in your prayer to Him who fights for you.

Jesus Christ, the captain of our salvation, is fighting our battle and He has already won the victory. We fight *from* victory, not *toward* victory.

When you take over and fight in your own strength, you cannot win the battle. If you lose, you know that you have taken over. God ordained that you "stand and see the salvation of the *Lord* on your behalf" (2 Chronicles 20:17, KJV).

Not from any merit or ability on our part do we win in this battle, but through the strength of the Lord. He defeated Satan at the cross and has given us all we need to be "more than conquerors." We are to march forward as soldiers of Christ, claiming victory by His strength and His power. See 1 John 5:4.

Conclusion and Application

What a thrill to be in the army of the living God! You can believe Him for the victory in the battles of your life right now. He has the power to overcome any habit in *your* life or any problem you are facing.

Closing Prayer

Attitude Makes the Difference

Opening Prayer

Discussion Starter

(To start the discussion, use the question that introduces this lesson on the bottom of page 55 in the student's book.)

Lesson Development

(Ask one of the group members to summarize the paragraphs appearing at the opening of this lesson in the student's book. Note the diagram and discuss it.)

Leader's Objective: To show group members how to look at life from God's perspective and to lead them to begin trusting God and thanking Him for all situations

LESSON 7

Bible Study

God's People in Trouble

In Exodus 14:1–4, the Israelites experienced an unrecognized blessing. As you read, notice the human viewpoint of the people and God's viewpoint as seen in Moses.

1. How did the Israelites react to apparent danger (Exodus 14:10–12)?
   (They became very frightened.)

2. Notice how Moses reacted. Why do you think he commanded the people as he did (Exodus 14:13,14)?
   (He had great confidence in God.)

3. What did God accomplish in their hearts and minds through this experience (Exodus 14:31)?
   (They learned to trust God and to believe Moses.)

Victory or defeat occurs in the mind before it occurs any place else. God has called on us to first maintain a correct mental attitude.

The Bible tells us "perfect love drives out fear" (1 John 4:18). If the Israelites had loved God sincerely, they would have trusted Him and not been seized with fear.

Instead, their fear led to torment. As they traveled through the wilderness, they began to complain—to Moses and to the Lord. They were discontent because they were not in Egypt. They had forgotten how hard their bondage had been. How true this is of human nature. We remember the good of the past, but not the bad.

Moses was in the same situation as the others, but he trusted God while they doubted. He gave the glory to God! He told the people to watch what God would do. God was Moses' only hope—and God did not let him down!

The people saw God in action! It is so thrilling to be present when God does a mighty work. God must teach us to trust Him; it is not a part of our nature. When everything is going well, we often do not credit God, but our own ingenuity. He has to bring us to the place where we recognize that we cannot do anything in our own wisdom and strength —then He moves in and works. See Psalm 37:5 and 1 Peter 5:7.

4. Think back to a crisis in your life. How did those around you respond?

How did you react?

How could you have improved your attitude?

List ways God has worked through difficulties in your life, and has shown these difficulties really to be blessings.

We often think we are enduring something no one else ever has. Yet we can learn important lessons and gain real comfort from others who have been through a similar trial.

Taking the Proper Attitude

1. List some things the Bible guarantees when you are tempted or tested (1 Corinthians 10:13).
(My temptation is common to all. God won't let it be too great for me; He will provide a way of escape; I will be able to endure it.)

God has promised that we will not be tempted above what we are able to withstand. It is never right to think we cannot endure the temptation. If we cannot resist a particular thing, God will not allow us to be tempted in that way.

To find the way to escape, the Christian should immediately go to God's Word. When we do not seek His answer to the problem, we fall deeper into the temptation.

God promises that we will be able to bear the temptation. Always remember that we can "do everything through him who gives [us] strength" (Philippians 4:13). All power in heaven and earth is ours. We have all the resources we will ever need in Jesus Christ.

2. How can the Bible's guarantee in Romans 8:28 be true that everything will work out for good to those who love God?
(God promised; God's purpose will be done.)

When have you ever doubted God's work in your life?

❷ Does Romans 8:28 refer to everyone?

This verse includes qualifications. One is that the promise is limited to those "who love God." Love for God brings trust. Therefore, you know that whatever comes is under the Father's control.

Why?

3. What response to tribulation does God expect from you, according to Romans 5:3–5?
(I am to rejoice in them.)

What are the results of tribulations? (See also James 1:3.)
(Perseverance, proven character, hope.)

4. What is the purpose of unrecognized blessings according to:

2 Corinthians 1:3,4
(So I can comfort others.)

Hebrews 12:5–11
(That I may share His holiness, be trained by the discipline, receive the peaceful harvest of righteousness.)

5. Read 1 Thessalonians 5:18 and Hebrews 13:15.

What response does God command in *all* situations?
(That I give thanks.)

The second qualification is those "who have been called according to His purpose." God's purpose is fulfilled in those who are yielded to Him. Until we come to the point in our lives where we can accept His will, we will not see His perfect will being accomplished.

❓Why do suffering, heartbreak, and tragedy come into a Christian's life?

Philippians 1:29 says:

It has been granted to you on behalf of Christ not only to believe on him, but also to suffer for him.

These things come to *accomplish God's divine purpose.* All sunshine and no rain creates a desert. *To mold our Christian character,* God not only gives us times of blessing and encouragement, but also allows times of trouble and difficulty. Most of us want to escape these at all costs, but God does not always intend for us to escape.

In times of trial we *learn to trust God and draw close to Him.* We learn of the comfort He can give; we learn of the provision He can make; and we learn how weak and self-centered we really are. We learn to see God's power in a new way.

Suffering sometimes *exposes a rebellious attitude.* The world can see no meaning in suffering, no purpose for it; but for the Christian, the hand of a loving God, who is tenderly disciplining His children, sends a blessing in disguise through suffering. We must learn to accept God's victory in suffering and difficulties.

How can you rejoice and give thanks when sorrow and tragedy come?

Contrast this with the attitude of the Israelites in Exodus 14:1–12.

(The Israelites complained and worried, just the opposite of thankfulness.)

LIFE APPLICATION

1. List the methods by which an attitude of trust can become a reality for you. (See Ephesians 5:18; Galatians 5:16; 1 Thessalonians 5:17; Romans 10:17.)

2. With what trial in your life do you need to trust God right now?

3. What do you think the unrecognized blessings in that trial could be?

4. How can you receive those blessings?

❖ ❖ ❖

❷ What is the advantage in giving thanks in all things?

First, we acknowledge God's authority in our lives. We show our trust in His faithfulness. As Moses did, we see the glory of God manifested, and enjoy it because we look for His way out rather than our own.

Then, we understand more clearly when we think from God's point of view. Thanking Him reminds us that He is in control of the situation. We don't have to fall apart trying to manufacture an answer.

Conclusion and Application

One of the greatest lessons we can learn in the Christian life is to give thanks in all things. That can change the course of our lives. We need to stay in such close fellowship with the Lord that we have His mind in all circumstances.

Closing Prayer

❖ ❖ ❖

Recap

Opening Prayer

Discussion Starter

(Discuss how Christ abiding in us provides the basis for bearing fruit, waging spiritual warfare, and dealing with temptation. Talk about which area currently seems to be the greatest struggle in your students' lives and how they plan to use God's Word to help them in those areas.)

Lesson Development

(Any appropriate material from previous lessons that was not sufficiently covered could be used at this time, and you also may deal with any point that the group members may not understand as well as they could.)

(Then go over the remaining Recap questions and answers. This material will benefit both the students and you by giving you a deeper appreciation of God's Word.)

Leader's Objective: To review the concept of living the Christian life by allowing Christ to live in the believer; to help the student deal with temptation he faces

The following questions will help you review this Step. If necessary, reread the appropriate lesson(s).

1. In your own words, what does the abundant Christian life involve?

2. Envision and describe the abundant life you desire for yourself.

   What part does bearing fruit have?

   What part does spiritual warfare play?

3. How do you know your picture of the abundant life is consistent with God's view?

LIFE APPLICATION

1. What specific steps do you still need to take to make the abundant life a reality for you?

2. List verses from Lesson 6 that can help you deal with temptations you face. Each week, update this list to include additional temptations and the verses to help you deal with them.

❖ ❖ ❖

Conclusion and Application

A careful, prayerful sincere study of these great truths will, if claimed in faith, change your life so that you will never be the same.

These keys unlock the door to a full and abundant Christian life, but a key is no good unless it is used. Search the Scriptures diligently and make these great doctrines true in your everyday experience.

(See the chart in the student's book and discuss it.)

Closing Prayer

The Christian and the Holy Spirit

Moving Beyond Discouragement & Defeat

STEP 3

Who Is the Holy Spirit and Why Did He Come?

Opening Prayer

Discussion Starter

(Hold up an unlit candle and read Ephesians 5:8, "You were once darkness, but now you are light in the Lord." Then say:)

Until the Holy Spirit of God lights the candle of man's spiritual life, he cannot see and know God. Man is spiritually dead (point to the unlit candle), but when the Holy Spirit takes up residence at the time of spiritual birth (John 3:3,6), he becomes spiritually alive (light the candle).

❓What differences do you think that would make in a person's life?

The majority of Christians know very little about the Holy Spirit. All of us have heard sermons about God the Father, and many on God the Son, but a sermon about God the Holy Spirit is unusual. The Holy Spirit is equal in every way with God the Father and God the Son. The Holy Spirit vitally affects everything about our lives as Christians. In fact, His presence or absence in a person's life makes the

Leader's Objective: To introduce students to the person and ministry of the Holy Spirit and to encourage them to surrender their lives to His direction and control

LESSON 1

Bible Study

Who Is the Holy Spirit?

1. Personality (a person) is composed of intellect, emotions, and will. In 1 Corinthians 2:11, what indicates that the Holy Spirit has intellect?
   (He knows the thoughts of God.)

   What evidence do you observe in Romans 15:30 that the Holy Spirit has emotion?
   (Love of the Spirit.)

   How does the Holy Spirit exercise His will as recorded in 1 Corinthians 12:11?
   (He works: He distributes as He wills.)

2. Find the one word that describes the nature of the Holy Spirit in each of the following references.

   Romans 8:2 *(Life.)*

   John 16:13 *(Truth.)*

   Hebrews 10:29 *(Grace.)*

   Romans 1:4 *(Holiness.)*

3. What is His function or role?

   John 14:16,26
   (To counsel, to remind us of what we have learned.)

   1 Corinthians 3:16
   (To dwell in the believer.)

   John 16:13,14
   (To guide to all truth, to disclose things of Christ.)

difference between spiritual life and death. We are born spiritually through the ministry of the Holy Spirit according to John 3:1–8.

Lesson Development

(Encourage students to read the article, "Experiencing the Power of the Holy Spirit" at the beginning of their book on their own time if they have not already done so.)

(Ask one of the group members to read the paragraph appearing at the opening of this lesson in the student's book.)

❓Would you consider God a person (a personality)? Why or why not?

The Holy Spirit is the Spirit of God.

For this reason, I kneel before the Father, from whom his whole family in heaven and on earth derives its name. I pray that out of his glorious riches he may strengthen you with power through his Spirit in your inner being (Ephesians 3:14–16).

❓What is the particular ministry of the Holy Spirit mentioned here in Paul's prayer?

(Read Ephesians 3:17–19.)

❓How are the other persons of the Trinity mentioned?

The Old Testament records the work of the Holy Spirit in the following areas:

◆ *Creation:* Genesis 1:2,3; Job 26:13; Psalm 104:30

Acts 1:8
(To empower the believer for witnessing.)

4. What specific actions does the Holy Spirit perform?

Acts 13:2
(Calls believers for special work.)

Acts 8:29
(Directs the serving believer.)

Romans 8:14
(Provides leadership for the sons of God.)

John 16:7,8
(Convicts the world of sin, righteousness, and judgment.)

Romans 8:26
(Intercedes for us when we pray.)

2 Thessalonians 2:13
(Sanctifies believers.)

5. What are His attributes?

Hebrews 9:14
(Eternal.)

Psalm 139:7
(Present everywhere.)

1 Corinthians 2:10,11
(Knows the things of God.)

Why Did He Come?

1. What is the chief reason the Holy Spirit came (John 16:14)?
(To glorify Christ.)

2. What will be a logical result when the Holy Spirit controls your life?

◆ *Revelation:* 2 Timothy 3:16; 2 Peter 1:2

◆ *Power for service:* Exodus 31:3; 1 Samuel 16:13; 2 Chronicles 15:1,2

The Holy Spirit was active in the ministry of Jesus in the following ways:

◆ *Birth:* Matthew 1:18–20; Luke 1:30–35

◆ *Baptism:* Matthew 3:16

◆ *Miracles:* Matthew 12:28

◆ *Message of new birth:* John 3:5,6

◆ *Resurrection:* Romans 8:11; 1 Peter 3:18

The life of the Lord Jesus and the ministry of the disciples depended upon the Holy Spirit. We must depend upon Him even more.

Why would the Holy Spirit seek to glorify Christ?

The Holy Spirit glorifies Christ because He is "the Way" (John 14:6), and He came "to seek and to save what was lost" (Luke 19:10).

3. How does the following diagram compare with your life?

1. Write one new insight you have gained from this lesson concerning the Holy Spirit.
2. In what area of your life do you believe the Holy Spirit needs to be more in control?
3. What will be the result when He is in control?

❖ ❖ ❖

(See the diagram in the student's book.)

Conclusion and Application

People often give the impression that God is an impersonal force which can be exploited for a life of well-being. This is wrong. God is a person, and through His Spirit He wants to control and use us for His own glory and our own good. We do not use God—He uses us.

Closing Prayer

The Holy Spirit's Relationship With You

Opening Prayer

Discussion Starter

 As a Christian, how are God the Father, God the Son, and God the Holy Spirit individually related to you?

God the Father: Source of life, source of all that is holy and good.

God the Son: God manifest in flesh, our Savior, provides way of salvation.

God the Holy Spirit: Regenerates, gives new life; seeks to instruct, encourage, lead, motivate, inspire, and empower us.

Lesson Development

(Invite one of the group members to read the paragraphs appearing at the opening of this lesson in the student's book. Note the diagram and discuss it.)

❖

Leader's Objective: To show that successful Christian living is based upon the Holy Spirit's control of our lives, and to lead students to allow that relationship to be vitally real in their daily lives

171

LESSON 2

Bible Study

The Work of the Holy Spirit

1. When you became a Christian (that is, at the time of your spiritual birth), the Holy Spirit did a number of things for and in you. What are they?

   1 Corinthians 3:16
   (Lives in me.)

   Ephesians 4:30
   (Sealed me as God's child for eternity.)

   1 Corinthians 12:13
   (Baptized me into the body of Christ.)

   2 Corinthians 5:5
   (Became God's pledge, His guarantee.)

2. Explain in your own words what the Holy Spirit does for the Christian according to the following verses:

   Romans 8:16
   (Testifies with our spirit that we are God's children.)

   Romans 8:26,27
   (Helps our praying, intercedes for us according to God's will.)

The Results of Being Filled With the Holy Spirit

1. Can a person be a Christian and not have the Holy Spirit dwelling in Him (Romans 8:9)? Explain.

There is a story about three men who all claimed ownership of the same house. The first man was the builder. He drew up the plans, built the house, then put it up for sale. The second man was the buyer. He paid the price to buy the house. He owns the house, but a third man now lives in it. So it is with us. God the Father created us; God the Son redeemed us—bought us—with His precious blood at Calvary, and God the Holy Spirit has come to live within us.

> Don't you know that you yourselves are God's temples and that God's Spirit lives in you (1 Corinthians 3:16)?

It is almost inconceivable that the great creator of the universe, God Himself, comes to live in us when we receive Christ, but He does!

The Holy Spirit initiates the new life and then wants to fill (direct and control) the believer.

Paul certainly was Spirit-filled and his message was powerful. Note his testimony in 1 Corinthians 2:4,5.

❓How did he speak?
(With the Spirit's power.)

(No. If we do not have the Spirit, we do not belong to God.)

2. What is the main reason to be filled with the Spirit (Acts 1:8; 4:29,31)?
   (To have power for witnessing and be able to speak with boldness.)

3. What work of the Holy Spirit is necessary for successful Christian living and service (Ephesians 5:18)?
   (He must fill us.)

LIFE APPLICATION

1. Complete the chart below.

2. Are you filled with the Holy Spirit?

   How do you know?

   If not, what makes you think you are not filled?

3. Do you really desire to be filled with the Holy Spirit?

   Why?

 What does he contrast?
(The Spirit's power and man's wisdom.)

 How can you have this boldness and power?
(By asking for and receiving the Holy Spirit's power.)

Conclusion and Application

(Discuss possible ways students can fill out the "Life Application" chart.)

It is evident that the Holy Spirit plays a major role in the life of the Christian. God carries out His purpose in the life of the Christian through the control of the Holy Spirit. To be a successful Christian, you must yield to His direction and control.

(Do not ask students to discuss their answers to the last two questions in class.)

Closing Prayer

❖ ❖ ❖

Why So Few Christians Are Filled With the Holy Spirit

Opening Prayer

Discussion Starter

(Ask students to write four or five things that they believe would keep an individual from experiencing the direction and control of the Holy Spirit and living a Spirit-filled life. Discuss those things together.)

Galatians 5:25 says, "If we live in the Spirit, let us also walk in the Spirit" (NKJ).

❓What does Paul mean by "living" as opposed to "walking"?

Lesson Development

(Invite one of the group members to summarize the paragraphs appearing at the opening of this lesson in the student's book. Note the diagram and discuss it.)

The battle for the Spirit-filled life is fought within the heart of the Christian.

A key reason many Christians are not directed and controlled by the Holy Spirit, and the battle for a Spirit-

Leader's Objective: To guide group members in understanding the barriers to living a Spirit-filled life, to help them identify those barriers in their own lives, and to lead them to surrender those barriers to God

L E S S O N   3

Bible Study

The Heart's Battlefield

1. How does Paul describe himself in Romans 7:19–24?
   (He is not in control; he is wicked, evil, a prisoner of the law of sin, and he wants to do good but cannot.)

   How does this description make you feel?

2. In your own words, explain why so many Christians are unhappy, according to Galatians 5:16,17.
   (Flesh and Spirit oppose each other, creating conflict.)

Why the Battle Is Often Lost

1. According to each of the following verses, give one reason so few Christians are filled with the Holy Spirit.

   Psalm 119:105
   (They don't use the lamp, the Word of God.)

   Proverbs 16:18
   (Pride.)

filled life is lost, is a lack of knowledge of the Word of God. Let me give you an example.

A young Christian who loved the Lord Jesus Christ and wanted to serve Him was eager to get married. He was in the Armed Forces in France. He became very fond of two French women and didn't know which one he liked better.

One day he walked into a large church and sat in one of the pews. Asking God to guide him, he looked up at the stained glass windows and saw two words: "Ave Maria." Strangely enough, the name of one of the French women was Maria. He thought, "Have Maria, have Maria! I'll ask her to be my wife." But, sad to say, that woman was not a Christian.

If that man had been reading God's Word diligently, and if he had read and digested 2 Corinthians 6:14—"Do not be yoked together with unbelievers"— he would never have looked to a stained glass window for guidance. If the Word of God was dwelling in him richly, the Spirit of God would have shown him clearly that he could not ask a non-believer to be his wife. The Spirit-filled life is tremendously practical.

Pride was the sin of Satan (Isaiah 14:12–14). Pride was also the first sin of mankind as Adam and Eve wanted to be something they were not (Genesis 3:5,6). The self-centered Christian cannot have fellowship with God, for "God opposes the proud, but gives grace to the humble" (1 Peter 5:5).

Proverbs 29:25
(Fear of man.)

One of the greatest tragedies of our day is the difficulty of telling a Christian from a non-Christian (generally speaking). We are not to be "conformed any longer to the pattern of this world, but be transformed" (Romans 12:2). The world should know that we are different.

All around us are people with hungry hearts who would respond to the gospel if we would be brave enough to let people know where we stand.

Luke 9:26
(Ashamed of Christ and of His words.)

"Martin Luther, the great Protestant reformer, stood fearlessly before the Holy Roman Emperor and the Diet of Worms as an Archbishop questioned him about his writings.

"Luther replied, 'The books are all mine, and I have written more.'

"'Do you defend them all, or do you reject a part?' asked the Archbishop. Luther replied aloud, 'This touches God and His Word. This affects the salvation of souls. Of this Christ said, "He who denies me before men, him will I deny before my Father."'

"Luther was given a day to think it over and asked the next day to recant his statements. Luther replied, 'Unless I am convicted by Scripture and plain reason—I do not accept the authority of popes and councils, for they have contradicted each other—my conscience is captive to the Word of God. I cannot and I will not recant anything, for to go against conscience is neither right nor safe. Here I stand, I cannot do otherwise. God help me'" (Bainton, *Here I Stand, A Life of Martin Luther,* p. 144).

2. What is another barrier between you and the Lord that keeps you from being filled with the Spirit (Psalm 66:18)? *(Cherishing sin.)*

What else can divert you from being filled with the Spirit (1 John 2:15–17)? *(Love of the world.)*

3. Lack of trust in God also will keep you from being filled with the Holy Spirit. Read John 3:16, Romans 8:32, and 1 John 3:16. Describe how these verses help you trust God fully.

Basically, the reason most Christians are not filled with the Holy Spirit is that they are unwilling to surrender their wills to God.

LIFE APPLICATION

1. Examine the diagram on the preceding page, and write here any of those or other barriers you are aware of between yourself and God.

2. Prayerfully consider, then answer this question:

God will not fill an unclean or unyielded vessel. He wants you to confess all known sin, and make restitution where you can. See 1 John 1:9; Exodus 22:3,5,6,12.

Love for material things and desire to conform to a secular society is the spiritual disease of many Christians. Every Christian should make careful and frequent evaluation of how he invests his time, talent, and treasures to accomplish the most for Christ.

Some people are afraid that, if they surrender to God's will, He will take something away from them or make them unhappy. Nothing could be further from the truth. When a person chooses to do God's will, that person will be fulfilled:

Selfward: Find the inner longings of his own heart gratified (Psalm 16:11; 23:5; 63:5; John 4:13,14; 7:37,38)

Godward: Glorify God (Matthew 5:16; John 15:8; 1 Corinthians 6:20; Ephesians 1:6)

Manward: Bring salvation and blessing to others (Luke 24:47,48; Acts 4:13; 9:15; 1 Corinthians 4:9; 2 Corinthians 4:10,11; Galatians 1:16; Philippians 1:20)

Conclusion and Application

(See the diagram in the student's book.)

The most unhappy people in the world are not the unbelievers, but Christians who resist the will of God for their lives! The Christian who refuses to do the will of God must be

"Am I willing to surrender my will to God?"

3. If you are, pray this prayer with all of your heart to turn your life over to God.

Dear Father, I need You. I acknowledge that I have been directing my own life and that, as a result, I have sinned against You. I thank You that You have forgiven my sins through Christ's death on the cross for me.

I now invite Christ to again take His place on the throne of my life. Fill me with the Holy Spirit as you commanded me to be filled. I pray this in the name of Jesus.

As an expression of my faith, I now thank You for taking control of my life and for filling me with the Holy Spirit. Amen.

prepared to pay the price of disobedience. "As we sow, so shall we reap."

A number of years ago, a man resisted the call to ministry in Sweden. He stubbornly resisted God's will even through the death of his wife and daughter. He went into business and prospered, only to be robbed by his own son. In his older years, as he languished with cancer, he said, "I know that I am saved, but oh, the loss, as I soon will be ushered into His presence only to give an account of a whole life of disobedience."

God is a loving Father in whom we can trust without reservation, as a son trusts an earthly father who has proven his love. Romans 14:23 says, "Everything that does not come from faith is sin." And Hebrews 11:6 says, "Without faith it is impossible to please God." Many Christians grieve the Holy Spirit because of their unbelief.

Closing Prayer

How You Can Be Filled With the Holy Spirit

Opening Prayer

Discussion Starter

Suppose you are a counselor. A new Christian comes to you and asks, "Don't you think one's conversion experience and sinful background determine the success in personal witnessing, in Christian work, and in Christian growth? I do not have the power 'X' has because he has such a tremendous background."

❓What would you say?

❓What does determine success?

Lesson Development

(Ask one of the group members to read the paragraph at the opening of this lesson in the student's book.)

To try to live the Christian life or do service for God apart from His Spirit is like trying to operate a car without gas. It doesn't work!

Leader's Objective: To discuss how one is filled with the Holy Spirit and to pray with those who desire to be filled with the Holy Spirit

Bible Study

What You Must Know

1. What is the *command* found in Ephesians 5:18? *(To be filled with the Holy Spirit.)*

2. What is the *promise* found in 1 John 5:14,15? *(God will answer our request to be filled with His Spirit because that is according to His will.)*

3. According to these Scriptures, why do you need to be filled with the Spirit?

   Galatians 5:22,23
   (To have the fruit of the Spirit in your life.)

   Acts 1:8
   (To have power to witness.)

   The fruit of the Spirit is never an end in itself, but only a means to the end. We win men and women to Christ, which in turn brings glory and honor to Him (John 15:8).

What You Must Feel

1. What is one prerequisite to being filled with the Spirit, according to Matthew 5:6?
   (We must hunger and thirst after righteousness; we must desire to be filled.)

The Holy Spirit was responsible for our new birth. We are "born of the Spirit" (John 3:5,6). The Holy Spirit living in us makes us conscious of God's presence and gives us the assurance that we are children of God.

The Spirit Himself testifies with our spirit that we are God's children (Romans 8:16).

The Holy Spirit guides our lives.

Those who are led by the Spirit of God are sons of God (Romans 8:14).

Our hope of the resurrection lies in the power of the Holy Spirit.

If the Spirit of him who raised Jesus from the dead is living in you, he who raised Christ from the dead will also give life to your mortal bodies through his Spirit, who lives in you (Romans 8:11).

Since the Holy Spirit inspired the writing of the Bible, we cannot understand its true meaning apart from His control.

We pray with His assistance according to Romans 8:26, and we witness in His power according to Acts 1:8.

The Holy Spirit lives in every believer from the moment he receives Christ. However, the Spirit does not continue to control the life in the sense of filling unless we want Him to do so and are willing to trust and obey Him.

Read John 7:37–39. Pick out the verbs in verses 37 and 38 *(come, drink, believe)*. When one thirsts one must come to Christ, drink, and believe. Some come to Christ because they thirst, but they do not believe (trust, rely on, have faith in).

2. How are you applying this to your life?

What You Must Do

1. If your desire to be filled with the Spirit is sincere, what will you do now (Romans 12:1,2)?
   (Present your body as a living sacrifice; be transformed.)

   This means there can be no unconfessed sin in your life. The Holy Spirit cannot fill an unclean vessel. He waits to fill you with His power.

2. How then are you filled with the Holy Spirit (Matthew 7:7–11; John 7:37–39)?
   (Ask; come to Jesus.)

3. Will the Holy Spirit fill you if you ask Him?
   (Yes.)

   How do you know (1 John 5:14,15)?
   (When we pray according to God's will, He hears and answers.)

LIFE APPLICATION

1. You can be filled with the Holy Spirit only by faith. Prayer is one way of expressing your faith. If you truly desire to be filled with the Holy Spirit, you can pray this prayer now:

   Dear Father, I need You. I acknowledge that I have been in control of my life, and as a result, I have

❓According to verses 38 and 39, what can one expect will be the result in coming to Christ, drinking, and believing?
(An outflow of "streams of living water.")

(To illustrate the importance of having no unconfessed sin in your life, bring a clear glass that has a lot of food or drink residue in it. Pour clear water into the dirty glass and offer it to a group member. Then ask:)

❓How is offering someone a dirty glass of water like expecting to be used of God with unconfessed sin in your life?

(Then bring out a clean, crystal glass, pour fresh water into it, and offer it to the same student. Ask:)

❓How is this glass like us when we are filled with the Holy Spirit?

Conclusion and Application

The Spirit-filled life is the norm for the Christian life. It is for every Christian. With a Spirit-filled life, the Christian will experience the joy and reality of his Christian life; he will have power to witness. The simple prerequisites are confession, cleansing, and complete surrender to His will by faith.

❓Would you like to pray this prayer now?

sinned against You. I thank You for forgiving my sins through Christ's death on the cross for me. I now invite Christ to take control of the throne of my life. Fill me with the Holy Spirit as You commanded me to be filled, and as You promised in Your Word that You would do if I asked in faith. I pray this in the name of Jesus. As an expression of my faith, I now thank You for taking control of my life and for filling me with the Holy Spirit.

2. What must you have when you ask Him to fill you (Hebrews 11:6)? *(Faith.)*

3. If you have asked the Holy Spirit to fill you, thank Him. God is dependable; His Word is true. If you are sincere, He has filled you.

4. What should be your attitude from this day forward (1 Thessalonians 5:18)?

Date of filling:

Your comments:

(Give the students a few moments of silence to pray the prayer in the student's book.)

(Continue with discussion of "Life Application" questions and answers as appropriate.)

Closing Prayer

How You Can Know When You Are Filled With the Holy Spirit

Opening Prayer

Discussion Starter

❷What do you think Paul meant when he said, "I no longer live, but Christ lives in me" (Galatians 2:20)?

❷What part do feelings play in your Christian life?

❷What part does faith play?

❷Do feelings and faith ever contradict each other? How?

Lesson Development

(It is important to have the students seriously consider the questions appearing at the opening of this lesson, just before the "Bible Study" begins. Your continuation of this study will depend on the responses. If some of the group members need to go back to Lesson 4, don't hesitate to do so.)

Let's look up and talk about these Scriptures:

John 4:34—Jesus' motive for living

Leader's Objective: To give group members the assurance that they are filled with the Holy Spirit and encourage them to continue their walk in the Spirit by faith

LESSON 5

Bible Study

Results of the Spirit-filled Life

1. What will the Holy Spirit demonstrate in and through your life as a result of His filling you (Galatians 5:22,23)?
   (His fruit: love, joy, peace, etc.)

   Which specific fruit of the Spirit are you most in need of?

2. Read Acts 1:8. How do you see this power at work in your life?

   How does John 15:16 apply to you today?
   (God chose me to bear fruit that will last.)

3. How do you identify with 1 Corinthians 12:1–11 and Ephesians 4:11?

4. What mannerisms, language, activities, and inconsistencies in your life do you think are hindering the Holy Spirit from developing His fruit, power, and gifts in you?

5. What happens as we are occupied with Christ and allow the Holy Spirit to work in us (2 Corinthians 3:18)?
   (We are transformed into His likeness.)

Fact, Faith, and Feelings

1. *Fact:* Why should we be filled with the Holy Spirit

John 7:37–39—An exuberant, abundant life flowing over into the lives of others

(You may want to make copies of the following list to distribute to your group members for their consideration or write the list on a flip chart for students to copy in their books.)

Checklist of Results of Being Filled With the Spirit

___ I realize my utter dependence on Jesus Christ moment by moment.

___ I look to Him in all things.

___ I am slow to speak, to act, to plan, until I have been in touch with Him.

___ I let Christ live His life through me, instead of trying in my own strength to live my life for Him.

___ I realize that He is Love.

___ I have given up self-love and made it the priority in my life to love others.

___ I experience boldness in my witness for Christ.

___ I produce fruit according to Matthew 4:19 and John 15:8.

❓Why should we make our feelings subordinate to fact and faith?

Feelings fluctuate, but fact does not change, and faith anchors.

(Ephesians 5:18)?
*(Because we are com-
manded by God to be.)*

2. *Faith:* What is our assurance that we have been
filled with the Spirit (1
John 5:14,15)?
*(God has promised to an-
swer our prayer when it is
in accord with His will.)*

3. *Feelings:* When you were
filled with the Spirit, did
you feel any different?

Do not depend upon feel-
ings. The promise of
God's Word, not our feel-
ings, is our authority.
The Christian lives by
faith in the trustworthi-
ness of God Himself and
His Word.

This train diagram illus-
trates the relationship
among fact [God and His
Word], faith [our trust in
God and His Word], and
feeling [the result of our
faith and obedience]
(John 14:21).

The train will run with or
without the caboose.
However, it would be fu-
tile to attempt to pull the
train by the caboose. In
the same way, we do not
depend upon feelings or
emotions, but we place
our faith (trust) in the
trustworthiness of God
and the promise of His
Word.

(Ask volunteers to share about
times when they let feelings rule and
what happened. Talk about what could
have happened if they had let faith rule
the situation.)

Feelings are an important part of
the Christian life. God created our feelings and we should glorify Him with
them. But we should not let them
become more important than our faith
or let them hide the facts from us.

(Note the train diagram in the
student's book and discuss it.)

Conclusion and Application

(Have students fill out the "Life Application" questions without giving answers aloud.)

The Christian is filled with the Holy Spirit by faith. He continues to be filled and controlled by *faith*. Evidence that he is living a Spirit-controlled life will be seen in the fact that he is becoming more like Christ and a more fruitful witness for Him (Matthew 4:19 and John 15:8).

(Allow students to share times when they let their faith rule, which resulted in great things for God's kingdom.)

Closing Prayer

LIFE APPLICATION

Though you may not be aware of a change immediately, with the passing of time you will see some evidence of your being filled with the Spirit. If there is no change, the Holy Spirit is not in charge.

1. Do you think a person can be filled with the Holy Spirit and not be aware of it? Explain.

2. Ask yourself these questions:

   ◆ Do you have a greater love for Christ?

   ◆ Do you have a greater love for God's Word?

   ◆ Is prayer more important to you?

   ◆ Are you more concerned for those who do not know Christ as Savior?

   ◆ Are you experiencing a greater boldness, liberty, and power in witnessing?

   If you can answer yes truthfully to these questions, you undoubtedly are filled with the Spirit.

3. What does that assurance mean to you now?

4. If your answer was no to any of those five questions, what do you suppose that indicates?

5. What will you do to change your attitude or actions?

How You Can Continue to Be Filled With the Holy Spirit

Opening Prayer

Discussion Starter

(Use role playing to help group members identify their problems. Ask three individuals to briefly play the following roles:)

◆ A Christian who has unconfessed sin, and who lacks faith to claim 1 John 1:9 and the filling of the Holy Spirit as in 1 John 5:14,15.

◆ A Christian who has been defeated by sin, but is now using 1 John 1:9 to rebound. Discuss how long a Christian has to remain defeated (only until he realizes his need for confession and cleansing).

◆ A Christian just returning from meeting a friend to whom he has successfully witnessed. Discuss what a witnessing Christian indicates (that he is Spirit-filled and controlled).

(Discuss the roles played and why the characters reacted as they did.)

Leader's Objective: To help each student experience the Spirit-filled life as a moment-by-moment reality

LESSON 6

Bible Study

How to Be Filled Continually

Read Ephesians 5:18. In the original Greek, "be filled" means "keep on being filled constantly and continually." Living a godly life is a vital part of this process.

1. What characterizes the life of a Christian who is "being filled" constantly and continually (John 15:1–11; Galatians 5:16–25)?
   (He walks in the Spirit, he glorifies the Father by bearing much fruit.)

2. Which two commandments do you think are most important to living the Spirit-filled life (Matthew 22:36–40)?
   (Love God; love your neighbor as yourself.)

   Why?
   (Because it is a command of our Lord and all the law and the admonitions of the prophets depend on these two commandments.)

We have become so used to depending on feelings instead of facts in the Christian walk that we tend to doubt God's Word and inwardly question whether He will do what His Word says He will. Many of you have come to realize that you have been living a powerless Christian life and you honestly asked the Holy Spirit to fill you.

Now, a few days later, you may be doubting the validity of this filling because there has been no big emotional reaction or drastic change.

Remember that what God says is fact, and whether your response was calm assurance, excited enthusiasm, or no definite emotional reaction at all, you still can be positive that the Holy Spirit has filled you if you've met the qualifications we discussed in Lesson 4. These qualifications are surrendering your will to Christ, asking in faith, and expecting Him to fill you.

Lesson Development

(Ask one of the group members to summarize the paragraphs that appear at the opening of this lesson in the student's book.)

For a person to become Spirit-filled, he must take these three basic steps:

◆ *Confess* sin and receive cleansing (1 John 1:9).

◆ *Claim* God's will and purpose, which is the filling of the Holy Spirit (Ephesians 5:17,18; Romans 12:1,2; Acts 1:8). This is done through prayer (1 John 5:14,15).

◆ *Believe* God's promise and act in faith (Hebrews 11:6 and James 1:6).

3. In your own words, explain the concept of Spiritual Breathing (see pages 41 and 42).

    Exhale (1 John 1:9)

    Inhale (Ephesians 5:18; 1 John 5:14,15)

    How can Spiritual Breathing enable you to live a godly life and be filled continually with the Holy Spirit?

(Take time to go through Spiritual Breathing with your students using the diagram in the student's book and referring to pages 41 and 42 of the article.)

4. To be filled continually with the Holy Spirit, you must abide in Christ. Read John 15:1–11.

    How can you do that (John 14:21; John 15:10)? *(By keeping His commandments.)*

    What does the example of the vine and branches in verses 1–8 mean to you in your Christian life?

Abiding in the Spirit is *expressed* in love (1 John 3:23). God, who is love, can manifest Himself only to those who are willing to love others. See John 3:16; 1 John 3:16, 3:1; 4:8; 4:19; John 13:1; 15:9.

5. Do not grieve the Holy Spirit.

    Read Ephesians 4:25–32. How do you grieve the Holy Spirit? *(By sinning.)*

    Which commandment in that list do you need to pay special attention to?

    How can you get rid of sin in your life (1 John 1:9)? *(By confessing it and accepting forgiveness and cleansing.)*

    According to Romans 8:13, what does the Holy

Think of how a child can grieve his or her parents by having a rebellious attitude.

❓How is this like grieving the Holy Spirit?

Spirit want to do for you?
(Put to death the misdeeds of the body.)

6. Spend time daily in prayer and Bible study.

What do these verses teach about the role of prayer in the life of the Spirit-filled believer?

Hebrews 4:15,16
(It is vital so we may receive mercy and find grace to help in time of need.)

James 5:16
(We may be healed.)

1 Samuel 12:23
(It would be sin to stop praying for those we are concerned about.)

James 1:5
(Prayer is our means of gaining wisdom from God.)

Acts 4:31
(We may receive boldness.)

What do these verses tell us about the role of God's Word in the Spirit-filled life?

Romans 1:16
(It is the power of God for salvation of everyone who believes.)

Hebrews 4:12
(It judges our thoughts and our hearts' intents.)

2 Timothy 2:15
(It helps us understand God's truth.)

2 Timothy 3:16,17
(It shows us doctrine, reproof, correction, and training in righteousness,

Spending time daily in prayer and Bible reading is vital to abiding in Christ. God's Word and prayer are the conduits that allow us to experience the fullness of the Holy Spirit at work in us. Prayer is like water to a thirsty branch and God's Word is like nourishment.

❓How have you seen God's Word at work in your life that would indicate you are filled with His Spirit?

There is an interesting parallel between Ephesians 5:18, which admonishes us to be consistently and continually directed and empowered by the Holy Spirit, and Colossians 3:16, which admonishes us to "let the Word of Christ richly dwell within you." The result of both letting the Word of Christ dwell in you and being filled with the Holy Spirit will be that you will talk much about the Lord, quoting psalms and hymns, and making music to the Lord.

and we may be prepared for good works.)

7. Obey God's commandments.

   According to these verses, what role does obedience have in the Spirit-filled life?

   John 14:15
   (Shows our love for Christ.)

   John 14:23–26
   (Gives the basis for fellowship with the Father.)

8. Witness for Christ.

   According to Acts 1:8, for what purpose was the Holy Spirit given?
   (To give believers the power to witness for Christ throughout the world.)

(Talk about how being filled with the Spirit, spending time with God each day, obedience, and witnessing are interrelated. Discuss what would happen if one area began to decline in a Christian's life.)

LIFE APPLICATION

The Spirit-filled life is an obedient and abiding life. It can be experienced daily as you:

- ◆ Love God with all of your heart
- ◆ Practice Spiritual Breathing
- ◆ Spend time daily in prayer and Bible study
- ◆ Obey God's commandments
- ◆ Witness for Christ

1. How is the Holy Spirit's fullness and power evident in your life?

2. List any areas of your life in which the Holy Spirit is not in control.

Conclusion and Application

The Spirit-filled life is not one of obligation. Do not make this list a reason to consider yourself a failure. Instead, use the list as a guideline to keep yourself on track and to discover which areas you can strengthen.

To have a continuous, day-by-day, Spirit-filled life is God's norm for the Christian and results from cleansing, and uncompromising faith that believes God and claims His promises to be truth *each day*, moment by moment.

List the areas in which the Holy Spirit is in control.

What practical steps will you take this week to give the Holy Spirit full control of those areas that you have not surrendered to Him?

3. Have you realized a victory today over a sin you confessed yesterday?

Describe.

Closing Prayer

(Observe a period of silent prayer to give students an opportunity to confess sin and appropriate God's forgiveness. Then finish by praying aloud.)

Recap

Opening Prayer

Discussion Starter

(Ask for and discuss any questions anyone in the group may have about the person and ministry of the Holy Spirit as presented in the previous six lessons.)

(Then talk about how the previous lessons have produced changes in their lives. Ask students to share insights they have gained, and exciting new ways God is using them because of what they have learned.)

Lesson Development

(Any appropriate material from previous lessons that was not sufficiently covered could be used at this time, and you also may deal with any point that the group members may not understand as well as they could.)

(Then go over the remaining Recap questions and answers. This material will benefit both the students and you by giving you a deeper appreciation of God's Word.)

Leader's Objective: To be sure students understand who the Holy Spirit is and why He came; to review how to be filled and how to walk continually in the Spirit

LESSON 7

The following questions will help you review this Step. If necessary, reread the appropriate lesson(s).

1. Is the Holy Spirit a personality or an impersonal force?
   (He is a personality.)

   How do you know?
   (He has intellect, emotions, and will.)

   What is the chief reason the Holy Spirit has come?
   (To glorify Christ.)

2. What is the *command* of Ephesians 5:18?
   (To be filled with the Holy Spirit.)

3. What is the *promise* of 1 John 5:14,15?
   (Whatever we ask that is according to God's will, He will give us.)

4. Name as many reasons as you can that Christians are not filled with the Holy Spirit.
   (They don't know the Word of God, are proud, fear man, are ashamed of Christ, have wickedness in their hearts, do not trust in God, and love the world.)

LIFE APPLICATION

1. What should be your motives for being filled with the Spirit?

2. How can you be filled with the Spirit?

Conclusion and Application

Every day can be an exciting adventure for the Christian who knows the reality of being filled with the Holy Spirit and living constantly, moment by moment, under His gracious control. God commands every Christian to be filled with the Holy Spirit, and not to be filled or controlled by Him is an act of disobedience.

(If any in your group still do not have assurance that they are filled with the Holy Spirit but indicate a desire to do so, lead them in the prayer in Lesson 4.)

3. How do you know you
   are filled with the Holy
   Spirit?

4. How can you continue to
   be filled with and walk in
   the Spirit?

Closing Prayer

The
Christian
and **Prayer**

Unlocking
the Secrets
of a
Successful
Prayer Life

STEP 4

Purpose of Prayer

Opening Prayer

Discussion Starter

❓Why do you pray?

❓Why do you think we should pray?

Lesson Development

(Encourage students to read the article, "Discovering the Secret of Successful Prayer" at the beginning of their book on their own time if they have not already done so.)

(Ask one of the group members to summarize the paragraphs appearing at the opening of this lesson in the student's book. Note the diagram and discuss it.)

Leader's Objective: To help group members understand the basis for scripturally sound and meaningful prayer

LESSON 1

Bible Study

Why Prayer Is Important

Read John 14:13, 1 Thessalonians 5:17, Acts 4:23–33, and Matthew 9:38.

Identify at least three reasons for prayer.

1) *(To glorify God.)*

2) *(That we may be granted boldness to witness for Christ.)*

3) *(That laborers may be sent forth into His harvest.)*

(Other reasons may be listed.)

The Apostles' Motive

Read Acts 4.

1. What problem did the apostles face?
   (Persecution and threats for preaching the resurrection of Christ.)

2. Why did they not ask God to remove the persecution?
   (They were not concerned about personal safety and comfort.)

3. For what did they pray (verse 29)?
   (Boldness.)

   Why is this significant?
   (So they could speak God's Word confidently and boldly.)

4. What was their real motive (John 14:13)?
   (To glorify the Father.)

Prayer is not an "escape hatch" to get us out of trouble. It is not merely something to make life easy for us. It is a means of glorifying God, whatever the cost may be to us. Prayer that moves God is prayer that seeks first the kingdom of God and His righteousness. In Acts 4:31, God answered the prayer of the apostles by filling them with the Holy Spirit so that they could speak the Word of God boldly.

Other reasons for prayer that we might list—communion with God, adoration, confession, thanksgiving, supplication—share the common purpose of glorifying God. If we pray merely for personal pleasure—and not to glorify God—we pray, for the most part, in vain.

Your Motives for Praying

On the basis of your personal experience, list at least four reasons you pray.

1)

2)

3)

4)

God's Motives In Teaching Us About Prayer

Read John 3:5–8 and John 4:23,24.

1. In what form does God exist?
   (Spirit.)

   What must happen to us before we can have fellowship with Him?
   (We must be born again—of the Spirit.)

   What kind of worship does He desire?
   (That which is in spirit and in truth.)

   What is His delight (Proverbs 15:8)?
   (The prayer of the upright.)

2. List some purposes of prayer from each of the following Bible references:

   Matthew 7:7
   (To seek God's supply.)

   Matthew 26:41
   (To avoid temptation.)

As we pray, it is important to realize that prayer is a spiritual activity and must be motivated and carried out by the Holy Spirit. The person who is not a Christian:

> ...does not accept the things that come from the Spirit of God, for they are foolishness to him, and he cannot understand them, because they are spiritually discerned (1 Corinthians 2:14).

For this reason, so much of prayer is an empty experience for the non-Christian. This is also the reason prayer can be a dull experience for the Christian who does not understand the work of the Holy Spirit within him.

Qualifications for effective prayer are wrapped up in two phrases taken from John 15:7: "If you abide in Me" and "My words abide in you" (NKJ). Abiding in Christ means total dependence on Him.

There are at least three ways to cross the Pacific Ocean. You can swim, depending totally on your own strength. In this case you would go a few miles at the most, and then drown.

You can paddle in a canoe, partially depending on your own strength. You might get several miles farther, but the first strong wind would overturn you.

Or you could travel on an ocean liner or in a plane. This would mean totally committing yourself to another to do what you cannot do. This would allow you to complete your trip and arrive safely at your destination.

In the same way, abiding in Christ means total dependence on the

Luke 18:1
(To not give up.)

3. From your understanding of these passages, what do you think God wants you to realize about Him?

Prayer Meets the Heart's Needs

1. According to 2 Corinthians 3:5, what is the source of the Christian's sufficiency?
(God.)

How do you tap into that source?
(Through prayer.)

2. Read Psalm 63. Note the elements of worship and write below the word or phrase that describes how we should worship God; include references (for example, "My soul thirsts for you—Psalm 63:1").

strength, power, and ability of another. We do not trust ourselves even in part. Lack of abiding—laboring in our own strength, being out of fellowship with God—makes our prayer lives empty and vain.

Christ's words also must abide in us. His words must remain in our hearts and control our lives. In the military, a soldier who refuses to obey orders can be court-martialed. An employee who refuses to obey his supervisor is fired. A student who does not obey instructions fails the course. The Christian who, whether from ignorance or unwillingness, does not obey God's commandments recorded in the Bible will see his whole life suffer—especially his prayer life.

"Right praying" requires right living.

Prayer satisfies the longings of our hearts. One reason for prayerlessness is a loss of our "first love" for God and a lack of desire to seek God.

❓Do we seek God for Himself alone—apart from all He can give us?

Exodus 33:12–17 records Moses' pleas for the presence of God after Israel's sin with the golden calf. In verse 15 Moses said,

If your presence does not go with us, do not send us up from here.

God had said He would send an angel, but this was not enough for Moses. Moses wanted the best—God's presence with him.

(See the chart in the student's book.)

1. What conclusions can you now make concerning your relationship with God in prayer?

2. Begin a prayer list. Keep a record of the things for which you pray.

❖ ❖ ❖

Conclusion and Application

The Christian's fellowship with the Father goes two directions:

◆ God speaks to us in His holy Word. The Bible is the Father's message to His children.

◆ We have the privilege of speaking directly to God in prayer. Prayer can be the Christian's constant delight, his refuge in the moment of distress, his resource in time of struggle, his solace in the hour of need.

(See the chart in the student's book.)

Closing Prayer

(Invite each person to pray silently that God will reveal unconfessed sin so it can be confessed and not hinder the effectiveness of his prayer. Close with a brief prayer.)

To Whom Should We Pray?

Opening Prayer

Discussion Starter

(Ask each group member to list these four names on a piece of paper: Jesus, God, Holy Spirit, and his own name. Now assign one or two of the following Scripture passages to each person and have him relate the Scripture verse to the proper names:)

Hebrews 4:14–16

1 Timothy 2:5

Isaiah 59:2

Ephesians 6:18

Matthew 6:9

Romans 8:26

John 14:6

1 John 3:21,22

Jude 20

❖

Leader's Objective: To show the divine operation of the Father, Son, and Holy Spirit in our prayers and to help students have a deeper appreciation of the great privilege of prayer

❓What do these verses show about how the Father, the Son, and the Holy Spirit are involved in prayer?

Bible Study

To Whom Do We Pray?

1. According to Matthew 6:6, to whom should we pray?
   (Our Father in heaven.)

2. From the following passages, give several reasons for your answer:

   1 Chronicles 29:11,12
   (God owns everything.)

   Matthew 6:9
   (Jesus told us to pray to the Father.)

   John 16:23
   (The Father will give us what we ask for.)

3. Meditate on the principles contained in the following excerpt from *How to Pray* by R. A. Torrey.

   How do you approach God when you pray?

   How can you better focus your attention on Him?

   Think about a time when you particularly sensed God's presence when you prayed. What made this time of prayer different from others? Why?

Through Whom Do We Pray?

Read John 14:6 and 1 Timothy 2:5.

1. How many mediators are there between God and man?
   (Only one.)

Lesson Development

(Ask one of the group members to summarize the paragraphs appearing at the opening of this lesson in the student's book. Note the diagram and discuss it.)

(Invite a student to read the quote from the student's book.)

(Share your personal thoughts on each of these questions.)

A college student at an eastern university was once invited to accompany a friend to Washington, D.C. The college student had no idea that anything out of the ordinary would happen, but when they arrived in Washington, his friend took him to the White House.

Who is this mediator?
(Jesus.)

2. On the basis of Hebrews 4:14–16, describe the qualifications of our great high priest.
(He sympathizes with our weaknesses and has been tempted in all things as we are yet without sin.)

3. What are the requirements for a prayer relationship according to 1 John 3:21–23?
(We are to obey His commandments, believe in Jesus Christ, and love one another.)

4. What does unconfessed sin in our lives do to our prayer fellowship with God (Psalm 66:18)?
(The Lord will not listen to our prayers.)

5. God's Word promises in 1 John 1:9 that if we confess our sins He will forgive us. The word "confess" means to "agree with." This involves naming our sins to God, acknowledging that He has already forgiven us through Christ's death on the cross, and repenting of our sins (turning away from or changing our attitude toward them).

Follow these steps for confessing your sins:

Here they spent the day with the President and his wife, as their guests.

It turned out that the friend had known the President for years, and through him the college student was able to spend a day he would never forget. This would have been impossible on his own initiative, but when an acquaintance of the President opened the way for the student, he received a priceless privilege.

How is this like what Jesus has done for us in giving us access to God?

The way to God is opened for us through Christ and our relationship with Him.

Think of a time when you knowingly had unconfessed sin in your life. What happened?

(Take time during class to follow the steps for confessing sins. Pass out

◆ Ask the Holy Spirit to reveal any sin in your life.

◆ Write it down on a sheet of paper.

◆ Confess the sin to God and ask Him to forgive you.

◆ Receive His forgiveness by faith according to 1 John 1:9.

◆ Write the verse across the sin.

◆ Throw away the paper.

6. God honors those who truly pray in His Son's name. What is the promise recorded in John 15:16 and 16:23?
(The Father will give us what we ask for.)

What did Jesus promise in John 14:12–14?
(We can ask for anything in His name and He will do it.)

7. The name of Jesus means everything to God. He lifted Jesus to the highest place in the heavenly sphere and elevated His name far above all others in heaven and on earth.

From the following passages, describe the significance and standing given to the name of Jesus:

John 20:31
(Son of God.)

Acts 2:38
(Forgiveness is in His name.)

sheets of paper for your students to use. Be sure to do the exercise yourself at the same time.)

God gives us double security that He will answer our prayers when we ask in Jesus' name. First, God the Father guarantees that He will give us what we ask for. Second, Jesus promises to answer our prayers. Therefore, our prayers must be very important to God and we can have confidence that He hears us and answers (see also 1 John 5:14,15).

(You may want to spend a few moments praising God for Jesus' name right now.)

Acts 3:6,16; 4:10,30
(Healing comes from His name.)

Acts 19:17
(High honor.)

Acts 4:12
(Salvation.)

Mark 9:37
(We do good works in His name.)

Philippians 2:5–11
(Name above all names.)

8. Improperly used, the name of Jesus does not bring results. To many people, the name of Jesus has become a powerless incantation, a run-together phrase, leaving them bewildered over unanswered prayer.

According to the following verses, how can we use Jesus' name properly and receive our answer from God?

1 John 5:13–15
(If we believe in His name, our prayers will be answered.)

Ephesians 5:20
(Give thanks to God in Jesus' name.)

Colossians 3:17
(Do everything in Jesus' name.)

John 15:16,17
(Bear fruit and the Father will give us whatever we ask in Jesus' name.)

James 4:3; John 14:13
(Bring glory to the Father in Jesus' name.)

When asked how Jesus' name could be used improperly, most of us would immediately think of cursing. But as Christians we can sometimes misuse His name in different ways.

❓How have you seen Jesus' name used improperly by Christians?

❓How can we make the mistake of using Jesus' name too lightly?

Many Christians have a holy regard for Jesus' name. Can you think of someone you know who is a good example of using Jesus' name with reverence?

❓How does this person bring glory to the Father?

❓What fruit have you seen in his or her life?

By Whom Do We Pray?

Read Ephesians 6:18 and Jude 20.

Andrew Murray, noted author and authority on prayer, wrote:

1. According to Romans 8:26,27, why does the Holy Spirit need to help us pray?
   (We don't know how to pray as we should.)

   How does He help us pray?
   (He intercedes for us.)

   Why does God answer the prayers of the Holy Spirit?
   (Because the Spirit of God intercedes according to the will of God.)

2. What, then, should be our relationship with the Holy Spirit (Ephesians 5:18)?
   (We should be filled with the Holy Spirit.)

3. As we exercise the privilege of prayer, what does God do about our anxiety (Philippians 4:6,7)?
   (He gives us His peace which transcends all understanding.)

   Give an example of how this has worked in your life.

4. Why should we cast our troubles on Him (1 Peter 5:7)?
   (Because He truly cares for us.)

(Ask a student to read the quote from the student's book.)

We are to pray *in the Spirit.* This has already been discussed in earlier lessons, but we should note again that unless our prayer is prompted by the Holy Spirit and consistent with the Word of God, it can never be effective before God. Only the filling and prompting of the Holy Spirit can produce vital, believing prayer. No matter how we work up our emotions, no matter what our feelings, no matter how great our desperation—unless God the Holy Spirit is behind our praying, it is fleshly, self-centered, powerless prayer.

How should we, then, prepare for prayer?
We ask God to fill us with His Spirit.

We cannot afford to neglect this priceless privilege. No wonder prayer accomplishes so much; no wonder it does what nothing else can do.

C. H. Spurgeon said years ago:

You have no place in which to pour your troubles except into the ear of God. If you tell them to your friends, you but put your troubles out for a moment, and they will return again. Roll you burden onto the Lord, through prayer, and you have rolled it into a great deep out of which it will never by any possibility rise. Cast your trouble where you cast your

Think back to a time when you did this. How did He answer your prayer?

What did the answer mean to you?

LIFE APPLICATION

1. List any new insights into prayer that you have gained from this lesson.

   Describe how you will use these insights to have a more well-rounded prayer life.

2. Write down at least one new way in which you want to apply prayer in your life right now.

   ❖   ❖   ❖

sins; you have cast your sins into the depths of the sea, *there* cast your troubles also. Never keep a trouble half an hour before you tell it to God in prayer. As soon as the trouble comes, quick, the first thing, tell it to your Father in prayer.

Continual prayer means continual freedom from burdens and anxieties. It is the only way to be a happy, joyful Christian.

Conclusion and Application

That God *desires* our fellowship is one of the most amazing facts in Scripture. It is so staggering that it is difficult to grasp its significance.

This fact should inspire us with a desire to seek God's face. The usual concept—that we read our Bibles and say our prayers for our own benefit and satisfaction—will fade into insignificance. This simple thought of His desire for our fellowship can carry us through times of darkness and give us patience to persevere through trials.

Closing Prayer

(Thank and praise God for the privilege of prayer. Begin to develop a fellowship of prayer within your group to help apply the principles you will learn in these lessons. List praises, thanksgivings, and requests that your students share to note the changes in their prayers as the study progresses.)

A Guide to Effective Daily Prayer

Opening Prayer

Discussion Starter

(Ask group members to define the following:)

◆ Adoration

◆ Confession

◆ Thanksgiving

◆ Supplication

(Then proceed with:)

We can categorize this prayer pattern in two phases: giving to God (adoration, confession, thanksgiving) and receiving from God (supplication).

❷ Which category are you least familiar with?

❷ Which category do you use most in your devotional life?

Leader's Objective: To teach students a simple guide to use in their daily prayer times

LESSON 3

Bible Study

Adoration

1. Why should we praise God?

   Jeremiah 32:17
   (He made heaven and earth; nothing is too hard for Him.)

   1 John 4:10
   (He loved us and sent His Son to die for us and pay for our sins.)

   Philippians 1:6
   (He began a good work in us and will complete it.)

2. What is the best way for you to show your gratitude toward God, and your faith and trust in Him in all circumstances (Philippians 4:6)?
   (By not worrying and by praying about everything with thanksgiving.)

   What would you conclude that God expects of us (1 Thessalonians 5:16–18)?
   (He wants us to be joyful, pray continually, and give thanks in every circumstance.)

   If you sometimes find it hard to praise God, read some of the Psalms (Psalms 146–150 in particular).

3. How do you communicate your adoration to God?

Lesson Development

(Invite one of the group members to summarize the paragraphs appearing at the opening of this lesson in the student's book. Note the diagram and discuss it.)

(For each of these four categories, encourage your students to share how their prayer life has been enriched by using that particular element of prayer.)

Adoration: Paying honor to a divine being; regarding with fervent devotion and affection.

❓How is adoration different from thanking God?

Adoration is adoring God, telling Him how much you love Him, praising Him for who He is.

Thanking God is telling Him how grateful you are for what He has done for you.

Confession

Read Isaiah 59:1,2.

1. What will hinder fellowship with God?
   (Iniquities, sins.)

2. Psalm 51 was David's prayer after he had fallen out of fellowship with God. What did David conclude that God wanted of him (Psalm 51:6,16,17)?
   (The truth, his broken spirit, and his contrite heart.)

3. Read Psalm 32:1–7.

   What was David's observation about confession?
   (It brings forgiveness and deliverance.)

   What was his observation about not confessing his sin (verses 3,4)?
   (It made him feel very old and continually under God's heavy hand.)

4. What should you do when you find that your fellowship with God is broken (1 John 1:9)?
   (Confess your sin and accept His forgiveness.)

   What sin in your life is keeping you from fellowship with God?

   How will you deal with that sin?

Confession: Admitting one's faults, especially confessing one's specific sins. The Greek word means "say the same thing with." We agree with God about our sins.

In confessing sin, note these principles:

◆ We do not need to feel "spiritual" to confess our sins. If we have sin we need to confess, it is a sign that we are not spiritual at the moment anyway. But the time to confess it is immediately after we realize we have sinned.

◆ Confession should be honest and sincere, but beware of torturous self-examination or unhealthy extremes of introspection.

Lord Wariston, a devout young man of the 17th century, described himself in his diary as being God's "poor, naughty, wretched, useless, passionate, humorous, vain, proud [man] . . . the unworthiest, filthiest, passionatest, deceitfulest, crookedest . . . of all thy servants." However true, this cataloging of sins seems tainted with a bit of pride in the thoroughness of his self-condemnation.

◆ We must be willing to accept God's forgiveness and then change behavior appropriately. Some Christians confess their sins but still retain their guilt feelings and self-pity because they are not able to believe and accept the fact that God cleanses from all unrighteousness.

Thanksgiving

Let us never be guilty of being ungrateful to God.

1. How often should we give thanks (Hebrews 13:15)?
   (Continually.)

   For what should we praise Him (Ephesians 5:20)?
   (For all things.)

   Why (1 Thessalonians 5:18)?
   (It is God's will in Christ for us.)

2. What about a situation that seems adverse (Romans 5:3,4)?
   (We should still rejoice.)

3. How do you practice thankfulness when you pray?

   As you go about your daily life?

4. Make a list of each problem, disappointment, heartache, or adversity that concerns you. Begin to thank God for each one. Doing so demonstrates your trust in Him.

Supplication

1. Intercession.

   An example of intercession is provided in Colossians 1:3. What was Paul's prayer for the Christians of Colosse?
   (He thanked God for their faith and labor.)

   Many times our efforts in leading people to Christ are fruitless because we

Thanksgiving: Offering thanks, especially to God; a prayer expressing gratitude.

To fail to give thanks in all things is to sin against God, just the same as violating the Ten Commandments is sin against God. After Job lost his money and his family, he worshiped God and said, "Blessed be the name of the Lord" (Job 1:2).

If, in the next twenty-four hours, you were to lose your whole family and every cent you have, what would your attitude be? If you were filled with God's Holy Spirit and recognized that He controls all things, it should be one of praise and thanksgiving.

Supplication: Imploring God; a humble petition or entreaty.

Christians often do not realize the importance of intercession. The first chapters of almost all of Paul's epistles show that he continually prayed for his converts. He also asked them to pray for him (Romans 15:30,31, etc.).

Early in your Christian life, you should try to form prayer partnerships with your friends. This will bring you

forget the necessary preparation for witnessing. The divine order is to first talk to God about men, and then talk to men about God.

If we follow this order, we will see results. Prayer is really the place where people are won to Christ; witnessing is just gathering in the results of prayer.

As you meditate on the above, list the requests you can make to God for Christians and non-Christians.

2. Petition.

Why should we expect God to answer our prayers (Matthew 7:9–11; Romans 8:32)?
(He gives good gifts; He loves us so deeply.)

According to Psalm 84:11,12, what has God promised to do?
(He will not withhold any good thing.)

What part does belief have in our prayers (Mark 11:24; James 1:6,7)?
(Believing is necessary if we are to receive.)

Faith is necessary for answered prayers. What else is required (Matthew 6:9,10; 1 John 5:14,15)?
(We must ask according to God's will.)

Why will God not answer some prayers (James 4:3)?
(We ask with the wrong

closer together and will profoundly affect your life.

(Discuss this with your group and encourage them to form prayer partnerships either with each other or with a Christian outside your group.)

❓What part do feelings play in our prayer life?

Although feelings can enrich our communication with God, they should not determine the extent of our prayer. Just as we live by faith based on the facts in God's Word, we pray by faith and on the prayer promises God has given us in His Word. Our feelings will often follow as we pray by faith.

❓Think of a time when God said no to your prayer request. What happened?

❓Why does God sometimes say no to our requests?

❓Share about a time when God answered your prayer in a completely different way than you expected. What did that answer teach you about prayer? About God?

motives, for our own gain.)

How does this relate to your prayer life?

3. Explain 2 Corinthians 12:7–10 in light of Romans 8:28.

What does this passage teach us about apparently unanswered prayer?
(God answers our prayers in ways that are for our best but not always in the way we ask.)

LIFE APPLICATION

1. Add other requests to the prayer list you began at the end of Lesson 1.

2. Begin using the ACTS system for prayer during your daily time alone with God. After several days, note here how your prayers have changed.

3. List daily situations in which you could use praise and thanksgiving to help you react in a godly manner.

Now follow through by applying praise and thanksgiving in these circumstances.

Conclusion and Application

Once again we are faced with the importance of prayer. We can be careful to use these methods and procedures, but they in themselves will not make us great prayer warriors. To learn to use these things effectively, we must pray in faith.

Closing Prayer

How to Pray With Power

Opening Prayer

Discussion Starter

(Ask students to name several sources of power such as electricity, nuclear power, or hydroelectric power. Discuss how each of these sources of power originate. Then discuss how prayer is only as powerful as the God we pray to. As a group, describe the power of God.)

? What are some things you can do to be sure your prayers get answered?

Lesson Development

(Invite one of the group members to summarize the paragraphs appearing at the opening of this lesson in the student's book. Note the diagram and discuss it.)

Leader's Objective: To help students discover the great power available through prayer and how to release that power

LESSON 4

Bible Study

Power for Answered Prayer

Read Acts 12:5–18.

1. How did Peter's fellow Christians respond to his imprisonment (verse 5)?
(They prayed for him.)

What was God's answer to their prayer (verses 6–11)?
(Peter was miraculously released.)

What was their response to God's answer (verses 13–16)?
(They didn't believe it; they were astonished.)

How does seeing God answer your prayers in a powerful way change your feelings about prayer?

2. What do the following Bible references tell you about the qualities God demands in a person for powerful prayer?

Hebrews 11:1,6
(Faith.)

Romans 12:1,2
(Yieldedness.)

Mark 11:25
(An attitude of forgiveness.)

1 John 3:22
(Obeying His commandments.)

Ephesians 5:18
(The filling of the Spirit.)

These Christians had a serious problem from which there was no conceivable escape. Peter was an important leader in the early church, and his death might have meant catastrophe for the early church. James had already been killed, and it looked as if Peter would be also.

We should not despair when prayer seems to be the only solution, because prayer is more effective than anything else we can do.

Only those who live for God and put Him first in their lives are assured that their prayers will be answered. If your prayers are powerless before God, perhaps the difficulty is not just in your prayers, but in your life. Perhaps you are not surrendered to God's control in some area. Perhaps some sin is hindering you.

Dr. R. A. Torrey tells the story of a woman who said she did not believe the Bible any more. When he asked her why, she replied, "Because I have tried its promises and found them untrue. The Bible says," she continued, "'Whatsoever we ask believing, we shall receive.' Well, I fully expected to get things from God in prayer, but I did not receive them, so the promise failed."

Dr. Torrey then turned her to 1 John 3:22:

> Whatsoever we ask, we receive of Him, because we keep His commandments, and do those things that are pleasing in His sight.

Then he asked, "Were you keeping His commandments and doing those things pleasing in His sight?"

She confessed that she was not. Her trouble was not the Bible's promises; it was her own disobedience.

Conditions to Answered Prayer

1. Why is it necessary to ask in accordance with the will of God (1 John 5:14, 15)?
   (God will not answer anything that is contrary to His will.)

❓Would God really be doing the best thing for us if He answered prayers that were not His will?

A baby playing in the kitchen might see a shiny steel knife and want it. Yet his mother, knowing the danger of giving it to him, keeps it from his grasp. Many times, things we want with all of our hearts will ultimately bring misery and spiritual weakness in our lives and thus are outside of God's will.

2. Write out John 15:7 in your own words and state what it teaches about conditions to answered prayer.

❓Why is it necessary to abide in Christ and allow His Word to abide in us, so our prayer may be answered?

We noted above that we must pray *in the will of God*. But the important question is, how do I know the will of God when I pray? The answer is, through God's Word, which establishes the general principles of Christian living. Many times we pray outside the will of God because we do not know the Word of God.

John 16:13 says, "He will guide you into all truth."

If we put all of our dependence on Christ, He will guide our prayers by the Holy Spirit. This experience becomes true in our lives as we walk close to God and spend much time in prayer with Him.

3. What is the value of several Christians praying for something as opposed to just one (Matthew 18:19)?
   (It increases our power in prayer.)

There are times, of course, when God answers the prayer of just one individual. But when several share the burden of a prayer, the Scripture teaches that there are greater results. Paul, for example, requested others to pray for him (Ephesians 6:18,19).

When many pray, many have a chance to witness God's power instead of one. When many pray, a closer fellowship both with God and with one another results. Seek a prayer partner and share your prayer burdens. Christians in the same work crew, class or school, family, etc., should meet together for prayer. There is *power* in united prayer.

Prevailing Prayer

During his lifetime, George Mueller recorded more than 50,000 answers to prayer. He prayed for two men daily for more than 60 years. One of these men was converted shortly before Mueller's death and the other about a year later. As in Mueller's experience, we do not always see the answer to our prayers. We must leave the results to God.

One of the great needs of today is for men and women who will begin to pray for things and then pray repeatedly until they obtain what they seek from the Lord.

1. How long do you think we should pray for someone or something (Luke 18:1–8)?
   (Continuously.)

Many Christians become impatient waiting for a prayer to be answered. They want to see results immediately. But one fruit of the Spirit is patience.

God waited many years before He sent Christ. He may wait many more years before He sends Him the second time. He waited patiently for years while some of us lived without knowing or wanting to know Him. Even today He bears patiently with all kinds of weaknesses and rebellious attitudes. So, if He requires us to wait days, weeks, even years before prayers are answered, we should have no complaints. Through waiting patiently our faith grows and our characters are refined.

Why do you think God honors prevailing prayer?

What part do our feelings play in prevailing prayer?

2. What did the following men accomplish through prayer?

Moses (Exodus 15:22–25)
(He made bitter water become sweet.)

Samson (Judges 16:28–30)
(He killed more Philistines at his death than he did in his life.)

Peter (Acts 9:36–41)
(He raised Tabitha from the dead.)

Elijah (James 5:17,18)
(He prayed that it would not rain. It didn't rain for three and a half years. Then he prayed that it would rain and it did.)

3. How do these examples help you gain greater confidence to pray?

4. Give an example of what God has done for you or someone you know as the result of prevailing prayer.

(We pray whether our feelings are right or not. As we pray, many times God will help us by giving us peace, happiness, or other feelings.)

❓What other biblical examples can you think of that demonstrate prevailing prayer?

❓How did God honor these prayers?

Job, Daniel, Hezekiah, and many others repeatedly asked God for help. God did not always give an instantaneous answer, but He always worked out events for the best.

(To begin the discussion for question 4, give an example of prevailing prayer from your life. You may want to also thank God for the privilege of talking to Him as your Father after students who want to have shared.)

1. Examine your prayer life in light of the conditions for answered prayer. What conditions are lacking for you to have open communication with God?

   How much do you really believe and trust God when you pray?

2. Write down one prayer request for which you are having to exercise "prevailing prayer."

3. List two Scripture verses that you can claim in relation to this prayer request.

   1)

   2)

Conclusion and Application

Our culture values power—political power, financial power, electrical power, muscle power. But secular thinking disregards the power of prayer. As Christians, we have the greatest resource in the universe—God's power—available to us at all times. When we realize the privilege God has entrusted to us, our lives and ministries will be revolutionized for good.

Closing Prayer

God's Promises About Prayer

Opening Prayer

Discussion Starter

Think about this statement:

"God helps him who helps himself."

❓ Is this statement true or false?

❓ Why?

Lesson Development

(Ask one of the group members to summarize the paragraphs appearing at the opening of this lesson in the student's book. Note the diagram and discuss it.)

Leader's Objective: To show the student that God answers prayer in every area of life, and to lead him to a more active prayer life

LESSON 5

Bible Study

What God Has Promised Concerning Prayer

Look up the following verses and identify the condition and promise in each.

1. Jeremiah 33:3

    Condition:
    (Call to God.)

    Promise:
    (He will answer, and tell us great and unsearchable things.)

2. Matthew 21:22

    Condition:
    (Ask; believe.)

    Promise:
    (We will receive whatever we ask for.)

3. 1 John 5:14,15

    Condition:
    (Ask according to His will.)

    Promise:
    (He hears us, and we have what we ask of Him.)

At the time God made this promise, Jeremiah was being held captive by the unbelieving rulers of Israel. Israel had strayed far from God. They were a nation given to idolatry, and the horrible judgment of Babylonian captivity was about to descend on them.

God showed Jeremiah (as recorded in the rest of chapter 33) that a day was coming when He would utterly transform and change this idolatrous nation. What a marvelous revelation! What an encouragement to the heart of God's prophet!

Often, we are so wrapped up in our earthly circumstances we lose our heavenly vision. We need to take our eyes off the discouragement of self and circumstances. We need to realize that God has "great and mighty" things to show us about our individual relationships with Him and what He can do for and through us. We need only call upon Him to receive these things.

Hebrews 11:6 says:

Without faith it is impossible to please God.

This is a stumbling block for most of us because we are tempted by Satan to doubt God's love and willingness to provide for us. Sin entered the human race because Eve began to doubt God's Word (Genesis 3:1–6).

We cannot believe God for just anything, however, because sometimes it is not His will to do the things we ask. We must therefore ask God to lead us to ask for the right things, and when He does, He will give us the faith to believe.

The problem is not that God refuses to answer prayer or is ungenerous; the problem is that we do not ask according to His will (Philippians 2:13).

❓How can we know His will?

◆ By studying the Word of God.

◆ By thinking carefully about whether our prayer is for the glory of God and according to His will, or just something to gratify selfish desires.

> When you ask, you do not receive, because you ask with wrong motives, that you may spend what you get on your pleasures (James 4:3).

◆ By asking the Holy Spirit to lead us.

> Those who are led by the Spirit of God are sons of God (Romans 8:14).

❓What does it mean to ask in the name of Jesus?

It means far more than saying "in Jesus' name" glibly at the end of a prayer. To ask in the name of Jesus means to ask on the basis of the authority Christ has given to us. We are to ask in His authority, for His glory, so that "the Son may bring glory to the Father" (John 14:13).

4. John 14:14

Condition:
(Ask in Jesus' name.)

Promise:
(He will do it.)

5. Which promise do you need most to apply to your own prayer life right now and why?

What God Will Provide Through Prayer

In the following verses, identify God's promises concerning:

God says He will supply your *needs*, not necessarily your desires—according to His riches in glory. If you had a

1. Material needs
   Philippians 4:19
   (He will meet all our needs.)

   Psalm 84:11
   (He withholds no good thing.)

2. Guidance
   Proverbs 3:5,6
   (He will make our paths straight.)
   Psalm 32:8
   (He will instruct and teach us in the way we should go, and counsel us and watch over us.)

3. Spiritual needs
   Ephesians 1:3
   (He has blessed us with every spiritual blessing.)
   Philippians 4:13
   (We can do everything through Christ who gives us strength.)

benefactor with a million-dollar fortune, would you worry about where tomorrow's meals were coming from? God's fortune is far greater than a paltry million, so we do not have to worry about His ability to supply.

God gives only *good* things. Sometimes the things that are good for us in the long run may not make us happy for the moment. Sometimes it is good for us to go through testings, and we need to consider these as gifts from God also (James 1:2–4).

God does not promise to show us the whole future at once, but He does promise to guide us day by day. However, this comes only as we "trust in the Lord." Before making any important decision, we should always pray for guidance; and in even the little things of life, we should have an attitude of surrender and trust.

The greatest needs of life are things that God alone can satisfy. Spiritual needs include happiness and satisfaction in our hearts, victory over sin, and courage to overcome Satan and face trials. The Bible promises that God will supply these generously— more so than any other kind of blessing He gives. God does not allow every person on earth to be a material millionaire—some people live in elegant mansions and some life in one-room shanties—but God made *all* Christians spiritual millionaires. What we need to do is accept the possessions He has given us.

Why God Is Dependable

1. List reasons you can trust Him to keep His promises.

    Psalm 9:10
    (God has not forsaken anyone who has trusted in Him.)

    Psalm 115:11
    (He is our help and shield.)

    Isaiah 26:4
    (He is everlasting.)

    Nahum 1:7
    (God is good, a refuge in trouble, and He cares for those who trust Him.)

    2 Samuel 7:28
    (His words are trustworthy, and He keeps His promises.)

2. In what particular circumstance of your life do you presently need to trust Him more and for what?

    These promises are real—believe them; claim them; live by them.

List on this chart at least three things you need to pray for, and a verse for each that promises God's provision.

❖   ❖   ❖

❓Who is the most dependable person in your life and why? How does that person make you feel?

Many times we take God's dependability for granted. He's always available to listen, to show His love, and to be a friend. He wants us to totally depend on Him for everything, yet He also wants us to remember to thank Him for giving us His dependable love. I challenge you to write down several instances where God's dependability has meant a lot to you this week, then thank Him for each one.

Conclusion and Application

Through this Bible study we see again how important prayer is. It is like the pipe that carries water from the great city reservoir into our homes. If the pipe is plugged, all the water is held back and nothing comes through. Prayer is our channel to God.

(See the chart in the student's book.)

Closing Prayer

Planning Your Daily Devotional Time

Opening Prayer

Discussion Starter

Many young Christians know almost nothing about devotional time, and many older Christians are very lax in their practice of this foundational element for a victorious, effective, fruitful Christian life.

❓How do you think having a consistent devotional life could make a difference in your life?

❓What is your greatest obstacle to having a daily devotional life?

Lesson Development

(Ask one of the group members to summarize the paragraphs appearing at the opening of this lesson in the student's book. Note the diagram and discuss it.)

Leader's Objective: To explain the meaning of devotional time and its importance as a daily practice; to lead group members to establish regular devotions

Bible Study

Establish a Definite Time

A daily devotional time should be set aside for personal worship and meditation in which we seek fellowship with the Lord Jesus Christ. Once begun, this fellowship can be continued throughout the day (Psalm 119:97; 1 Thessalonians 5:17).

(Invite one of the group members to read this paragraph in the student's book and have another one look up and read the two Scriptures.)

1. In obedience to Christ's command, what did His disciples do after His ascension (Acts 1:13,14)? *(They gathered for prayer, and prayed continually.)*

2. Although different individuals' schedules will vary, many people prefer the morning hours, before the responsibilities of the day begin.

   We should meet regularly with God. Our devotional life cannot be haphazard or intermittent if we are to have sound spiritual health.

   David was called a man after God's own heart. What time did he set aside to communicate with God (Psalm 5:3)? *(Morning.)*

   Name two characteristics of the devotional life of Jesus (Mark 1:35).

   1) *(It was in the early morning.)*

   2) *(He went to a solitary place.)*

   In this instance, Jesus had just finished an extremely busy day. He was worn out, but not too tired to get up and pray. He recognized that the effectiveness of His ministry depended on time alone with God. *A person who is too busy for time with God is too busy.*

3. When is your best devotional time?

   None of us can say that we do not have time for

prayer and Bible study. We all can make time for things that we really want to do. Whether the period is long or short, set aside some time.

4. Make your devotional time unhurried. Don't think about your next responsibility. Concentrate on your fellowship with the Lord. A definite time every day will do much to help. A brief period with concentration is better than a long devotional time with your mind on many things.

How many minutes can you set aside daily for your time with God?

Choose a Definite Place

Avoid distraction by finding a quiet, private place of worship. If privacy is impossible, you will need to learn to concentrate. If you cannot have a devotional time in your own home or room, perhaps one of the following places will be suitable:

♦ A nearby chapel

♦ A corner of the school library

♦ Your office (before or after hours)

Name three other places you might find appropriate for your private prayer and Bible study.

1)
2)
3)

Suppose that for every day you spent at least twenty minutes in prayer, someone would give you a thousand dollars.

❷Would you be more diligent and faithful in your prayer life than you are now?

❷Is it possible that you and I would be willing to do for money what we would not be willing to do for God?

Mark 1:35 records how Christ selected a place where He could be alone and without distraction. This is essential in our devotional time, too. We must be able to turn all of our time and attention to God. If possible, select a place of beauty, such as a church, or some place surrounded by nature. Sometimes, if this is impossible, you can sing a hymn to yourself or play a recorded song to transform your devotional period into a time of real worship.

Goal and Content of the Devotional Time

1. We should have a reason for everything we do. "Aim at nothing and you will surely hit it." Our purpose for prayer should be to establish personal fellowship with God and to fulfill our own spiritual needs.

   A brief time of meeting with God in the early morning and walking in vital union with Him throughout the day, "practicing the presence of God," is more meaningful than spending an hour or more in a legalistic way and forgetting Him for the rest of the day.

   During our devotional time, we should be concerned with learning where we have failed and with rededicating ourselves to the task before us. We should use the time to regroup our forces after the battles of the previous day and plan for the next day's attack.

   What particular spiritual need do you feel today?

   What battles did you have yesterday?

2. The devotional time should include Bible study, prayer, personal worship, and quiet meditation. These aspects of the devotional time are so closely related that you

Two things are important in your devotional time: First and foremost, it should be God-centered—a time to worship, praise, and thank Him, a time to show your love for Him. Second, you should get something out of it. When reading the Bible, we learn more about God. When praying, we find our burdens lifted and gain strength and help for the activities of the day.

Remember, you cannot lead anyone higher than you have gone. You cannot enrich anyone beyond your own actual spiritual experience. So it is absolutely essential for the Bible to be central to your devotional time.

Prayer is one of the most important disciplines of the Christian life. John 4:23 reminds us that the Father *seeks* those who worship Him in prayer.

can actually engage in all at the same time.

For example, begin by reading a psalm of thanksgiving or praise. As you read, your heart will respond and you will continue to praise and worship God from a grateful heart.

Turn now to another portion of Scripture, such as Romans 8. Interrupt your reading to thank God for each truth that applies to you as a Christian. You will be amazed at how much you have to praise and thank God for, once you get started.

After you have read and prayed for a while, remain in an attitude of quiet, listening for instructions from God. Write down any thoughts that come to mind and pray about these.

Supplementary activity may include memorizing Scripture or reading from a devotional book or hymnal.

3. Study Matthew 6:9–13. Paraphrase this prayer in your own words, using expressions meaningful to you.

(Share personal examples of how God has used your devotional time to help you grow and to answer your prayers. Also share what has worked for you in planning and implementing a consistent, daily time with God.)

(Discuss the diagram in the student's book.)

Conclusion and Application

We need to grasp the strategic importance of the devotional time in the life of the Christian.

Andrew Murray writes in *God's Best Secrets:*

> There is no true, deep conversion, no true, deep holiness... no abiding peace or joy, without being daily alone with God. There is no path to holiness but in being much and long alone with God.

> What an inestimable privilege is the institution of daily secret prayer to begin every morning. Let it be the one thing our hearts are set on, seeking, and finding, and meeting God.

Complete these statements:

1. I have set aside the following definite time in the day for daily devotional time:

2. I have decided on the following place:

3. My purpose for setting aside a definite time and place for my devotions is to:

4. I will include the following activities during my devotional time:

Closing Prayer

(Read Psalm 145 as a prayer of praise, then spend several minutes letting each group member who wishes to pray briefly. Finish with an appropriate closing.)

Recap

Opening Prayer

Discussion Starter

❓ How has what you have learned in this study series about prayer changed your life?

❓ What have you seen change in your life because of your renewed commitment to a daily devotional time?

Lesson Development

(Any appropriate material from previous lessons that was not sufficiently covered could be used at this time, and you also may deal with any point that the group members may not understand as well as they could.)

(Then go over the remaining Recap questions and answers. This material will benefit both the students and you by giving you a deeper appreciation of God's Word.)

Leader's Objective: To deepen the students' understanding of the importance of prayer and assist them in their resolve to spend definite time daily in fellowship with their heavenly Father

The following questions will help you review this Step. If necessary, reread the appropriate lesson(s).

1. Why is prayer so important?

2. To be more effective in prayer, what conditions mentioned in Lessons 4 and 5 are you now meeting that you weren't meeting before?

3. Fill in the words to complete the suggested guide for prayer content:

A

C

T

S

1. Are you presently following the ACTS guide? (Remember, a guide is not mandatory, it is just helpful.)

   If you use another system, what is it?

2. How has your understanding of power and promises in prayer been broadened?

3. What specific time and place have you set aside for daily prayer and devotions?

   Time:

   Place:

(Use this lesson to help your students plan their devotional time. Ask group members to give suggestions on how they make their devotional time more meaningful. Then go through the steps to having a daily time with God so students can see how to plan or make changes to their own. Emphasize having a relationship with God, not merely fulfilling a planned schedule. Say:)

Whenever your devotional routines become too cumbersome or boring, change them. The goal of time with God is not to be tied to a certain plan or schedule but to have quality time with God every day.

Conclusion and Application

The world knows so little about what is accomplished through prayer. It is one of the most important things any Christian can do. Through prayer, men and women can be brought to Christ. Christians can be strengthened, holiness infused into their lives, circumstances altered, tragedies averted, perplexing problems solved, governments and kingdoms overturned, forces of evil defeated, and Satan rendered helpless. We have such a great privilege that it would be foolish not to spend time and effort in prayer.

What adjustments do you need to make for it to be more effective (more or less time, different place, etc.)?

4. Memorize and remember:

Effective praying is simply asking God to work according to His will and leaving the results to Him.

Closing Prayer

(Designate a short time of silent prayer for students to make a personal, private commitment to spend definite time daily in prayer. Then pray aloud.)

The Christian and the **Bible**

Growing Through the Study of God's Word

STEP 5

The Book of Books

Opening Prayer

Discussion Starter

Second Timothy 3:16,17 makes two claims for the Bible.

❓ What are they?

❓ If you were a non-Christian and you wanted seriously to investigate Christianity, how would you evaluate these two claims?

❓ What would be your criteria for the first claim?

❓ The second?

Lesson Development

(Encourage students to read the article, "Living By the Book" at the beginning of their Study Guide on their own time if they have not already done so.)

(Ask one of the group members to summarize the paragraphs appearing at the opening of this lesson in the student's book.)

Leader's Objective: To help students discover the uniqueness of the Bible and to motivate them to want to know more about it

LESSON 1

Bible Study

Various Names of the Bible

List the various names the Bible is called according to the following references:

1 Corinthians 15:3,4
(The Scriptures.)

Ephesians 6:17
(Sword of the Spirit; Word of God.)

Construction of the Bible

1. To become familiar with your own Bible, leaf through it and look at these divisions and books as you progress through the lesson. If possible, use a Bible with headlines to help you answer the questions.

   The Bible is composed of two main sections: the Old Testament, containing 39 books, and the New Testament, containing 27 books.

2. Read Genesis 1 and Revelation 22. From these two chapters, summarize the scope of the contents of the Bible.
   (God is eternal. He was at the beginning and will be at the end. His plan for mankind will be fulfilled completely.)

Divisions of the Old Testament

The Old Testament can be divided into five parts:

Turn to the table of contents in your Bible so we can survey the composition of the whole Book.

There are two objectives in this survey:

1) To see the practical value of getting familiar with the books of the Bible (Many students feel lost when asked to look up verses, so emphasize that the table of contents is there to be used. This will save them time and embarrassment.)

2) To gain a better grasp of the Bible's composition

Genesis records the creation of the universe and of man, and it shows how man was created to have fellowship with God. But because of man's stubborn self-will, he chose to go his own independent way and fellowship with God was broken. Genesis gives the first promise of the coming Redeemer (3:15), and shows the establishment of the Jewish nation through which that Redeemer was to come.

1. *Pentateuch.* The first five historical books, written by Moses, also are called the books of the Law. List these books:
(Genesis, Exodus, Leviticus, Numbers, Deuteronomy.)

Identify at least four major events recorded in these books.
(Some are: Creation, Abraham offering Isaac to the Lord, Moses leading the Israelites out of Egypt, conquering the Promised Land.)

2. *Historical Books.* The next twelve books tell of the establishment of the kingdom of Israel, of Israel's repeated turning from God to sin, and finally of the Assyrian and Babylonian exile—God's punishment. List these twelve books as follows and identify a main character in each section:

First three (pre-kingdom era):
(Joshua, Judges, Ruth.)

Next six (duration of the kingdom):
(1 and 2 Samuel, 1 and 2 Kings, 1 and 2 Chronicles.)

Last three (exile and post-exile period):
(Ezra, Nehemiah, Esther.)

3. *Poetry.* Of the next five books, Psalms—the Hebrew hymn book—is probably the best known.

Exodus is the story of Israel's leaving the bondage of Egypt and beginning their journey to the Promised Land. While on their journey, God gives the Law by which His nation is to live.

Leviticus contains detailed instructions of the Law.

Numbers and *Deuteronomy* tell of Israel's wandering in the wilderness and coming to the Promised Land.

❓What examples from these five books have inspired you?

Paul tells us in the New Testament that these narrations of Hebrew history were given to be examples to us.

❓Which historical event in these twelve books has meant the most to you? Explain.

List the five books of poetry.
(Job, Psalms, Proverbs, Ecclesiastes, Song of Solomon.)

Describe how God has used one of these books to comfort and strengthen you in a difficult situation.

4. *Major Prophets.* Written shortly before Israel was taken into captivity and during the exile, these books prophesy the coming Messiah and other world events. They also contain warnings of impending disaster if Israel did not turn from her wicked ways. List the five books of the Major Prophets.
(Isaiah, Jeremiah, Lamentations, Ezekiel, Daniel.)

Identify at least one major prophecy in each.
(Israel will be restored—Isaiah 49; a future king will occupy David's throne—Jeremiah 23; the Lord's compassion on Israel—Lamentations 3; judgment on Israel's enemies—Ezekiel 25–32; the end times—Daniel 12.)

5. *Minor Prophets.* These last twelve books of the Old Testament are called minor only because they are shorter, not because they are less important. They mainly concern Israel and the coming Messiah. List all twelve.
(Hosea, Joel, Amos, Oba-

❓Many modern hymns are based on the Psalms. Can you name a few?

Some of these prophecies have already been fulfilled and others are yet to be fulfilled. A knowledge of these prophecies is essential to understanding how completely Christ fulfilled the role of Messiah.

Many people avoid the Major and Minor Prophets because the books seem hard to understand. But they contain many important historical stories, prayers, teachings, and inspiring examples of men and women who lived for God despite adverse situations.

diah, Jonah, Micah, Na-hum, Habakkuk, Zepha-niah, Haggai, Zechariah, Malachi.)

Read one of the books and summarize its main points.

Divisions of the New Testament

The New Testament can also be divided into five parts.

1. *Gospels.* The first four books of the New Testament tell of Christ's life and ministry. List them here.
   (Matthew, Mark, Luke, John.)

   What was Jesus' last command to His disciples (Matthew 28:19,20)?
   (To go to all the world and preach the good news of Christ to everyone.)

   How does this apply today?
   (God is still asking us to help reach the world for Christ.)

2. *Acts.* This history of the early church, which also describes the ministries of Peter and Paul, consists of only one book. For practice, write it here.
   (Acts.)

   What is its significance for us today?
   (It's a pattern for churches and for individuals in ministry. It also shows the roots of our faith.)

(Read Ephesians 6:17.)

❓Why do you think the Bible is called the Sword of the Spirit?

(After hearing comments from several group members, explain how the Holy Spirit uses the Word to teach and convict and how we need to be familiar with it so that we are able to use this sword effectively.)

The Gospels record the life of Jesus, which stands as a transition between the Old and New Testaments.

❓In what ways do the Gospels show a change in how God is dealing with people?

Compare the writing in the New Testament books with a modern-day book on any subject. Notice how concise the Bible is. The words carry a meaning that has both depth and simplicity.

3. *Pauline Epistles and Hebrews.* Thirteen of the epistles (letters) were written by Paul, and were named for the church or individual to whom they were sent. Although the author of Hebrews is not identified, many believe Paul also wrote that fourteenth epistle. List all fourteen.
(Romans, 1 and 2 Corinthians, Galatians, Ephesians, Philippians, Colossians, 1 and 2 Thessalonians, 1 and 2 Timothy, Titus, Philemon, Hebrews.)

Write down your favorite verse in each book and describe why it is meaningful to you.

4. *General Epistles.* There are seven general epistles, and they are named not for the recipients but for the authors. List them here.
(James; 1 and 2 Peter; 1, 2, and 3 John; Jude.)

Identify one major truth in each book, and tell how you will apply each truth to your life.

5. *Revelation.* The last book of the New Testament is one of prophecy. It describes the end times and the triumph of Christ in His second coming. Write the name of it here.
(Revelation.)

Describe the central message of the book (Revelation 22:12–17).

How would you describe Paul's role in the formation of the New Testament?

Why do you think God waited so long to touch Paul's life?

(Be sure to share your favorite verse also. Encourage students to give reasons why the verses mean so much to them.)

Why do you think it's important to read and study Revelation?

(Jesus Christ is the beginning and the end and is the only One who can give us living water.)

What are its promises to those who overcome (chapters 2,3)?
(He will eat of the tree of life, will not be hurt by the second death, will have a new name, will rule nations, will have his name in the book of life, will dwell in God's temple, and will sit with Jesus on the throne.)

What warning does the writer of this book give (22:18,19)?
(Do not add to or take away from God's words.)

LIFE APPLICATION

1. What new insight about the composition of the Bible have you gained from this study?

   How will this help you in your daily life?

2. To know the Bible well and to be able to find Scripture references quickly, you should memorize the names of the books in the order in which they appear. Master one group, and then go on to the next.

   Focus on one division each week until you have memorized all the books of the Bible. Review these frequently until they are fixed in your mind.

(Encourage students to read through Revelation in one sitting this week. Tell them not to stop at things they don't understand or things that may intrigue them. Instead, instruct them to read quickly to get an overview and a feel for this book.)

Conclusion and Application

(Ask students to share what the Bible means to them and how it has changed their lives in specific ways.)

Today, commit to memory the books of the first division, the Pentateuch, and write them again here:

1) *(Genesis.)*
2) *(Exodus.)*
3) *(Leviticus.)*
4) *(Numbers.)*
5) *(Deuteronomy.)*

Closing Prayer

The Central Person of the Bible

Opening Prayer

(To set the tone for this lesson, begin by praising God for His Son and thanking God for what Jesus has done for us.)

Discussion Starter

(Divide the group members into pairs to discuss the following questions. Then have the pairs report their insights to the group.)

❷ How do we determine that Christ is the central person of the Bible?

❷ Why is it important to do so?

Lesson Development

(Ask one of the group members to summarize the paragraphs appearing at the opening of this lesson in the student's book. Note the diagram and discuss it.)

Leader's Objective: To show group members that the unity of the Bible lies in one theme—Jesus Christ and all that He is and has done

LESSON 2

Bible Study

What Christ Said About Himself and the Old Testament

1. What did Christ say of the Scriptures in John 5:39?
   (They testify about Christ.)

2. Read Luke 24:25–27,44–48.

   What was Christ's claim concerning the Old Testament teaching about Himself?
   (Everything in the Old Testament was written about Him.)

   What parts of the Old Testament did Christ say referred to Him (verse 44)?
   (Law of Moses, Prophets, and Psalms.)

   What do you think Christ wants you to understand about the Old Testament from verse 26?
   (The prophets wrote about Christ's death.)

   From verses 46, 47?
   (Christ's death and resurrection will be preached all over the world.)

What the Apostles Said About Christ and the Old Testament

1. What does Peter conclude in Acts 3:18?

Christ also made other claims about Himself. He declared He was God. (Read John 10:30.) He professed to be the only way to God. (Read John 14:6.) He claimed His words were eternal. (Read Mark 13:31.) He said He had divine authority. (Read Matthew 28:18.) Jesus' character and ministry offer abundant evidence to support His radical claims.

One of the many remarkable features of Christianity's foundation is the phenomenon of fulfilled prophecy. Suppose there were only 50 predictions in the Old Testament (instead of over 300) concerning the first coming of Christ, giving details of the coming Messiah that meet in the person and work of Jesus. The probability of chance fulfillment is calculated by mathematicians to be less than one in 1,125,000,000,000,000 (1125 x 10^{12}).

Jesus' friends considered Jesus the only God and Savior. The testimonies of Christ's closest followers are recorded in the New Testament. Peter begins one of his epistles, "Simon Peter, a

(Christ is the fulfillment of Old Testament prophecy.)

2. Keeping in mind that the New Testament had not yet been written, how did the apostle Paul use the Old Testament to show that it contained the "good news" of Christ (Acts 17:1–3)?
   (He proved to the Jews through the Old Testament that the Messiah had to suffer and die and rise from the dead.)

3. What three things occurred in Christ's life that Paul said were taught in the Old Testament (1 Corinthians 15:3,4)?
   1) *(Christ died.)*
   2) *(Christ was buried.)*
   3) *(Christ arose.)*

4. What does Paul conclude in Romans 15:8,9 about the ministry of Christ?
   (Christ became a servant to fulfill Old Testament promises and to glorify God.)

Old Testament Prophecies Concerning Christ Fulfilled in the New Testament

All of the more than 300 Old Testament prophecies about the first coming of the Messiah were fulfilled in the life of Christ. Here are a few of them.

1. Compare these Scripture references and record the prophecies fulfilled.

   1 Samuel 16:19, Isaiah 11:1—Luke 1:31–33

servant and apostle of Jesus Christ" (2 Peter 1:1). John, the beloved disciple of Jesus, says of Him, "No one has ever seen God, but God the One and Only, who is at the Father's side, has made him known" (John 1:18). Stephen, the first martyr for Christ, called upon his Savior as he was being stoned, "Lord Jesus, receive my spirit" (Acts 7:59). And Paul writes, "we wait for the blessed hope—the glorious appearing of our great God and Savior, Jesus Christ" (Titus 2:13). Each person knew Jesus, believed His claims to be God's fulfillment of prophecy, and suffered great persecution to spread the "good news" to others.

Could Jesus have manipulated events to make it seem as if He fulfilled these predictions? No ordinary person has ever selected the time, place, or family into which he was born. Only someone with supernatural power could choose the timing of our Savior's birth.

(Descendant of Jesse/ David, was "father" of Jesus.)

Genesis 3:15—Galatians 4:4; Hebrews 2:14
(Seed of the woman/God's Son born of a woman.)

Numbers 24:17—Matthew 2:2,9
(A star from Jacob/Magi saw star when Jesus was born.)

Isaiah 9:6—Matthew 1:23
(A son to be given who will be called "Mighty God"/ virgin's Son to be Immanuel, "God with us.")

Isaiah 40:3—Matthew 3:1–3
(A voice crying in the wilderness/John the Baptist came crying from wilderness.)

Zechariah 9:9—Matthew 21:1–11
(King coming riding on a donkey/Jesus entered Jerusalem in triumph on a donkey.)

Psalm 69:21—Matthew 27:34
(Gall and vinegar to be given/gall and vinegar given.)

Psalm 34:20—John 19:33,36
(No bones to be broken/no bones broken.)

Job 19:25–27—Galatians 3:13; 1 John 3:2
(Redeemer expected/ Christ is the expected Redeemer.)

(If time allows, ask three students to read the following verses, then discuss them briefly as a group:)

◆ Matthew 5:17,18

◆ Luke 4:16–21

◆ John 5:39,40

2. What is your impression after seeing these Old Testament prophecies and their New Testament fulfillment?

Christ, the Central Person of the New Testament

1. The four Gospels are the history books of Christ's ministry. (Read Matthew 1:1; Mark 1:1; Luke 1:1–4; John 20:30,31.)

   In what ways did the disciples know Jesus (1 John 1:3)?
   (They had seen and heard Him.)

   Do the four Gospels purport to record all that Jesus did (John 20:30)?
   (No.)

   Why were the historical facts and teachings of Jesus Christ written (John 20:31)?
   (That we might believe Jesus is the Christ and might have life in His name.)

2. The Book of Acts is a historical account of the acts of the Holy Spirit through the apostles.

   Who wrote it (Luke 1:1–4 and Acts 1:1)?
   (Luke.)

   How do you think the passage in Luke applies to the Book of Acts?
   (Luke investigated everything he wrote about.)

3. The Epistles are letters written to show the church the practical outworking of the life of

Jesus is not only the central Person of the New Testament, He is also the central Person of history. No other person has influenced the world for good more than Jesus. Charles Spurgeon, an English theologian, wrote:

Christ is the great central fact in the world's history. To him everything looks forward or backward. All the lines of history converge upon him. All the great purposes of God culminate in him. The greatest and most momentous fact which the history of the world records is the fact of his birth.

❓What are we to do with these teachings according to Matthew 28:19,20?

Christ in the lives of those who wrote them. By example, they teach us regarding our membership in the body of Christ, and about our privileges, responsibilities, and destiny.

Read Colossians 2:6–8.

What are Christians to do?
(Live in Christ.)

How are we to do it?
(By being firmly rooted in faith.)

Of what are we to beware?
(Human traditions.)

What would you say our greatest responsibility is?

4. The Book of Revelation is the only New Testament book of prophecy. Read Revelation 1:1–3.

   This book is the revelation of whom?
   (Jesus Christ.)

   What is its purpose?
   (To show what must take place.)

   Who gave such knowledge?
   (God gave it.)

   How was this knowledge given, and to whom?
   (God gave it to Christ, and Christ gave it to John through His angel.)

   How will studying the Book of Revelation affect your life and under what conditions?

The influence of Jesus is revolutionizing our world. Christianity has spanned cultural diversities, prejudice barriers, and political differences. Wherever the true message of Jesus has gone, people and nations have been changed, resulting in new life, new hope, and new purpose for living.

❓How have you seen this truth in your life?

❓What is the warning recorded in Revelation 22:18,19?

(Blessed—happy—is he who reads, hears, and takes to heart the things written there.)

LIFE APPLICATION

1. How will recognizing Jesus as the central figure of the entire Bible affect your Old Testament reading?

2. What do you see as your individual responsibility in fulfilling the commands of this person? See John 15:16 and Matthew 28:19,20.

3. Memorize the twelve Historical Books and write them again here:

   Pre-kingdom era (3)
   (Joshua, Judges, Ruth.)

   Kingdom era (6)
   (1 and 2 Samuel, 1 and 2 Kings, 1 and 2 Chronicles.)

   Exile and post-exile era (3)
   (Ezra, Nehemiah, Esther.)

   Review the names of all the books learned earlier.

Conclusion and Application

It is not merely in the isolated predictions, which are fulfilled with precision, but it is also in the entire Old Testament that one finds the patriarchs and prophets looking forward to something yet to come—the Messiah.

Jesus' life and work give a fullness of meaning to the whole Old Testament that it could not otherwise have. This total fulfillment provides us with firm ground for the belief that the Old Testament not only *did* lead to Christ, but *was intended*, by the God whose partial revelation it records, to lead to Christ.

Closing Prayer

Authority of the Old Testament

Opening Prayer

Discussion Starter

 What is meant by the inspiration of the Bible?

 What part did God play and what part did the writers play in writing the Bible?

(As you discuss the questions, consult 2 Peter 1:21; 2 Timothy 3:16; and Hebrews 1:1.)

Lesson Development

(Ask one of the group members to summarize the paragraphs appearing at the opening of this lesson in the student's book.)

❖

Leader's Objective: To give students confidence in the authority of the Old Testament

Bible Study

Testimony of Its Writers

The phrase, "thus saith the Lord," or its equivalent, occurs more than 2,000 times in the Old Testament.

1. Write out the statements concerning inspiration made by the following writers:

   David (2 Samuel 23:2)
   (The Spirit of the Lord spoke to me.)

   Isaiah (Isaiah 8:1,5,11)
   (The Lord spoke to me.)

   Jeremiah (Jeremiah 1:9)
   (The Lord touched my mouth.)

   Ezekiel (Ezekiel 3:4)
   (Speak My words to them.)

   What is different about each? What is the same?
   (The message and the way it was delivered were unique; the Lord told them what to speak.)

2. What two statements of Moses in Exodus 31:18 and 32:16 show that God actually wrote the Ten Commandments?
   ("The tablets of stone inscribed by the finger of God; the writing was the writing of God.")

3. What statement made by David shows that the pattern for the temple was dictated by God (1 Chronicles 28:19)?

When people are criticized or persecuted for what they say, they will usually trim their talk to suit the listener's applause. Jeremiah 23:16,17 provides a good description of the false prophet who lacks God's inspiration and cannot resist conformity.

The character and truthfulness of these biblical writers offer strong evidences for their divine inspiration:

◆ Isaiah 6:1–8 declares the prophet's awareness of his own inadequacy, his unworthiness to deliver God's message.

◆ Amos 7:12–14 records the prophet's answer to royal orders to stop prophesying or get out. (See also Peter's response in Acts 4:19,20.)

("The Lord...gave me understanding in all the details of the plan.")

Testimony of Christ

The New Testament had not been written during Christ's earthly ministry, and His references to the Scriptures refer to the Old Testament writings. He never once denied or made light of Old Testament Scriptures; He related Himself to them as their fulfillment. He said:

> These are the Scriptures that testify about me (John 5:39).

1. How did Christ describe those who did not believe the Old Testament prophecies (Luke 24:25)?
   (Foolish, slow.)

2. What is the result of not believing in the Old Testament (John 5:46,47)?
   (If they did not believe Moses, they would not believe Christ.)

3. What did Christ think of His responsibility concerning Old Testament prophecy (Matthew 5:17, 18)?
   (He came to fulfill all the Law and the Prophets.)

4. What was Christ's view of the story of man's creation as recorded in Genesis (Matthew 19:4–6)?
   (It was fact—God had created male and female.)

5. What authority did Christ use to answer:

The Old Testament can and should be evaluated independently regarding its claims. Nevertheless, it is inseparably linked to Christ. The final evaluation, therefore, rests upon the testimony of Christ.

James I. Packer, in his book *Fundamentalism and the Word of God*, says:

> Christ's claim to be divine is either true of false. If it is true, His Person guarantees the truth of all the rest of His teaching (for a divine person cannot lie or err; therefore, His view of the Old Testament is true). If His claim is false, there is no compelling reason for us to believe anything else that He said. If we accept Christ's claims, therefore, we commit ourselves to believe all that He taught—on His authority. If we refuse to believe some part of what He taught, we are in effect denying Him to be the divine Messiah—on our own authority.

Satan (Matthew 4:4,7,
10)?
("It is written.")

Men (Matthew 22:29–32,
43–46)?
(The Scriptures.)

6. Summarize Christ's attitude and view of the Old Testament.
(He treated it as the Word of God and infallible.)

Testimony of the Apostles

It is evident from their inspired writing that the apostles of Christ considered the Old Testament Scriptures prophetic and inseparable from the authority, power, and ministry of Christ.

1. *Peter.* From whom did the apostle Peter say the writings of the Old Testament came (2 Peter 1:21; Acts 1:16)?
(The Holy Spirit.)

   How did Peter feel about the Old Testament historical account he recorded in 1 Peter 3:20?
(He accepted it as fact.)

   Who did Peter say were inspired by God (Acts 3:20,21)?
(The holy prophets.)

2. *Paul.* How much of the Old Testament is inspired by God, according to Paul in 2 Timothy 3:16?
(All of it.)

   What did Paul believe the Old Testament to be (Romans 3:2)?
(The very words of God.)

Historical accuracy is established on three foundations: geography (and topography), ethnology, and chronology. In all three areas, modern science has been building a stronger and stronger case for the Bible during the past hundred years of extensive research in the Near East.

We are discovering the following piece by piece:

◆ The peoples, places, and events of Scripture are to be found in the same locale and under the precise geographical circumstances as those described in the Bible.

◆ Whenever statements are made in the Bible concerning kinship, origin, or customs of peoples, these statements can be depended upon to be in accordance with the finds of archaeology.

◆ When we compare events in the Old Testament with the records on the tombs and monuments of Egypt—or with the records of Babylonia, Assyria, and elsewhere—we find that the different parts of the chronology fit extremely well, in spite of the unscientific chronologi-

3. *James.* Acceptance of the Old Testament writing is evidenced in the Book of James by references to whom?

   2:21 *(Abraham.)*

   2:25 *(Rahab.)*

   5:11 *(Job.)*

   5:17 *(Elijah.)*

4. *John.* One of the many evidences that John believed the Old Testament is his acceptance of which story (1 John 3:12)?
   (Cain's slaying Abel.)

LIFE APPLICATION

1. The writers of the Old Testament, Jesus Christ the Son of God, the apostles of Christ, and the early church fathers all say of the Old Testament, "This is the inspired Word of God." What do you say? (See John 8:47 and 1 John 4:6.)

2. Describe how the information in this lesson gives you confidence in the authority of the Old Testament.

3. Write down several proofs of the authority of the Old Testament that you could use to explain to someone who doubts it.

4. Repeat the names of the five books of poetry until you have committed them to memory. Then write them here:

cal systems that the ancient cultures used.

❷ If you were to explain to a non-Christian why the Old Testament is the Word of God, what would you say?

❷ Which parts of the Old Testament are hardest for you to accept? Why?

❷ How has this lesson helped you believe in every part of the Old Testament as Scripture?

Conclusion and Application

The prophets lay down high standards as characteristic of the Word of God:

◆ Above and beyond the ways of man; effective and invincible (Isaiah 55:6–11)

◆ Eternal (Isaiah 40:8)

The writers of the Old Testament were fully convinced that their messages met these standards, and they would be the first to discard them if they did not. Such was the quality of their objectivity and devotion to God's truth.

(Job, Psalms, Proverbs, Ecclesiastes, Song of Solomon.)

5. Review all the names of the books you learned earlier.

Closing Prayer

Authority of the New Testament

Opening Prayer

Discussion Starter

Some people who have not examined all the evidence attempt to discredit the authority of Scripture.

 If I were someone who doubted, what valid reasons could you give me for your belief in the authority of the New Testament?

Lesson Development

(Ask one of the group members to summarize the paragraphs appearing at the opening of this lesson in the student's book. Note the diagram and discuss it.)

❖

Leader's Objective: To help students discover the absolute reliability of the Now Testament, and to increase their confidence in the entire Word of God

LESSON 4

Bible Study

Authority Given the Apostles by Christ

1. What four things did Christ say the Holy Spirit would do for the apostles (John 16:12–15)?

   1) *("Guide you into all truth . . .)*

   2) *(tell you what is yet to come . . .)*

   3) *(bring glory to me . . .)*

   4) *(by taking from what is mine and making it known to you.")*

   Why do you think the apostles could not know all the truth at that time?
   (They did not fully understand what Christ would do for them.)

   How would they in the future?
   (They witnessed Christ's death and resurrection.)

2. What authority did Christ give the apostles (John 17:18; 20:21)?
   (As God sent Him, He sent them.)

3. On what basis did Christ select the apostles to bear witness of Him (John 15:26,27; Luke 24:46–48)?
   (They had been with Him and had witnessed His death and resurrection.)

   How did Paul fit in according to Acts 9:3–6; Acts 26:13–15, and 1

The New Testament was written during the first century while eyewitnesses of recorded events still lived. Since legends require several generations to develop and spread, there was insufficient time lapse between Jesus' life and the writings for legends to distort the writings.

For the *earliest* written reports, read 1 Thessalonians 1:10 and Galatians 1:1 (dated A.D. 50, just 20 years after the event). Also note 1 Corinthians 15:3–9 with its statement that, *25 years after the event,* there were *several hundred* eyewitnesses still alive to tell the story.

For the *latest* written witness, read John 20:26–31 and 1 John 1:1–3, dated about A.D. 90–95. And we have a portion of a manuscript of John's Gospel that experts have dated at A.D. 125, only 30 years after the original writing.

Corinthians 15:7–9?
(He saw a heavenly light and heard the voice of Christ.)

4. What authority did Christ give Paul (Acts 26:15–18)?
(Christ appointed Paul a servant and witness.)

How do we fit into this as witnesses?

(We can tell others what God has done in our lives.)

The Apostles Wrote Under Christ's Authority

1. *Paul.* What does he call himself at the beginning of the book of Romans?
(A slave or servant of Christ.)

From whom did Paul receive what he preached (1 Corinthians 11:23; Galatians 1:11,12)?
(From the Lord; through a revelation from Jesus Christ.)

What was Paul's authority and purpose (2 Corinthians 5:20)?
(An ambassador for Christ.)

Read 2 Peter 3:15,16. What did Peter think about Paul's writings?
(He wrote according to wisdom given to him by God.)

What did he think about those who misuse the New Testament?
(They are headed for destruction.)

The strength of Paul's witness lies not only in the fact that he claimed, along with the others, to have seen the risen Christ personally, but that he also became fully convinced that *all* the aspects of the resurrection story were true. And, as James Martin comments in *Did Jesus Rise from the Dead?*, "such a man would accept the Christian case only if he were left with no alternative."

❓Considering Peter's personality, why do you think God included him as a New Testament writer?

Many of us can identify with Peter who was a common man with an impetuous nature. The changes in Peter's attitude because of the work of the Holy Spirit gives a striking example of how God can use all types of people.

2. *Writer of Hebrews.* Where did the writer of Hebrews get his authority (Hebrews 1:1,2)?
(Through the Son of God.)

3. *James.* What did this half-brother of Jesus (Jesus's Father is God) call himself (James 1:1)?
(A servant of God and of the Lord Jesus Christ.)

4. *John.* What does John claim as the authority for writing his epistles (1 John 1:1–3)?
(He had seen, heard, and touched the Word of Life, Christ.)

How was Revelation written (Revelation 1:1)?
(God gave the revelation to Christ, and He sent it to John.)

John was probably the closest to Jesus during His life on earth. John was privileged to see and hear things about heaven, then relay the glorious facts to us. Imagine how he must have felt to be entrusted with this part of God's message!

5. *Jude.* What does this other half-brother of Jesus call himself in Jude 1?
(A servant of Jesus.)

What do you think Paul, James, and Jude meant by saying they were servants of Christ?
(They were willing to do God's work rather than their own desires.)

6. *Peter.* What does he call himself (1 Peter 1:1)?
(An apostle of Jesus Christ.)

What does Peter make known (2 Peter 1:16)?
(The power and coming of the Lord Jesus Christ.)

Think of the authority of the Bible as a building. Christ is the foundation that holds everything up. The Old Testament is the first story. It is not complete without the second story, the New Testament. However, the New Testament cannot be completely understood without traveling through the Old Testament. Each story is a unit without the other, but the building is not complete without all its parts. Each biblical writer adds his own personality to the building but also conforms to the purpose the Master Builder has for the book.

7. On whose writings is the foundation of the church of Jesus Christ estab-

lished (Ephesians 2:20)?
(The apostles and prophets, with Christ Himself as the chief cornerstone.)

8. What is the gospel of Christ, according to the apostles (Romans 1:16)?
(The power of God for salvation.)

9. Why were the apostles confident that they wrote correctly about Christ (2 Corinthians 4:5,6)?
(God gave them the light of knowledge.)

LIFE APPLICATION

1. God has miraculously preserved His Word for us. Although the above study should convince us that the New Testament is the Word of God, what is your greatest assurance that it is God's Word (John 16:13; 8:47; 18:37)?
(Some possible answers are: the Holy Spirit guides us into truth; we hear what God says; Jesus testifies to this truth.)

2. How does the information in this lesson help you trust the Bible more than you may have in the past?

   How will you use the deeper trust in:

   Witnessing?

   Praying?

   Daily living?

3. Commit to memory the names of the five books

We can have confidence in using and trusting God's Word to build up our faith, for comforting others, for showing us the right path, and for reaching others with the exciting news of Jesus Christ.

❷ How have you used God's Word in these ways?

❷ How has using God's Word in your daily life increased your confidence in the authority of the Bible?

❷ How does the Bible prove its power?

Conclusion and Application

The fact that we, in the twentieth century, still have access to the Word of God is living proof that God's Word does not pass away. Throughout the centuries many desperate attempts to destroy the Bible have been to no avail. God Himself will not permit it.

of the Major Prophets. Then write them here. *(Isaiah, Jeremiah, Lamentations, Ezekiel, Daniel.)*

4. Review the names of all the other books you have previously learned.

Closing Prayer

The Power of God's Word

Opening Prayer

Discussion Starter

 What would your answer be if you were challenged by someone with: "I don't believe the Bible is the Word of God. I can't go along with a lot of the miracles, and I don't understand much of it. Do I have to believe in the Bible 100 percent— from cover to cover—to become a Christian?"

Lesson Development

(Ask one of the group members to summarize the paragraphs appearing at the opening of this lesson in the student's book. Note the diagram and discuss it.)

❖

Leader's Objective: To help students experience the power of God's Word in their daily lives

Bible Study

The Word of God

Tell what God's Word is or what it does, or both, according to the following Scripture references (use a dictionary for the definition of key words if needed).

1. What it is:

   Hebrews 5:12–14
   (Milk, word of righteousness.)

   Philippians 2:16
   (Word of life.)

   Ephesians 6:17
   (Sword of the Spirit.)

2. What it does:

   1 John 2:5
   (Perfects the love of God in us.)

   John 12:48
   (Will judge the one who rejects Christ.)

   Romans 10:17
   (Gives faith.)

   John 15:3
   (Cleanses.)

3. Both:

   1 Peter 1:23
   (Is imperishable seed, gives new birth.)

   John 8:31,32
   (Is truth, makes free.)

   John 17:17
   (Is truth, sanctifies.)

   1 Peter 2:2
   (Is pure milk of the Word, helps one grow in respect to salvation.)

Through the written Word, God speaks His living Word to us day by day, hour by hour. As a result, we learn one thing Jesus both practiced and taught in His wilderness temptations:

> Man does not live on bread alone, but on every word that comes from the mouth of God (Matthew 4:4).

❓How does God's Word help us think more clearly?

James I. Packer said:

> Man's mind becomes free only when its thoughts are brought into captivity to Christ and His Word; till then, it is at the mercy of sinful prejudice and dishonest mental habits within, and of popular opinion, organized propaganda and unquestioned commonplaces without. Tossed about by every wind of intellectual fashion and carried to and fro by cross-currents of reactions, man without God is not free for truth. Only as his thoughts are searched, challenged and corrected by God through His Word, may man hope to rise to a way of looking at things which, instead of reflecting merely passing phases of human thought, reflects God's eternal truth. This is the only road to intellectual freedom.

❓What must occur in a person's life for that person to understand and know God and His plan for his or her life (John 3:3)?
(New birth.)

A young woman once picked up a certain book to read but soon laid it

Hebrews 4:12 (5 things)
(Is living, active, sharper than two-edged sword, divides soul and spirit, judges thoughts and intents of heart.)

How to Understand the Word of God

1. Read 1 Corinthians 2:14.

   No one can understand the Word of God by his own ability. Why?
   (Natural man does not accept things of the Spirit of God.)

2. Describe in your own words a natural man's reaction to spiritual things.

3. Explain in your own words how one must come to understand the Word of God. See 1 Corinthians 2:7–12 and Romans 8:5–9.

   Why do some individuals deny the authority of Scripture, the deity of Christ, the inspiration of the Bible, and other basic teachings in the Word of God?

   What should be our response to them?

LIFE APPLICATION

1. When we approach the Word of God, what is the first thing we should understand (2 Peter 1:20, 21)?

2. What is one way the power of the Bible mani-

down, finding it too dull and difficult. Shortly afterward she met a young man to whom she was attracted. During their courtship, she learned that he was the author of this book. She began to read the book a second time, and this time she read it from cover to cover.

❓Why did she have a change of attitude about the book?

Now the young woman knew and loved the author.

❓How is this like when we became Christians?

When we come to know and love Jesus Christ, His Book—the Bible—becomes alive and vital to us.

Directing a non-Christian who is investigating biblical authenticity to Christ does not deny a rightful place for historical research and hardheaded scientific examination of the Bible. But a sole emphasis in these areas *misses the point.* Lay down this challenge to the non-Christian: *Begin where the Bible applies to you and can be tested by you.*

Conclusion and Application

You have the same teacher that great Bible scholars have—the Holy Spirit. Every time you sit down to study the Bible, ask the Holy Spirit to show you the things He wants you to learn from His Word, and to help you understand difficult sections.

fests itself, according to 2 Timothy 3:15?

3. How have you experienced that power in your life recently?

4. The twelve books of the Minor Prophets are probably the most difficult of all to learn and remember. Give extra diligence to memorizing this division, then write the names here.
(Hosea, Joel, Amos, Obadiah, Jonah, Micah, Nahum, Habakkuk, Zephaniah, Haggai, Zechariah, Malachi.)

Closing Prayer

The Need for God's Word

Opening Prayer

Discussion Starter

God has promised to guide us by
His Word.

❷ Why do you think He felt this
was necessary?

❷ How would you describe your
dependence on God's Word?

Lesson Development

(Ask one of the group members to
summarize the paragraphs appearing
at the opening of this lesson in the student's book. Note the diagram and
discuss it.)

Leader's Objective: To help
students discover the essential value
of God's Word and to increase their
desire for it as daily spiritual food

LESSON 6

Bible Study

What We Should Know About the Bible

Read Psalm 119.

1. What does the psalmist call God's Word in the following verses of Psalm 119?

   Verse 1 *(The law of the Lord.)*

   Verse 2 *(His statutes.)*

   Verse 4 *(His precepts.)*

   Verse 5 *(His decrees.)*

   Verse 6 *(His commands.)*

   Verse 7 *(Righteous laws.)*

   Verse 43 *(Word of truth.)*

   Verse 72 *(Law from His mouth.)*

   Verse 105 *(Lamp and light.)*

   Verse 123 *(Righteous promise.)*

2. What does this tell you of the importance of knowing God's Word?

3. When does God discipline His children (Psalm 119:126)?
   (When His law is broken.)

4. What value does the Word have for us (Psalm 119:72)?
   (More than thousands of gold and silver pieces.)

5. What is necessary in order to learn the Word (Psalm 119:73)?
   (God-given understanding.)

Certain essentials for physical health and growth find parallels in our spiritual lives. Without proper food, air, rest, and exercise, our bodies suffer. So, too, without spiritual food, air, rest, and exercise, our spiritual lives suffer.

❓What are these spiritual equivalents of food, air, rest, and exercise?

◆ *The Christian's food:* The Word (1 Peter 2:2; Matthew 4:4)

◆ *The Christian's breathing:* Prayer (1 Thessalonians 5:16–18; Philippians 4:6,7)

◆ *The Christian's rest:* Abiding in Christ (Matthew 11:28–30; John 15:10)

◆ *The Christian's exercise:* Witnessing (Acts 1:8)

In this Step, we have been studying the first of these necessities—the Word of God.

Here is a visual method of demonstrating how we "eat" the Bread of Life. Hold your Bible in your hand with a firm grip, noting that it takes all five fingers for the firmest grip. Then put the book down and count off on your fingers the following ways of appropriating the Word:

1) Hearing (little finger)
2) Reading (next finger)
3) Studying (middle finger)
4) Memorizing (index finger)
5) Meditating (thumb)

Hearing and Meditating: We attend church services and we hear the Word

How God's Word Affects Our Feelings

1. According to these verses in Psalm 119, what does the psalmist recognize is accomplished by respecting and learning God's Word?

   Verse 7 *(An upright heart.)*

   Verse 8 *(Will not be forsaken utterly.)*

   Verse 9 *(Can keep our way pure.)*

2. From Psalm 119:10–16, list at least three attitudes of the psalmist that show his love for the Word of God.

   (Could include: He sought God with all his heart; hid His word in his heart; rejoiced in following His statutes; meditated on His precepts; considered His ways; delighted in His decrees; would not neglect His word.)

3. Why is adversity sometimes good for us (Psalm 119:67 and 71)?

   (It makes us obey His Word and learn His decrees.)

4. From these verses in Psalm 119, what is the reaction of those who love Christ when His Word is not kept?

   Verse 136 *(They weep.)*

   Verse 158 *(They loathe the faithless.)*

5. How can we have great peace (Psalm 119:165)?

   (By loving God's law.)

preached. Psychologists say that most of what we retain from a worship service will be inspirational; we will actually *remember* only about 5 percent of what we heard (little finger), though that percentage might run as high as 15 percent depending on how much meditation (thumb) goes into the hearing.

Pick up your Bible and hold it with the thumb and little finger only. Hearing is vitally important. Romans 10:17 tells us that "faith comes by hearing" the Word of God. But 5 percent or even 15 percent does not give a very strong grip on the Word of God, does it? It would not be difficult for someone to take this Bible away from you when you're holding it like this.

Reading: Reading enables us to get an overview of the Scriptures, and this is absolutely essential. But we remember only about 25 percent of what we read. Now hold the Bible with the thumb, little finger, and the next finger. When we add personal reading of the Bible to hearing, we certainly have a firmer hold on God's Word, but it's still a rather weak grip, wouldn't you say?

Studying: To appropriate God's Word, we must study it. We retain up to 50 percent of what we study. Studying differs from merely reading in that we use a pencil. We may make notes, outlines, or word studies, and file them away for future reference. Or, we may make notations in the margins of our Bible concerning related passages, chapter outlines, and paragraph titles.

Results of Appropriating God's Word

1. Read these verses in Psalm 119, and write what affect the Word has on us when we do the following:

   Know and memorize the Word (verse 98)
   (Makes us wiser than our enemies.)

   Meditate on it (verse 99)
   (Gives us more insight than all our teachers.)

   Obey it (verse 100)
   (Helps us understand more than the aged.)

   Follow it (verse 105)
   (Enlightens us—it is a lamp to our feet and a light to our paths.)

   What does the Word give us (verse 130)?
   (Light and understanding.)

2. According to Psalm 119, what should we do as a result of appropriating the Word?

   Verse 11 *(Not sin against God.)*

   Verse 32 *(Have a heart that is set free.)*

   Verse 63 *(Be a friend to those who fear God.)*

   Verse 74 *(Hope in His Word.)*

   Verse 157 *(Not turn from His statutes.)*

   Verse 176 *(Not forget His commandments.)*

Sometimes we may write a synonym above a difficult word.

Memorizing: Memorizing may seem like child's play—something that is done in the Children's Department in Sunday school. But think again.

❓Have you ever heard of a doctor, physicist, lawyer, or stock broker who has not memorized many basic elements of his profession?

❓What good would a football or basketball player be if he refused to memorize the plays?

We memorize the things that are absolutely essential, the things we dare not forget. When we memorize, we do not retain 5 percent or 25 percent or 50 percent, but 100 percent.

Hold the Bible with all your fingers now. When you add memorization to your methods of learning and understanding God's holy Word, you have the firmest grip.

LIFE APPLICATION

1. What impresses you most about Psalm 119?

2. List three ways in which you recognize your personal need for God's Word today.

3. Many people can recite the four books of the Gospels. Can you? Add the one book of New Testament history, and write all five books here. *(Matthew, Mark, Luke, John, Acts.)*

Since this division is quite easy, go ahead to the next division, the Pauline epistles and Hebrews. That division is harder to learn so you should get started on it now.

Conclusion and Application

We need a sure word for the age in which we live; we need clearly spoken directions. This is what God promises to those who study His Word.

Closing Prayer

Private Bible Study Methods

Opening Prayer

Discussion Starter

(Rather than using a separate discussion starter, for this lesson just read and discuss the various points as appropriate for your group.)

Lesson Development

(Ask one of the group members to summarize the paragraphs appearing at the opening of this lesson in the student's book. Note the diagram and discuss it.)

(You may want to briefly use each of these study methods during your group session. For the Book Study, begin with Ephesians; for the Chapter Study, use Philippians 2; for the Topical Study, select one of the topics listed in the Student book; for the Character Study, use Jonah.)

(Divide your group time into four periods, then work together on each type of study. The hands-on experience will help your students continue using these Bible study methods after the

Leader's Objective: To encourage and motivate students to begin serious personal Bible study

LESSON 7

Bible Study

Proper Attitude for Bible Study

When you personally received Christ as your Savior and Lord, you began a great adventure. That great adventure is mapped out in the pages of the Holy Scriptures. As you read and study the Bible in the power of the Holy Spirit, you will receive meaning, strength, direction, and power for your life. You will learn and claim the many great promises God has reserved for His own.

Approach the Bible in prayer; with reverence, awe, and expectancy; with a willing mind; and with a thirst for truth, righteousness, and fullness in the Lord Jesus Christ. When you come with a humble and contrite heart, you can trust God the Holy Spirit to reveal God's truth to you, and you will experience the cleansing power of His eternal Word.

Above all, as you study God's Word, be eager to obey all that He commands, and rejoice in the knowledge that you are an ambassador for Christ, seeking men in His name to be reconciled to God.

1. How do you feel about Bible study?

2. What do you see at this point as your main pur-

session is over. Also, bring several of the Bible study tools listed in the lesson to show students and to let them use during the group session.)

You have been reading a number of Bible books as you have progressed through the study of these *Ten Basic Steps To Christian Maturity*. This program of study is designed to help you become familiar with the basics of Bible knowledge *and* develop good habits of regular, systematic feeding upon the Bread of Life.

The first eight Steps in the series are based on the book method of Bible study, so if you have worked from the Introductory Step through Step 4, you are familiar with it already.

Step 9, lessons 3, 5, 6, and 7 are designed to whet your appetite for the inspiration and education to be found in character studies. Once the taste has been created through the *Ten Steps,* you will be eager to get going on your own!

pose in studying God's Word?

3. Have you established a definite goal regarding Bible study?

Tools Needed

First, obtain at least two translations of the Bible. Study the various translations. You would not expect to learn much about the physical laws of our universe without diligent and persistent study. Should you expect to acquire much knowledge of God and the unsearchable riches of His Word without studying with equal diligence and persistence?

As funds are available, you will want to secure a topical Bible, a concordance, and a Bible dictionary. Additional Bible study books are helpful and can be added as convenient. However, always remember, Bible study involves just that—studying the Bible. The other items are merely tools to assist you in getting the rich truths God has for you in His Word.

As you consider each study of the Scriptures, may I suggest you record God's Word to you in a journal. This will not only result in a deeper, more serious study, it will also give you a written record of how God speaks to you and of your response to Him.

1. List the tools you now have.

(Discuss how each tool can help you in Bible study:)

More than one translation of the Bible—gives alternate meanings for the same verse. Good for comparison.

Topical Bible—Organizes verses according to topics. Lists additional references on each topic it covers. Gives an explanation of the topic.

Concordance—Lists additional references for key words.

Bible dictionary—gives pronunciation and meanings for words in the Bible and Christian terminology.

2. List the additional tools you desire in the order in which you plan to obtain them.

Suggested Methods

1. *Book study.* The Bible contains many books. Yet the divine plan of God to redeem men in Christ Jesus runs through the whole of it. Be careful to consider each book as a part of the whole. Read it through. Following these suggestions will help make your study more meaningful:

   ◆ *Mark and underline* as God speaks to you through His Word.

   ◆ *Outline* it.

   ◆ *List* the names of the principal characters; tell who they are and their significance.

   ◆ *Select* from each chapter key verses to memorize and copy them on a card to carry with you.

   ◆ *List* teachings to obey and promises to claim.

   ◆ *Consider* the characteristics revealed of God the Father, God the Son, and God the Holy Spirit.

   Which book would you particularly like to study using this method? (It is best to start with one of the shorter ones.)

(Suggest that students may be able to find these resources in their church library.)

(Use Ephesians 1:1–14 to demonstrate the Book Study method. Ask a student to look up "predestined" and "adoption" in a topical Bible and read the entries.)

How effective do you think this study method will be for you? Why?

What do you think are the advantages of using this method?

2. *Chapter study.* To get a grasp of the chapter, answer the following questions:

   ◆ What is the principal subject of the chapter?
   ◆ What is the leading lesson?
   ◆ What is the key verse? (Memorize it.)
   ◆ Who are the principal characters?
   ◆ What does it teach about God the Father?
   ◆ What does it teach about Jesus Christ?
   ◆ What does it teach about the Holy Spirit?
   ◆ Is there any example for me to follow?
   ◆ Is there any error for me to avoid?
   ◆ Is there any duty for me to perform?
   ◆ Is there any promise for me to claim?
   ◆ Is there any prayer for me to echo?

   Choose a chapter from the book, and apply these questions.

3. *Topical study.* Take an important subject—such as grace, truth, prayer, faith, assurance, justification, regeneration, or peace—and, using a topical Bible and a concordance, study the scope of the topic throughout the Bible.

   You will find it necessary to divide each topic into sub-topics as you accumulate material; for ex-

(Ask students to read Philippians 2 silently. Then discuss the questions as a group. Use the Bible dictionary to find out who the Philippians, Timothy, and Epaphroditus were.)

❓How effective do you think this study method will be for you? Why?

❓What do you think are the advantages of using this method?

(Invite the students to pick one of the topics listed in their books and use the concordance at the back of their Bibles or one you brought to class to find additional references on the topic. Then ask students to look up and write information on the topic they chose. When they finish, ask:)

❓How effective do you think this study method will be for you? Why?

ample, forms of prayer, prayer promises, examples of prayer in Scripture, Christ's teaching on prayer, Christ's ministry as we pray, the ministry of the Holy Spirit in prayer.

What topic do you plan to study first?

How much time have you scheduled for it?

4. *Biographical study.* There are 2,930 people mentioned in the Bible. The lives of many of these make extremely interesting biographical studies. Why is it important to study the characters of the Bible (1 Corinthians 10:11; Romans 15:4)?
   (As examples, warnings, to encourage us.)

Using a concordance, topical Bible, or the proper name index in your Bible, look up every reference in the Bible of someone you would like to study.

Name the person you would like to study.

State your reason for choosing that particular person.

Answer the following questions:

♦ What was the social and political atmosphere in which he (or she) lived?

♦ How did that affect his life?

❓What do you think are the advantages of using this method?

(Begin a character study on Jonah. Ask students to select three questions in the Biographical Study section to answer about Jonah. A study Bible like the *Thompson Chain Reference Bible* provides sections with character studies that will help your students.)

(Then look up Jonah 4:10,11 in several different translations and note the differences between the versions.)

(When students have finished, ask:)

❓How effective do you think this study method will be for you? Why?

❓What do you think are the advantages of using this method?

- ◆ What do we know of his family?
- ◆ What kind of training did he have in his youth?
- ◆ What was accomplished by him during his life?
- ◆ Was there a great crisis in his life? If so, how did he face it?
- ◆ What were his outstanding character traits?
- ◆ Who were his friends? What kind of people were they?
- ◆ What influence did they have on him?
- ◆ What influence did he have on them?
- ◆ Does his life show any development of character?
- ◆ What was his experience with God? Notice his prayer life, faith, service to God, knowledge of God's Word, courage in witnessing, and attitude toward the worship of God.
- ◆ Were any particular faults evident in his life?
- ◆ Was there any outstanding sin in his life?
- ◆ Under what circumstances did he commit this sin?
- ◆ What was its nature and its effect on his future life?
- ◆ What were his children like?

◆ Was there some lesson in this person's life that will help to enrich your life?

By the time you complete the studies outlined in this series of booklets, you will have been introduced to each of these four methods. You already have taken the first step in the book study method by reading the Book of Acts.

Lessons 2 and 4 of *Step 2: The Christian and the Abundant Life* were chapter studies. You will soon be ready to apply these as well as the other two methods to more advanced work in your own individual Bible study.

When you have completed Step 10 of the *Ten Basic Steps,* you will be ready to launch out into one profitable Bible study after another. However, it is recommended that you complete the *Ten Steps* series to lay a foundation in God's Word before you move to more advanced, individual work.

LIFE APPLICATION

1. Which method interests you most now?

2. How do you expect to benefit from serious study of the Bible?

3. Select one method and use it over the next week. Use the other methods in the following weeks.

4. Complete your memorization of the Pauline epistles and the last book of prophecy. Write them all here:

Pauline epistles and Hebrews
(Romans, 1 and 2 Corinthians, Galatians, Ephesians, Philippians, Colossians, 1 and 2 Thessalonians, 1 and 2 Timo-

Conclusion and Application

If you were a college professor and your students never read the textbook for your class, what would you say? Would you think they deserved to pass the course? Would you have a hard time teaching those students?

The Christian life is so much more exciting than a mere college course. What a privilege we have to sit under the Holy Spirit's teaching and read the book that God wrote! I challenge you to take your time of Bible study seriously. Enjoy this Book of books. And develop a life-time habit of savoring its words daily.

thy, Titus, Philemon, Hebrews.)

General epistles and prophecy
(James; 1 and 2 Peter; 1, 2, and 3 John; Jude; Revelation.)

Remember, always study the Bible with the following:

◆ A pencil
◆ A notebook
◆ A prayer
◆ A purpose

Closing Prayer

Recap

Opening Prayer

Discussion Starter

(Begin this lesson with an oral review of the names of the books of the Bible and the divisions into which they fall.)

❷ Do you think a non-Christian should study the Bible?

❷ Why or why not?

Lesson Development

(Any appropriate material from previous lessons that was not sufficiently covered could be used at this time, and you also may deal with any point that the group members may not understand as well as they could.)

(Then go over the remaining Recap questions and answers. This material will benefit both the students and you by giving you a deeper appreciation of God's Word. Students should have completed question 1 on their own before class, so begin with question 2.)

Leader's Objective: To increase students' appreciation of the importance of the Bible, its authority and inspiration, its purpose, and what daily Bible study can do for the individual Christian

LESSON 8

The following questions will help you review this Step. If necessary, reread the appropriate lesson(s).

1. On a piece of paper, write the divisions of the books of the Bible and the names of each book in each division. Review any division you do not know well.

2. How would you explain the statement, "Christ is the central person of the Bible?"
   (The Old and New Testaments are a testimony of what Jesus has done for us.)

3. Who do you think is the real source of the authority of the Scripture?
   (God.)

   Describe how this is evident in biblical history.

4. Name at least three things the Word of God accomplishes that indicate its supernatural power.
   1) *(New birth.)*
   2) *(Fulfilled prophecy.)*
   3) *(Changed lives.)*

   Write down several changes that the Bible has made in your life. Be specific.

5. Why do you need the Word of God?
   (It is essential for spiritual growth and well-being.)

6. What steps do you still need to take to be fully

(For this lesson, bring your Bible study journal to help your students with their journal.)

(Encourage students to list prayer requests for other members of the group to use after the group study is over.)

(When you get to the "Life Application" section, invite students to ask questions or give suggestions on how to continue using their notebooks.)

prepared for serious study of the Bible?

7. Review the names of the books of the Bible and write them one final time. Be sure the spelling is correct.

LIFE APPLICATION

1. Begin a journal of what you are learning through your Bible study. Buy a small notebook and record:

   ◆ The portion of Scripture you are studying

   ◆ The method you are using

   For each day of study, record the following:

   ◆ Date

   ◆ Lesson that is important to you

   ◆ How you can apply it to your life

   ◆ Results of previous lessons you have applied to your daily situations

   Also, write down prayer requests and answers as well as verses you have memorized.

   When you finish the study, begin again with another portion of Scripture.

2. Periodically review your journal to see how you are growing spiritually and to remind yourself of important lessons you have learned.

Conclusion and Application

We can readily see the importance of and the need for the Word of God.

Someone has said, "Sin will keep me from this Book, but this Book will keep me from sin."

That is in accord with Psalm 119:11:

> I have hidden your word in my heart that I might not sin against you.

Closing Prayer

(Give the students a few minutes for silent prayer in which to make any commitments they feel necessary, especially regarding the study of God's Word. Then close by thanking God for His Word and what it has done in your life.)

The Christian and **Obedience**

Living Daily in God's Grace

STEP 6

Obedience—The Key to Knowing God's Will

Opening Prayer

Discussion Starter

The importance of obedience cannot be overemphasized. We are encouraged to discipline our children to save them from spiritual bankruptcy (Proverbs 23:13,14). We are admonished to teach our spiritual children the importance of obedience (2 Timothy 2:2). As a disobedient child becomes a problem, so will the disobedient Christian become a problem to himself, to others, and especially to the Lord if he does not learn to obey in his early Christian experience.

❓What kinds of problems do you think a disobedient Christian could create?

Lesson Development

(Encourage students to read the article, "Living Daily in God's Will" at the beginning of their book on their own time if they have not already done so.)

(Ask one of the group members to summarize the paragraphs appearing at the opening of this lesson in the stu-

Leader's Objective: To help students desire to know God's will and be completely obedient to Him regardless of their circumstances

289

Bible Study

Disobedience of King Saul

Read 1 Samuel 15.

1. What was God's command to Saul through Samuel?
   (To utterly destroy Amalek, its people, and their possessions.)

2. Describe how Saul rationalized his actions (15:7–9).
   (He decided that some things were too good to destroy so he spared Agag, the king, and he spared the best of the sheep and cattle.)

3. Was Saul's repentance sincere?
   (No.)

4. The main principle illustrated is stated in verse 22. What is it?
   (Obedience is better than sacrifice.)

5. What are some ways Christians rationalize disobedience today?

Obedience of Paul

Read Acts 9:1–22.

1. What was God's command to Paul (here called Saul)?
   (Go into the city where he would be told what to do next.)

2. How did he comply?
   (He did exactly what God told him to do.)

dent's book. Note the diagram and discuss it.)

God was displeased with Saul and dissolved his kingship (verses 11,23). Saul called his actions 100 percent obedience (verses 13,20); he also tried to blame the disobedience on his people (verses 15,21). Samuel called it rebellion, arrogance, and rejecting the Word of the Lord (verse 23).

❓How do you determine whether what you are doing is obedience or merely sacrifice?

❓How can you keep from falling into this trap?

Paul's background is found in Philippians 3:4–6: circumcised (physical sign of a Jewish covenant), people of Israel (pride of family), Pharisee (pride of religion), and zealous persecutor of the church (pride of conviction).

We see the transformation of his life in Acts 9: called by God (verse 6), a chosen instrument to be God's witness

3. Why was Paul's obedience so important at this particular time?
   (He was demonstrating his changed attitude toward God.)

4. How do you think Paul's obedience illustrates the truth of the principle in 1 Samuel 15:22?
   (Paul did not have to do penance for what he had done in the past. He just had to repent and obey.)

Obedience of Ananias

Read Acts 9:10–22.

1. What was God's command to Ananias?
   (To find Saul and lay his hands on him so Saul would receive his sight.)

2. What was Ananias' reaction?
   (Fear.)

3. How did he finally respond?
   (Complete obedience.)

4. Why was his obedience so essential at this particular time?
   (Ananias was an essential part of God's plan to use Paul in building the church.)

5. How does his obedience indirectly influence you?
   (God used Paul to reveal to mankind the most abundant life ever possible.)

(verse 15), sight restored (verses 8,17), filled with the Spirit (verse 17), baptized (verse 18), to preach Christ (verse 20).

It took a lot of faith for Ananias to obey God. Saul was one of the foremost enemies of the church. Ananias was literally taking a chance with his life in contacting Saul. But his obedience resulted in one of the most strategic events in the early church. God changed Saul's name to Paul, and used him to give us many books of the New Testament. Through Paul, many churches were formed and many people became Christians. Ananias was the link to this chain of events.

Our obedience also has far-reaching results. When we do what God asks—even if the task seems extremely hard at the moment—God blesses our obedience in tremendous ways.

1. How would you have felt in Ananias' place?

2. What is the most important thing this lesson teaches you about obedience?

3. What specific area of weakness in your life do you need to bring into obedience to Christ?

4. What steps will you take to become obedient in this area?

Conclusion and Application

There is a great instrument for finding God's will. It is so simple that even a child can understand it. Sometimes even the weakest people have used it to achieve mighty things for God. The name of the instrument is *obedience*.

Perfect obedience can bring perfect happiness when we have perfect confidence in the power we are obeying.

Closing Prayer

Insincere Obedience

Opening Prayer

Discussion Starter

Consider an apple tree. We cannot produce an apple tree by taking a bushel of apples and pinning them on an oak tree.

How is this like using outward obedience to God to solve the problems of the heart?

Can someone claim that he has the right attitude and true faith in God and not demonstrate his faith by his good works?

James writes:

You foolish man, do you want evidence that faith without deeds is useless (James 2:20)?

Lesson Development

(Ask one of the group members to summarize the paragraphs appearing at the opening of this lesson in the student's book. Note the diagram and discuss it.)

❖

Leader's Objective: To show students that true obedience affects the inward attitude to produce the outward act

Bible Study

An Example of Insincere Obedience

Read Acts 4:32—5:11.

1. At one time, Jerusalem Christians held goods as common property. Each Christian put his funds into a common treasury, which then supplied the needs of the Christian community.

   What made them willing to give up personal possessions (verse 32)?
   (They were of one heart and mind.)

2. One writer has said that many today view the local church as if it were a restaurant where all kinds of people meet for a short time, sit down together in the same room, then part, not knowing or caring anything about each other.

   What is your estimation of the fellowship in our churches today compared with the fellowship of the Jerusalem Christians?

   What kind of attitude did the early Christians display?
   (Unselfishness, desire to tell others about Jesus.)

   Do you think this is true in your church?

Because of insincere hearts, Ananias and Sapphira gave money to God—not to please Him, but only to please men. Obedience not backed by the right attitude is unacceptable, and sooner or later it will reveal itself in sin.

Suppose these two had been given the job of handling the funds of the church. No doubt they would have been dishonest in this area also. Note these things about the sin of Ananias and Sapphira:

The sin was within the fellowship of the church. The church is rarely harmed or hindered by opposition from without; it is perpetually harmed or hindered by perils from within. Persecution of the early church made it stronger, but hypocrisy within the church is a sin that can cause Christian disunity and do irreparable harm to the Body of Christ.

The sin of Ananias and Sapphira was not in refusing to contribute to the church, nor was it in the amount they gave, nor that they held back part of the price. There was no rule that they should give, or not give, a certain amount. *Their sin was pretending they had done more than they had*—in other words, hypocrisy.

God was more severe in dealing with Ananias and Sapphira than with Saul who was involved in the murder of Christians. When confronted with their sin, they tried to cover up their lie. Saul, on the other hand, immediately repented and changed his ways. Repentance is always the first step of obedience when sin is present.

What can you do to improve the fellowship in your church?

3. When Barnabas sold his land, which was probably valuable, and gave the money to the church, no doubt other Christians praised his devotion.

How do you think Barnabas' action might have influenced Ananias and Sapphira?
(They wanted the same kind of praise from others.)

4. What do you suppose motivated Ananias and Sapphira to sell their possessions and give money to the church?
(Pride, jealousy.)

5. How did their motive differ from Barnabas' motive?
(They acted out of selfish motives; Barnabas had a godly attitude.)

Importance of Our Christian Testimony

1. How can it be possible to study the Bible, share Christ with others, or attend Christian meetings, and yet be committing sin when you think you are pleasing God?
(You are only doing those things as outward obedience, not from the heart.)

2. What did Christ say was wrong with the people of His day (Mark 7:6)?
(They honored Him with

One thing that made Christ angry, against which He gave His severest rebuke, was the sin of hypocrisy. What scorching, blasting words He said to people who pretended to be religious!

❓How does your attitude affect your testimony?

Sometimes we begin with a godly attitude, but gradually it deteriorates. We may not even realize how we have changed.

their lips, but their hearts were far from Him.)

3. Why is your heart attitude just as important to God as your outward action?
   (Your attitude determines the sincerity of your actions.)

Attitude in Giving and Prayer

Read Matthew 6:1–8.

1. Each of us has a tendency to do things for the approval of our friends. When this desire becomes our sole motivation, our attitude is wrong. Think of a person you know who has a godly attitude toward giving. How do his actions differ from those described in Matthew 6?

2. List some ways you can help keep your giving sincere.

3. Public prayer is not wrong in itself. When you pray aloud with others, to whom are you talking?
   (God.)

4. How can you make your public prayers a testimony to how much you love God?
   (Make them sincere and honest.)

LIFE APPLICATION

1. Read 1 Corinthians 13:1–3. In terms meaningful to you, paraphrase these three verses.

❓What are some outward signs you can look for to help you determine when your inward attitude is not in line with your actions?

❓How can you avoid having this happen?

Conclusion and Application

(Assign two or three group members to each give a present-day example of types of hypocrisy, then add:)

Hypocrisy toward God. We tell God we are surrendered to Him when we

2. On the basis of this passage, what would you say is the relationship between love and sincere obedience?
(Sincere obedience comes out of love.)

3. What action or activity in your life needs a change in motivation?

4. How do you expect that change to affect other people with whom you come in contact?

5. How do you expect that change to affect your life?

are not, instead of honestly expressing our feelings—no matter how sinful they may be—and obtaining His forgiveness.

We claim to love Him and His will. He who said, "I am the truth," never compromised with untruth! Be *honest* in prayer. If you do not want to do God's will on any issue, it is far better to tell Him so and ask for His help, rather than hide your feelings because you think dedicated Christians are not supposed to have such feelings.

Hypocrisy toward other believers. We try to put on a show of being dedicated, sincere Christians, experiencing victory in most of our life when in reality we are defeated and in desperate trouble. Do not broadcast your defeats before others, or wallow in self-pity, but don't be afraid to seek help from mature Christians when you need it.

Hypocrisy toward non-Christians. We tell them we are Christians and that God has given us the power to live differently; we read our Bibles; we attend church. But we become just as frustrated, worried, or exasperated as they do under pressure. Or, even worse, our lives show drastic moral inconsistencies—we sin in sex, drinking, drugs, money, or other areas. Our lives will never be perfect. But we must ask Christ to enable us to live godly lives if we are to impact the non-Christian world for Christ.

Closing Prayer

Personal Purity

Opening Prayer

Discussion Starter

❓What is sexual temptation, and what do you think is the best way to resist it?

Lesson Development

(Ask one of the group members to summarize the paragraphs appearing at the opening of this lesson in the student's book. Note the diagram and discuss it.)

Jesus speaks in the Sermon on the Mount of two things: an *outward requirement* and an *inward reality.*

❓Why is meeting the outward requirement without the inward reality unacceptable to God?

The Sermon on the Mount is the classic condemnation of external religion, which is largely obedience to laws and rules. Mark 7:1–23 illustrates this as it was in Jesus' day. In our own time, many believe they are justified before God if they are outwardly

Leader's Objective: To motivate group members toward purity in both their thoughts and their actions

LESSON 3

Bible Study

Purity and the Mind

1. What does Christ say of impure thought (Matthew 5:27,28)?
   (It shows a wicked heart, which is as much a sin as outward sinful actions.)

2. List the things on which we are to think (Philippians 4:8).
   (Whatever is true, noble, right, pure, lovely, admirable, excellent, and worthy of praise.)

   Why does the human mind not want to think on these things (Romans 8:7)?
   (Its nature is fleshly and hostile toward God—unable to be subject to the law of God.)

3. What are some things in our modern life and homes that naturally lead to impure thoughts?
   (Some television and radio programs, ads, fashions, reading materials.)

4. How do we gain victory over impure thoughts (Galatians 5:16)?
   (By living in the Spirit.)

   What can we do to avoid thinking impure thoughts (Romans 13:14)?
   (Live moment by moment for Jesus; do not think about how to gratify evil desires.)

moral, cultured, polite, considerate, and refined.

Many philosophers and social reformers believe that the basic solution to our problems is an external one, merely the improvement of our environment through legislation and welfare programs. Jesus stands against all such thinking. He says:

> Nothing outside a man can make him "unclean" by going into him. Rather, it is what comes out of a man that makes him "unclean" (Mark 7:15).

Many Christians diligently read their Bibles, pray, attend church, and even witness for Christ, but God does not accept their works because they do not have the right attitude.

A policeman was shot to death by a gunman in California, and a Michigan business executive accidentally shot his best friend while hunting. In the case of the policeman, a search was made for the killer and he was prosecuted. In the case of the business executive, there was no prosecution—it obviously was not his fault. He even received sympathy.

Both gunmen had done the same thing—they had shot and killed another human being. But the thoughts in their hearts were entirely different.

> As [a man] thinks within himself, so he is (Proverbs 23:7, KJV).

Evil thoughts will eventually result in evil actions. The source of personality is within the thought processes.

5. Apply these verses to the things you listed in question 3. How will you handle each area of temptation?

Note: Temptation in the thought life is not the same as sin. Evil thoughts may pass through the mind, but sin comes from dwelling on the thought.

How can we avoid some temptations (2 Timothy 2:22)?
(Flee the evil desires and pursue righteousness.)

As we live each day in vital union with Christ, we are to claim the strength, power, and protection that He provides. The victory over impure thinking does not come from us, but from Christ.

Purity and the Opposite Sex

1. What does the Bible say about the sexual relationship in its proper place (Hebrews 13:4)?
(Within marriage, it is honorable and pure.)

2. When tempted by immorality, what is a Christian to do (1 Corinthians 6:18)?
(Flee immorality.)

Why?
(The immoral person sins against his own body, which is the temple of the Holy Spirit.)

3. List some things you can be certain will help you when you are tempted (1 Corinthians 10:13).
(Knowing that it is common to man, you are not the only one, you will not be tempted beyond what you can handle, God will provide a way of escape, you can endure it.)

We are to give no occasion, no opportunity to the flesh to fulfill its impure desires. Any choice you face in life will find two voices calling you, each in opposite directions:

1) The flesh is influenced by Satan.

2) The spirit is influenced by Christ.

We often fail because we put ourselves in positions where we will be tempted. To look at or read something that promotes sinful thoughts and then expect God to protect us from sin is equivalent to leaping from a building and asking God to keep us from falling!

God promises *unconditional* forgiveness, based not on how guilty we feel or if we promise never to do it again, but rather on the promise of His faithfulness. He alone is faithful and just. He alone can forgive.

When God forgives sin, He also removes it and forgets it. Unconditional forgiveness provides complete cleansing.

4. Write in your own words the warnings against immorality found in the following Scriptures:

Proverbs 6:26

Proverbs 6:32

1 Thessalonians 4:3–8

Purity and Forgiveness

1. Write in your own words what the following verses say about God's forgiveness:

Psalm 103:12

Isaiah 43:25

1 John 2:1,2

2. What must we do to obtain God's forgiveness (1 John 1:9)?
(Confess our sins; agree with God concerning them.)

LIFE APPLICATION

1. What area of impurity in your life do you need to face and deal with?

2. What are you doing or have around you that increases the temptation?

The most difficult aspect of keeping our hearts right before God by confessing our sins is admitting that a particular thing we have done is sin. The human personality is constructed to prefer rationalizing or justifying wrong rather than admitting the wrong.

❓To whom does the "we" in 1 John 1:9 refer?

It refers to believers.

The Greek meaning of the word *confess,* "to agree with" [God], implies being specific, naming the sin.

❓What is wrong with praying, "Lord, forgive me for all of my sins"?

It is too general. Unless we identify the sin, we will probably not forsake it.

❓When should we confess sin?

We should confess our sins the moment we realize we have sinned.

The *instant* we recognize that we have failed God, or are unkind or unfaithful to a friend, we need to confess the sin to God and ask forgiveness of that person.

Conclusion and Application

As Christians, we often forget that our relationship with God depends on our being cleansed, moment by moment, and not on an attitude of "anything goes if I am sincere, or if I am trying."

(Give students time to reflect on and fill out these three questions. Do not ask anyone to reveal their answers.)

3. Choose an appropriate verse or passage from this lesson, apply it to your situation, and write the result you expect to attain.

Closing Prayer

(Use the prayer time to allow students to commit to doing what they have recorded in the "Life Application" questions. Close by asking God to help each of you deal with persistent temptation.)

No Matter What Others Think

Opening Prayer

Discussion Starter

Jerome Hines, the famous Metropolitan Opera star, had the privilege of singing at a Presidential Prayer Breakfast, which was attended by the President of the United States, members of the Cabinet, the House of Representatives, the Senate, and the Supreme Court. Before he began, he clearly told of his faith in Jesus Christ. He minced no words. His stand was strong and dynamic.

Other Christians, when presented with golden opportunities, become afraid and never say a word for their Lord.

❓ What do you think is the reason for the difference?

❓ In what kinds of situations do you have difficulty sharing your faith?

Leader's Objective: To motivate students to overcome the fear of what others think and be able to obey God more fully

LESSON 4

Bible Study

Peter's Renunciation

Read Matthew 26:57–75 carefully.

1. Peter knew and loved Christ in his heart, but when it came time to openly identify himself as a follower of Christ, what did he do (verse 58)?
   (He followed Jesus at a distance.)

2. Note the contrasts between Christ and Peter:

   Who accused Christ (verse 59)?
   (The chief priests and the whole Sanhedrin.)

   Who accused Peter (verses 69,71)?
   (Two different servant girls.)

   How did Christ answer His accusers (verse 64)?
   (He boldly told them who He was.)

   How did Peter answer his accusers (verses 71–74)?
   (He said he didn't know Jesus.)

   What happened to Jesus because He told the truth (verses 67,68)?
   (He was spit upon, beaten with fists, and slapped.)

   What was the result when Peter told those lies (verse 75)?
   (He remembered what Jesus had said and wept bitterly.)

Lesson Development

(Ask one of the group members to summarize the paragraphs appearing at the opening of this lesson in the student's book. Note the diagram and discuss it.)

❓ Which of Peter's characteristics do you identify with?

❓ Have you ever found yourself in a situation where it was very difficult to witness? What happened?

❓ What makes it so hard to be bold for Christ?

Before the resurrection of Christ, Peter had a human concept of Jesus' mission. Because of the resurrection, Peter understood why Jesus came to earth. After the resurrection, he understood that Christ is the Messiah who must suffer for our sins and be raised again for our justification. That was the message Peter preached!

3. Some have said that Christ's teachings are only for weaklings, cowards, neurotics, and those who need some kind of crutch. As you look at the examples here of Christ and Peter, how would you evaluate such a statement?

4. Describe what Jesus' example means to you in facing your peer pressures.

Peter's Restoration

1. After Christ's resurrection, what did the angel announce to the women in Mark 16:7?
   (They were to go tell the disciples—and Peter—that Jesus would meet them.)

   Why did the angel single out Peter's name from all the rest?
   (To reassure Peter that Christ loved him and forgave him.)

2. Upon what basis can Christ restore you even though you have denied Him?
   (Christ's forgiveness is complete. He has paid for every sin we've committed.)

Peter's Transformation

1. Less than two months later at Pentecost, Peter stood up from among the disciples to give a bold defense of the Christian

Peter's Example

◆ *His strong faith* (Matthew 16:13–16; 26:33): He promised Christ that he would never be ashamed of Him.

◆ *His denial* (Matthew 26:69–75): He denied knowing Christ in front of several people.

◆ *His transformation* (Acts 2:14–41): He boldly preached the good news about Christ before thousands of people.

The Scripture makes a point of showing us that God still considered Peter a valuable member of His team.

❓How does Peter's restoration make you feel?

faith to a ridiculing crowd (Acts 2:13–15).

What shocking thing did Peter fearlessly tell the crowd (Acts 2:36)?
(That they had crucified Jesus, who was both Lord and Christ.)

2. What made this dramatic difference in Peter's life (Acts 1:8; 4:8)?
(At Pentecost, he was filled with the Holy Spirit.)

3. And what resulted (Acts 2:37–41)?
(Three thousand people repented and became Christians.)

4. Compare the actions of the disciples during the crucifixion (Luke 22:47–62; 23:49; Matthew 26:56) and during this account in Acts. What part does Christian fellowship and unity play in standing up to peer pressure?
(During the crucifixion, the disciples scattered; after the resurrection, they were united in boldly witnessing. Christian fellowship and unity help us be bold for Christ.)

LIFE APPLICATION

1. How do you think having natural courage and boldness compares to being filled with the Holy Spirit?
(Natural courage fluctuates with situations and is dependent on a person's personality. The Holy

Peter preached the good news about Christ again before all the leaders in Jerusalem who had been responsible for the death of Christ (Acts 4:8–20). Everyone marveled at his boldness.

He preached about Christ yet again before the religious leaders, claiming that he must obey God rather than men (Acts 5:29–42).

Because of Pentecost, Peter had within him the power to tell others the good news of the gospel. It was a power that rested not in self, but in the Holy Spirit who lived within him.

Conclusion and Application

Many professing Christians have no power or authority in their lives. They want to be men of God, but they are defeated by an overwhelming sense of the fear of man.

The only way to overcome that fear is to yield to God, become obedient to Him, and be faithful to the command,

Spirit is always able to give us boldness.)

2. Write Proverbs 29:25 here in your own words.

3. If we know and love Christ in our hearts, why must we also take a bold and open stand for Him (Matthew 4:19; 10:32; 16:24)?

(Jesus commands us to witness; we must acknowledge God publicly; we must deny ourselves to follow Christ.)

How do these verses relate to your present attitudes?

4. To whom do you particularly need to confess Christ and take a bold stand for Him (Romans 10:13–15)?

Why?

"Be filled with the Spirit" (Ephesians 5:18).

If you want power and authority and if you want to be a man or woman of God, you must let the Holy Spirit have full and complete control of your life.

Closing Prayer

(Use this prayer time to encourage students to make a commitment to greater boldness in witnessing and to ask God to fill them with His Spirit.)

Taming the Tongue

Opening Prayer

(Thank God for any opportunities your students have had to boldly speak out for Christ in the past week.)

Discussion Starter

❓ Why should we control our tongue?

❓ Why do you think the Scriptures devote most of a chapter in the Epistle of James, plus numerous passages in other books, on taming the tongue? And why does Christ Himself have so much to say about the tongue?

Leader's Objective: To lead students to realize the importance of the tongue, how it reflects what is in our hearts, and how it must be controlled if we are to be obedient to God

Bible Study

Effects of the Tongue

Read James 3:1–13.

1. Though we may study our Bibles faithfully, attend Christian meetings regularly, and even talk to our friends about Christ, one thing marks us as really mature Christians.

   What is it?
   (When we do not stumble in what we say.)

2. When you control your tongue, what else will happen (verse 2)?
   (You will be able to keep the whole body in check as well.)

3. James compares a wicked tongue to an incorrectly handled steering mechanism on a ship. What would happen if the ship were an oil tanker in rocky water?

   How does this relate to the damage of "spilled" words?

4. What does it take to start a forest fire in a drought?
   (A small spark.)

   What does it take to put out a forest fire?

   What damage can be caused by just a few words of gossip that you pass on?

Lesson Development

(Ask one of the group members to summarize the paragraphs appearing at the opening of this lesson in the student's book.)

An unruly tongue can wreck one's Christian life.

❓What is the origin of evil speech?

Jesus said,

> Out of the overflow of his heart his mouth speaks (Luke 6:45).

The tongue is not something independent; it merely reflects the condition of the heart. Therefore, controlling the tongue requires that the heart totally submit to Christ.

Controlling the tongue also keeps us from inconsistency and hypocrisy. James 3:9–12 points out how a person's tongue can reveal his inconsistent life.

Many Christians know all the "language," can pray eloquently, and speak as if they were very holy. But in almost the same breath their gossiping tongues betray their hypocrisy. Remember, your everyday speech is like a large neon sign telling everyone what you *really* are. (Summarize with James 1:26:)

> If anyone considers himself religious and yet does not keep a tight rein on his tongue, he deceives himself and his religion is worthless.

5. Give an example from your own life in which you suffered from the "fire" of someone's destructive words.

   How did you respond?

   How would you respond today?

   Why?

(Caution students about naming people when responding to question 5. Discuss the results of destructive words instead of trying to place blame on someone.)

Sins of the Tongue

1. Name the sins of the tongue that are condemned in the following references in Proverbs:

   6:16–19
   (A lying tongue, a false witness who lies, and one who stirs up dissension.)

   11:13
   (A gossip who betrays a confidence.)

   15:1
   (Harsh words that stir up anger.)

   17:9
   (Repeating an account of someone else's transgression.)

   27:2
   (Self-praise.)

   Give examples of how you may have been hurt by or how you may have offended another in each of these areas.

2. Read Ephesians 4:29.

   How does this apply to profanity, obscene language, off-color jokes, and so on?
   (They should not come out of our mouths.)

   The tongue can do so much damage with so little effort. All sin is sin. But some sins do more damage than others. Many times we have sins in our lives for which God will hold us accountable, but which are not so public. Note the difference between harboring a secret grudge and spreading lies openly.

   We can also cause a lot of hurt feelings by telling half-truths or by not defending the truth. As a rule of thumb, if you speak in love and kindness, your words will generally be good.

What else can you name that could be included here?

What does this verse say we should do instead?
(Build each other up.)

Significance of the Tongue

Read Matthew 12:33–37.

1. For what shall we give account to God?
   (Every careless word we speak.)

2. What illustration does Christ use to explain good and bad words?
   (A good tree with good fruit, and a bad tree with bad fruit.)

3. How does He apply it?
   (Our mouth speaks from what's in our heart.)

4. What, then, is the real source of an evil tongue?
   (An evil heart.)

5. How does this relate to attitude?
   (Attitude also comes from the heart.)

6. What is the only solution to taming the tongue for a believer (Galatians 5:16)?
   (Live by the Spirit.)

LIFE APPLICATION

1. How will you obey the instructions indicated in James 1:19 in your own life?
   How about James 1:26?

2. Think about the attitudes expressed through your

Another form of evil speaking is using sarcastic humor that cuts another person down. As Christians, we can lovingly see the humor in people's actions, but we should be careful not to let our humor harm anyone.

The test of a Spirit-filled life is how we speak in difficult situations. It's easy to speak kindly when your spouse surprises you with a gift. But how about when he or she forgets to pay a bill on time? It's easy to say gracious words when you get the award for employee of the month. But how about when a co-worker lashes out at you in front of your colleagues? Spirit-filled living means relying on Him moment by moment to give you the attitude and actions that will please God.

Conclusion and Application

The tongue does not function by itself. It is completely controlled by the mind. It responds to thought impulses.

Many times we try to control our tongue without changing our attitude. That cannot be successful for long.

words in the past week. Ask yourself these questions, and answer them honestly.

What attitude do I need to confess and make right with God?

To whom do I need to go and ask forgiveness because he or she has been affected by my words?

Since a person's tongue is controlled by his mind, the mind must be renewed (Romans 12:2). Renewal involves conformity—not to the world—but to Christ as the work of the Holy Spirit conforms us to Christ's image (Romans 8:28,29). When our mind is renewed, our tongue will follow suit.

Closing Prayer

The Key to Inner Security

Opening Prayer

Discussion Starter

(Read or relate the following to your group:)

In 1923 a very important meeting was held at the Edgewater Beach Hotel in Chicago. In attendance were nine of the world's most successful financiers ... men who had found the secret of making money. Twenty-five years later let's see where these men were:

The president of the largest independent steel company, Charles Schwab, died bankrupt and lived on borrowed money for five years before his death. The president of the largest utility company, Samuel Insull, died a fugitive from justice and penniless in a foreign land. The president of the largest gas company, Howard Hopson, went insane.

The greatest wheat speculator, Arthur Cotton, died abroad, insolvent. The president of the New York Stock Exchange, Richard Whitney, was released from Sing Sing Penitentiary. The member of the President's Cabinet, Albert Fall, was pardoned from prison so he could die at home. The greatest "bear" on Wall Street,

Leader's Objective: To show students that physical, material, and spiritual security depend on Christ and our obedience to Him

Bible Study

The Rich Fool

Read Luke 12:13–34.

1. What was foremost on the mind of the man in verse 13?
   (His inheritance.)

2. Why did Jesus deny his request?
   (Jesus did not come to provide material blessings.)

   In light of this, why do you think He denies some of our requests?
   (He knows they are not the best for us.)

3. Why was the man in the parable a fool?
   (The man in the parable concentrated on building his material wealth but failed to build his relationship with God.)

4. How do people today make the same mistake this man made?
   (Acquiring things or money becomes more important than knowing or serving God.)

5. Name some illustrations Jesus used in verses 24–28 to show the uselessness of worrying about material things.
   (God feeds the ravens; we can't add to our height; God clothes the lilies and grass, and He will clothe us.)

6. Give some examples from recent events that

Jesse Livermore, died a suicide. The head of the greatest monopoly, Ivan Krueger, died a suicide.

The president of the Bank of International Settlements, Leon Fraser, died a suicide. All of these men learned well the art of making a living, but not one learned how to live. (From Billy Rose, *Pitching Horseshoes,* 1948. The meeting at the Edgewater Beach Hotel was a youth congress.)

❓What do you think this tells us?

Lesson Development

(Ask one of the group members to summarize the paragraphs appearing at the opening of this lesson in the student's book. Note the diagram and discuss it.)

Many books by well-meaning Christians give the impression that, if we receive Christ, we are guaranteed an improvement in our material condition. A recent advertisement told of a book that explained how the author had discovered the secret of making money and guaranteed that the readers who faithfully followed his formula would prosper. The secret, it said, was taken from the teaching of Jesus.

But the blessings of Christianity are not material, though these frequently incidentally result. They are spiritual and eternal. We must be careful not to make Christ just a divine bill-payer!

show how true verse 34 is.

7. How does this parable help you put your priorities in order?

A Follower of Christ

Read Philippians 4:10–19.

1. How did Paul react to the lack of money?
   (He had learned to be content either with money or without it.)

2. Where did Paul obtain the strength to face adverse circumstances?
   (From Christ who strengthened him.)

3. Is it easier for you to handle humble circumstances or prosperity?

   Why?

4. How does having your priorities straight affect material changes in your life—whether for the better or worse?
   (It's easier to accept these changes and use them for God's glory.)

5. Study verse 19. Why do you think God promises to supply our needs, but not necessarily our desires?
   (He wants us to be satisfied in Him, not satisfied in our possessions.)

6. Read 1 Timothy 6:17–19. How do these verses compare with the world's view? Be specific.
   (The world opens up savings accounts, builds bigger houses, creates bigger

The man in the parable probably thought that *after* he had expanded his fortune he could straighten out his life with God. God says "this night" your soul shall be required. All his efforts to accumulate material wealth were useless.

? In what ways can we be overly concerned about material things to the neglect of the spiritual? (See 1 John 2:15,16.)

? What is the difference between *using* the things of the world and *loving* them?

When we love *things* more than God, we are guilty of one of the worst kinds of sins.

? What kind of security can be found in money?

? In family relationships?

? In possessing clothes and goods?

? In God?

C. T. Studd was a wealthy, young Cambridge student famous for his skill as a cricket player. He studied the Scripture, especially the story of the rich, young man to whom Jesus said,

corporations, buys more luxuries to say, "Look what I have" or to feel secure. Christians who lay up spiritual treasure already have riches and security that they will never lose.)

7. Against what things did Paul warn the rich in Philippians 4:10–19?
   (Be content with what they have.)

8. What did he exhort them to do?
   (Be generous and willing to share, lay up treasure for themselves as a foundation for the coming age.)

   Why?
   (So they could take hold of the abundant life.)

9. How would your obedience to these verses affect relationships in the following:

   Your family?

   Your church?

   Your neighborhood?

Christ Himself

1. In your own words, write what Jesus Christ did for us according to 2 Corinthians 8:9.
   (Could include: He was rich, but became poor for our sakes, so we through His poverty could become rich.)

"One thing you lack: go, sell everything you have and give to the poor, and you will have treasure in heaven. Then come, follow me" (Mark 10:21).

C. T. Studd felt impressed to do exactly what the rich, young man had failed to do. In simple obedience to the black and white statements of God's Word, he gave away a substantial inheritance. He put God to the test and found that He never fails those who trust Him—neither he nor his wife nor their children ever lacked the necessities of life. He went as a missionary to China, India, and Africa, and through his ministry hundreds of thousands of people were won to Christ.

Consider what he said:

Seeing that some 40 years ago at God's command I left mother, brethren, friends, fortune, and all that is usually thought to make life worth living, and have so continued ever since, I have been called fool and fanatic again and again, yet lived to prove that the worldly counselors were the fools. 'Cursed is he that trusteth in man' does not make a very good pillow for a dying man, but there is much comfort in the other one, 'Blessed is he that trusteth in the Lord.'

The life of C. T. Studd was a testimony to the world that when a believer is obedient to the commands of Jesus Christ, every *need* in life will be supplied.

2. Read 2 Corinthians 9:7,8.

   Because of what Jesus Christ has done for us, we should be willing to invest part of our income in His work. When we give toward His work, what should our attitude be (verse 7)?

   (It should come from our hearts willingly and cheerfully.)

3. Note the use of the words *all* and *every* in verse 8. Why can you be cheerful even though you may give sacrificially to God's work?

   (God is still supplying all your needs.)

   When you have done this, what has been the result?

LIFE APPLICATION

1. Think about the circumstances of your life. What part do they play in your search for security?

2. In which areas of your life do you feel greedy or materialistic?

   How have these feelings affected your spiritual well-being?

3. List on this chart your most important possessions. Prayerfully yield each one to God. Then write down one way you can show that it belongs to Him.

The One who spoke of detachment from material things was Himself detached. Jesus, the creator and ruler of the universe, owned no property and often had no place to sleep (Matthew 8:20). He had every right to live in a palace with servants and riches. But He chose to live humbly so He could accomplish His mission.

Conclusion and Application

God will give us what we need to do His will. And He expects us to give out of faith that He will supply. Faith always needs an action to complete it. The way to show our faith in God's ability to supply our needs is to give generously.

(See the chart in the student's book.)

Closing Prayer

Recap

Opening Prayer

Discussion Starter

(Assign students to complete the first two statements of the Recap study in their books. Then ask:)

❓ Why do you think God requires inward obedience from the heart rather than outward conformance to rules and regulations?

❓ What difference does it make?

Lesson Development

(Any appropriate material from previous lessons that was not sufficiently covered could be used at this time, and you also may deal with any point that the group members may not understand as well as they could.)

(Then go over the remaining Recap questions and answers. This material will benefit both the students and you by giving you a deeper appreciation of God's Word.)

Leader's Objective: To help group members better understand the difference between true obedience and outward conformity and make a commitment to obey God from the heart

LESSON 7

The following questions will help you review this Step. If necessary, reread the appropriate lesson(s).

1. Complete the following statements:

   True obedience to God *is not...*
   (Sacrifice or outward conformity to rules and requirements.)

   True obedience really *is...*
   (An attitude of the heart that willingly and joyfully conforms to God's will.)

2. How is your obedience expressed in the following:

   Your attitude toward God's will?

   The sexual purity of your life?

   The degree of satisfaction you find in your possessions?

   Your courage in witnessing for Christ?

   Your speech?

   The true motivation for your actions?

   (Ask your students to pick the area of obedience that concerns them most. Instruct them to look up verses from a chapter dealing with that topic and write down specific ways God helps us obey Him. Then ask students to think of a hypothetical situation showing how the verses could apply in someone's life. When the students finish, discuss each situation. If no one selects an area, invite students to give an example from their lives.)

3. Describe the result of a young child's obedience to his parents. Compare it to a Christian's relationship with his heavenly Father.

   How has your obedience to God benefited your life?

   (Use your Bible concordance to look up verses that describe God's role as a father. Discuss how these verses assure you of His love and care for us.)

LIFE APPLICATION

1. List the area from this study that concerns you most.

2. Review the verses that pertain to that area.

3. Write down at least three ways you can grow in that area.

   1)
   2)
   3)

4. Commit this area to the Lord, asking Him to fill you with His Holy Spirit and to help you grow in this area.

Conclusion and Application

(With your group, work through the questions in the "Life Application." Do not ask members to mention their area of concern aloud. Encourage students to commit that area to God.)

Closing Prayer

(Pray for each group member by name, asking God to help that person obey in the area he listed. Then pause for a few moments of silent prayer to allow students to make their commitments. Close by thanking God for giving us the power to obey Him.)

The *Christian* **Witnessing** *and*

Bringing Words of Hope to the World Around You

STEP 7

Why We Witness

Opening Prayer

Discussion Starter

A young man rushed home from a Billy Graham meeting to the apartment he shared with a friend. They had roomed together for several years. "I have to tell you something!" he exclaimed to his friend. "Tonight I invited Christ to be my Savior, and He's changed my life."

His friend smiled. "Wonderful. I've been hoping you would do that. I've been living the Christian life all these years hoping you would trust Christ as your Savior."

The new Christian's eyebrows rose. "You live such a perfect life! I kept trying to do the same, but couldn't. Tonight I invited Jesus to be my Savior because I failed to live up to your standard. Why didn't you tell me why you can live the way do you? Why didn't you tell me how I could know Christ, too?"

 After hearing this illustration, what would you say to a person who claims to witness for Christ only through the way he lives?

Leader's Objective: To demonstrate the reason for verbally witnessing for Christ

LESSON 1

Bible Study

What Is a Witness?

1. Describe what a witness testifies to in a courtroom.
   (Tells what he has experienced.)

   How is that like sharing your faith in Christ?
   (We are to tell what Christ has done for us.)

2. What are you admonished to do in Psalm 107:2 (use *The Living Bible*)?
   (Speak out! Tell others He has saved you.)

   Why is this hard for you to do?

3. How have you followed this admonishment today?

   This week?

   This month?

   If you have not, what is keeping you from witnessing?

The Motivation for Witnessing

1. What did Jesus command you to do (Mark 16:15; Matthew 28:19, 20)?
   (Go into all the world and preach; make disciples of all nations, teach them.)

2. Read Acts 20:24–27,31, 32.

   How important would you say Paul's ministry of

Lesson Development

(Encourage students to read the article, "Take the Challenge; Experience the Adventure" at the beginning of their Study Guide on their own time if they have not already done so.)

(Ask one of the group members to summarize the paragraphs appearing at the opening of this lesson in the student's book. Note the diagram and discuss it.)

❓What is a witness?

A witness is any Christian who bears testimony to the death, burial, and resurrection of Jesus Christ by his actions and by his words.

Romans 10:14 says:
> How can they believe in the one of whom they have not heard?

❓What do you think this verse says about our responsibility to witness with our lips?

A witness is one who first receives the gospel himself, then proclaims that truth to others. One can never teach or testify to a truth that he does not first personally believe and practice.

(Ask if any student has served as a witness in a court case. If so, invite him to tell what happened. Then relate his experience to how we are to serve as witnesses for Christ.)

witnessing was to him?
(More than life itself.)

Why?
(He wanted to complete the task that God had given him.)

3. Read 2 Corinthians 5:14, 15.

   What caused Paul to witness?
   (The love of Christ, His death for all.)

   What attitude should we have about what Jesus has done for us?
   (We should no longer live for ourselves, but for Him.)

   How should that change our lives?
   (We should do what He asks us to do, not live for our selfish desires.)

4. What does Jesus Christ say about the one who is ashamed of Him (Luke 9:26)?
   (The Son of Man will be ashamed of that person.)

   How should this affect your witness?

5. If you are faithful to follow Jesus, what does He promise to do (Matthew 4:19)?
   (He will make you fishers of men.)

   How has He helped you do this?

The Message

1. We are called Christ's ambassadors in 2 Corinthians 5:18–20. (An am-

The biblical position on witnessing is as follows:

◆ People are lost without Christ and hungry for God (Matthew 9:37,38; John 4:28–39).

◆ Jesus Christ is the only Savior (John 14:6; Acts 4:12; 1 Timothy 2:5).

◆ We have a commission and responsibility (Acts 1:8).

◆ Those who spread the gospel are blessed (Romans 10:15).

◆ The early church was active in witnessing (Acts 4:2,31; 5:42; 8:4; 15:35).

◆ The Lord added new believers to the church (Acts 2:41,47; 4:4; 11:18).

Christ, who is our example, did the following:

◆ *Talked with individuals*
Nicodemus (John 3:1–21)
The Samaritan woman (John 4:1–42)

◆ *Talked with groups*
Crowd of 5,000 people (John 6:1–15)
In the temple (John 8:1–12)
The Pharisees (John 8:13–59)
The disciples (John 13:1–17)

Our responsibility is the same:

◆ *Talk with individuals*

◆ *Talk with groups*
Family
Close friends
Others as appropriate

bassador is one who is appointed to represent his country in a foreign land.) Reflect on the duties of an ambassador.

How do these relate to the Christian life and to witnessing about your faith in Christ?
(God relays His message through us; we are not citizens of this world, but of God's kingdom; our lifestyle reflects on God's reputation; our authority comes from God, not from any man; non-Christians will know what God is like through our example.)

2. Why did Jesus say He came into this world (Luke 19:10; Mark 10:45)?
(To seek and to save what was lost.)

3. As a representative of Christ, what would be your message to those who do not know Him personally? Write your answer in words you could use with a non-Christian.

4. How does Paul express the message in 1 Corinthians 15:3,4?
(Christ died for our sins, was buried, and raised again according to the Scriptures.)

LIFE APPLICATION

1. Take several moments to reflect on what your relationship with Jesus Christ means to you. Complete this statement:

Other reasons for witnessing include the following:

◆ It is our responsibility (Ezekiel 3:18)

◆ To glorify God (John 15:8)

◆ So our prayers will be answered (John 15:16)

❷ What have you found effective in witnessing for Christ?

(If your students have never written out a three-minute testimony, now might be a good time to do that.)

Acts 20:17–38 is an example of how Paul felt about those to whom he witnessed. Compare Acts 20:20,21 and Ezekiel 33:9.

❷ How important did Paul consider the message he was bringing?

Conclusion and Application

The desire to witness is not natural to us. Satan uses our old nature, which is still within us, to keep our hearts cold to the spiritual needs of our friends.

Because Christ rose from the dead and lives in me, I . . .

Isn't this truly the greatest, most joyful news you could ever share with another person?

2. Based on your obedience to Christ's command to share your faith with others, what conclusion do you think He would draw about your love for Him?

3. Why do you believe it is important that you, personally, be a witness for Christ?

4. Can you think of at least two people with whom God led you to share Christ during the past week?

1)

2)

How did you respond?

How would you like to respond?

But if we remember what Christ has done for us and what it will mean to us if those friends come to know Him too, our desire to witness can be awakened. And when we rely on the Holy Spirit to do His work in and through us, we often see great victories.

Closing Prayer

Jesus Shows How to Witness

Opening Prayer

Discussion Starter

 Suppose you want to share your Christian faith with someone you know. How would you begin?

Lesson Development

(Ask one of the group members to summarize the paragraphs appearing at the opening of this lesson in the student's book. Note the diagram and discuss it.)

In Lesson 1 we considered why we witness. Many reasons were suggested. An additional reason is that we would never have received Christ if someone had not witnessed to us. We are debtors to Christ and to the person who introduced us to Christ, so we in turn must tell others.

One reason so few Christians witness for Christ is that they don't know how to go about it. But our Lord has given explicit instructions on why and how to witness.

❖

Leader's Objective: To show the students new approaches and techniques of witnessing as illustrated in Christ's example

---

LESSON 2

Bible Study

Example of Jesus

Read John 4:1–42.

1. What everyday experience did Jesus use as an opportunity for witnessing?
   (Being thirsty.)

2. What do you think is the advantage of beginning a conversation on the level of a person's immediate interest?
   (They can relate to what you are telling them.)

   Think of an occasion in which you used a person's special interest to share Christ with him. How did he respond?

3. List some of your natural opportunities to witness for Christ.

4. Why do you suppose Jesus sent all twelve of His disciples to buy provisions when two of them could have done it?
   (He wanted an opportunity to talk with the woman alone.)

5. Who spoke first, Jesus or the woman of Samaria?
   (Jesus.)

   Why is this significant when considering how to witness?
   (He was willing to talk with anyone who had a need regardless of race, creed, or social status.)

Jesus gave us examples from His own life to follow. These methods have been recorded in the account of His discussion with the Samaritan woman in the fourth chapter of John.

He began His conversation with her on a topic of interest to both of them. Jesus was sitting by the well at noontime when it was hot, and he was thirsty. When she came to draw water, He asked her for a drink.

It was unheard of for a Jew to speak to someone from Samaria, let alone talk to a Samaritan woman. To the Jews, Samaritans were half-breeds who were held in contempt. Yet Jesus challenged this woman with His own claims about Himself and her need for what He could do for her.

6. What did Jesus do repeatedly when the woman tried to divert His attention from her sin and her need?
(He had a set purpose and would not be sidetracked; He kept bringing the subject back to her need.)

Jesus was tactful, kind, and considerate in His dealings with the woman. He answered her questions, but He always returned to her problem.

Responses of the Samaritan Woman

1. How did the woman first respond to Jesus' approach?
(With surprise and disbelief.)

How does verse 15 indicate that her attitude changed?
(She asked Him for the living water.)

What do you think brought it about?
(He was genuinely interested in her and He talked to her about a need she had.)

2. What did Jesus say that demonstrated His divine powers?
(He knew about her husbands.)

3. How did Jesus describe God (verse 24)?
(As a Spirit.)

Why is this statement important?
(To know God, we must understand who He is and how we can worship Him.)

4. Who was the woman looking for and why?
(For the Messiah. He

Jesus was a good listener and did not force His witness, which is a necessary characteristic in witnessing! Often we must listen and hear the other person's viewpoint before we can give the gospel message. The non-Christian often has misconceptions that he will discover are wrong as we patiently listen.

*would tell them every-
thing.)*

5. What did Jesus claim
   about Himself?
   *(He said He was the Mes-
   siah.)*

Effectiveness of Jesus' Witness

1. How effective was the approach Jesus used in witnessing to this woman of
   Samaria?
   (Very effective.)

2. What was the result of
   His witness?
   *(She believed, and imme-
   diately went to tell others.)*

3. How did the people to
   whom she witnessed re-
   spond?
   *(Many believed in Jesus
   and came to hear Him.)*

   Why?
   *(She convinced them that
   she had met the Messiah.)*

"Sound Barriers"

Sometimes witnessing can
seem like breaking a sound
barrier, like when an airplane accelerates to super-
sonic speed. Introducing the
subject of Jesus can produce
much stress and nervous-
ness.

The *first sound barrier* occurs when we first mention
the name of Jesus Christ and
the value of knowing Him.
Once we turn the conversation from dating, fashions,
politics, work, sports, or any
other topic to spiritual
things, we have broken the

The Samaritan woman knew very
little about Jesus, but she told the
people in her town what she had seen,
heard, and felt. Many in the town came
to hear Christ because of her report,
and many believed when they heard
Him.

Our responsibility is to share the
good news about Jesus Christ with
everyone who will listen. They will not
believe because of what we say, but
because of what God the Spirit says to
them through the written Word. As
we become more skillful in using His
Word, we become more effective in
introducing men and women to Christ.

(Discuss how each of these sound
barriers makes your students feel.
Encourage group members to relate
examples from actual situations on
how they have overcome each barrier.)

first barrier. It is sometimes hard to do, and it does not always come easily.

The *second sound barrier* comes when we present the gospel. That nervous feeling returns once again. We must blast through this one also because many people, when they understand who Jesus Christ is and what He has done for them, *will* want Him in their lives.

The *last barrier,* asking the person to receive Christ right now, is the most difficult. But this is the most important step. Often we tell the person how to become a Christian and then just leave him high and dry. Until we ask the person to trust Christ as his or her Savior and Lord, our witness is not complete.

LIFE APPLICATION

1. Think of the last time you encountered the first barrier. How did you begin your conversation about Christ?

   How could you have handled it better?

2. How did the person respond when you asked him to receive Christ?

   If the person did not receive Christ, how could you have been more effective in your approach?

3. What is the one thing you have learned from Christ's example that you

(Also give examples from your witnessing experiences. Often, talking about times when you failed to break one of these barriers can help you gain insights on a better way to approach and overcome barriers.)

Conclusion and Application

Christ demonstrated clearly that the woman accepted His message because He helped her understand who He was and all that He said. Obedience to what Christ says is what brings us to fully understand and know Him.

The only real way to learn to witness and become effective at it is to *do* it. It is only by trying that one ever succeeds. The Word of God says: "He who wins souls is wise" (Proverbs 11:30). You will be amazed at how many people will appreciate your concern for them and be genuinely grateful that you talked to them.

can apply most in your own witnessing?

4. What do you think hinders your witnessing most?

List some practical ways you can overcome it.

Closing Prayer

Qualifications for Witnessing

Opening Prayer

Discussion Starter

(Brainstorm about qualifications your students think are necessary in the lives of those who desire to be effective witnesses for Jesus. Write the qualifications on a flip chart or chalkboard and checkmark each quality that you find in the lesson. At the end of the session, note each quality that has not been checked and discuss how important it is to your witness.)

Lesson Development

(Ask one of the group members to summarize the paragraphs appearing at the opening of this lesson in the student's book. Note the diagram and discuss it.)

Leader's Objective: To help students take a personal inventory of their spiritual qualifications for witnessing

L E S S O N   3

Bible Study

Philip's Opportunity

Read Acts 8:26–40.

1. According to verses 26 and 27, why do you think God called Philip for this particular assignment?
   (He was obedient.)

2. To whom did Philip witness (verse 27)?
   (An Ethiopian eunuch who was court official and treasurer for the queen.)

3. Who told Philip to join the chariot (verse 29)?
   (The Holy Spirit.)

   Does the Holy Spirit lead us in this same way today?
   (Yes.)

   Describe an example from your life.

4. How did Philip respond?
   (He ran up to the chariot.)

5. How did Philip approach the man (verse 30)?
   (He asked the Ethiopian if he understood what he was reading.)

6. Was the man ready?
   (Yes.)

   Why?
   (He was reading God's Word.)

   What was his response?
   (He wanted Philip to help him understand what he was reading.)

7. What Old Testament passage was the Ethiopian

(Read Acts 8:1–8.)

You will notice that persecution did not stop Philip. It only opened the door for a vital witness in Samaria.

God sent an angel to command Philip to leave a revival where many were responding to the gospel and go to the desert. Philip was humble and obedient. He was God's key man, and God depended on him because he was dependable.

The Word of God is the only effective means of opening up the minds and hearts of people to the gospel. Philosophy, sociology, and other studies will not meet the needs of the heart of man. The reading of God's Word had so prepared the Ethiopian for Philip's witness that the man asked Philip who Isaiah was speaking about.

The Holy Spirit had prepared the Ethiopian's heart. However, God used a man to win him. Philip had earned the right to be used.

reading (verses 28,32, 33)? *(Isaiah 53.)*

To whom did this refer? *(Christ.)*

8. What was Philip's message?
(The good news of Jesus.)

Philip's Qualifications

1. Philip demonstrated at least eight qualities that contributed to his effectiveness for Christ. Place the appropriate verses after the following words:

   ◆ Knowledge of the Word of God *(35)*

   ◆ Boldness *(30)*

   ◆ Compassion *(30)*

   ◆ Humility *(27)*

   ◆ Obedience *(27, 30)*

   ◆ Receptivity, sensitivity to guidance *(27, 30, 35, 38)*

   ◆ Tact *(30)*

   ◆ Enthusiasm *(27, 30, 40)*

2. Reflect on each of these qualities. How are they at work in your life?

   Which ones do you have difficulty with?

   List ways you could strengthen these areas.

Possible Hindrances to Our Witnessing

After each hindrance, describe how it affects your witnessing.

1. *Spiritual lethargy*

   If you are not excited about something, chances

After Philip had baptized the Ethiopian, God's Spirit brought Philip to Azotus. The miraculous way the Holy Spirit transported Philip from place to place indicated God's delight in using him.

(Discuss why each of these qualities will help make us more effective in our witnessing.)

God does not want us to wait until we feel we have mastered each of the qualities before we witness. God wants us to be faithful to witness and to be building these qualities into our lives as we go. Sometimes the experiences we encounter as we introduce others to Christ will help us build good qualities.

(When discussing these hindrances, do not ask students to reveal personal answers unless they want to. Instead, emphasize how the hindrance can affect witnessing in a general way and encourage students to write in their books how it affects them personally.)

are you won't tell many people about it. For many Christians, the excitement of the Christian walk has been dulled by everyday distractions, materialistic pursuits, and unconfessed sin. Like the believers in Ephesus, these men and women have left their first love.

How it affects my witnessing:

2. *Lack of preparation*

Personal dedication to Christ and understanding how to witness and what to say are imperative. Preparing your heart through prayer gives you the right attitude and opens yourself to the power of the Holy Spirit.

How it affects my witnessing:

3. *Fear of man*

We possibly will be persecuted by unbelievers, as well as believers, but the fear of man will prove to be a snare (Proverbs 29:25). Christ said of those who feared to confess His name, "They loved the praise of men more than the praise of God."

How it affects my witnessing:

4. *Fear of failure*

"They won't believe; they won't accept such simple truth." Certainly some will reject or neglect the gospel, but you should

❓Since spiritual lethargy can creep up without being noticed, how can you recognize it in your life?

We can avoid spiritual lethargy by walking close to God and asking Him to reveal the attitudes of our heart (Psalm 139:23,24).

❓What happens when you aren't prepared for witnessing and you encounter a particularly difficult situation?

You won't have the guiding of the Holy Spirit or you won't know how to handle the situation.

❓How can you conquer this fear?

We can witness for God's glory. Focusing on Him keeps our eyes off the situation. Praying for those we want to witness to will give us love for them and will help remove our fear (1 John 4:18).

❓If someone rejects your witness, is that a sign of failure?

No. It may mean that they are dealing with conviction of sin or that their hearts haven't been totally prepared

never believe the lie of Satan that people are not interested. Christ said, "Open your eyes and look at the fields! They are [present tense... 'now'] ripe for harvest" (John 4:35).

Jesus said, "The harvest is plentiful but the workers are few. Ask the Lord ... to send out workers into his harvest field" (Matthew 9:37,38).

How it affects my witnessing:

5. *Fear that the new Christian will not go on and grow in the Lord*

Review the parable of the sower (Matthew 13:1–23). Every seed of the Word of God will fall on one of these types of soil: path, rocky, thorny, or good. Some new Christians will become disciples. Keep up the faithful search for these disciples!

How it affects my witnessing:

6. *Lack of practical "know-how"*

As a result of thousands of surveys, we have found that the vast majority of Christians today not only believe they should share their faith, but they also really want to. However, they don't receive the practical hands-on training that will ease their fears and help them

for God's message. Your witness may start them searching for God.

❓How would you define failure in witnessing?

Christ did not convert everyone He encountered. The scribes and the Pharisees spent much time with Jesus and saw His miracles and His compassion. Yet they did not accept Jesus as their Savior. Sometimes we set unrealistic standards for witnessing—such as seeing almost everyone we speak to come to Christ. This sets us up for a feeling of failure.

❓How can the parable of the sower in Matthew 13 encourage us when someone we have introduced to Christ does not grow as we hoped?

Through the parable we see that not everyone will respond as we hope they will. It is God who produces growth in people's lives; it is our responsibility to be faithful to do His work.

❓How would you rate your "know-how" in witnessing?

❓If you received training in how to share your faith, how did that help your fear of not knowing what to say?

witness effectively. The result is a guilt trip: They know they should, but they hesitate because they don't know how.

How it affects my witnessing:

LIFE APPLICATION

1. Which hindrance is the greatest problem for you?

   Why?

   What steps will you take to overcome it?

2. Have you let distractions, lethargy, materialism, or unconfessed sin rob you of your excitement in Christ?

   In what ways?

3. In a time of quiet prayer, ask God to reveal any unconfessed sin in your life. After reading 1 John 1:9, confess any such sin, and ask for God's cleansing and forgiveness.

4. Look back through the list of qualities in Philip's life and identify the ones you would like to have God develop in your life.

5. Spend some time in prayer, asking God for those characteristics to be developed in your life and witness.

Conclusion and Application

When we witness, we do not find it easy to be prayerful, tactful, compassionate, or humble. It is Christ in us who gives us the right attitude. It is not what we are or were, but what He is in and through us that draws others to Him. Our responsibility is to deny self and daily take up the cross, and let Him live His resurrection life through us. We must invite Him, His Spirit, and His Word to be central in our lives.

(Ask students to turn to the sections titled "How to Share Christ With Others" and "Four Spiritual Laws" in the back of their Study Guides. Encourage them to read through both sections before the next session so they can share their questions and insights with the group.)

Closing Prayer

Witnessing and the Word of God

Opening Prayer

Discussion Starter

(Invite students to ask questions and share insights about "How to Share Christ With Others" and "Four Spiritual Laws" from the back of their books. You may want to give each student a copy of the "Four Spiritual Laws" booklet and encourage them to use the booklet in a witnessing situation before the next session. You can obtain copies of the "Four Spiritual Laws" booklets from a local Christian bookstore, mail-order distributor, or NewLife Publications.)

One of the most important areas in which many Christians fail in living a life for Christ is in memorizing and effectively using the Word of God. This can be a hindrance to sharing our faith in Christ. Let's look at the important link between the Bible and witnessing.

Leader's Objective: To demonstrate to students the value of memorizing and using Bible verses when witnessing

LESSON 4

Bible Study

Peter's Witness

Read Acts 2.

1. Of all the disciples, why was Peter the least qualified to witness for Christ, and yet the most qualified, as suggested above and in Acts 2?
   (He had denied Christ, but he had a thorough knowledge of the Old Testament on which to base his preaching.)

2. How much of Peter's sermon involves quotations from the Bible (such as from Joel, David, etc.)?
   (More than half.)

   How much Scripture memorization do you suppose Peter had done in his early life?

3. What part does the Holy Spirit play . . .

   In those who share Christ's message (John 14:26)?
   (He will teach and bring to remembrance what Jesus has said.)

   In those who hear Christ's message (John 16:8–11)?
   (He will convict of sin, righteousness, and judgment.)

4. What part does prayer play (Acts 2:42–47)?

5. What did Peter say to convince them of sin (Acts 2:23,36)?

Lesson Development

(Ask one of the group members to summarize the paragraphs appearing at the opening of this lesson in the student's book. Note the diagram and discuss it.)

Peter had no notes to which he could refer. His address was impromptu and based upon Old Testament Scripture that he had studied from an early age.

No doubt the disciples studied the Scriptures as they traveled with the Lord Jesus. Often He explained or expounded the Scriptures to the disciples as they journeyed.

The success of what Peter said was due entirely to the Word of God affecting the hearts of the hearers through the Holy Spirit.

Peter's first sermon after Pentecost contained the Word of God and was preached in the power of the Holy Spirit.

The Holy Spirit used the Old Testament to convict Peter's listeners about their sins—particularly the sin of crucifying Christ.

(They had crucified the one whom God had sent.)

6. List some great things Peter preached about God (verses 24,34,35,38, 39).
(He raised Christ; conquered our enemies; made Jesus Lord and Christ; gave us the Holy Spirit.)

The Crowd's Response

1. How many became Christians that day?
(3,000.)

2. List the emotions experienced by the hearers before and after conversion.
(Bewilderment, derision, repentance, joy.)

3. Why did some listeners react in anger first?
(Peter told them about their sin.)

The Power of the Word

1. Summarize Isaiah 55:11.
(The Word of God will do what God intends it to do.)

2. According to Hebrews 4:12, how does the Word of God affect the non-Christian as you witness?
(Judges the thoughts and attitudes of the heart.)

3. In Ephesians 6:17, what is the Bible called?
(The sword of the Spirit.)
Why?
(Because it penetrates soul and spirit.)

As you will see in more detail in Lesson 6, it is the Holy Spirit who brings

The Spirit of God uses the Bible to exalt the Son of God through whom people become the children of God.

The Word of God is the most effectual tool in dealing with people about their need of Christ. Their questions are only truly answered in the Bible. There is convincing power only in a presentation of what the Word of God has to say. Therefore, we should keep bringing the non-Christian back to what God says rather than what we think. Our opinions are always secondary to what God actually says in His Word.

men to grips with the issues as we witness.

The Value of Scripture Memorization

Committing portions of Scripture to memory is the best way to know the Word of God, and as a result, to know Christ. Also, by having the promises and commands of the Word memorized, we can apply them to any life situation at a moment's notice, especially when we want to use them in an unexpected witnessing opportunity.

1. List some things God has promised us (2 Peter 1:2–4).
   (Abundant grace and peace; everything we need for life and godliness; participation in the divine nature and escape from corruption in the world.)

2. List some ways that memorizing Scripture will help you, according to the following verses:

   1 Peter 2:2,3 and Hebrews 5:12–14
   (To grow in respect to salvation, grow to be teachers, and learn to distinguish good from evil.)

   Joshua 1:8 and Psalm 1:1–3
   (We will be careful to do everything written in it; be prosperous and successful; be fruitful.)

   Psalm 32:8
   (God will instruct us and

We are to set aside our hearts for the Lord God according to 1 Peter 3:15. Then we are to be ready to give a scriptural answer to any question men can ask concerning the hope (which is actually a firm conviction) of our salvation, with gentleness, humility, and respect for them as individuals. We must study the Scriptures diligently if we are to be effective witnesses for Christ.

The psalmist says clearly that it is the Word of God that keeps the Christian from sinning against God and the Word is the means by which the Christian purifies his or her life.

❓What does God mean by success?

teach us how to live; He will counsel and watch over us.)

3. List some ways, mentioned in the following references, in which God's Word will nourish your growth:

    Romans 10:17
    (Hearing God's Word will deepen my faith.)

    Psalm 119:11
    (Hiding the Word in my heart will keep me from sin.)

    Psalm 119:165
    (Will give me great peace and keep me from stumbling.)

4. Name one thing for which God's Word was absolutely essential, according to 1 Peter 1:23.
    (We are born again through it.)

LIFE APPLICATION

1. List specific ways in which the preceding Bible verses will help you in your witnessing.

2. Which verse do you believe you need the most?

3. Memorize that passage.

4. How will you apply it?

 How is that different from what the world means by success?

 How did God use the Bible to bring you into His family?

Conclusion and Application

Christians who have been used most successfully are those who have memorized the Word of God systematically and then obeyed it. To introduce men and women to Christ, we must learn the Scriptures, and memorizing is a vital part of the process.

Closing Prayer

Witnessing and Prayer

Opening Prayer

Discussion Starter

(Invite students to share their experiences in using the "Four Spiritual Laws" with non-Christians. Be sure to relate your experiences also.)

 Have you ever wondered why some people see fruit in their witness for Christ and others do not?

 Why do you think some Christians seem to have more joy in witnessing than others?

Prayer is the place where people are won to Christ; preaching and personal witnessing simply gather in the fruit. If we really believe this, we will certainly spend more time praying before we witness.

❖

Leader's Objective: To demonstrate the vital part that prayer plays in effective witnessing for Christ, and to motivate students to pray with faith for those who need Christ

LESSON 5

Bible Study

What the Early Christians Prayed For

Read Acts 4.

1. What problem did these Christians face?
   (Persecution and danger.)

2. What do you think would have happened to Christianity if they had stopped witnessing?
   (It would not have spread.)

3. How important is the soul-winning witness to the cause of Christ today?
   (It is essential to the growth of the church, and to glorify God.)

   Give two specific examples.

   1)
   2)

4. How did these Christians solve their dilemma:

   Before magistrates?
   (They told the truth about Jesus.)

   In private?
   (They prayed.)

   In public?
   (They preached Christ.)

5. What protected them (Acts 4:21)?
   (The people were praising God.)

6. For what did they pray?
   (Boldness to speak God's Word.)

Lesson Development

(Ask one of the group members to summarize the paragraphs appearing at the opening of this lesson in the student's book. Note the diagram and discuss it.)

The early Christians did not pray that they might be spared from persecution, nor did they keep silent in the midst of personal danger. They wanted power and boldness to proclaim Christ.

Today, boldness is a scarce commodity in Christian circles. We are afraid of what men will think of us or do to us. But God has not given us a spirit of fear, but a spirit of power, of love, and of a sound mind (2 Timothy 1:7). We need to pray for boldness!

The Answer to Their Prayer

The answer to their prayer was immediate and definite. They prayed, and God answered as He had promised. None could stand against them, and they were victorious in Christ.

(Invite students to share times when their prayers had an immediate answer.)

1. How can you profit from their courage, prayer, and effective witness?

2. Successful praying is simply asking God to work according to His will and leaving the results to Him.

   From this statement, what part does faith play in your prayers?
   (My responsibility is to pray in faith and God gives the answer.)

   ❷Is faith a feeling you work up when you pray? If not, then what is faith in prayer?

   Give an example.

3. In what ways can other people depend on your courage, prayer, and witness?

4. Someone has said, "Prayer is not an argument with God to persuade Him to move things our way, but an exercise by which we are enabled by His Spirit to move ourselves His way."

   How does this statement help us understand our role in witnessing?
   (We are always to depend on His Spirit and His power.)

   In our willingness to share our faith?
   (We are to be willing because we know God wants us to witness.)

Many people mistake feeling confident with having faith. Feelings are dependent on many things such as circumstances, emotional and physical well-being, or maybe even the weather. Faith is rooted in our confidence in God and our belief that He can and will answer according to His will. We may not always have the feelings to match our faith.

The Christian's Opposition

1. How were the witnessing Christians of the early church persecuted? (The Book of Acts gives several examples.)
   (They were put in prison, killed, beaten, and ridiculed.)

2. In your opinion, who is the author of resistance to Christian witness?
   (Satan.)

   Why?
   (Satan does not want anyone to receive Christ as Savior, so he puts up as many barriers to witnessing as possible.)

   How does knowing this help you have more courage?
   (I can expect resistance, ask God to help me overcome my fears, and be prepared when I witness.)

God's Timing

1. Success in witnessing is simply taking the initiative to share Christ in the power of the Holy Spirit and leaving the results to God. How do you react when a person does not receive the gospel right away?

   How should you react?

2. God's will does not operate according to our timetable. Think of a situation when God's answer to your prayer did not come at the time you expected.

Although many believe that Satan does not exist, the Word of God verifies his presence and speaks of his work against God in concrete terms. But Satan cannot overcome and defeat a praying Christian. Jesus told Peter, "Watch and pray so that you will not fall into temptation" (Matthew 26:41). Battles are being waged in the heavens between Satan's forces and Christ and His angels.

We do not struggle against flesh and blood, which appear tangible, but against powers that energize this world system, and against spiritual corruption that is all around us.

❓According to Ephesians 6:11–13, what should we do to help us in our battle?

It is the prayers of the believers that bring victory on earth and in heaven. God has included us in the battles and victories of the ages, and nowhere can we have a more powerful part than in the field of prayer.

These Scripture passages show unique answers to prayer of people facing opposition:

◆ Jehoshaphat (2 Chronicles 20:1–30)

◆ Hezekiah (2 Chronicles 32:1–23)

◆ Peter in prison (Acts 12:1–17)

◆ Paul and Silas in prison (Acts 16:25–40)

(Take a few minutes to pray for boldness. Invite group members to pray for each other specifically. By now, your group members should know each other well enough to lift

How did He answer that prayer?

Relate the timing of this incident to waiting on God for His harvest.

LIFE APPLICATION

1. What specific opposition have you encountered recently, and how did you deal with it?

2. How could you have handled it better?

3. Which special friends or loved ones have been on your heart recently?

   Have you ever felt that a particular situation was hopeless?

   How can prayer change that attitude?

4. Look up verses that you can use when you feel a situation is hopeless. Put these verses on a card in your Bible so you can review them and pray over them the next time you get discouraged about witnessing. Use the index in your Bible to find appropriate verses.

5. What principles have you learned from this study to help you in your prayer and witness to these people?

   Think of each person by name and apply the principles you have learned to each situation.

each other up in the areas they need to grow in their witness for Christ. Also pray for non-Christians that group members have mentioned. Thank God for the opportunities your group has had to share their faith in Christ with others.)

Conclusion and Application

Prayer is the God-ordained way to bring Christ into the lives of men and women so they can find the abundant life here on earth and perfect life in heaven. We must pray for those without Christ. Praying for them will motivate us to reach out and share Christ with them.

(Invite the students to give examples of people who have come to know the Lord as a result of their prayers or the prayers of someone else. If they cannot give any instances, relate a few of your own experiences.)

(References you can suggest to help your students get started are 2 Peter 3:9; Philippians 4:13; and 1 Timothy 2:4.)

6. List at least one prospective witnessing situation and spend a few moments praying specifically for God's leading and empowering through your life.

7. Continue to pray without ceasing, but instead of begging and pleading with God, thank and praise Him by faith that He is going to answer your prayer in His perfect timing.

(Encourage students to continue using the "Four Spiritual Laws" during the week.)

Closing Prayer

(Pray for those people your students have listed in question 6 of the "Life Application." Then close by using the suggestions in question 7.)

Witnessing and the Holy Spirit

Opening Prayer

Discussion Starter

 What do you think is the most important attribute we must have to witness and see results?

 What part does the Holy Spirit play in witnessing?

Lesson Development

(Invite one of the group members to summarize the paragraphs appearing at the opening of this lesson in the student's book. Note the diagram and discuss it.)

No amount of persuasiveness or imagination or ability on our part will ever move any person to receive Jesus Christ as Savior apart from the work of the Holy Spirit in His convicting and regenerative power. Salvation, as the psalmist says, is of the Lord—totally and completely.

❖

Leader's Objective: To demonstrate to students the vital necessity of the Holy Spirit to our witness, and encourage total dependence upon Him

Bible Study

Work of the Holy Spirit in a Believer's Life

Read Acts 6 and 7, and underline every mention of the Holy Spirit.

1. What part did the Holy Spirit play in Stephen's life?
   (He controlled Stephen, gave him courage to witness, and produced results.)

2. What spiritual indictment did Stephen pronounce upon his hearers that cut them to the heart?
   (They were resisting the Holy Spirit, just as their fathers did.)

3. As a Spirit-filled man, Stephen had two purposes that were his greatest concerns, as seen in his desire to witness and in his dying prayer.

   What were they?

   1) *(To present Christ as He is to men as they are.)*

   2) *(That men's sins might be forgiven.)*

4. How do these concerns show the fullness of the Holy Spirit in Stephen? (Compare Galatians 5:22, 23; 2 Corinthians 5:14,15.)
   (He showed fruit of the Spirit and a selfless life, living for the One who died for him.)

Stephen, the first Christian martyr, was an ordinary man. Yet he had a tremendous testimony for Christ. As you read Acts 6 and 8, you will not find the speaking techniques or witnessing methods that Stephen used to introduce people to Christ. However, he was fearless, and moved multitudes with the sincerity and power of his life and witness for Christ.

By examining his life, we will discover the reason for his effectual witness—the person and work of the Holy Spirit who produced in him a mighty likeness to the Son of God. The Holy Spirit gave Stephen the courage, the witness, and the results.

Stephen did not compromise his message regardless of circumstances. He told people what was wrong with them. He spoke of the person of Christ, not of pious platitudes.

One result of being filled with the Spirit is selflessness. Stephen did not fear what man could do to him nor was he defeated by self-consciousness. The Holy Spirit did not play a part in his life, but the Holy Spirit *was* his life. Stephen was full of the Holy Spirit.

The presentation of the person of Christ always brings a reaction from the hearers. In the case of Stephen, rejection and anger resulted in his death. Another reaction is acceptance of Christ and the person bearing the message about Him.

The work of the Holy Spirit always produces conviction of sin in the heart of the sinner, but the reaction to the Spirit's conviction is not always the same.

Work of the Holy Spirit in Witnessing

1. What is the ministry of the Holy Spirit (John 15:26; 16:13,14)?
   (To testify about Christ and glorify Him.)

2. How is it accomplished in a person who witnesses of Christ (Acts 1:8; 6:10)?
   (The Spirit gives that person power, favor with others, and the ability to communicate more effectively.)

   How is it being accomplished in your life?

3. What will the Holy Spirit do for the witnessing person (Acts 4:31)?
   (He will give him guidance, power, and boldness.)

4. What will the Holy Spirit do for the person receiving the Good News (1 Corinthians 2:10–12)?
   (Open the person's understanding to the thoughts of God.)

5. How does that passage compare with 2 Corinthians 4:3,4?
   (Satan blinds people's hearts to God but the Holy Spirit opens their hearts to God's love.)

6. It is the Holy Spirit who brings us face to face with the facts regarding our condition and our need.

(Invite students to share about times when their witnessing produced adverse reactions. Ask:)

❓ Did the reaction necessarily mean you presented Christ in a wrong way?

❓ How do you feel when you are confronted with a sin you have committed?

❓ Does it sometimes take time for you to admit your sin and confess it to God? Why?

❓ How does this relate to a person who is confronted with the fact that he is a sinner doomed to an eternity without God?

This action is called "convicting, reproving, exposing, bringing to light."

If we were to witness on our own, we would accomplish nothing. But when the Holy Spirit uses our witness, He brings a person face to face with important facts, presenting them so forcefully that these facts must be considered.

What are these facts (John 16:7–11)?
(Man is sinful, God is righteous, and the world and its rulers will be judged.)

7. What promise does God give us regarding His Spirit (2 Corinthians 1:21,22)?
(He will put His Spirit in our hearts as a deposit, guaranteeing that we will always belong to God.)

LIFE APPLICATION

1. Record the names of at least three persons to whom you believe God would have you speak about Christ within the next week.

   1)
   2)
   3)

2. Ask the Holy Spirit to prepare these individuals, freeing their minds so they can make a logical, intelligent choice to receive Christ as Savior.

❓How will realizing the intense pain involved in the conviction of sin help your reaction to people who reject or get angry at your witness?

❓How can you use these facts to increase your compassion for non-Christians?

Conclusion and Application

The power evidenced in Stephen's life and ministry and in the life and witness of the early church can be ours if we will only receive it. How do we appropriate it? By yielding our lives completely to Christ and inviting the Holy Spirit to fill us and control us.

All we have to do to place Christ on the throne of our life is ask the Holy Spirit to fill and control us.

❓Would you like to do that right now as we conclude in prayer?

3. Study "How to Share Christ With Others" on pages 65–67. Practice reading through the *Four Spiritual Laws* booklet with a friend.

4. Ask the Holy Spirit to lead you to these individuals at the proper time, and to speak through you in giving them the message of Christ.

   As you witness, remember that it is the Holy Spirit who penetrates the mind of the other person, revealing spiritual truth.

5. Are you sure you are prepared? If not, review the earlier lessons in this Step.

Closing Prayer

(Give students time to silently ask the Holy Spirit to fill and control them. Then close by thanking Him for filling you and for giving power and boldness for witnessing.)

Recap

Opening Prayer

Discussion Starter

(Bring something that is impossible to assemble without directions, such as an intricate model airplane or a jigsaw puzzle without a picture of the finished piece. Ask several students to try to assemble it without directions. Then ask:)

❓Is is frustrating to do something without knowing how? Why?

❓How successful are you at doing something you have never done before without directions?

Many times that's what we expect from non-Christians. We want them to become Christians, but we never show them how. That's why witnessing is so important. Without a verbal explanation of how to receive Christ as Savior, non-Christians may never find the joy and full life we enjoy as children of God.

Leader's Objective: To emphasize the Importance of witnessing and to review the qualifications, methods, and resources available

The following questions will help you review this Step. If necessary, reread the appropriate lesson(s).

1. What is the most important reason you have learned to witness for Christ?

2. How have you overcome the problem that most hinders your witnessing?

3. What is the next most troubling hindrance for you, and how do you plan to overcome it?

4. Summarize why you think a knowledge of the Word of God is important in witnessing.

5. How will prayer specifically help you?

6. Why do you think the Holy Spirit does not speak of Himself?

LIFE APPLICATION

1. Write a three-minute testimony of your personal experience with Christ. Briefly share three things:

   1) What your life was like before your decision

   2) Why and how you received Christ

   3) How Christ has changed your life

   List benefits of knowing Christ. Explain in greater detail what it is like to be

Lesson Development

(Any appropriate material from previous lessons that was not sufficiently covered could be used at this time, and you also may deal with any point that the group members may not understand as well as they could.)

(Then go over the remaining Recap questions and answers. This material will benefit both the students and you by giving you a deeper appreciation of God's Word.)

(Go through pages 65–76 in the student's book. Ask group members to select a partner and practice going through the "Four Spiritual Laws." If you already did this in Lesson 6, discuss ways to introduce the "Four Spiritual Laws" to friends you want to witness to and practice these suggestions.)

Conclusion and Application

(Encourage students to write a three-minute testimony if they haven't already done so. Help them understand that by writing it they will clarify and organize it in their own minds. Rewriting as needed will help them make their testimonies more concise and powerful. Invite a couple students to share their testimony.)

John 15:16 reminds us that Christ has chosen us to be His witnesses. When He asks us to do something, He always gives us what we need to accomplish the task. A clear understanding of His call, of His methods of witness-

a Christian. (Attach your testimony to this lesson.)

2. Begin a prayer diary listing those whom God has laid on your heart to share your faith in Christ. Record:
   ◆ Their prayer needs
   ◆ Their responses to your witness
   ◆ Their spiritual growth

3. List the opportunities God has given you to witness for Him in the past month. Then praise and thank God for them.

ing, and of the power available to us through His Holy Spirit will make it easier to do God's work. Our role is to fully surrender our lives and allow Him to work through us for His glory.

(If you have not already done so, read aloud "A Challenge" on pages 63 and 64 of the students' books.)

Closing Prayer

(Give your group members time for silent prayer to fully surrender themselves to the Lord and to appropriate the fullness and power of the Holy Spirit for witnessing. Then close with a prayer of thanksgiving.)

The Christian and Giving

Rejoicing In His Abundance, Sharing His Resources

STEP 8

God's Ownership Over All

Opening Prayer

Discussion Starter

A steward is not the owner of what he manages. He does not possess the estate. The true owner has the right to demand an accounting from the one he has entrusted with his possessions.

❖ What kind of accounting do you think God should be able to require from us? Why?

Lesson Development

(Encourage students to read the article, "Rejoicing in His Abundance, Sharing His Resources" at the beginning of their Study Guide on their own time if they have not already done so.)

(Ask one of the group members to summarize the paragraphs appearing at the opening of this lesson in the student's book. Note the diagram and discuss it.)

Leader's Objective: To show that God owns everything including our lives and to encourage absolute surrender to His Lordship

LESSON 1

Bible Study

Creation and Fall of Man

1. After what pattern did God create man (Genesis 1:26)?
   (After Himself, in the image of God.)

   Theologians have long debated just what it is in man that constitutes the image of God. That image seems to include the basic characteristics of personality: intellect, emotion, and will. Adam and Eve had intellect (Genesis 2:19), emotion (Genesis 3:10), and will (Genesis 3:6), just as God does.

2. What did man do to bring about separation between himself and God (Genesis 3:1–7)?
   (Disobeyed God's command not to eat of the tree of the knowledge of good and evil.)

   Note: This passage gives important insight into the character of sin. Adam did not get drunk or commit immoral acts. He and Eve merely asserted their independence from God, rebelled against His command, and took control of their own lives. *Sin is being independent of God and running your own life.*

3. How did the sin of man affect his:

Man is not *physically* in God's image, because "God is Spirit" (John 4:24). Man is not *morally* in God's image, because man is sinful and God is holy (Romans 3:23). How then are we made in God's image? With intellect, emotions, and will—the elements of personality.

Man was given intellect to know God, emotions to love God, and a will to serve God. Man was created not only *by* God, but *for* God. The most intelligent animals lack any God-consciousness, but God and man can communicate. Of all His earthly creatures, man alone can have real fellowship with God.

Man fell from fellowship with God, not vice versa. Earth's first couple, Adam and Eve, decided that they could no longer depend on God to give them the best, but that they could gain what they thought God could not give them. They removed their lives from divine control. "Godlessness" is an attitude of being independent of God, which results in dishonesty and immoral acts.

Ephesians 2:1 tells us that, because of sin, man became spiritually dead. Total chaos invaded humanity. And man could no longer know God (1 Corinthians 2:14).

Intellect (2 Corinthians 4:4)?
(Man is blinded to the light of the gospel of the glory of Christ.)

Some non-Christian scholars have suggested that Jesus fed the 5,000 with five loaves and two fishes by hiding the bread in a cave and having His disciples secretly pass it out to them.

Millions of intelligent people believe in such obvious foolishness. They say that Jesus did not exist, or that God does not exist (He is our imagination); even that death does not exist, or that sin does not exist. Others teach that Adam is God, that Jesus married Mary and Martha and had children, that only 144,000 will be saved in the end times to reign with Jesus. Atheism and the cults of our day illustrate the blindness of the natural human mind.

Emotions (Jeremiah 17:9)?
(The heart is more deceitful than all else and is desperately sick.)

Man's emotions also became perverted. He could not love God.

The brutalities of many ideologies including Naziism and Communism, the love for sex that drenches our society, the crime and violence rampant in our cities, the pursuit of wealth above all things, and the worship of idols throughout history are testimony to this.

Will (Romans 6:20)?
(All are slaves to sin.)

The will of man is now enslaved— the non-Christian is the servant (bondslave) of sin. Therefore man cannot serve God. That is why Adam and Eve hid from God, became afraid of God, and became ashamed before God. After they sinned, their sweet communion with God was broken.

4. How did this act of rebellion affect the world (Romans 5:12)?
(Sin and death entered into the world and spread to all men.)

Reconciliation

1. How did God bring us
   back and reconcile us to
   Himself (Romans 5:8–
   10)?
   *(While we were yet sin-
   ners, Christ died for us.)*

2. What has God given us to
   enable us to live for Him
   (John 14:26)?
   *(A Counselor, the Spirit of
   truth, the Holy Spirit.)*

Our Responsibility

1. God now has restored us
   to a position of fellowship
   similar to what Adam
   had. What does that declare about our present
   relationship with God (1
   Corinthians 6:19,20)?
   *(We are not our own; we
   belong to God because He
   has bought us.)*

2. What, then, is to be our
   response to God (Romans
   12:1,2)?
   *(We are to present our
   bodies to God and be transformed in our minds.)*

3. Many people attempt to
   compromise and give
   God less than full allegiance. How did Jesus regard that practice in

Adam's act of independence ruined
the human race, and yet God in His
grace, at the price of Christ's blood,
has redeemed us and restored us. The
Christian who refuses to submit to the
Lordship of Christ *repeats Adam's sin
all over again.*

❓Who is the Holy Spirit (Romans 8:9)?

He is the Spirit of God and the
Spirit of Christ.

❓Where does the Holy Spirit live
(Galatians 4:6)?

He lives in the hearts of believers.

❓What has he come to do (Acts 1:8;
Galatians 5:22,23)?

The Holy Spirit came to empower
believers for witnessing, and to produce
godly fruit in the lives of believers.

❓How must I cooperate (Acts 4:31;
Ephesians 5:18–20)?

We are to pray and be filled with
the Holy Spirit.

Because God has redeemed us
with the precious blood of His Son,
Jesus Christ, all we have belongs to
Him. And we are His stewards.

Foundational to all understanding
of stewardship is that God entrusts us
with the responsibilities of His kingdom. He has put into our hands the
administration of all that He owns.
The Christian steward realizes that in
Christ "we live and move and have our
being" (Acts 17:28). God is our pre-
eminent Master. The whole of our
life—our personality, influence, material substance, everything—is His,

Matthew 12:30?
(He said, "He who is not with me is against me." There is no middle ground.)

4. In Revelation 3:15,16, how did Jesus describe His attitude toward those who will stand neither for nor against Him?
(They are lukewarm, repulsive to Him; He would "spit you out of my mouth.")

5. What logical choice did Elijah present to the people (1 Kings 18:21)?
("If the Lord is God, follow him; but if Baal is God, follow him.")

If Elijah's logic is true, we must take one of two positions. If we determine that Jesus Christ is Lord and God, we must serve Him loyally. If He is not, He is an imposter and Christianity is obviously a hoax. If this were true, we should dissuade men from being Christians. It is one or the other! We must stand either with Christ or against Him, but never try to stand in between.

1. Read Isaiah 48:17–19. What blessings would you lose by going your own way and failing to

even our successes. He holds us accountable for how we manage what He has given us.

A young boy put it well when he responded to a question on the meaning of stewardship. "It means that life is a ship loaded with a cargo of many things on its way to many people in many places," he said. "God is the Owner, but I am the captain of the ship, and He holds me responsible for the distribution."

The divine perspective helps us understand our purpose for living as Christians. Once we have committed ourselves to serving Jesus as Lord of our lives, we must take one more step in our stewardship: representing Him to the world.

Apart from the command to love God and others, our Lord's most important command is to "Go into all the world and preach the good news" and "make disciples of all nations" (Mark 16:15; Matthew 28:19). I am not here merely to enjoy the good life. I am here as a child and a servant of God to invest my time, my talent, and my treasure to seek and to save the lost. This is what our Lord came to do nearly 2,000 years ago, and what He commanded His followers to do generation after generation until His blessed return.

Conclusion and Application

The Bible speaks of God's ownership of man as being twofold: 1) God created man in the beginning; and 2) He redeemed man, or brought him back,

recognize God's owner-
ship?
*(Lack of peace and right-
eousness.)*

2. How much of your life are
   you willing for God to
   control?

   How much of it does He
   control?

3. Is there something in
   your life that you have
   not surrendered to the
   control of your heavenly
   Father?

   What is it and how will
   you now deal with it?

4. What do you think God
   will do with your life if
   you surrender it all to
   Him?

after man turned from Him and became enslaved in sin. And what a price
God paid—the death of His only Son!

In view of this, it would be foolish
for us to turn back to the things of the
world. But it shows true wisdom when
we surrender fully to God's will and
the control of the Holy Spirit.

Only by acknowledging God's
ownership will we truly experience the
blessings God has prepared for us.

Closing Prayer

(Give students a moment for silent
prayer of confession and dedication
and then close with a prayer of thanksgiving.)

Examples of Perfect Giving

Opening Prayer

Discussion Starter

❓In what ways do you think God demonstrated to us how to be a good steward?

Lesson Development

(Ask one of the group members to summarize the paragraphs appearing at the opening of this lesson in the student's book. Note the diagram and discuss it.)

Leader's Objective: To show how God has set the example of good stewardship and to motivate students to live a Spirit-controlled life

![LESSON 2]

Bible Study

Stewardship of God the Father

1. Read John 3:16. What was God's greatest gift to mankind?
   (His Son Jesus.)

2. What else does God give us (Romans 2:4,7; 1 John 5:11)?
   (Kindness, tolerance, patience, honor, eternal life.)

3. Read John 3:34, 10:10, and 14:16. What has the Father given us to enable us to live abundantly?
   (The Holy Spirit.)

4. List some characteristics of God's nature that make giving a priority with Him.
   (Loving, generous, merciful, forgiving.)

Giving began with God the Father. His supernatural expression of giving was in the sacrifice of His only Son that we might receive forgiveness for our sins. God continues to give of Himself today in love, forgiveness, peace, purpose, and power. The Source of all life, He continues to also provide food, air, water, shelter, and clothing.

Stewardship of God the Son

1. List acts of Christ that indicate perfection in His stewardship (Philippians 2:5–8).
   (He did not insist on His right to be equal with God, made Himself nothing, became like a servant, took on human form, humbled Himself, was obedient to death on the cross.)

2. What was Christ's supreme purpose in life (John 6:38; Hebrews 10:7)?
   (To do the will of God.)

Christ was perfect in every aspect of His life. Imagine it! A life without a single moment of sin. Those who were closest to Him—His disciples—would certainly have seen any flaws that would have been in His character. But they testify strongly to His sinlessness.

Wilbur Smith, in his book *Have You Considered Him?*, explains:

Fifteen million minutes of life on this earth, in the midst of a wicked and corrupt generation—every thought, every deed, every purpose, every word, privately and publicly, from the time He opened His baby eyes until He expired on the cross, were all approved of God. Never once did our Lord have to confess any sin, for He had no sin.

Here was One who...never shed a tear of repentance; never regretted a single thought, word, or deed; never needed to asked divine pardon; was never concerned about the salvation of His own soul; and boldly faced all His present and future enemies in the absolute certainty of His spotless purity before God and man.

Jesus was perfect in obedience. His one objective was to obey His Father's will.

❓What was the most important aspect of His Father's will that Jesus came to do (Luke 19:10; 1 Timothy 2:3–4)?

He came to seek and save the lost.

❓How well did He fulfill His Father's will (John 8:29; 2 Corinthians 5:21; 1 Peter 2:22; 1 John 3:5)?

He accomplished the Father's will without sin.

But was Christ sent merely to give us an example—merely to show us a model of life to which we could never attain? No! The Scripture says He came to save us *from* (not *in*) our sins (Matthew 1:21). He promised:

Blessed are those who hunger and thirst for righteousness, for they will be filled (Matthew 5:6).

Jesus was perfect in His dependence on God. He modeled the absolute surrender God wants from us.

Jesus told His disciples that His leaving was good for them because He would send the Holy Spirit to live in

3. Read John 12:23–33.

As part of God's will for Jesus, what was involved (verses 23,27,32,33)?
(A particular kind of death: crucifixion.)

In verse 24, Jesus uses the example of a grain of wheat that is planted in the earth. In what sense does a grain of wheat have to "die" to bring forth fruit?
(It is buried and looks dead.)

How does that apply to us (compare verse 25)?
(We must identify with Christ's death to receive life; we must put to death our old sinful nature.)

If, as a Christian, you are unwilling to make any sacrifice to reach others for Christ, to suffer any hardship, to face any self-denial, to suffer any persecution, but instead you want everything to be comfortable, easy, and effortless, how will this affect your fruit-bearing?

4. List some characteristics of Christ's nature that make giving a priority with Him.
(Humble, willing to sacrifice, loving.)

Stewardship of God the Holy Spirit

1. What are some duties the Holy Spirit performs as God's steward, as revealed in the following verses?

John 16:7–11
(Convicts the world of sin, righteousness, and judgment.)

In what way does this convicting ministry of the Holy Spirit help us in evangelism?
(Prepares people's hearts for God's message.)

John 16:13
(Guides us into truth, will tell us what is to come.)

Note: In a general way, the Holy Spirit guides the believer into spiritual truth. In a specific way, He guided the apostles and early Christians in proclaiming the truth of the gospel and in writing

them (John 16:7). The Holy Spirit is also called the Spirit of Christ. As Christ lived in absolute dependence on His Father (John 5:19,30; 6:57; 8:28), so we are to live in absolute dependence on Christ in the power of the Holy Spirit. The Scripture commands:

> Just as you received Christ Jesus as Lord, continue to live in him (Colossians 2:6).

When we came to Christ, we came as sinners, as people who had no strength and had to depend on Jesus Christ absolutely. We surrendered ourselves to Him (Romans 5:6–9). He did the rest.

The Holy Spirit's example of giving shows us the power of accomplishing God's will without calling attention to Himself. He is equal to God—He is God. Yet He is willing to put aside His glory to do God's work in and through us and to give us life.

❷ How have you seen the Holy Spirit work to prepare someone's heart for the gospel message?

❷ How did that make you feel?

the New Testament Scriptures.

Romans 5:5
(Pours out the love of God into our hearts.)

Romans 8:14
(Leads the sons of God.)

Romans 8:16
(Testifies with our spirits that we are children of God.)

Romans 8:26
(Helps our weakness; intercedes for us in prayer.)

2. When the Holy Spirit controls a person, who is glorifed (John 16:14)? *(Jesus Christ.)*

3. List characteristics of the Holy Spirit's nature that make giving a priority with Him. *(Is a Helper, Counselor, guides, does not want glory for Himself.)*

LIFE APPLICATION

1. How does the giving nature of God the Father inspire you to give?

2. How can you best apply to your life the example that Jesus set? Be specific.

3. What does the Holy Spirit want to do in your life at this time?

4. List ways you can cooperate as suggested in Acts 4:31, Ephesians 5:18–20, and Romans 12:1,2.

❓In what specific ways have you experienced the Holy Spirit pouring out the love of God through you?

The Holy Spirit's purpose is to glorify Christ, and He does so by empowering and enabling you and me to glorify God by the way we live. His resources are at our disposal.

Conclusion and Application

God manifests Himself in three persons: God the Father, God the Son, and God the Holy Spirit. All three have the mind and attributes of God. There is never conflict or disagreement among the three. Yet each demonstrates different characteristics of the one God. This is called the trinity.

We can never understand the divine mystery of three Persons in one, but we can better understand how God gives in many different ways by seeing the perfect stewardship of each Person of the trinity.

Closing Prayer

Stewardship of Our Time

Opening Prayer

Discussion Starter

One morning, a farmer told his wife he was going out to plow the "south forty." He got off to an early start so he could oil the tractor. He needed more oil, so he went to the shop to get it. On the way to the shop, he noticed the pigs weren't fed, so he went to the corncrib where he found some sacks of feed. The sacks reminded him that his potatoes were sprouting. When he started for the potato pit, he passed the woodpile and remembered that his wife wanted wood in the house. As he picked up a few sticks, an ailing chicken passed by. He dropped the wood and reached for the chicken. When evening arrived, the frustrated farmer had not even gotten to the tractor, let alone the field!

? How is this story like living life in the fast lane in our culture?

? How can lack of control in time management thwart God's plans?

Leader's Objective: To help students understand the importance of wisely using their time and to demonstrate how they can be better stewards of their time

Bible Study

Right Attitude About Time
Read Psalm 90:12.

1. What should be our prayer concerning the use of the time that God gives us?
   (That we might use it wisely.)

2. Why is the proper use of our time today so important (James 4:13–15)?
   (We don't know about tomorrow; life is short.)

3. What does God demand of us in the stewardship of our time (Psalm 62:8)?
   (That we trust in Him at all times.)

   When do you find this hardest to do?

4. What does Christ admonish us to do as stewards of time until He comes again (Mark 13:33–37)?
   (Be on the alert. We don't know when He will return.)

5. If we are wise stewards and heed the commands of our Lord, how will we use our time (Ephesians 5:15,16)?
   (We will be wise, making the most of our time.)

   What does making use of our time have to do with wisdom?
   (How we use our time shows how wise we are. If we waste our time, we are foolish. If we live purposefully, we are wise.)

Lesson Development

(Ask one of the group members to summarize the paragraphs appearing at the opening of this lesson in the student's book. Note the diagram and discuss it.)

God expects us to fruitfully invest whatever He gives us. Often we think of God's blessings in terms of money or material goods. But time is also a gift of God—one that He has given all of us equally each day. We are expected —in fact, commanded—to use our time wisely.

The Bible confirms that God intends to help us make the most of our lives. Consider, for example, the promise of Psalm 32:8:

> I will instruct you (says the Lord) and guide you along the best pathway for your life; I will advise you and watch your progress (TLB).

Christ's ministry on earth lasted only three and a half years. Yet He fit all the activities necessary to accomplish God's purpose for Him into this short span of time. He said to His heavenly Father:

> I have brought you glory on earth by completing the work you gave me to do (John 17:4).

By focusing on what was important, Jesus accomplished in His brief ministry a more significant mission than any other person in history. He launched a worldwide movement that has continued for nearly 2,000 years.

With evil days?
(Time is like money. We buy a little every day. We can buy up opportunities to do good or waste our time on evil pursuits. Then our days become evil.)

Right Relationship With God

1. As wise stewards concerned over the use of our time, what will we want to understand (Ephesians 5:17)?
(The will of the Lord.)

2. What is necessary in order to know fully the will of God concerning the duties of our stewardship (Ephesians 5:18)?
(To be filled with the Holy Spirit.)

3. What will the Holy Spirit give the faithful steward to enable him to perform the duties of stewardship (Acts 1:8)?
(The power to do what God asks us to do.)

4. In whose name should the steward perform these duties (Colossians 3:17)?
(The Lord Jesus Christ.)

5. What should be our attitude as we utilize the time over which God has made us stewards (Ephesians 5:19–21)?
(An attitude of praise and thanksgiving, making music in our hearts to the Lord.)

When you are walking in the Spirit—when God is in control of your life—you will know what He wants you to do, for He will put His thoughts in your mind, and you will find that you are doing the right thing (Philippians 2:13).

Proverbs 3:5,6 confirms the fact that, if you "trust in the Lord with all your heart" and "in all your ways acknowledge Him," He will direct your path in life.

The most crucial quality in a disciple is *power* from God. This enables him to be sensitive to God moment by moment and to be able to fulfill what He asks him to do.

Two other key qualities are *direction* and *action*. A disciple should be increasingly willing to follow the commands and principles of God's Word in his daily response to God, others, and himself. He should seek to be a person of action, willing to take the initiative not only in sharing the message of Christ with non-Christians, but also in ministering meaningfully and practically to fellow Christians.

6. How would you describe such a useful and joyous life (John 10:10)?
(Abundant.)

Most Important Use of Time

1. As wise stewards who know and are obedient to the will of God, what will we spend much of our time aggressively doing (Mark 16:15)?
(Preaching the gospel to all creation.)

2. What does God say about a soul winner in Proverbs 11:30?
(He is wise.)

3. Of what value is a soul according to Christ in Mark 8:36,37?
(More than the whole world.)

4. What is the greatest thing that has happened in your life? *(Receiving Christ as Savior.)*

5. What, then, is the greatest thing you can do for another?
(Introduce him to Christ.)

6. What happens in God's presence when one repents and receives Christ (Luke 15:7,10)?
(There is joy in heaven in the presence of the angels.)

7. How did Paul feel about those whom he had won to Christ (1 Thessalonians 2:19,20)?
(They were his glory and joy.)

The familiar passage in Matthew 28:19,20 says:

> Therefore go and make disciples of all nations, baptizing them in the name of the Father and of the Son and of the Holy Spirit, and teaching them to obey everything I have commanded you. And surely I will be with you always, to the very end of the age.

A godly steward uses his time in the following ways:

◆ Actively serving his Lord

◆ Winning others to Christ

◆ Helping build them in their faith

◆ Sending them forth as spiritual multipliers to win and build others for the Savior

Just as someone introduced us to Christ and changed our lives eternally, we too need to use our time to introduce others to Him. We can find no better use of time than that.

Keeping track of how you spend your day can be of great value in evaluating the stewardship of your time. On a sheet of paper, record the number of hours spent on business, class, sleep, Christian service, recreation, etc. Place the total hours per week used in each activity on the chart below.

1. Determine what blocks of time are wasteful. How could you use them to serve the Lord?

2. List ways to tithe your time that can be worked into your present schedule.

Conclusion and Application

Do you seek to live for Christ where you live and work? Are you actively helping to fulfill the Great Commission? Are you prepared to serve God in the area in which He leads you? I challenge you to use the chart to plan your time wisely for God's purposes.

(Go through the chart at the end of this lesson in the student's book.)

Closing Prayer

(Lead students in a prayer of commitment to use their time wisely.)

Stewardship of Our Bodies

Opening Prayer

Discussion Starter

How do you determine your standard of morality? By your conscience? The crowd? Circumstances? Christ?

How is it possible to keep His standards?

Lesson Development

(Ask one of the group members to summarize the paragraphs appearing at the opening of this lesson in the student's book. Note the diagram and discuss it.)

Leader's Objective: To motivate each student to dedicate his body to the Lord and live by the Spirit

LESSON 4

Bible Study

The Spirit and the Body

Read 1 Peter 4:1,2 and Hebrews 10:1–10.

1. How did Jesus regard His body (1 Peter 4:1,2)?
   (He used it for the glory of God.)

2. What does Christ's sacrifice mean to us (Hebrews 10:10)?
   (He has made us holy through His sacrifice.)

   Look up the word *sanctified* in a Bible dictionary. How does the word relate to your stewardship?

3. What do you learn about the body of the Christian from Romans 8:8,9 and Romans 12:1?
   (It is the only thing we can present to Christ for service.)

4. Express in your own words the additional reasons given in 1 Corinthians 6:19,20 for being a good steward of your body.

   How are we to do this (Galatians 5:16; Romans 12:1; Matthew 26:41)?
   (Live by the Spirit; present ourselves to God; watch and pray to guard against temptation.)

Individual Parts of the Body

1. The tongue

   Why is it so important to be a good steward of the

   Conversion means to change one's mind, resulting in a change in one's lifestyle. To be converted to Christ one must change his mind about who Christ is and what He did on the cross to present us to God perfectly restored to righteousness. Romans 8:8 says, "those controlled by the sinful nature cannot please God." We are to have the mind and Spirit of Christ.

   God prepared a body for Christ to offer (verse 5) and we, too, need to offer our bodies to the Father. Our lives will be used either to further the cause of Christ or to hinder His purposes and further the desires and plans of Satan. The impact of our lives depends on who we yield our bodies to.

   We reflect God's nature to the world when we glorify Him in our bodies. Second Corinthians 4:7 says, "We have this treasure [the gospel of Christ] in clay jars to show that this all-surpassing power is from God and not from us." The showcase of the gospel is the body of a Christian. Our bodies should be clean, empty of selfish desires, and filled with Christ.

   Ask volunteers to read Proverbs 6:16,17,19 and 1 Peter 3:10.

   ❓What is God's attitude toward sins of the tongue?

tongue (James 3:2–6; James 1:26)?
(Though small, it controls our entire body and the course of our life.)

What should you know concerning its use (Matthew 12:36)?
(We will give an account in the judgment for every careless word we speak.)

List areas in which you misuse your tongue.

How has this affected your life?

How should you use your tongue properly (James 3:9,10; Ephesians 4:29; Proverbs 21:23; Psalm 39:1; Proverbs 4:24)?
(Praise God; build up others; guard my tongue; keep my tongue from sin; do not talk corruptly.)

2. The heart

What must we understand about the heart (Jeremiah 17:9)?
(It is deceitful and sick.)

How can we counteract our natural tendencies (Psalm 139:23,24)?
(Continually pray for God's searching and leading.)

What condition of heart does God require (Psalm 51:17)?
(A broken spirit and a contrite heart.)

What kind of heart does God look for and why (2 Chronicles 16:9; Matthew 5:8; 2 Thessaloni-

❓How will controlling your tongue help you live longer?

Some schools of thought today say that controlling our words can lead to repressive anxieties. But having an uncontrolled tongue can also damage physical and mental health. What then is the answer? It is letting Christ live in us and fill us with His Spirit, which leads to peace and righteous speaking.

❓Why should we be stewards of our hearts?

Because our actions proceed from what is in our heart. Jesus said:

Woe to you, teachers of the law and Pharisees, you hypocrites! You are like whitewashed tombs, which look beautiful on the outside but on the inside are full of dead men's bones and everything unclean. In the same way, on the outside you appear to people as righteous but on the inside you are full of hypocrisy and wickedness (Matthew 23:27,28).

The things that come out of the mouth come from the heart, and these make a man "unclean." For out of the heart come evil thoughts, murder, adultery, sexual immorality, theft, false testimony, slander. These

ans 3:5; Psalm 15:1,2)?
(One that is fully commit-
ted to Him so He can
strengthen it; a pure heart;
a heart with love and per-
severance; a righteous
heart.)

3. The mind

What is your responsibil-
ity in being a steward of
your mind (1 Peter 1:13)?
(To prepare it for action,
to be self-controlled; to
hope.)

Whose mind should you
have and which qualities
should you strive for
(Philippians 2:5–8; 1 Corinthians 2:12–16)?
(The mind of Christ.
Spiritual thoughts, accept-
ing the Spirit's words, hu-
mility.)

What is the result of
keeping your mind fo-
cused on God (Isaiah
26:3)?
(You will have perfect
peace.)

How can you keep your
mind on Him (Philippi-
ans 4:6,7; Deuteronomy
11:18)?
(Give thanks in prayer for
everything; pay attention
to what God says.)

4. The hands

What does God think
about the work of your
hands (Proverbs 12:14,
24)?
(It will reward us and help
us become leaders.)

How did the apostles feel
about the importance of

are what make a man "unclean"
(Matthew 15:18–20).

❓How can our thought lives be pure?

By thinking on the things of
God . . . occupation with Christ!

We demolish arguments and
every pretension that sets itself up
against the knowledge of God, and
we take captive every thought to
make it obedient to Christ (2 Corinthians 10:5).

Praying about everything keeps
us focused on God rather than on our
problems. Thanking God helps us
remember that God has our lives in
His control.

❓How does the work of our hands
in our jobs affect our testimony
for Christ?

When our work is below standard,
it reflects on our witness. For example,
if we are not prompt at getting our
work done because of time mismanage-
ment or things under our control, our

what their hands had done (Acts 20:34,35; 1 Thessalonians 4:11,12)? *(They worked so they could support themselves and give to others; they could win others' respect and not become dependent.)*

How can we use our hands to glorify God?

Proverbs 31:20 *(Help the needy.)*

Ephesians 4:28 *(Work, doing something useful so we can share with others.)*

Deuteronomy 15:10,11 *(Be open-handed with others.)*

Ecclesiastes 9:10 *(Work with all of our might.)*

5. The feet

Contrast the feet of those who do evil with those who do good (Isaiah 59:7; Romans 3:15; Isaiah 52:7; Psalm 119:101,105; 56:13). *(Evil: they rush into sin; quick to kill. Good: proclaim peace, good tidings and salvation; obey God's Word; do not stumble.)*

How do Romans 10:15 and Ephesians 6:15 relate to evangelism? *(Feet symbolize readiness to go and tell others about Christ.)*

6. The eyes

What is the importance of the eyes (Matthew 6:22, 23)? *(The eyes disclose the attitude of the heart.)*

co-workers will assume that Christ has not made a good impact on our daily life. This applies to every area of our work, including our attitude, our honesty, and the way we treat others.

❓ How can the work of our hands in doing good deeds open the way for our testimony?

People are much more receptive to what we say when we first prove that we care about them.

In the King James version, living the Christian life is translated as walking with Christ. "Walking with" implies side by side, slow enough to communicate and to maintain a steady pace for a long time.

❓ How do the eyes reflect what's in the heart?

Today the world tries to entice us in many ways, especially through visual stimulus. The danger is that we

Describe what this means to you.

What sins can we commit with our eyes?

Proverbs 21:4 *(Haughtiness and pride.)*

Jeremiah 22:17 *(Set on dishonest gain.)*

Proverbs 27:20 *(Dissatisfaction.)*

Matthew 5:28 *(Lust.)*

1 John 2:16 *(Lust, cravings.)*

What privilege did the apostles have (1 John 1:1–3)? *(They saw Jesus.)*

How can we avoid temptation (Psalm 19:8; 119:37; 121:1,2; 123:1)? *(Let His commands give light to our eyes; turn our eyes away from worthless things; look to God for hope and help.)*

7. The ears

Write down ways we can misuse hearing.

Proverbs 21:13 *(Shut our ears to the cry of the poor.)*

2 Timothy 4:3,4 *(Listen to false teachers.)*

What can listening to God give us?

Romans 10:17 *(Faith.)*

John 5:24 *(Eternal life.)*

How can you apply James 1:19,22 to your daily life? Give specific examples.

Sexual Expression

1. Compare the sexual sins in 1 Corinthians 6:9,10,

will become so accustomed to visual temptation that we will not even notice ourselves sliding into sin.

❓How can we guard against this subtle trap?

Our eyes can lead us to good or to evil. As the lamp of the mind, our eyes can be an effective tool to build us up in our Christian faith. Read Psalm 119 sometime this week and see how God regards reading His Word.

Our minds record everything we hear, whether we consciously remember it later or not.

❓How can we counteract what the world may be throwing at us through our ears?

We can avoid listening to things that do not build us up. When we cannot avoid hearing sinful things, we can keep our minds set on the Lord and His Word and be in continual prayer.

We find in 1 Thessalonians 4:3–8:

It is God's will that you should be sanctified: that you should avoid sexual immorality; that each of you

13–18 with marriage in 1 Corinthians 7:1–8.
(Immoral: doing what the body is not meant for; God will destroy those who are immoral. Marriage: fulfilling God's purpose for sex; thwarts temptation.)

2. God considered David a man after His own heart, yet what was David's great sin (2 Samuel 11:2–5,14–17,26,27)?
(Covetousness, adultery, murder—rebellion against God's laws.)

3. What is God's stern judgment against misusers and abusers of sex (1 Corinthians 6:9,10)?
(They will not inherit the kingdom of God.)

Why is it especially tragic if a Christian becomes involved in the misuse of sex (1 Corinthians 6:15–18)?
(He sins against his own body, which is the temple of the Holy Spirit.)

How serious is sexual lust, according to Christ (Matthew 5:28)?
(It is equal to actual adultery.)

4. How can the application of the following verses enable you to overcome sexual lust?

Philippians 4:8
(The mind is to dwell on honorable and pure things.)

should learn to control his own body in a way that is holy and honorable, not in passionate lust like the heathen, who do not know God; and that in this matter no one should wrong his brother or take advantage of him.

The Lord will punish men for all such sins, as we have already told you and warned you. For God did not call us to be impure, but to live a holy life. Therefore, he who rejects this instruction does not reject man but God, who gives you his Holy Spirit.

Whatever the standard of the non-Christian, the standard for the Christian is clear: His body is a sacred trust from God; he should restrict and preserve his body's functions for the purpose designed by God.

(Read these additional scriptures that help in dealing with sexual temptation:)

Flee the evil desires of youth, and pursue righteousness, faith, love and peace, along with those who call on the Lord out of a pure heart (2 Timothy 2:22).

Clothe yourselves with the Lord Jesus Christ, and do not think about how to gratify the desires of the sinful nature (Romans 13:14).

The Biblical View of Sexual Expression

Sex is a gift of God, good and holy, to be expressed only within the marriage bond. Sex needs marriage and marriage needs sex. The two are interdependent in the design of God.

◆ Genesis 2:18–25—God said it was not good for man to be alone, so He instituted marriage.

Psalm 119:11
(Memorized Scripture keeps us from sin.)

1 Corinthians 10:13
(God will provide a way of escape.)

Romans 6:11–13
(Sin is not our master; we have the ability to resist; we can offer ourselves to God.)

1 Thessalonians 4:3–5
(Avoid temptation.)

Psalm 119:9
(Live according to God's Word.)

List things in your life that tempt you to have impure thoughts. How can you apply these verses to each?

LIFE APPLICATION

1. How does stewardship of each individual part of the body affect each part? *(It helps us put our attitude under God's control and serve God.)*

   How could it affect the body as a whole? *(If one part of the body is out of control, the whole body is out of control.)*

2. How would you apply 1 Thessalonians 5:22 to the following:

   The use of your tongue?

   The desires of your heart?

"A helper suitable for him" (verse 18) literally means a helper who will in every way complement and supplement him.

In verse 22, we can see clearly that it was God who first brought man and woman together.

The Bible views the body as the vehicle for the expression of spiritual values. Thus, sex cannot be separated from the love that gives it true meaning.

◆ Ephesians 5:22–25,28—Marital love is compared to Christ's love for the church.

◆ 1 Corinthians 7:3–5—Christ instructs us about the relationship between husband and wife.

◆ 1 Peter 3:8—These attitudes provide the basis for a rewarding sexual relationship.

Conclusion and Application

To keep our bodies pure for Christ, we must:

◆ Dedicate them to God (Romans 12:1,2).

◆ Yield the body's members not to sin, but to God (Romans 6:11–13).

◆ Live by means of the Holy Spirit (Galatians 5:16,17).

As Christians, we must guard against being guilty of *spiritual* immorality. (See James 4:4–8; Jeremiah 3:1,13,14; Matthew 22:37.)

We can show the world who Christ is and what He is like by giving our

The control of your mind?

The work of your hands?

Where you go?

What you see?

What you hear?

Your conduct with members of the opposite sex?

bodies completely to God and living a joyful, Spirit-filled life.

We are examples to the world in our speech, conduct, love, faith, and purity. Do all to the glory of God!

Closing Prayer

(Give group members an opportunity to surrender themselves in silent prayer to Christ by giving Him all that they are and all that they have to be used in His service. Then close with a prayer of thanksgiving.)

Stewardship of Our Talents and Gifts

Opening Prayer

Discussion Starter

Each of us has been given at least one spiritual gift from the Holy Spirit according to 1 Corinthians 12:7. A great variety of gifts are given.

❓ What do you think is the difference between a spiritual gift and a natural ability?

Lesson Development

(Ask one of the group members to summarize the paragraphs appearing at the opening of this lesson in the student's book. Note the diagram and discuss it.)

Leader's Objective: To lead students to surrender their talents and abilities to God for His use and glory

LESSON 5

Bible Study

Natural Gifts

1. What talents and natural abilities do you have?

2. How did you acquire them or improve on them?

3. According to 1 Corinthians 4:6,7 and Exodus 4:11, what should your attitude be about them? *(We should not become arrogant; we have nothing that was not given to us.)*

4. How would you apply Colossians 3:17 to the stewardship of your natural gifts? *(We are to do all and use all in the name of the Lord Jesus, thanking the Father through Him.)*

Spiritual Gifts

1. Major passages on spiritual gifts in the Bible are:
   - Romans 12:3–8
   - 1 Corinthians 12:1–31
   - Ephesians 4:4–8,11–16
   - 1 Peter 4:10,11

   From these passages make a composite list of spiritual gifts (combine any two that might be identical). Across from each one, give your brief definition of the gift. (You

Whether a certain ability you have is the result of being spiritually gifted or naturally talented really is not that important. What matters is that you develop that gift or ability to its fullest potential through the control and empowering of the Holy Spirit. And that you use your gift and ability according to God's will and for His glory.

Within the body of Christ, each of us has a unique function. True, two people might have similar functions—just as a body has two hands that function similarly. But those two hands are not identical. Just try to wear a left-hand glove on your right hand! You and I might have similar abilities, but we are not identical. We are unique creations of God.

Therefore, we should not look upon our abilities with pride or be boastful of them. On the other hand, we should not be envious or look with disdain on others because of their different abilities.

Each of us has the obligation to *use* our gifts in a scriptural way. We would be poor stewards of what the Holy Spirit has given us if we do not use our abilities for God.

We must also use our gifts to glorify Christ—not to glorify ourselves, or to glorify some other person, or even to glorify the gift itself.

It is important to exercise our gifts in the power and control of the Holy Spirit—never through our own, fleshly efforts. When we exercise our gifts in the power of the Holy Spirit, Christ is

may wish to consult a concordance or a Bible dictionary.)

Spiritual Gift:

(Teaching)

(Helps, service, mercy)

(Leadership)

(Giving)

(Wisdom, knowledge)

(Faith)

(Healing, miracles)

(Prophecy)

(Discerning of spirits)

(Tongues)

(Exhortation)

(Apostleship)

(Evangelism)

(Pastoring)

2. What are some reasons God has given gifted people to the church (Ephesians 4:11–16)?
   (To prepare God's people for the work of service, to build up the body of Christ, for unity in the faith, knowledge, maturity, and growth of the body in love.)

3. Why will two people not exercise the same gift in the same manner (1 Corinthians 12:4–6)?
   (The Spirit gives different kinds of gifts.)

glorified and Christians are built up in the faith.

Following are brief definitions of spiritual gifts (refer to the chart in the student's book):

Teaching—Ability to explain information to others so they will be edified and can apply the information to their lives.

Helps, service, mercy—Similar gifts for building up the body of Christ. Helps is more task-oriented; service is people-oriented; and mercy is used for the sick, elderly, injured, or those who are unable to care for themselves.

Leadership—Ability to set spiritual goals and motivate and direct the activities of others to accomplish the goals.

Giving—Ability to acquire money for the purpose of giving it to others to carry out the work of God.

Wisdom, knowledge—Wisdom is the ability to discern the mind of Christ in applying specific knowledge to needs within the body of Christ. Knowledge is the ability to discover, accumulate, analyze, and clarify information and ideas for the growth and well-being of the body of Christ.

Faith—Ability to discern with extraordinary confidence the will and purposes of God in the growth and well-being of the Church.

Healing, miracles—Being the vessel through which God performs acts outside the ordinary laws of nature.

Prophecy—Ability to proclaim God's Word to others, not the ability to foretell the future.

4. Though some spiritual gifts seem to be of greater value than others (1 Corinthians 12:28–31), what ideas does Paul stress to keep Christians from personal pride because of those they may possess (Romans 12:4,5; 1 Corinthians 12:12–26; 1 Corinthians 13; Ephesians 4:11–16)?

(There are many members with different functions; we are one in Christ; we need each other; there should be no division; we should care for one another, and suffer and rejoice with each other; love is most important; unity and maturity in love is our aim.)

5. List several principles that describe what your attitude and responsibilities should be toward your spiritual gifts (Romans 12:3–8).

(We are not to think more highly of ourself than we should; we are to exercise our gifts in ways that result in the maximum glory of God.)

Discerning of spirits—Ability to discern whether things said and done are of God in the power of the Holy Spirit or are of Satan or the flesh.

Tongues—Ability to speak to others or to God in a language or utterance never learned by the speaker to glorify Christ.

Exhortation—Ability to minister words of comfort, consolation, encouragement, and counsel to others.

Apostleship—Ability to give leadership to a number of churches and to show wisdom and authority in spiritual matters related to these churches.

Evangelism—Ability to share Christ and open minds of unbelievers to the gospel when it is shared.

Pastoring—Ability to shepherd believers in a local church and care for the interests of those believers God has committed in his care. This gift is not restricted to clergy but may involve the pastor and lay leaders.

Some of the gifts of the Spirit are supernatural enhancements of abilities common to all men—like *wisdom*. Other gifts—such as *teaching*—are granted by the Holy Spirit to only some of the members of the Body.

In addition, some gifts we acquire instantly, while others we develop. The gift of tongues at Pentecost was *instantaneous,* while the gifts of preaching and teaching are *developmental*.

The developmental gifts are developed by the Holy Spirit within us over a period of time, and usually require some hard work on our part.

Remember that whatever God calls us to do, He will enable us to do. In developing our gifts, three elements play a part:

◆ The empowering of the Holy Spirit

◆ Dedicated work on our part

◆ Time for the work of the Holy Spirit, coupled with our efforts, to bring about maturity in our lives and in the use of the gifts He has given us

Some believers try so hard to discover or receive additional spiritual gifts that they do not develop and use their own known gifts and abilities to do God's will.

Do not go to extraordinary lengths to discover your spiritual gifts. Rather, fully surrender yourself to Jesus Christ as Lord and Master and ask to be filled with the Holy Spirit. Then seek God's direction in your life. He will lead you into areas where He wants you to serve, which will allow you to use your gifts. Through faith and hard work, you can accomplish what God has called you to do.

Spiritual gifts can be a vibrant part of your supernatural life. But do not place such emphasis on gifts that your life becomes off-balance. The gifts of the Spirit are given for glorifying Christ *in love*, for equipping the saints *in love,* and for unifying the body of Christ *in love* (1 Corinthians 13:1–3).

Follow these steps to more fully understand your part in the Body of Christ:

1. Realize that you have at least one spiritual gift, probably more (1 Corinthians 12:11).

2. Pray that God will make your gifts known to you.

3. Determine which of your activities the Lord seems to bless and inquire of other mature Christians who know you well what your spiritual gifts might be.

4. List here what you believe your spiritual gifts are.

5. Seek to develop your gifts in the power of the Holy Spirit.

6. Realize that you may have other gifts of which you are not presently aware, so exercise various gifts. Be aware that you are accountable to God for stewardship of your spiritual gifts.

Conclusion and Application

The apostle Paul explains the wonderful truth:

> It is God who works in you to will and to act according to his good purpose (Philippians 2:13).

God's Holy Spirit is at work in our lives, empowering and controlling us—but we must, as a matter of our own wills, consecrate our lives to God and sometimes work hard and long to accomplish what God calls us to do.

If the Lord asks you to serve Him in some particular way, such as teaching, ask the Holy Spirit in faith to empower you to become an effective teacher. The Holy Spirit may make you a great teacher overnight, but this is unlikely. So if it does not happen, do not be discouraged.

Have faith! Continue to ask and believe that the Holy Spirit will give you spiritual gifts. They might be developmental in nature, and you might have to work hard to develop your gift. But remember, "Faith without works is useless" (James 2:20, NASB).

(Go through the chart in the student's book.)

Closing Prayer

Stewardship of Our Possessions

Opening Prayer

Discussion Starter

(Ask each individual to estimate how much of his material wealth is given over to God for His use. Show the results of poor stewardship according to Luke 6:38. Then ask:)

 How much do you think good stewardship of possessions has to do with a person's lack of power and victory and the provision of needs in his life?

Lesson Development

(Ask one of the group members to summarize the paragraphs appearing at the opening of this lesson in the student's book. Note the diagram and discuss it.)

❖

Leader's Objective: To encourage students to begin giving faithfully to God's work both in their local churches and throughout the world

Bible Study

Money—The Old Testament Standard

1. What did God command those under the Law of Moses to do (Leviticus 27:30; Malachi 3:8–10)?
   (Set aside a tithe and bring it to the storehouse.)

2. What would you say the "storehouse" is (Deuteronomy 12:5,6,11)?
   (A place where God's name is proclaimed.)

3. How much is a tithe (Genesis 14:20; Hebrews 7:2)?
   (A tenth, ten percent.)

Money—The New Testament Standard

1. As believers in Christ, we are under grace, rather than the Old Testament Law. Whereas the Law in itself did not provide eternal life for those who attempted to keep it (Galatians 2:16), we have received life by the favor of God though we do not deserve it and could not possibly earn it.

   Therefore, do we have a higher or lower motivation and standard for stewardship of our possessions than those under the Law?
   (A higher motivation.)

2. How did Jesus regard a person's responsibility in

In the Old Testament, a tenth of all produce, flocks, and cattle was declared sacred to Jehovah. These tithes were a symbol of the people's recognition and acknowledgment that the whole land belonged to God.

(Read Genesis 14:19,20.)

Abram gave ten percent of all that God had given him in battle to Melchizedek, priest of the most High God. Abram gave a tithe to show that God had given success in battle.

❓How does the following verse relate to giving?

Do not conform any longer to the pattern of this world, but be transformed by the renewing of your mind. Then you will be able to test and approve what God's will is—his good, pleasing and perfect will (Romans 12:2).

that area (Matthew 23:23)?
(It should be practiced.)

3. Read 2 Corinthians 8—9.

In this passage, Paul attempts to encourage the Corinthian church to give financially to help needy Christians. He first points them to the example of the Macedonian church.

What was the attitude of the Macedonians in giving their money to God (2 Corinthians 8:2–5)?
(Overflowing joy and rich generosity.)

In light of this, what do you think God is interested in?
(Our attitude in giving.)

Nevertheless, why is giving money an important part of our Christian life (2 Corinthians 8:7; 9:12, 13)?
(It supplies needs, shows our thanks to God, is a gracious act.)

In what sense does the one who "sows" (gives) sparingly reap sparingly (2 Corinthians 9:6)?
(Lack of joy, love and adventure, doesn't see God's work through himself.)

What kind of attitude does God want you to have in giving (2 Corinthians 9:7)?
(Cheerfulness.)

When is it hard for you to give that way?

Giving is one of the greatest privileges we enjoy. Think of it! God has need of nothing, yet we have the privilege of giving *things* to the God of the universe. How can we resist giving in gladness?

On this earth, we enjoy the privilege of giving for only about 75 years. Compare this with the immeasurable treasure that we will inherit with Christ in heaven. Romans 8:16,17 says:

> The Spirit himself testifies with our spirit that we are God's children. Now if we are children, then we are heirs—heirs of God and co-heirs with Christ.

For all of eternity we will enjoy riches that we do not deserve to enjoy, that were given to us, that were paid for by the death of the Son of the everlasting God. In heaven we will not have the priceless privilege of giving.

God's Priority for Missions

1. Who is the great example of giving (2 Corinthians 8:9)?
   (The Lord Jesus Christ.)

2. In your own words, summarize the last command Jesus gave His disciples (Matthew 28:19,20).

3. Read John 14:21,23,24. Describe how this relates to fulfilling the Great Commission.
   (We will obey Christ's command to help fulfill the Great Commission because we love Him.)

4. Oswald Smith said, "If you see ten men carrying a heavy log, nine of them on one end and one man struggling to carry the other, which end would most need your help? The end with only one man." This illustrates how inequitably the evangelized nations have been using their resources to help fulfill the Great Commission.

   What percentage of your giving is going to overseas missions?

   To home missions?

5. Prayerfully consider what kind of adjustments you feel the Lord is leading you to make in your missions giving. Record your decisions here.

One exciting part of giving is that we can give money where we live that will help introduce people to Christ on the other side of the world—or in our own community. We become partners with the Body of Christ everywhere.

Consider adopting a part of the world as your special area. Put up a map of that country or area, then start a prayer diary. Research the needs of your area, obtain information about mission groups and missionaries that work there. You may want to correspond with someone to find out how you can give to further God's work in that area.

God will reward our faithfulness in giving. While supplying their needs, God used a difficult time financially in the lives of Wesley and Patricia to teach them much about budgeting and God's principles of giving.

Wesley underwent major back surgery and was unemployed for several months. As a self-employed truck driver, he received no disability or worker's compensation. The only income they had came from Patricia's small salary and their savings.

Even so, they continued giving to their church and supporting three missionaries. As the couple trusted God to meet their needs, money came from many sources—from the sale of various things, overtime at Patricia's job, a forgotten paid-up insurance policy, and anonymous gifts.

"Whenever it looked like we just couldn't make it financially," Patricia

Other Possessions

1. To whom do you and your possessions belong (Psalm 50:12; 1 Corinthians 6:19,20)?
   (The Holy Spirit of God.)

2. What should be your motive in the use of whatever you possess (1 Corinthians 10:31)?
   (To glorify God.)

LIFE APPLICATION

1. What is your understanding about tithing? Describe your view in a short paragraph.

2. What is the difference between "giving" and "tithing"?
   (Giving is supplying out of what you own; tithing is giving God back part of what He owns and you manage for Him.)

   Which one describes your practice and why?

3. Ask yourself, "Is my heart attitude one of joy and gratefulness as I give?" How do you express your attitude?

4. List some Christian groups or churches that are working to fulfill the Great Commission in which you would like to invest financially.

says, "the Lord would open up another avenue and provide for us."

On one occasion God provided by helping Patricia find a sizable error in the family checkbook. As the deadline approached on a bill for $700, Patricia spent the morning in prayer asking God to meet their need. As she prayed, their bank statement arrived in the mail. To her surprise, she discovered that she had neglected to write down a $600 deposit the previous month. That amount plus what she had available brought her account balance up to the amount needed—with $75 to spare.

"Thankfully, my husband has returned to work," Patricia says, "but God used that time to stretch and strengthen our faith in Him."

God can do and will do more than we ever expect when we give our possessions to Him.

Conclusion and Application

According to Revelation 4:11, everything was created for the Lord's pleasure. This includes our material possessions.

Obedience to our heavenly Father in giving is the natural and spiritual outgrowth of our faith. An attitude of obedience softens the soil of our heart for fruitfulness in every good work, and gives testimony to God's ownership of our possessions.

Closing Prayer

Trusting God for Our Finances

Opening Prayer

Discussion Starter

 How do you know when your finances are controlling you?

 How do you get them back under control?

Lesson Development

(Ask one of the group members to summarize the paragraphs appearing at the opening of this lesson in the student's book. Note the diagram and discuss it.)

❖

Leader's Objective: To challenge students to fully surrender their finances to God

LESSON 7

Bible Study

Recognize That God Is Worthy of Your Trust

1. Read Psalm 12:6. How much can we trust God?
   (God's words or promises are flawless.)

2. What will happen if you make God's promises the foundation of your financial security (Proverbs 3:5,6)?
   (He will make your path straight—give you His kind of prosperity.)

3. List the financial areas that are hardest for you to put into God's hands. Prayerfully dedicate them to Him.

The first step in learning to trust God is to recognize that He is worthy of your trust. We cannot separate God from His character. He is perfect in truth. We can count on God to do as He says because the One who created the heavens and the earth and who set the laws that govern the universe is more capable of providing our needs than we could ever imagine.

Realize That God Wants You to Live a Full and Abundant Life

1. Read John 10:10. How does this promise apply to financial freedom?
   (We will not be weighted down with financial burdens.)

2. Does abundant life mean having all the money or possessions you want?
   (No.)

   Why or why not?
   (Abundant life is not dependent on physical possessions.)

3. Do you feel you have abundant life right now?

Our Lord promises to give every obedient Christian an overflowing, joyous life regardless of his financial position.

If you obey the Lord in your stewardship, "your gift will return to you in full and overflowing measure" (Luke 6:38, TLB) and you will live a joyous, abundant life. He will reward your obedience, for faith places you in position for God's continued blessings.

If not, what is keeping you from it?

Substitute Faith for Fear

1. How does fear interfere with your trust in God? *(Fear is the opposite of faith so it cancels our trust.)*

2. Read 2 Timothy 1:7. Contrast the two kinds of spirits mentioned. *(Timidness; power, love, and self-discipline.)*

3. Write down the financial areas that make you fearful. Surrender these to the Lord.

One emotion that can undermine our faith and throw us back into financial bondage is fear. When anxiety over the future grips us, we lose the ability to trust God for our needs.

By obeying God's will in our lives, however, we substitute faith for our fear. When we actively obey His commands, we establish our faith firmly and open our lives to His abundant blessings.

A good way to build your trust is to study the attributes of God. Begin with characteristics such as loving, forgiving, merciful, faithful, truthful, and all-powerful. Use the concordance at the back of your Bible to find references that contain these words. Record your insights.

Ask God to Supply Your Needs

1. What is the difference between needs and wants? Be specific. *(Needs are essential to living; wants are the extras we would like to acquire. Food is a need; a steak dinner is a want.)*

2. Why do we lack good things (James 4:2,3; John 15:7)? *(Our motives are wrong and we aren't abiding in Christ.)*

3. Faith requires action. According to 1 John 5:14,15:

   a) As an act of your will, ask God to supply your needs.

Be content with what God provides. Such an attitude rarely finds its way into our materialistic society. Even among Christians, contentment is not often evident. Many believers misunderstand what it means. Contentment is not merely satisfaction with one's position in life. Rather, it is knowing God's plan and living at peace within it. Contentment in the financial sense means living within the resources God gives us, while striving to make the best use of our assets for His glory.

b) Expect Him, as an expression of your faith, to provide for your needs.

Keep Your Heart and Motives Pure

1. What wrong motives do we sometimes display (James 4:3)?
   (Greed, selfishness.)

   What is the result?
   (God will not answer our prayers.)

2. Write down the wrongful motives that you battle.

   Then:

   a) Confess them to God.

   b) Claim the power of the Holy Spirit to help you rely on Him to supply your needs.

Take a Step of Faith

1. What is essential to your Christian walk (Hebrews 11:6)?
   (Faith.)

2. One way to enlarge your faith is to make a "faith promise"—one that is greater than you are capable of fulfilling according to your present income. It is not a pledge that must be paid. Rather, it is a voluntary "promise" based on your faith in God's ability to supply out of His resources what you cannot give out of your own. You give as God supplies.

Trust in God by itself will not enable us to continue to live abundantly. We must also keep our heart and motive pure. Just like a seed planted in dry, parched soil, our faith cannot produce without the right conditions for growth.

Sometimes God requires a further step of faith. Dr. Oswald J. Smith had a burning, driving passion "to bring back the King through world evangelization." The entire ministry of his People's Church in Toronto centered on this vision. The high point of each year was the four-week Annual Missionary Convention. To Dr. Smith, raising support for missions was the prime duty of every individual—from the toddlers in the primary department to the college-and-careers, the filing clerk and millionaires, the homemakers and retired seniors.

Each year, he would challenge them to decide on a "faith promise" that they felt God would put into their hands to give to missions above their regular

Describe a time in which God led you to give above your means.

What was the result?

If you have never made a "faith promise," you may want to do so now after prayerfully considering various worthwhile investments you can make for God. Keep a careful record of your giving and how God supplied your needs in a special way.

LIFE APPLICATION

1. Read Luke 6:38. How does this verse apply to financial freedom?
   (When we give, we will receive in the same measure we gave.)

2. Suppose a new Christian confides in you that he is afraid to give God control over his checkbook. How would you advise him?
   (God is better able to manage your checkbook than you are; God loves you so much that you can trust Him with anything; God is all-wise and knows the future, who better to trust with your checkbook?)

3. Review the steps to trusting God for your finances. Which of these steps are weak areas in your life?

giving—even if they could not see a way in their budget. No one received a reminder, and miraculously each year more than the amount came in.

The basis of this concept is faith in God's ability to supply out of His resources what we cannot give out of our own. During a missions convention, a small boy captured the spirit of faith promise giving. Printing his name and address on a faith promise card, he vowed to give twenty-five cents a month for missions. Then across the bottom of the card in uneven block letters, he scrawled: "My daddy will pay this."

Conclusion and Application

As your faith in God and His love and trustworthiness grows, I encourage you to prayerfully make a faith promise—one that is greater than you are capable of fulfilling according to your present income. Take God at His word to supply from His unlimited resources and make a generous faith promise to help fulfill the Great Commission.

Then expect a miracle! God has promised in His Word: "Call to Me, and I will answer you, and show you great and mighty things, which you do not know" (Jeremiah 33:3, NKJ). With our faith and trust, we link our finite lives with the infinite God—the God of love, power, wisdom, and sufficiency. We tie ourselves into His inexhaustible supply of answered prayer. We become His instruments for changing the world.

Why do you find them difficult?

What could you do to strengthen them?

4. Read the steps to "Financial Breathing" listed on page 18. Breathe financially for any areas in which you do not follow good stewardship principles.

5. Prayerfully consider the faith promise God would have you make. Write that promise here.

Closing Prayer

Our Accountability to God

Opening Prayer

Discussion Starter

Imagine that Jesus Christ returned to earth today and walked into this room and asked you: "How have you used the time, treasure, and talents I have given you?"

How would you feel?

How would you answer?

Lesson Development

(Ask one of the group members to summarize the paragraphs appearing at the opening of this lesson in the student's book. Note the diagram and discuss it.)

Leader's Objective: To motivate students to be faithful stewards by being accountable for what God has given them and commanded them to do

LESSON 8

Bible Study

The Christian at Christ's Coming

1. According to 2 Corinthians 5:10, what will Christ do when He comes again?
   (He will judge each Christian for the deeds done in the body.)

2. Notice that Paul says "we all." Who is this primarily for?
   (Christians.)

   Note: Our sins have already been judged in Christ (Romans 8:1). The judgment here is of our works since the time we became a believer.

3. Read 1 Corinthians 3:11–15. God's judgment of our works is compared to the reaction of certain materials to fire. According to this passage, what is God most interested in regarding the works we do for Him (verse 13)?
   (The quality of the work.)

   How is it then possible for us to spend long hours working for God, but have no reward whatsoever?
   (We are doing the good works with the wrong attitude.)

   A Christian's works may be rejected, but what can he himself still be sure of

Romans 14:12 says,

> So then, each of us will give account of himself to God.

❓What kind of feelings do you have when thinking about giving an account before God?

We are warned in 1 John 2:28:

> And now, dear children, continue in him, so that when he appears we may be confident and unashamed before him at his coming.

When Christ comes, as His stewards we should:

◆ Watch (Matthew 24:42)

◆ Be ready (Matthew 24:44)

Matthew 25:14–29 relates the parable of the servants (also see 1 Corinthians 4:2). The master gives the first servant five talents, and the second servant two talents. He gives the third servant one talent. A talent is a considerable amount of money. The first two servants invest their money and double the number of talents they have. When their master returns, he praises them and calls them good and faithful servants. The third servant hid his one talent, and his master calls him wicked and lazy.

(verse 15)?
(He will be saved.)

The Time of Christ's Coming

1. The judgment of the Christian will take place when Christ comes again. When will that be (Acts 1:6,7)?
   (It is not for us to know— only God knows.)

2. On what should we concentrate until He comes (Acts 1:8; Matthew 28:19,20; Mark 16:15)?
   (Being His witnesses.)

3. Why has Christ waited so long already before coming (2 Peter 3:9)?
   (He does not wish for any to perish, but for all to come to repentance.)

The Earth at Christ's Coming

Read Mark 13. This chapter foretells the world conditions as Christ's coming approaches. As we see the world today becoming more like this, we know His coming is drawing nearer.

1. What will we see happening in religion (verses 5,6,21,22)?
   (Many people will come claiming to be Christ and will mislead many others.)

2. What will the world situation be (verses 7,8)?
   (Wars, rumors of wars, nations against nations.)

3. What will occur in nature (verse 8)?
   (Earthquakes and famines.)

Christ will come again, not as a meek child in a manger, but in all His glory (Revelation 19—20). Light dispels darkness and reveals what had been hidden by it. In the same way, the radiance of the risen Christ will reveal the sinfulness of man and will expose the kind of life we have been living. He came the first time to die. This time He comes to judge. We do not know when He will come, but we are admonished to watch for Him.

❷ Do you see evidences of these things beginning to be fulfilled today?

❷ What are these evidences?

❷ How does the imminent return of Christ make you feel?

❷ Are you prepared for His return?

4. What will the attitude be toward true believers (verses 12,13)?
   (They will be hated because of Him.)

5. Describe in your own words what you think Christ's coming will be like (verses 26,27).

Preparing for Christ's Coming

1. As a believer, what are you to do as His coming draws near (Mark 13:33)?
   (Be alert.)

2. How will obedience to that instruction affect the following:

   Your employment?

   Your social life?

   Your worship?

   Your giving?

LIFE APPLICATION

1. As faithful stewards of God's resources, our primary responsibility is to help fulfill the Great Commission. If God were to call you into account for your stewardship, what would you say to Him (Luke 16:1,2; Hebrews 4:13; 1 Peter 4:5)?

   How can you be more faithful in your giving to help reach your world for Christ?

2. In what ways are you storing up treasures in heaven?

3. Look over your spending for the past month. What

Dr. J. Sidlow Baxter gave this illustration of the second coming of Christ:

A Scotchman and his two sons were returning from a fishing trip. The younger son said, "I can see her now, my precious wife, waiting at home for me—oh yes, she is indeed a faithful one."

The elder son said, "My wife will not only be waiting, but she will be perched on the window sill watching for me to come home. That is what I call faithfulness."

The father Scotchman said, "Sons, I can show you where your mother, bless her dear heart, excels them both. She will not only be waiting and watching for me to come home, but she will be fixing my dinner as well!"

Conclusion and Application

A father and his two teenage sons were setting out on a month-long camping trip in the mountains. They had packed their equipment and drawn their map. On the morning they were to leave, each dressed in his hiking clothes with a sense of excitement.

Ready for their big adventure, the boys gathered their gear and hurried out the door. "Boys! Come back here and sit down for a minute," their father called. "There's one more item we need before we start."

The boys looked at each other and groaned. "Oh, Dad!" the older one exclaimed. "We've gone over our plans and equipment several times to make sure we haven't forgotten anything."

percentage did you give to God's work?

4. To plan your giving for the next year, go through the chart on the following page some time this week.

Stewardship Plan

1. Begin by asking God how much and where He wants you to invest your time, talents, possessions, and money. Write these ideas here.

2. Prayerfully develop a systematic plan for giving each month in each of these areas:

   ◆ Time

   ◆ Talents

   ◆ Possessions

   ◆ Money

3. Plan to set aside some time and resources for needs you may become aware of at your church, in your neighborhood, or other places.

4. Dedicate your plan to God. Ask Him to use your resources to bring the greatest glory to His name.

5. Begin to implement your plan with a joyful heart, expecting God to bless you through your stewardship.

"Yes, you've been very thorough," the father agreed. "But what I'm talking about will determine whether our trip will be a magnificent experience or a huge disaster."

"Tell me what it is and I'll go buy one," the younger son joked.

His father laughed, then sobered. "We can't buy it at any price. There'll be times during our trip when you'll feel so tired you can barely plant one foot in front of the other. You may have to sleep cold and wet. Our food supply may run low. Each of us must firmly resolve to devote every ounce of his strength to last through the month. If we commit all our strength, will, and wisdom to what lies ahead, this trip will be the most thrilling expedition we ever take together."

The boys nodded enthusiastically. "We're willing and ready!"

"Let's go, then!" the father announced, shouldering his pack.

Life is too short to be wasted; in fact, the most precious possession we have is time. God wants our lives available to Him, that He might use us to do His will. The urgency of the hour demands Christian discipleship. We do not know when Christ will come; so we must live every day as if it were our last. We want to be able to say with the writer of Revelation, "Amen. Come, Lord Jesus."

Closing Prayer

Recap

Opening Prayer

Discussion Starter

(Invite volunteers to tell about Christians they know who are examples of godly stewardship. Then discuss the good qualities the Holy Spirit has produced in their lives that help them give.)

Lesson Development

(Any appropriate material from previous lessons that was not sufficiently covered could be used at this time, and you also may deal with any point that the group members may not understand as well as they could.)

(Then go over the remaining Recap questions and answers. This material will benefit both the students and you by giving you a deeper appreciation of God's Word.)

Leader's Objective: To be sure students have a good understanding of stewardship and of what good stewardship toward God means personally to them

LESSON 9

The following questions will help you review this Step. If necessary, reread the appropriate lesson(s).

1. Define "Christian steward" in your own words. *(Managing our possessions for God.)*

2. Why are we referred to as Christian stewards? *(God owns everything and has given us responsibility to manage what He has given us.)*

3. Summarize your responsibilities as a steward of God as you now understand them.

LIFE APPLICATION

1. List several things over which you exercise stewardship.

2. What is the most important thing for you to realize about your attitude toward stewardship?

3. In which particular areas of your life have you seen a change for the better in your Christian stewardship?

4. Read about the *Sound Mind Principle* on the following pages. Use the steps included to help you make financial decisions.

We have seen again that God is the sovereign owner of everything, and that His standards of stewardship as expressed by Christ and by the Holy Spirit are perfect. We have looked at how we can become good stewards of out time, of our bodies, of our gifts, and of our possessions, and we have seen how we will be accountable to God for the exercise of our stewardship responsibilities. It remains now only for us to decide to allow God to rule in our hearts and through the power of the Holy Spirit to produce the growth toward maturity that He desires in us.

Conclusion and Application

(After making sure your students understand what stewardship is and how they can apply it to their lives from the questions in this lesson and the "Life Application," spend time discussing the "Sound Mind Principle" on pages 74–77 in the student's book. Then ask one or two volunteers to talk about ways they can apply the "Sound Mind Principle" to a decision they must make in the next few weeks. If students hesitate to share, tell about a decision you must make.)

Closing Prayer

(Use this time to give students an opportunity to commit themselves to godly stewardship in the decisions they will be making soon.)

Exploring **the Old**

Testament

Discover
God's Pattern
of Promise &
Blessing

STEP 9

The Drama Begins

Opening Prayer

Discussion Starter

Of the 39 books of the Old Testament, Genesis is perhaps the most important. It answers one of the great mysteries of all time, the mystery of how things came into existence. This book deals with the origins of the world, man, woman, sin, marriage, and the nations.

❷ How else is Genesis significant to us today?

Lesson Development

(Encourage students to read the article, "Discovering God's Pattern of Promise" at the beginning of their Study Guide on their own time if they have not already done so.)

(Ask one of the group members to summarize the paragraphs appearing at the opening of this lesson in the student's book. Note the diagram and discuss it.)

Leader's Objective: To teach students the relevance of Genesis to today's living

LESSON 1

Bible Study

Origin of Man

1. How did our world come into existence (Genesis 1)?
   (It was created by God.)

2. What was the condition of the world and everything that was in it at this time (Genesis 1:10,12,18, 21,25)?
   (Good.)

3. How did the first man come into existence (1:27)?
   (God created him.)

4. Was he an intelligent being at this time (2:20)?
   (Yes.)

   How do you know?
   (He gave all the animals and birds names that they still have.)

5. How was the first woman brought into existence (2:21,22)?
   (She was fashioned from a rib taken from the man.)

Origin of Sin

1. What was man's commission from God (1:28–30)?
   (To increase in number, subdue the earth, rule over living things.)

   What was man's relationship with God at this time (1:28)?
   (He was blessed by God.)

2. How would you describe Satan's personality char-

The opening phrase of Genesis, "In the beginning God," places God the creator at the center of the stage. This is more a story of the creator than one of His creation. As you read the next three chapters of Genesis, you will see that man is the climax of God's creation.

According to Genesis 1:26, God made man in His own image.

❓What is the image of God?

The image of God is what mankind now possesses that makes him different from any other created being (Genesis 9:6; 1 Corinthians 11:7; James 3:9).

The qualities that make man different from any created being are the capacities of morality, rationality, spirituality, immortality, and dominion over lower creation.

Spirituality refers to the life that was breathed into Adam by God in Genesis 2:7, making him a spiritual being.

When created in the image of God, man and woman possessed "original" righteousness and holiness (Genesis 1:31; Ecclesiastes 7:29). This was *lost* through sin and is restored in Christ through sanctification. As believers grow in faith, they become like the image of Christ (Colossians 3:10; Ephesians 4:24).

In the future, the redeemed will have a perfect body (Philippians 3:21). The reference to immortality applies to the soul. Originally the body was immortal, but this immortality was lost through sin (Romans 5:12, 6:23; 1 Corinthians 15:20–21). The Christian

acteristics when he appeared as a serpent, confronting Eve (3:1–5)?
(Sly, crafty, deceitful.)

How has he used these same personality characteristics in confronting you?

3. Whose word did Satan question (3:1)? *(God's.)*

Did Eve answer truthfully (3:2,3—look particularly at the last phrase of verse 3, then at 2:17)?
(No, she added to what God had said.)

4. In light of 1 John 2:16, analyze the temptation and list the three parts of it (3:6).

 1) *(Cravings of sinful man.)*

 2) *(Lust of the eyes.)*

 3) *(Boastful pride of life.)*

5. Why was it wrong for Adam and Eve to eat of this tree (2:16,17)?
(It was an act of disobedience to God's command.)

Sin's Result

1. What was the result of the sin of the man and the woman (3:7,8)?
(Their eyes were opened; they knew they were naked; they tried to cover themselves; they hid; their fellowship with God was broken.)

2. What was the penalty for sin for each of the following (3:14–19):

looks forward to receiving an immortal body fashioned in the image of Christ.

Genesis 3:1 introduces Satan indwelling a serpent for his attack upon creation. The book of Revelation pictures his punishment and, interestingly enough, uses the name *serpent*:

> The great dragon was hurled down—that ancient serpent called the devil or Satan, who leads the whole world astray. He was hurled to the earth, and his angels with him (12:9).

We learn here how sin came into the world and what it is. Sin is the greatest single problem of mankind. In Christ alone the Christian can face it with a realistic solution.

Christianity has revealed that man is not just a species of protoplasm, but that he is God's special creation. Man was created to have fellowship with God. We see how the fellowship was broken, and how it can be restored.

God's judgment was sure and just. Yet, even before the first sin, God had prepared a way to redeem mankind. The plan would cost God His Son's life

The serpent?
(He would crawl on his belly, eat dust, be at enmity with the woman and her seed, and suffer ultimate defeat.)

The woman?
(She would suffer pain in childbirth, her desire would be for her husband, and she would be subject to him.)

The man?
(The ground was cursed and he would have to work very hard for food.)

How was man's relationship with God altered (3:8–10)?
(He no longer walked with God; he now was fearful and ashamed.)

3. What did God promise regarding Satan's destiny (3:15)?
(He would be defeated by the woman's seed—Christ.)

The "seed of the woman" is the way the Bible describes the entrance of Christ into the world—conceived of the Holy Spirit, born of a woman, without a human father. (Compare Matthew 1:18–23.)

In light of this, explain the correlation between Christ's first and second coming and this verse.

LIFE APPLICATION

1. How does Adam's and Eve's sin affect you today

but would be the greatest demonstration of love ever given.

The only way a person can recover that intimate relationship with God is through receiving Christ as Savior and Lord and living moment by moment in the power of the Holy Spirit. Then we, too, can experience what Adam and Eve did when they walked with God in the garden.

In Christ's first coming, Satan struck Christ's heel through the crucifixion. However, Satan did not defeat Christ. In Christ's second coming, He will crush Satan's head by completely defeating him for eternity and throwing him in the lake of fire (Revelation 20:10).

Conclusion and Application

We have seen from Genesis the great spiritual events that have influenced

(Romans 5:12)?
(All men are under sin.)

2. Starting with Genesis 3:15, God begins to point to the time when the penalty for sin would be paid on man's behalf by the seed of the woman. In the chart on the next page, notice the prophecies pointing to Christ and their fulfillment in Him.

These are only a few of the more than three hundred Old Testament references to the coming of the Messiah that were fulfilled in the life, ministry, death, and resurrection of Jesus.

Look up all the references listed there regarding the promises and their fulfillment and read them.

What is the overall picture they present to you?

3. Read Romans 3:23 and 6:23. Describe what Jesus' death and resurrection mean to you.

the world. And we have learned that God is the creator and ruler of all things. This helps us realize our responsibility to Him as creator and gives us a glimpse of His omnipotent power. Anyone who denies God as creator automatically is faced with an empty, purposeless existence. But those who surrender their lives to Him find an abundant, joyful life.

(Go through the chart in the student's book.)

Closing Prayer

Adam Through Abraham

Opening Prayer

Discussion Starter

(Ask someone in the group to share how he has relied on God's promises in a difficult situation and how God was faithful to fulfill the promise. If no one in the group is able to do this, then share something from your life.)

Lesson Development

(Ask one of the group members to summarize the paragraphs appearing at the opening of this lesson in the student's book.)

Leader's Objective: To demonstrate successful living as a result of obeyng God's Word and failure as a result of disobedience

418

LESSON 2

Bible Study

Cain and Abel

1. In Genesis 4, two sacrifices are made. Evaluate each. Why was one acceptable to God and the other was not?
   (Cain's offering was just some of his fruit; Abel's was the choicest part of the best of his flock.)

2. What do you think verse 7 means?
   (A proper sacrifice was available to Cain if he wanted it.)

3. Read Hebrews 11:4. What part did faith play in Cain's and Abel's sacrifices?
   (Abel offered his sacrifice by faith, trusting God's requirements; Cain exhibited no such faith.)

4. Give at least one present-day example of the two types of sacrifices offered by Cain and Abel.
   (People who give money to the church for their own glory versus others who give to build up God's kingdom; people who serve others to make themselves feel good or to add up a pile of good deeds to their credit versus others who serve because they love those they serve.)

Noah

1. Why was God sorry that He had made man on the

(Read Hebrews 9:22.)

God was already setting up the system for sin sacrifice by requiring Cain and Abel to bring their sacrifices to Him.

Cain had no sense of sin or need for atonement. He did not listen to God's instructions, but did his own thing. Abel's sacrifice involved confession of sin and expression of faith in God's substitute.

(Read the parallel passages on the sacrifice of Cain and Abel in 1 John 3:12 and Hebrews 11:4.)

❷ How does Ephesians 2:8–10 relate to Cain's and Abel's sacrifice?

❷ How about 1 Samuel 15:22?

Noah gave evidence of his trust in God when he persisted in preparing the ark while almost everyone else made fun

earth (Genesis 6:5–7)?
(Because man was disobedient, wicked, and would not try to understand the ways of God.)

2. Why was Noah chosen by God to build an ark (6:8,9)?
(He had found favor in the eyes of the Lord.)

3. What do you think God accomplished through Noah? (Genesis 6:17–22; see also Hebrews 11:7.)
(He saved Noah's household; He condemned the world; and He taught the necessity of faith and obedience.)

Abraham

1. Abraham holds a unique place in the history of the world.

   Three religions point to Abraham as the founder of their faith: Christianity, Islam, and Judaism. On the basis of Genesis 12:2,3; 16:4,15; and 17:19, how does each faith trace its origins to Abraham?
   (Abraham was given the promise that he would be the one through whom God would bless the earth—ancestor of Christ and spiritual father of those who believe in Jesus; Abraham was the father Ishmael—ancestor of all Arabs; Abraham was the father of Isaac—ancestor of all Jews.)

2. Why do you suppose God made the request of

of him. Repercussions of faithless behavior are severe, but the blessings of obedience are unending.

Abraham's lack of faith in God's promise to provide a son resulted in the birth of Ishmael. Eventually, Ishmael's descendants followed the prophet Mohammed, who rejected the God of the Jews. Muslims and Jews have hated each other over the years and their enmity continues today.

Abraham is the spiritual father of the believing Jews, not the unbelieving—the father of Judaism that pointed to Christ (Romans 4:11–17). At Christ's death the veil of the Holy of Holies was torn in two. This was a sign that Judaism as God's chosen way to communicate with man and as the picture of redemption no longer existed—no temple, no blood sacrifice, no holy of holies. Instead, Christ became the only way to God.

Abraham recorded in Genesis 22:1,2?
(To test his faith.)

3. Study Genesis 22:8 and give your explanation of it.
(It is an example showing that God will provide the necessary sacrifice, and we can trust His promise.)

4. How does Abraham's willingness picture God's love for us?
(God willingly gave His Son for us.)

1. What important lesson have you learned from God's response to Cain?

2. Do you think you would have boarded the ark with Noah? Why or why not?

3. How have you and your family been blessed in Abraham as promised in Genesis 12:3?
(We receive eternal life through Abraham's line by Jesus' birth and through Abraham's faith.)

4. How can the story of Abraham offering Isaac to God in Genesis 22 help your faith to grow?

❖   ❖   ❖

(Read Genesis 17:15,16 and Genesis 22:8.) Isaac was a sacrifice of his father just as Christ was.

❓Describe the kind faith Abraham had. What elements stand out to you?

(Read Matthew 1:1.) This is an outline of Matthew. In chapters 1—25, Christ is Son of David, the king. In chapters 26—28, he is Son of Abraham, the sacrifice of His father.

Conclusion and Application

We can trust the promises of God because:

> God is not man, that he should lie nor a son of man that he should change his mind. Does he speak and then not act? Does he promise and not fulfill? (Numbers 23:19).

Spiritual problems usually arise from a problem in our view of the Bible. Either we do not trust God's promises, or we are ignorant of them, so we worry. These difficulties can be overcome by making God's Word a part of our lives. And when we confess our sin according to 1 John 1:9, we receive cleansing, and our fellowship with God is restored.

Closing Prayer

Moses, the Passover, and the Exodus

Opening Prayer

Discussion Starter

Susan is ready to start her last year at nursing school. A fine Christian guy has proposed to her. She loves him and would like to marry him. The problem is that when she was sixteen she felt God called her to go to foreign missions as a nurse.

 What should she do?

Lesson Development

(Ask one of the group members to summarize the paragraphs appearing at the opening of this lesson in the student's book.)

❖

Leader's Objective: To illustrate what it means to walk by faith and to motivate students to rest in the Lord so that He can use them in whatever way He chooses

Bible Study

Moses the Leader

1. Read Hebrews 11:23–29.

   Why do you think God chose Moses to lead His people?
   (He was a man of faith.)

2. Read Exodus 3 and 4.

   When God told Moses what He wanted him to do, how did He say the people would react (Exodus 3:18)?
   (They would listen to what Moses said.)

   Whose work was this going to be (Exodus 3:17, 20,21 and 4:12)?
   (God's.)

   Where did Moses fit in?
   (Moses was to be the leader to lead the people in God's name.)

3. In Exodus 4, how did Moses respond, and how did God handle those responses?

   Verses 1–9
   (He was afraid people wouldn't believe him, and God gave him miraculous proofs.)

   Verses 10–12
   (He pleaded slow speech and tongue. God assured him He would be with his mouth.)

   Verses 13–17
   (He didn't want to be the one to speak. God gave

This period of Moses' life illustrates the blessings of trusting God.

The "faith hall of fame" listed in Hebrews 11 contains names of some of the men and women made great, not by their own talent, but by their trust in God. No man *ever* counted for God without faith (Hebrews 11:6). Note the change that faith made in Moses' life as Hebrews 11 records:

Before faith	After faith
Had great opportunities; lost them (Exodus 2:11–15)	Accomplished tremendous feats—performed miracles; led Israel out of Egypt; gave Law; wrote first five books of Bible
Spent 40 wasted years (Acts 7:23,30)	Became one of history's greatest men, after he was 80 years old
Fled as a coward (Exodus 2:15)	Defied the greatest empire of his day, Egypt

The simple act of trusting God completely transforms a life. Note what God called Moses to do—defy the great ruler Pharaoh, with no backing but the promise of God. God usually calls us to do far greater things than we have ever imagined.

Note how well God had things planned for Moses—He has all things planned for us as well. But He expects us to fit into His plans for our own good and blessing.

him Aaron and a special staff.)

4. In Exodus 4:1, Moses said of the people, "What if they do not believe me?" When Moses was obedient, how did the people respond (verse 31)?
(They believed him, and they bowed down and worshiped God.)

The Passover

Read Exodus 12.

1. Why was God sending plagues at this time (verse 12)?
(To judge Pharoah and compel him to let His people go.)

2. What was the most vital instruction given to the children of Israel (verse 13)?
(To slay a perfect lamb and apply its blood to their doorpost.)

3. What are the correlations between Christ's death and the Passover as indicated in these Scriptures?

Exodus 12:3—John 1:29
(A lamb; Christ is the Lamb of God.)

Exodus 12:5,6—Isaiah 53:7; 1 Peter 2:22
(Without blemish; Jesus was sinless.)

Exodus 12:6—1 Corinthians 5:7
(To be slain; Christ was sacrificed for us.)

❖ How does knowing that Moses had weaknesses and felt inadequate help you trust God more?

Moses could have disobeyed God's call, with the result that he would have faded into oblivion. When we accept God's plan for our lives, we are the winners.

❖ How does the story of Moses confronting Pharoah show that God is in control of nations and rulers?

Note how clear this makes the issue of salvation. Salvation is based *solely* on what one does with Christ.

A man is either saved or lost. There is no in-between or second chance for "good" people, any more than there was an in-between for those who, whatever their social status and personality, refused to apply the blood.

Blood applied to the two doorposts (sides) and to the lintel (top) created what kind of picture?
(Complete protection.)

4. What do you suppose happened to those who disobeyed the instructions given through Moses?
(Their first-born died.)

What spiritual truth do you believe this illustrates?
(We are protected by blood.)

5. What does Exodus 12:29 teach about God being a respecter of persons?
(He is not. Pharaoh and the captives were equal.)

How does this apply to the condition of any person who has not received Christ?
(Anyone who does not receive Christ will suffer eternal death.)

The Exodus ("Going Out")

1. One of the most important events in the history of Israel occurred immediately following the Passover. What was it (Exodus 12:40,41)?
(All the Israelite people were freed from slavery.)

2. Compare Exodus 3:7,8 and John 3:16. How do you see them being related?
(Both show His love, His awareness of need, and

As humans we tend to be awed by position, wealth, and talent. But God accepts everyone on an equal basis—as sinners who need redemption.

❓ How does knowing this help you share your faith in Christ?

Paul compares our bondage in sin to slavery (Romans 7:14). We could not liberate ourselves, but Christ broke the power of sin and death over our lives. God has given us a new life, and Jesus promised to prepare a place

*His provision; both con-
tain promises.)*

3. One of the most remarkable and well-known mir-
acles in the world is
recorded in Exodus 14.
Summarize it here.
*(The parting of the Red
Sea.)*

What spiritual truth does
this experience suggest
to you?

4. While the Israelites were
in the wilderness, they
had many trials and hard-
ships. Several times in
the many years of wan-
dering before coming
into the land that had
been promised to them,
they failed God. (See
Exodus 17:1–7; 32:1–6,
15–20; and Numbers
21:4–9.)

What practical value do
these events recorded in
the Old Testament have
for you today (1 Corinthians 10:5–11)?
*(They were examples and
warnings to us.)*

What wrong attitudes
and sins were shown in
these examples?
*(Quarreling, complain-
ing, idolatry, sexual im-
morality, disobedience,
impatience.)*

5. In summary of the wilderness wanderings men-
tioned in 1 Corinthians
10:1–13, what is God's
promise to you?
*(No temptation will be too
great to bear, and God's*

for us when He ascended to heaven
(John 14:1–6).

   Crossing the Red Sea shows how
God goes before us and opens the way
for whatever He asks us to do. He also
protects us from the forces of evil that
are coming after us.

❓What Old Testament story has
helped you understand a biblical
principle?

❓How could the Israelites have
applied the principle in 1 Corinthians 10:13 to their situation?

help is always there—verse 13.)

Write out the verse that contains the promise, and claim it.

1. God asked Moses a question in Exodus 4:2. What was it?

   ("What is that in your hand?")

2. God expects us to use what we have. Moses used a rod; David used a sling; Gideon used lanterns, pitchers, and trumpets. What is in your hands?

3. How do you think God wants you to use what He has entrusted to you?

4. How can you use 1 Corinthians 10:13 in your daily life?

❖ ❖ ❖

Conclusion and Application

Israel's mistakes were made in spite of the fact that the people had witnessed tremendous miracles by God on their behalf. They committed idolatry (1 Corinthians 10:7) and sexual immorality (verse 8), they tested the Lord (verse 9), and they complained against God (verse 10). For these things God sent judgment upon them. (Read Galatians 5:7,8.)

The apostle Paul warns us about getting sidetracked in the race we are running for our faith. According to 1 Corinthians 10:12, it is possible for us to fall into the same types of sins despite our Christian maturity. When tempted, if we will appropriate God's promise given in verse 13, we can avoid falling into sin and God will be able to use us.

All we need to do is to surrender ourselves and whatever He has given us—our abilities and gifts and possessions—totally to Him for His use in accomplishing His purpose. When we trust in Him and His provisions and rest in His promises, He will work in and through us.

Closing Prayer

Law and Grace

Opening Prayer

Discussion Starter

 What is law?

 What is grace?

 What is the difference between the two?

Lesson Development

(Ask one of the group members to summarize the paragraphs appearing at the opening of this lesson in the student's book.)

❖

Leader's Objective: To help students be aware of the danger of legalism and to motivate them to live under grace instead of trying to keep any kind of law through self-effort

Bible Study

The Law

When the "Law" is mentioned, the thing that most commonly comes to mind is the Ten Commandments.

The Ten Commandments are listed in Exodus 20 and are repeated in Deuteronomy 5. They are as follows:

I. You shall have no other gods before me.

II. You shall not make for yourself an idol in the form of anything.

III. You shall not misuse the name of the Lord your God.

IV. Remember the sabbath day by keeping it holy.

V. Honor your father and your mother.

VI. You shall not murder.

VII. You shall not commit adultery.

VIII. You shall not steal.

IX. You shall not give false testimony against your neighbor.

X. You shall not covet . . . anything that belongs to your neighbor.

1. Jesus condensed these ten into two in Matthew 22:37–40. What are they?

   1) *(Love God with all your heart, soul, and mind.)*

In the New Testament, *law* describes the legal method of approaching God, seeking to be justified before Him by obeying His righteous standards.

The Law of Moses is the highest and best representative of the legal approach to God. All religions and moral systems that try to appease God approach Him legally *except* true Christianity. Of these legal systems, the Law of Moses is the only one ordained by God.

All who seek salvation or blessing on the basis of *obedience,* even if it is obedience to the Ten Commandments or the Sermon on the Mount, are approaching God by *law.*

❓ How is what Christ said a contrast to keeping the Law?

Christ's two commandments deal with the heart only, not outward obedience. When we love God, we want to serve Him and others.

2) *(Love your neighbor as yourself.)*

2. What was James' pronouncement concerning the seriousness of breaking even one of these laws (James 2:10)?
(If we stumble in one point, we are guilty of all.)

What the Law Does

Read Deuteronomy 29:29 and 30:11–20.

The Law of Moses was a covenant of works. God said, "You shall" and "You shall not." The laws were definite, and the attached penalties were definite if the conditions were not obeyed.

Webster defines law as "a rule of conduct or action prescribed by the supreme governing authority and enforced by a sanction." Law always implies two things: a standard and a penalty.

These laws were presented as God's standard of righteousness for that time. They were literally a yardstick for man. The New Testament reveals that "by the law is the knowledge of sin." Jesus Christ came to "fulfill the law," and now God's standard of righteousness is Christ Himself.

1. How are God's people to respond to the things He has revealed of Himself

❓How does fulfilling Christ's commandments result in keeping the Law?

When we love God first and others second, we will naturally fulfill the other laws.

James emphasizes the importance of the Law.

❓How do verses 12 and 13 of James 2 describe our relationship to the Law?

When we deal with others and their shortcomings, we should treat them with mercy so we will not fall under judgment of the Law. When we expect others to fulfill the Law, God will then expect us to live up to the Law's standards too.

The world uses a yardstick for almost every part of life. We have speedometers on our cars. We work a certain number of hours per day in our jobs. We measure ingredients in recipes. We are charged by how many gallons we use and how long the job takes, and we are graded in school. Yet the world expects God to look the other way when evaluating our morals. But God has His own yardstick—and no one can live up to His standards.

(Deuteronomy 29:29; 30:11,19)?
(Follow all the words of the law.)

2. Briefly, what is the summary of all the Law (Deuteronomy 30:16,20)?
(Love the Lord your God; walk in His ways; keep His commandments; obey His voice.)

3. How did Jesus Christ summarize the will of God for man in Mark 12:29–31?
(Love God with your heart, soul, mind, and strength; love your neighbor as yourself.)

4. On the basis of Matthew 5:17, what do you think was Christ's assessment of the Law?
(It was to be kept—He came to fulfill it.)

5. Read Romans 3:19–26.

   What does the Law reveal (verses 19,20)?
   (The knowledge of sin.)

   To what did the Law bear witness while failing to reveal it fully (verse 21)?
   (The righteousness of God.)

   How has a full revelation been made to us (verses 22–24)?
   (Through faith in Jesus Christ.)

Grace

1. The Living Bible translation of Romans 3:19–26 will help you understand God's grace. As you read

That's what makes the Mosaic Law impossible to live by.

❓Why do you think the world makes an exception to measuring or grading when it comes to morals?

The world is not interested in living up to God's standards. Since the world cannot rise to God's level, it tries to resolve guilt and expectations by pretending that morals do not matter or that they are different than every other law. The result is disasterous.

❓How do you think Christ fulfilled the Law? Give specific examples from the Ten Commandments.

Christ worshiped at the synagogue each Sabbath (Luke 4:16). He honored His mother (John 19:26,27). He was completely one with God the Father (John 10:30).

❓How will these verses come true at God's judgment seat?

When God judges each nonbeliever's life against the Law, no one will have an excuse. Each non-Christian will have to account for all of his sins and will have to pay for them.

Grace is an entirely different way of approaching God (Romans 6:14). Law and grace are two different systems ordained for two different purposes,

the following passage, underline the words that have special meaning to you.

The judgment of God lies very heavily upon the Jews, for they are responsible to keep God's laws instead of doing all these evil things; not one of them has any excuse; in fact, all the world stands hushed and guilty before Almighty God. Now do you see it? No one can ever be made right in God's sight by doing what the law commands. For the more we know of God's laws, the clearer it becomes that we aren't obeying them; his laws serve only to make us see that we are sinners.

But now God has shown us a different way to heaven—not by "being good enough" and trying to keep his laws, but by a new way (though not new, really, for the Scriptures told about it long ago). Now God says he will accept and acquit us—declare us "not guilty"—if we trust Jesus Christ to take away our sins. And we all can be saved in this same way, by coming to Christ, no matter who we are or what we have been like. Yes, all have sinned; all fall short of God's glorious ideal; yet now God declares us "not guilty" of offending him if we trust in Jesus Christ, who in

and are never to be mingled. Each is complete in itself.

We are under either one system or the other, not both. All Christians, whether they realize it or not, whether they enjoy the privilege or not, are under grace.

Grace is the kindness and love of God expressed toward us entirely apart from what we deserve (Titus 3:5,6; Romans 4:4,5). Under the Law, we earn whatever we get. Under grace, whatever we get is a free gift.

Since grace depends only on our accepting it, and not on what we deserve, it is in no way dependent on how good we are, and can *never* be limited by how bad we are (Romans 5:8). God did the most for us when we deserved the least from Him.

Our society is full of evidences that people cannot escape the desire to be morally acceptable. Eating disorders, ulcers, depression, and many other psychological and physical problems can come from the need to be better than we are. Tragically, the answer is not in becoming better or more moral in our own efforts, but in knowing that we are acceptable—even perfect—in God's eyes because of Jesus.

God cannot love us more than He already does. Knowing this, we can open ourselves to God's love and He will begin building our self-esteem that has been damaged by sin and from living in a harsh world. When we realize

his kindness freely takes away our sins.

For God sent Christ Jesus to take the punishment for our sins and to end all God's anger against us. He used Christ's blood and our faith as the means of saving us from his wrath. In this way he was being entirely fair, even though he did not punish those who sinned in former times. For he was looking forward to the time when Christ would come and take away those sins. And now in these days also he can receive sinners in this same way, because Jesus took away their sins.

2. Compare Romans 3:20 with Ephesians 2:8,9 and write your conclusions. *(The only way we can become righteous is through faith.)*

   How does keeping the Law make a person feel? *(Guilty.)*

   Should living under grace make you more eager to obey God or less? *(More eager.)*

   Why? *(We are serving out of love rather than out of fear.)*

LIFE APPLICATION

1. How would you explain the difference between Law and grace to some-

that we are perfect in God's eyes, we can respond fully to His love by loving Him, by being filled with His Spirit, then loving our neighbors and friends. As we love God and others, we will naturally keep the commandments we could not do in our own strength.

The progression of the Christian in His conversion and faith is as follows:

1) The Law reveals our sin.

2) Grace allows us to be reconciled to God through faith in Christ.

3) When we do, we become righteous in God's eyes.

4) Through faith and love we serve God, which leads us to greater maturity in the Lord and to fulfilling Christ's two commandments.

5) We begin doing the spirit of the Law through our love for God and others.

Conclusion and Application

Every believer in Christ receives God's inexhaustible love, power, and grace. Yet, because of the ignorance of their

one who was depending upon his own good works to please the Father?
(Grace is unmerited favor; Law is living up to a perfect standard.)

2. What is Christ's relationship to the following:

   The Law?
   (He fulfilled it perfectly.)

   Grace?
   (By paying for our sins, He allowed God to exercise grace on our behalf.)

3. What is your relationship to the following:

   The Law?
   (It revealed my sin.)

   Grace?
   (It opens the way for me to have a relationship with God.)

4. What difference will an understanding of Law and grace make in your desire to please God?

spiritual heritage and their own weakness, many Christians labor in misery and defeat, plagued with guilt and feelings of condemnation because they live as though still under law.

To them, God is a hard, exacting, and scrupulous taskmaster. They spend their lives trying to make up for sins, trying to earn His love and acceptance, trying to lift themselves toward heaven with their good works.

But the One Jesus lovingly called Father forgives freely, gives bountifully, and is a joy to know. He is the God of grace.

Closing Prayer

Deliverance and Forgiveness

Opening Prayer

Discussion Starter

❓ How does sin in our lives hinder our fellowship with God?

❓ How does your relationship as a parent or a friend help you understand the relationship between God and a Christian who sins?

Lesson Development

(Ask one of the group members to summarize the paragraphs appearing at the opening of this lesson in the student's book.)

Leader's Objective: To teach the students how to rest by faith in the promises of God, and to encourage them to keep an unhindered fellowship with the Lord by confessing sin

LESSON 5

Bible Study

Joshua and Deliverance

Joshua's name gives us some insight into the book. His name means "Jehovah is Salvation." It is carried over into the New Testament in the name of our Lord, "Jesus."

1. Read Joshua 1:1–9 and list God's promises to Joshua.
   (God would give Joshua every place he walked on, and strength and victory. God's presence and comfort, success and prosperity would be his. God would never leave him.)

   What was the condition on which these promises would be fulfilled?
   (Obedience to God's Law and Joshua's willingness to arise and go.)

   Which of these can you apply to your life?

   How?

2. In Joshua 7, why did God tell Joshua to stop praying?
   (Israel had sinned and disobeyed Him.)

   What does God say to you in Psalm 66:18?
   (That if you cherish sin in your heart, the Lord will not hear you.)

   How can you apply Numbers 32:23 to this passage?

❓ How much of Joshua 1:1–9 depended on Joshua?

❓ How much of our Christian life depends on us?

    The one who calls you is faithful and he will do it (1 Thessalonians 5:24).

    If we are faithless, he will remain faithful for he cannot disown himself (2 Timothy 2:13).

Notice Abraham's example of believing God as recorded in Romans 4:20,21.

When God gives a command, He also gives us the ability to obey. God was faithful to Joshua as He was previously to Moses—He is no respecter of persons (Joshua 4:23).

❓ To what lengths did God go to complete His will and promise to Joshua (Joshua 10:13,14)?

❓ Has God changed? See Hebrews 13:8: "Jesus Christ is the same yesterday and today and forever."

❓ If you do not deal with your sin, what will God do?

("Your sin will find you out.")

3. What happened after the sin was taken away (Joshua 8:1)?
(God's blessings were restored.)

4. What was Joshua's command to the people before he died (Joshua 23:6)?
(To be careful to keep all of God's law and not to turn away from it.)

5. How do the characteristics of Joshua as deliverer foreshadow Christ's work for us?
(Joshua led his people into the Promised Land; there he conquered the godless people living in the land. Christ also leads us into an abundant life. He conquers our spiritual enemies and helps us win battles over the world and our fleshly nature.)

David and Forgiveness

1. Read 1 Samuel 24 and 2 Samuel 5 and 12. As you read these chapters, list the verses that indicate the following characteristics of David:

Submissiveness
(1 Samuel 24:6,8,10,12, 15,22; 2 Samuel 5:19,20, 23–25; 12:13,23.)

Sincerity
(1 Samuel 24:11,12,13, 22; 2 Samuel 12:5,6, compared with 13.)

❓What is the importance of having your sin find you out?

❓Describe how you feel when you confess your sin and God forgives.

God graciously chose David as a young man and brought him out from feeding sheep and anointed him King of Israel.

When the Jewish new year ended in March, it was customary for kings to go to battle. David, however, sent Joab and stayed at home (2 Samuel 11:1).

Psalms 5:3; 63:1; and 143:8 reveal that as a rule David was faithful in meeting God daily and seeking guidance early. But 2 Samuel 11:2 shows a

Boldness
(*1 Samuel 24:4,8–15; 2 Samuel 5:7,17.*)

Trust in God
(*1 Samuel 24:6,10,12, 15; 2 Samuel 5:19,20,23-24; 12:29.*)

Leadership stature
(*1 Samuel 24:7,20,22; 2 Samuel 5:1–5,10,20,25; 12:29.*)

Sinful passion
(*2 Samuel 12:4,9.*)

Sorrow for sin
(*1 Samuel 24:5; 2 Samuel 12:13.*)

2. The nobility of David's character is seen in many of the recorded instances from his career, including some of those you have just read. He is described as a "man after God's own heart," and as such, he occupies a high position among the heroes of the faith. Jesus' title as the ruler of God's people is "the Son of David."

Many people, however, find the stories of David's terrible sins to be absolutely contradictory to this exalted position of spiritual leadership.

How can you hold up such a man as an outstanding example of "a man after God's own heart"?
(*David repented and changed his ways. He served God with all of his heart.*)

time when David arose in the evening instead of early morning. While walking on his balcony, he was overwhelmed with temptation at the sight of a beautiful woman.

A person who walks away from God always walks into trouble. David's sins included adultery (verse 4), murder (verse 15) and hypocrisy (verse 25).

The Bible says that man can enjoy sin only for a season, and Psalms 32, 38, and 51 all reveal David's distress and misery during this year's period of being out of fellowship with God.

David paid an awesome price for his sin:

◆ His child of adultery died (2 Samuel 12:18).

◆ One son, Amnon, committed incest (13:14).

◆ Another son, Absalom, committed murder and fought to take the throne from David (13:28,29).

◆ The same son suffered a dreadful, accidental death (Chapters 15—18).

David confessed and received complete forgiveness and restoration:

◆ He admitted his guilt (2 Samuel 12:13; Psalm 51:3).

◆ He prayed for the joy of his salvation to be returned (Psalm 51:12).

◆ He realized he must have a clean heart to be used of God (Psalm 51:13).

If you can answer this question, you will have grasped the essence of biblical faith. Read 2 Samuel 12 again, and then Psalm 32 and 51, which David wrote at that time. (You might find help in Romans 4:1–8 or Luke 7:36–50; 18:9–14.)

3. How did David's experience foreshadow the attitude of Jesus toward sinners? Be specific.
(It doesn't matter what we've done, God will forgive us. Jesus forgave the woman who had committed adultery, forgave those who crucified Him, and forgave the thief on the cross.)

4. How do Christ's roles as King and High Priest relate to deliverance and forgiveness?
(As King, He has the power to deliver us and the wisdom to lead us. As High Priest, He offered the sacrifice of His own body for our forgiveness.)

LIFE APPLICATION

1. What sin, or problem, do you need deliverance from today?

2. Read Proverbs 28:13. How can you appropriate it for your problem?
(Confess the sin.)

3. Read Joshua 24. Circle all the "I's" in verses 3 through 13 and notice all the things God accom-

❓How can David's life show you how to restore a Christian who has sinned?

Many Christians feel that some sins are unforgivable. But that is not how God considers sin. Jesus forgave Peter who denied Him three times. God also forgave David for his sins. We are to follow the example and forgive other Christians who have wronged us or who have hurt other people.

Conclusion and Application

The blessings of Christian experience depend upon obedience to Christ. Confession of disobedience restores the sense of right standing and the joy of our salvation. We do not wait to feel restored, but simply believe it, just as the Bible teaches in Proverbs 28:13:

> He who conceals his sins does not prosper, but whoever confesses and renounces them finds mercy.

plished for the people of Israel.

What do you need Him to accomplish for you?

Pray, asking in faith that God will work on your behalf in these areas.

4. How does your heart attitude compare with that of Joshua and David?

How can you use their example to live a more godly life?

❖ ❖ ❖

One of the best ways we can reflect God's qualities in our lives is to be truly forgiving to others. When our non-Christian friends see how we love in spite of differences and hurts, they will be more open to hearing about God's love for them.

Closing Prayer

Elijah: The Power of a Spirit-Led Man

Opening Prayer

Discussion Starter

Two Christians have the same background. One is fearless in his witness and the other is not. Instead, he is a spiritual "milquetoast."

❷ Why do you think that is?

❷ How do you think he could get a handle on his fear of witnessing?

Lesson Development

(Ask one of the group members to summarize the paragraphs appearing at the opening of this lesson in the student's book.)

❖

Leader's Objective: To encourage the students, through an examination of the life of Elijah, toward spiritually powerful Christian service

LESSON 6

Bible Study

Elijah

1. Read 1 Kings 17:1–7. Indicate whether the following statements are true or false.

   (T) The cessation of rain is dependent on all these factors: God lives; Elijah lived in His presence; and Elijah's word controlled the rain.

   (F) The Bible says that Elijah searched eagerly for the will of God.

   (T) The prophet obeyed orders for the immediate future, though he did not know how it would turn out.

   (F) Elijah thought the plan was absurd, and hesitated.

   (F) The brook dried up, proving he was right.

2. What step of duty have you not taken because you cannot see its outcome?

The Widow

1. Read 1 Kings 17:8–24. Indicate whether the following statements are true or false.

   (T) Strict, implicit obedience characterized Elijah.

Imagine you are Elijah. You are living in a day when your society has abandoned traditional morals. Your leader is worshiping Baal, the god of a foreign people—the Phoenicians. In fact, your king, Ahab, is married to a Canaanite woman named Jezebel and she hates anyone who worships Jehovah God. She talks Ahab into issuing death orders for anyone found worshiping God.

Then God asks you to confront Ahab. The message you are to give is that God will bring judgment upon the king for his wickedness.

❓How would you feel?

❓How is Elijah's society similar to the one in which we live?

God sent a famine on the land. But that did not change Ahab's heart. He still permitted the worship of Baal to be part of the kingdom.

When the Lord sent Elijah back to Ahab, the first person Elijah talked to

_(T)_ When her boy died, guilt turned the widow's eyes upon herself.

_(T)_ God desires to remove from our lives now the guilt that can cripple our faith in time of crisis.

2. Do you think it was humiliating to take a step of faith that made him dependent on a very poor widow?

3. Why do you think God deals with us in such a way?
   (He wants us to depend on Him and to let others get the blessing of serving.)

Ahab

1. Read 1 Kings 18:1–18. Indicate whether the following statements are true or false.

   _(T)_ Ahab was at least concerned for his animals.

   _(T)_ He had refused to acknowledge the real reason for the problem (verses 17, 18).

   _(T)_ Nevertheless, Elijah recognized the real reason (verses 17, 18).

2. Describe a time when you were the cause of a problem for others that you did not acknowledge.

   What was the result?

was Obadiah, a believer who was serving God in Ahab's palace.

❷ What does this say to you about the need for Christian unity during hard times?

❷ What had Obadiah done that showed his faith (1 Kings 18:12,13)?

❷ How has God worked in your life when you have had to depend on other Christians?

When Elijah once again confronted Ahab, he tried to make Elijah look like the troublemaker. Elijah put the blame where it belonged—on Ahab's sin.

❷ How is this like what happens when Christians stand up for what's right today?

3. How can you avoid this sin (Proverbs 3:5,6)?
   (Acknowledge God and He will help us keep on the right path.)

Prophets of Baal

1. Read 1 Kings 18:18–40. Write the verse number(s) in which Elijah did the following:

   (21) Rebuked the people for compromise

   (24) Challenged the enemies of God to a contest

   (27) Blasted them with withering sarcasm

   (33,34) Ordered water poured

   (36) Prayed to God to make Himself known

   (40) Ordered the priests executed

2. How can this incident apply to today?
   (We can display God's power to our corner of the world.)

3. Elijah's prayer in verse 36 provides a superb revelation of the Spirit-led life. Why do you think that is true?
   (Elijah acknowledged that all he did was the work of God in and through him.)

LIFE APPLICATION

1. Describe the relationship Elijah had with God.
   (He obeyed God and did what God wanted him to

Elijah put God to the test on the top of Mount Carmel before the entire nation. Elijah proposed a test by fire because Baal was a fire-god. He brought the test to Baal's strongest claim. (Read 1 Kings 18:27–29.)

Then Elijah let the prophets of Baal do their thing for an entire day. He knew the outcome—God would triumph.

Elijah also made the test uneven by pouring water on his own altar. No one watching could ever doubt that God had the greatest power.

❓What did Elijah pray?

(Read 1 Kings 18:36.)

God answered instantly and displayed His power by destroying the offering, the wood, the stones, and the dust.

Today we can also show God's power. Like Elijah, we can be the instrument God uses to prove His strength. When we love others, live by faith, and introduce others to Jesus through the power of the Holy Spirit, we demonstrate God's power.

Conclusion and Application

One characteristic of Elijah's life was that he dealt with people in different ways. He confronted Ahab. He was tender with the widow. And he encour-

do in God's power. He re-lied on, talked to, and obeyed God.)

2. How does your relation-ship and power with God compare to Elijah's?

3. How has God's power been exerted through you upon the lives of oth-ers?

4. What changes in your mental and spiritual thinking need to take place for you to find the power with God that you desire?

aged Obadiah. That is a characteristic of the Holy Spirit at work. As we let the Holy Spirit lead us, He will show us how to relate to all kinds of people. He will give us an increasing sensitivity to people's needs and the best way to pre-sent God's love to them.

Closing Prayer

Jeremiah: A Witness Who Stood Alone

Opening Prayer

Discussion Starter

❓In your experiences in dealing with people who need Christ, have you ever felt incapable of sharing your faith with them?

❓Why?

Lesson Development

(Ask one of the group members to summarize the paragraphs appearing at the opening of this lesson in the student's book.)

Leader's Objective: To encourage students to be faithful in the face of discouragements

Bible Study

Jeremiah's Call

Read Jeremiah 1.

1. When facing Scripture verses that command you to speak for Christ, have you ever felt, "Why, I could never do that, I have no training for it"?

   What did Jeremiah say (1:6)?
   (He did not know how to speak because he was too immature.)

2. To be effective in speaking, one must have something to say. Where do you get the right message (1:7–17)?
   (God will give us what He wants us to say.)

   In what way does God touch our mouths today (Ephesians 5:18)?
   (He fills us with His Holy Spirit who speaks through us.)

3. Opposition of the intensity that faced Jeremiah is unknown in America, although it is common in some parts of the world. How can these verses help us overcome situations we face (1:8,18,19)?
   (Remember that God has promised to be with us and deliver us.)

If we have hidden God's word in our hearts and are controlled by the Holy Spirit, the Spirit will call to mind the words needed to answer every person in every situation (John 14:26; Colossians 4:5,6).

Paul had a powerful testimony about persecution in 2 Timothy 3:10–12.

❷ What was it?

❷ What is the promise of God for a life of service to the Lord (Luke 18:29,30)?

Jeremiah's Arrest and Prayer

Read Jeremiah 19:14,15. In verse 14, we see that not only what Jeremiah said but also where he spoke (and to whom) were under the Lord's direct guidance. This was also observed in Elijah's life as one of the secrets of effectiveness. The secret is to be filled with God's Holy Spirit. He will lead us to those He wants us to touch. As a result, Spirit-filled Christians share their faith with others at every opportunity. The apostle Paul records in Colossians 1:28, "Everywhere we go we talk about Christ to all who will listen" (TLB).

Verse 15 was Jeremiah's unpopular message in a nutshell: condemnation upon the capital city, Jerusalem; the Babylonian armies would destroy the city. He advised the people to surrender and avoid the horrors of a siege that could not be resisted for long since God was on the enemy's side.

Read Jeremiah 20.

1. How did punishment affect Jeremiah's testimony (20:1–6)?
   (It just made it more sure and more specific.)

2. Verses 7–18 are an example of the abrupt interruptions interspersed throughout the book of Jeremiah. What do these prayers reveal about the

❓What are some practical lessons we can gain from standing alone with the Lord?

(Have several members suggest applications to life, then point out the following:)

◆ God's faithfulness (Lamentations 3:22,23)

◆ His mercy overcoming our distress (Psalm 103:17,18)

◆ Grace during human weakness (2 Corinthians 12:9,10)

◆ Confidence in God rather than in men (Hebrews 10:35,36)

◆ Communion of knowing and loving the Lord (Jeremiah 24:7)

Jeremiah's prayer indicates that although he was a strong witness, he had to deal with inner doubts and fears in prayer.

Jeremiah understood the total inadequacy of the flesh and the absolute capability of God to meet his every need. He unloaded his burdens and hardships on his Lord. He was completely open in the presence of God, hiding nothing. He was abiding in Christ, letting Him bear every weight, just as the branch allows the trunk of the tree to support it in a storm (John 15:4,5).

He was fearless in public because he dealt with and removed these fears through his private prayer life (see Philippians 4:6,7; 1 Peter 5:7).

apparent fearlessness of the prophet?
(Inwardly he was afraid and miserable; he wished he had never been born.)

3. Since his message brought him so much unpopularity, what did Jeremiah consider (20:8,9)?
(Not speaking, holding it all in.)

Why did he reject that idea?
(He could not withhold God's message.)

4. How did his enemies think they could get the best of him (20:10)?
(By denouncing and deceiving him.)

5. What thoughts restored His confidence (20:11)?
(The Lord was with him, like a mighty warrior.)

6. How can you relate Jeremiah's attitude to your experiences in witnessing for the Lord?

How can Jeremiah's example help you?

Jeremiah's Prophecy

Read Jeremiah 21.

1. How do you think feelings of despair and frustration influenced the prophet's obedience to God?
(Jeremiah felt bad sometimes but that did not keep him from obeying God.)

2. When asked by the government for a word of comfort and security, what response did Jere-

❓When gave you had similar feelings?

❓What might happen if you remain silent when the Bible instructs you to reprove unfruitful works in yourself and others (Ephesians 5:8–14)?

(Invite members of your group to share these experiences with one another in order to understand better what the text means.)

Being true to God and one's conscience is the source of peace and happiness.

❓What mental and even physical problems could Jeremiah have suffered if he had given in to pressures?

❓How do feelings of despair and frustration influence your obedience to God?

miah give (21:1–7)?
(God was going to fight against them and they would be taken into captivity.)

3. What decision did the prophet declare that his hearers must make (21:8–14)?
(To surrender and live, or to fight and die.)

On this chart, list discouragements you may be facing, and what you have learned from Jeremiah's life that will help you cope with them.

❖ ❖ ❖

God has given us the "ministry of reconciliation" (2 Corinthians 5:18). It is our privilege to share the gospel frankly, as did Jeremiah. Ours, however, is a message of life and freedom, not one of condemnation and captivity.

Conclusion and Application

(Go through the chart in the student's book.)

We are faithful, like Jeremiah, not because we will always see a favorable resolution of the difficulties, but because "the love of Christ controls us" (2 Corinthians 5:14). What we receive is far more than success.

Jeremiah had a personal relationship with God and, although he was sometimes despondent, he conducted his life not by feelings but by the principle of obedience to the One he loved. Suffering adds a deep quality to our lives.

Closing Prayer

❖ ❖ ❖

The Tabernacle

Opening Prayer

Discussion Starter

God's earthly dwelling place during Old Testament times was the Tabernacle. God, of course, cannot be confined to any one place, but the Tabernacle was where He met with the High Priest. Later when Solomon built the Temple, he fashioned it like the Tabernacle, and the Temple then became the dwelling place of God.

❷For whose benefit did God establish the Tabernacle—His or His people's?

❷Why?

Lesson Development

(Ask one of the group members to summarize the paragraphs appearing at the opening of this lesson in the student's book. Note the diagram and discuss it.)

Leader's Objective: To show how God has given us a picture of His Son in the Tabernacle and to help students use the picture to live victoriously

451

LESSON 8

Bible Study

The Furnishings

Read Exodus 25–27.

1. The Brazen Altar

    Read Exodus 29:36,37 and describe how the Altar was used.
    (The priests burned sacrifices on the altar for purification of sin.)

    Why do you think the Altar was placed just inside the entrance?
    (Before anyone can approach God, he must present a sacrifice for the purification of his sins.)

    Read Hebrews 13:10–16. How does the Brazen Altar reflect Christ's sacrifice?
    (Just as the priests offered a sin sacrifice for the people, Jesus offered Himself as the complete sacrifice for the world's sin.)

    What sacrifices are we to offer?
    (Sacrifice of praise to God; confess His name; and do good to others.)

2. The Laver

    Read Exodus 30:18–21 and describe the Laver and its use.
    (A bronze bowl with water in it; placed between the altar and the tent of meeting; priests washed their hands and feet in it so they would not die when they approached the Lord.)

The Bible calls the Tabernacle God's dwelling place because that was where He symbolically and physically showed Himself to man. He symbolically showed Himself through the furnishings and rituals of the Tabernacle, and He physically showed Himself through the cloud that surrounded the Tabernacle.

Twice a day, the priests would burn the blood and parts of an unblemished lamb on the altar. The parts not used were taken outside the city walls and burned completely. This signified the disgraceful death Jesus would die outside Jerusalem on Golgotha.

Jesus' sacrifice is the only offering that actually covers sin. The sacrifices the priests made on the Brazen Altar just looked forward to Christ's once-for-all sacrifice on the cross. (Read Hebrews 7:26–28.)

❖ In your opinion, how can a praise be a sacrifice?

What is the parallel in Ephesians 5:25–27?
(Christ cleanses the church with His Word [the Bible] so she is holy and blameless.)

What is our part (1 John 1:9)?
(To confess our sins.)

The cleansing is not the forgiveness we receive when we become Christians. It is what we do after we are children of God to be cleansed of our sins.

How does what the priests did at the Laver help us know that?
(The priests did not wash their entire bodies, only their feet and hands, which they used for service.)

Why is the Laver placed between the Altar and the Holy Place?
(The Altar signifies our entrance into God's kingdom through Christ's blood. The Laver signifies our need to have our hearts cleansed to have fellowship with God. Then we can approach God as our Father, which is a holy communion between us and Him.)

3. Table of Shewbread

Read Exodus 25:23–30 and Leviticus 24:5–9. Describe the Table and how it was used.
(It was overlaid with gold and had dishes made of pure gold. Twelve cakes and frankincense were put

(Read John 13:1–15.)

❓What do you think Jesus meant when He said Peter didn't need his whole body washed?

❓How does this incident bear out the symbolism of the ritual of cleansing at the Laver?

(Refer to the diagram of the tabernacle in the student's book.)

on the Table as a memorial to the Lord.)

How is the Shewbread a picture of Christ (John 6:32–35,50,51)?
(Jesus is the bread of life who came down from heaven and gave up His body for us. The bread is a symbol of His body.)

As Christians, God considers us priests (Revelation 1:6). When we partake of the Lord's Supper, what should our attitude be toward the bread (1 Corinthians 11:23,24)?
(We should eat it as a remembrance of what Jesus sacrificed for us and how He has given us eternal life.)

4. The Candlestick

Read Exodus 25:31–40; 27:20,21. Describe the Candlestick and how it was used.
(It was made of pure gold; hammered out of one piece; it had seven holders for candles; the priests continually burned pure olive oil in it.)

How is this a picture of Jesus (John 8:12)?
(Jesus is the light of the world—the light of life.)

How does this relate to our daily lives (John 12:35,36)?
(We should walk in Jesus' light.)

5. Altar of Incense

Read Exodus 30:1–8. Describe the Altar of In-

(Read Matthew 2:1–12 and ask this question:)

❓ What gifts did the wise men give Jesus?

Gold signified purity, and frankincense was for a remembrance. Myrrh was used in Jesus' burial as shown in John 19:39–42. The gifts the wise men brought were a picture of Christ's death and burial.

Imagine what candles meant to people before the invention of electricity. To them, a candlestick or an oil lamp was one of the basic necessities of life. Candles were also used for beauty. Every home had many candles and candlemaking was an art. Therefore, a candle meant many things.

(Read Revelation 21:22–27, then ask these questions:)

❓ What kind of temple will we have when Jesus reigns?

❓ Describe the light in that city. What does this say about the connection between light and life?

cense and its use.

(It was made of wood overlaid with pure gold; it was placed just before the veil that hid the Holy of Holies; the high priest burned incense on it every morning.)

The Altar of Incense is the reminder of our prayers, which are an incense to God. According to Revelation 8:3,4, what happens to our prayers?
(They go before the throne of God.)

What kind of attitude should we have toward prayer (Psalm 141:2)?
(My prayers are as sweet as incense to God; I should pray often and sincerely.)

Why do you think the Table of Shewbread, Candlestick, and Altar of Incense were placed inside the Holy Place?
(To enter the Holy Place, sin had to be atoned. Cleansing must be done to wash away any temporary uncleanness. Then the priest could enter. Inside, the Table and Candlestick pictured Christ's work for us as believers. The Altar of Incense signified immediate and personal access to God through prayer. None of these pieces dealt with man's sin and so were holy.)

6. Ark of the Covenant

The Holy of Holies was hidden by a veil. Inside we find the Ark, which

❓How do you think prayer is like a fragrance?

(Discuss how the high priest must have felt as he faced the Holy of Holies behind the costly, thick veil. He had to be perfectly clean to enter, otherwise he would die. Also, talk about how the rituals the high priest performed before he entered the Holy of Holies may have prepared his heart for this yearly atonement.)

was the dwelling place of God Himself. What was placed inside the Ark (Hebrews 9:4)?
(Manna, Aaron's rod, and the tablets of stone with the commandments God had given to Moses.)

What was on it (verse 5)?
(Cherubim and the mercy seat.)

Who was the only person allowed to enter the Holy of Holies (verses 6,7)?
(The high priest.)

Why was the Ark separate from the other furnishings?
(It was the dwelling place of God.)

Why was it placed in the Holy of Holies?
(God cannot look upon sin. To meet with Him, the high priest had to perform all the rituals to cleanse himself and prepare himself to meet God.)

Christ as High Priest

1. How was the Tabernacle set up and sanctified (Exodus 40)?
   (They set up the furnishings and curtains; anointed all with oil; put holy garments on the priests; anointed the priests with oil to consecrate them.)

   What significance did the cloud have?
   (It showed that God and all His glory was present.)

(Discuss what each item placed in the Ark might have stood for:)

◆ Manna was the reminder to the Israelites of God's provision for the people.

◆ Aaron's rod reminded the Israelites of God's miraculous deliverance for His people.

◆ The tablets of stone showed God's principles for living—the Ten Commandments.

❓Why do you think the Ark had a mercy seat on it?

The mercy seat symbolized that the only way to God is through His mercy.

❓How does this picture of the Holy of Holies help you better appreciate our privilege in knowing and fellowshipping with a holy, righteous God?

2. What part did Aaron play?
(Aaron was the first high priest.)

3. What happened to the veil at Christ's death (Matthew 27:50,51)?
(It was torn in two to expose the Holy of Holies.)

What did this signify?
(That God no longer dwelled in the Holy of Holies, but because of Christ's sacrifice, He now dwells in His children.)

4. Describe why Christ is the final High Priest (Hebrews 9:6–14).
(Being sinless, Christ gave an unblemished sacrifice. With His resurrection, He lives forever as our High Priest and His role will never cease.)

5. Compare the Old Covenant with the New (Hebrews 9:15–23).
(Old: Sealed with blood; death of the sacrifice; a copy of things to come. New: Sealed with blood; death of the sacrifice; the final, perfect sacrifice.)

6. Christ is both the sacrifice and the High Priest. Read Hebrews 9:24–28. Describe how this is so.
(Christ offered Himself as a sacrifice, in heaven in front of God the Father. Being perfect, He could be the unblemished Lamb. Being the Son of God descended through Aaron's line, He could also be our High Priest.)

(Read 1 Corinthians 6:19,20.)

❓If your body is the temple of God, how then should you treat it?

The Old Covenant was given to the Jewish people in the Old Testament. It was relayed to Moses at Mount Sinai. God alone gave the covenant. Its one condition was obedience to its laws.

The sprinkling of blood on the altar and the people's agreement to follow the Law sealed the covenant (Exodus 24:4–8). Over the years of Hebrew history, the people proved that God's laws could not be obeyed by mankind. But God had already prepared for the New Covenant. The prophet Jeremiah prophesied: (Read Jeremiah 31:31–34.) The New Covenant was sealed by Jesus' blood sacrificed on Calvary.

Since our sins are forgiven, we could become the temple of God. We only have to agree to it by receiving

What is the hope this gives us?
(Jesus' sacrifice is once for all, never needed again, and He is in heaven assuring us that His sacrifice is sufficient for us.)

LIFE APPLICATION

1. What has Christ done for us as recorded in Hebrews 10:10?
   (Sanctified us.)

2. How should we live accordingly (Hebrews 10:19–25)?
   (With a sincere heart; full of faith; hold fast to our hope in Him; encourage each other; meet regularly for fellowship.)

3. What have you learned from the Tabernacle that will help you live your daily life?

4. We must remember to keep the proper spiritual sequence in our Christian lives as we live victoriously for Christ. What has the Tabernacle taught you about this sequence?
   (Deal with sin first; keep remembering what Christ has done for us; walk in Christ's light; be fervent in prayer; thank God that we can approach Him today.)

How will you use this knowledge to live victoriously?

Christ as our Savior. The Holy Spirit can then indwell our bodies, fulfilling Jeremiah's words that God "will put [His] law in their minds and write it on their hearts." No longer will people come to God through outward obedience to a law, but would be renewed in their inner being by the Holy Spirit (2 Corinthians 3:7–18; 4:16–18.)

Conclusion and Application

God's dwelling place on earth is now in the hearts of believers. We have the Holy of Holies within us.

How does this make you feel?
(Read 2 Corinthians 6:16–18.)

Relating these verses to what we have learned, what will be the result of God living in us?

Closing Prayer

(Close by inviting students to thank God for Jesus and His sacrifice and telling the Lord what it means to them.)

❖ ❖ ❖

Recap

Opening Prayer

Discussion Starter

Someone has said that you can open the Old Testament, turn to any passage and see the red line of Jesus' blood drawn through it.

❓What do you think that means?

(Note the diagram in the Student's book and discuss it.)

Lesson Development

(Any appropriate material from previous lessons that was not sufficiently covered could be used at this time, and you also may deal with any point that the group members may not understand as well as they could.)

(Then go over the remaining Recap questions and answers. This material will benefit both the students and you by giving you a deeper appreciation of God's Word.)

Leader's Objective: To ensure that students understand the difference between law and grace and to bring them to a clear awareness of how the Law teaches our need for grace

The following questions will help you review this Step. If necessary, reread the appropriate lesson(s).

Now that we have gone through the Old Testament at a rapid pace, you have some idea of what it contains and what it teaches. Imagine yourself a Jew, possessing only the Old Testament.

1. Can you find God's plan for man in it? Write your conclusions here in your own words.

2. Why did Jesus of Nazareth have to come?
   (To become the sacrifice for our sins.)

3. How is Jesus pictured in the Old Testament through the following?

   Abraham *(The sacrifice of a loving father.)*

   Joshua *(Jesus delivered us from our enemies—sin and death—and has given us a new, abundant life.)*

   David *(Jesus has given us complete forgiveness.)*

   The Tabernacle *(Christ is our way to God.)*

4. List some examples of how the High Priest worked in the Old Testament (Exodus 25—27).
   (He sacrificed animals as sin offerings, kept bread on the table and oil in the lampstand, burned incense every morning, and once a year entered the Holy of Holies to sprinkle blood on

(Use this lesson to give an overview of the Old Testament rather than going into details about any one part of the Old Testament. Also, make sure your students have a clear understanding of the differences between law and grace and how this affects their Christian life.)

(You may want to go back and review the tabernacle diagram from Lesson 8 in the Student's book, showing how the Old Testament portrayed Christ.)

Conclusion and Application

(Ask these questions but do not require students to answer aloud:)

❓Do you understand why Jesus is the culmination of the Old Testament?

❓Have you confessed all known sin and appropriated the filling of the Holy Spirit to empower your life for service?

If you have not taken these steps before, I would encourage you to do so now. First confess your sins to God.

the Ark. God spoke to the priest concerning His commandments to the people.)

5. How is Jesus our High Priest (Hebrews 10)?
(He was the perfect sacrifice, given once for all.)

LIFE APPLICATION

1. How did your study of the Old Testament help you understand the New Testament better?

2. Using Hebrews 10:10–18, describe the differences between Law and grace.
(Law required continual sacrifice/grace required one sacrifice; law cannot take away sin/grace did; law is outward obedience/ grace provides obedience from the heart.)

   How does this affect the way you relate to God?

3. Using the diagram of the Tabernacle, list ways you can draw nearer to God.
(Brazen Altar: forgiveness of sin; Laver: keep sin accounts short with God; Table of Shewbread: remember Christ's sacrifice for me; Candlestick: let Christ be my light; Altar of Incense: pray often; Ark of the Covenant: remember that I am God's dwelling place.)

   Which is the most significant for you to do today?

4. Right now, thank God for His great sacrifice through Jesus Christ.

Then ask His Spirit to fill you on the basis of Ephesians 5:18 where God commands you to be filled. Lastly, by faith thank God that He has forgiven you and filled you with the Holy Spirit.

Closing Prayer

(As you close with an appropriate prayer, give your students an opportunity to make whatever commitments they are led to at this time.)

Exploring
the **New**
Testament

Discover the
Mystery of
God's Plan

STEP 10

Matthew

Opening Prayer

Discussion Starter

One Saturday morning, an accident occurred involving a van and a compact car. Four bystanders witnessed the collision: a lawyer, a writer, a housewife, and a teenager. When the police officer took their statements, each witness noted different details.

❓How do you think their testimonies might have differed?

❓In light of this example, why do you think we have four Gospels?

❓Why do you think the writers presented some of the same incidents in the life of Christ?

Lesson Development

(Encourage students to read the article, "Why the New Testament?" at the beginning of their Study Guide on their own time if they have not already done so.)

(Ask one of the group members to summarize the paragraphs appearing

Leader's Objective: To show students how Matthew presented Jesus as the King of kings and encourage them to make Him Lord of their lives

Bible Study

Genealogy

Of the four Gospels, only Matthew and Luke give Christ's genealogy. Compare Matthew 1:1–17 and Luke 3:23–38.

1. What differences do you find?
   (Matthew starts with Abraham; Luke goes back to Adam. Matthew gives genealogies in time sequence according to Jewish national history; Luke goes straight back to our human father Adam without interruption.)

2. Keeping in mind that Matthew presented Christ as King, why do you think Matthew wrote the genealogy the way he did?
   (Matthew wanted to show Christ's legal right to inherit the Jewish throne; he wanted to show how Christ came at the right time for Jewish prophecy to be fulfilled.)

at the opening of this lesson in the student's book.)

In the report of an accident, four witnesses give a clearer and more complete picture than one witness because of their different perspectives. That's why the Gospels present four accounts, each from a different point of view, but all in perfect harmony. They present a more complete portrait of Christ.

◆ *Matthew* presents Jesus as King, the Jewish Messiah. The book was written with the Jew in mind. (Read Matthew 5:17.)

◆ *Mark* presents Jesus as servant— serving, suffering, and finally triumphant. (Read Mark 10:45.) Mark was probably written at Rome and primarily for the Romans.

◆ *Luke* presents Jesus as the perfect man, as well as the divine Savior. The book was written with the Greek in mind. (Read Luke 2:11 and 19:10.)

◆ *John* presents Jesus as God. The book was written with everyone in mind. (Read John 1:14,34.)

One example of presenting different aspects of the same event is the genealogy of Jesus in Matthew and Luke. Many Bible scholars think Luke traces Mary's lineage whereas Matthew traces Joseph's line.

Matthew's list begins with Abraham because he was given the first promise of a coming eternal heir. Matthew gives the kingly line of David's throne, which had been unoccupied for six centuries. The Jews would not consider anyone to be Messiah unless He had the legal right to occupy David's throne.

Joseph, as Mary's husband, provided the legal (but not physical) right for Jesus to occupy David's throne. The genealogy in Luke gives Jesus the physical heritage to be the Messiah through Mary's blood line.

(Write this outline on a chalkboard or flip chart.)

The following outline presents the Sermon on the Mount as a series of contrasts—Jesus contrasts His view of the Old Testament with that of the Pharisees:

◆ *Spiritual reality transcends material society* (Matthew 5:3–16). Jesus gives the Beatitudes in these verses. The word "blessed" is the same as the word "happy," and describes someone who is truly satisfied. Blessedness is not associated here with material possessions or external righteousness, but with holy character, with real spirituality.

◆ *Internal purity transcends external piety* (Matthew 5:17—6:18). Jesus takes the Pharisees to task for their outward show of spirituality. He shows that true belief is of the heart, and that God's laws reach inside a man.

◆ *Godly faith transcends worldly anxiety* (Matthew 6:19–34). The Pharisees were "lovers of money," and Jesus rebukes materialism.

◆ *Brotherly love transcends critical judging* (Matthew 7:1–12). Jesus sees through another sin of hypo-

Sermons

In presenting his record of the life of Jesus, Matthew is careful to record the major sermons that Jesus preached. The longest sermon on record is the "Sermon on the Mount," which is found in chapters 5 through 7.

1. As you read this sermon, answer the following questions:

   Give one reason Jesus considers it important for His disciples to live according to the moral standards of the Old Testament Law and prophets (Matthew 5:16).
   (So others will praise God.)

   What promise does Jesus give that helps the Christian overcome his desire for man's praise as he does good deeds (Matthew 6:1–18)?
   (Your Father sees what you do in secret and will reward you.)

   What assurance does Jesus give to help the Christian overcome his anxiety over physical needs such as food and clothing (Matthew 6:25–34)?

(Your Father knows your needs and will take care of you.)

2. Read Jesus' sermons recorded by Matthew in the chapters listed below and write in your own words the verse that means the most to you:

Chapter 10

Chapter 13

Chapter 18

Chapters 24 and 25

A Vital Question

In Matthew 16:13, Jesus asks a question.

1. Why is answering this question so vital?
   (Understanding who Christ is determines whether we become children of God or are separated from God for eternity.)

2. Read verses 14–16. Why does Jesus say Peter's answer was revealed by the Father?
   (Peter did not learn this from other people or even from religious leaders. Only God can help us understand spiritual knowledge.)

3. How have you answered this question?

The Great Commandment

Read Matthew 22:34–40.

1. What does Jesus mean when He says that the

crites, judging unjustly. He commands us not to judge others.

◆ *True devotion transcends false doctrine* (Matthew 7:13–29). Jesus concludes by warning of false prophets, whom we are to avoid, and urging His listeners to put the sermon into practice.

First Corinthians 2:6–16 explains further the relationship between man's spirit and God's. These verses give us the assurance that we can understand God's heart toward us and others.

❓Why do you think a lawyer posed the question in verse 36 to Jesus?

Maybe because he was caught up in the ritual and intricacies of doing

whole Law and prophets depend on these two commandments?

(When we love God with our whole self, we will obey His commandments. When we love others, we will treat them as God wants us to. All the Old Testament laws are embodied in these two principles.)

2. How have you seen Jesus demonstrating the Great Commandment in Matthew's Gospel? Use specific examples.

(He healed the woman who touched His cloak; He stopped to help all kinds of people like the centurion; He fed 4,000; He forgave Peter; He gave up His life for us.)

The Great Commission

Read Matthew 28:18–20. Jesus gave His friends one last commandment before He ascended into heaven. Many call this commandment the Great Commission.

1. How is Jesus' goal different from that of human rulers?

(Many human rulers are selfish and try to change circumstances. Jesus has unconditional love and changes people's hearts.)

2. In your own words, paraphrase Christ's Great Commission.

3. What does the Great Commission mean to you?

every part of the Jewish law, but had no heart for the message of the rules. Jesus emphasized the attitude of the heart rather than the outward performing of laws.

Jesus, as King of kings, has all authority. He wants us to be part of His kingdom by:

◆ Enlisting soldiers for His army

◆ Baptizing them as a sign that they are part of His kingdom

◆ Training the soldiers how to take the enemy's (Satan's) territory and free the captives

The promise Jesus gives is that He is an active, ever-present King who will be by our side every step of the way.

LIFE APPLICATION

1. Which instruction from Jesus' sermons in Matthew do you need to pay particular attention to?

2. How will you apply that teaching to your life?

3. To let Christ rule your life, what areas do you need to turn over to Him? Be specific.

   Now ask Him to take control of each area.

4. List ways you can better apply the Great Commandment in your:

   Home life

   Work place

   Devotional life

5. How will obedience to Christ's command in Matthew 28:19,20 give your life purpose?

Conclusion and Application

As the link between the Old and New Testaments, the book of Matthew shows Jesus' right to be King of kings through His lineage and His authoritative teachings. The writer concludes the book with the commission the King gives His followers. When we see Jesus as the God-King, we will have no trouble surrendering every part of our lives to Him.

Closing Prayer

(Encourage your group members to surrender every part of their lives to Jesus and to commit themselves in helping fulfill His Great Commission.)

Mark

Opening Prayer

Discussion Starter

(For this lesson, you may want to be an example of service. You could serve refreshments to your group or volunteer to help group members in a practical way this week, such as babysitting, fixing a meal, tuning up a car, mowing grass, or shoveling sidewalks.)

❓If Jesus visited your church on Sunday, which of the following do you think He would most likely do?

◆ Sing a magnificent solo just before the sermon

◆ Receive a "Sunday school teacher of the year" award

◆ Help a sobbing preschooler find his way to his classroom

In his Gospel, Mark shows how Jesus came to serve. As Christians, that should be our desire too, yet as humans we can turn serving into a prideful event. We all fall into this trap at times in our lives. For example, we turn humble service of the Lord's Supper into an elevated position. We sing

Leader's Objective: To challenge students to apply Jesus' servant attitude and to exalt Him in their lives

471

worship songs in the choir merely to perform in front of a crowd. We fix a meal for a shut-in to receive thanks or add to our "Christian" reputation.

Think of a situation like this in your life.

❓What happened?

❓How did you feel about your actions and attitude?

Receiving recognition or being in the spotlight is not bad. In fact, we can glorify Christ in these positions. What is important is to have a servant attitude no matter what we do. When our hearts are right, we can serve others as Christ has served us.

LESSON 2

Bible Study

Jesus' Ministry

1. Read Mark 10:45. State Mark's objective for writing his Gospel.
   (He came to serve and to give His life for us.)

Lesson Development

(Ask one of the group members to summarize the paragraphs appearing at the opening of this lesson in the student's book.)

In Mark's Gospel, Jesus shows a pattern of service to others. He taught, He healed, He pardoned sinners, He suffered and died. Multitudes followed Him everywhere.

Imagine how tired Jesus must have felt. Crowds pushed and shoved to see Him. Everyone wanted something. The Pharisees were trying to catch Him in a wrongful act. He had so little time to teach and prepare His disciples for their work. He knew what lay ahead in a few short months—rejection and death.

2. Read Mark 1:20 and 3:13–35. How did Jesus choose His followers?
(He called them and expected immediate obedience.)

What do these passages say about the qualifications Jesus expects in His disciples?
(Availability, willingness to obey.)

3. In Mark 1:21–28, how was Jesus described as a teacher?
(Having authority, amazing, not like the religious teachers.)

4. One of the most striking ways in which the Gospel of Mark differs from Matthew is that it places greater emphasis on what Jesus did than what He said.

What were some of the things Jesus did that caused the religious leaders of His day to be so angry with Him (Mark 2:1–3:6)?
(Forgave sins, ate with tax-gatherers and sinners, disciples did not fast, picked grain on Sabbath, healed a man on Sabbath.)

Miracles of Jesus

1. Note the four miracles of Jesus, performed in Mark 4–5:43. List one characteristic of Jesus in each incident.

❓How do these accounts compare to how you were introduced to Jesus?

❓Why was Jesus described this way?
He taught the Scripture with authority, and He did miracles.

Jesus had a heart of love that displayed itself in patient service to everyone. He had time for children, the outcasts, the sick, the demon possessed, even for His enemies. His ministry truly was that of the Servant-King.

Miracles are supernatural manifestations of divine power in the external world, special revelations of the presence and power of God. The purpose of miracles is to arrest the attention of people, and win their acceptance of revealed truth.

Mark 4:35–41
(Unworried, confident, forceful.)

Mark 5:1–20
(Powerful, compassionate.)

Mark 5:21–23,35–43
(Unhurried, gentle, caring.)

Mark 5:25–34
(Sensitive, loving, did not discriminate.)

2. What one thing hinders Jesus from exercising His power and control in the lives of men (Mark 6:1–6)?
(Lack of faith, unbelief.)

Miracles were part of God's way of authenticating Jesus' mission. Jesus said that if He had not done works that no other ever did, they would not have sinned by disbelieving (John 15:24), indicating that He regarded His miracles as proofs that He was from God. Christ's miracles were always profound, helpful, illustrative of an important truth, and majestic.

Other miracles in Mark include the following:

Physical cures:

◆ Peter's mother-in-law (1:29–31)

◆ A leper (1:40–45)

◆ A paralytic (2:3–11)

◆ A man with a withered hand (3:1–6)

◆ A deaf and dumb man (7:31–37)

◆ A blind man (8:22–26)

Nature:

◆ Fed 5,000 (6:34–44)

◆ Jesus walked on water (6:45–52)

◆ Fed 4,000 (8:1–9)

◆ Fig tree withered (11:12–14)

Cure of demoniacs:

◆ A demoniac in the synagogue (1:21–28)

◆ The Syro-phoenician's daughter (7:24–30)

◆ The epileptic boy (9:14–29)

Jesus' Death and Resurrection

1. Compare Matthew's and Mark's accounts of Jesus' death and resurrection (Matthew 26–28; Mark

Considering the themes of Matthew and Mark, why do you think each author's account is written as it is?

Matthew's account of the Jewish King ends on earth; Mark includes the

14–16). What differences do you find?

(Matthew generally includes more details than Mark does; Matthew refers to more prophecies that Jesus fulfilled; Matthew ends with the Great Commission, Mark with the Ascension.)

How does having two accounts help you better understand Christ's sacrifice for you?

(We can see how Jesus was the fulfillment of the Old Testament and how He relates to us as common, ordinary people. He is both elevated as King and approachable as Servant.)

2. Describe how Christ the servant is exalted (Mark 16:1–20).
    (He had the power to rise from the dead; an angel announced His resurrection; He appeared to many believers; He ascended to heaven and sat at the right hand of God.)

3. How does Jesus combine the qualities of both a king and a servant?
    (He had power but was humble; He emptied Himself but will reign; He is just and merciful; He accepted worship but did not exalt Himself; He fulfilled prophecy of the kingly line but was submissive to His Father.)

ascension of the Servant. Matthew wants to prove Jesus is the King through prophecy; Mark writes an action-packed account. Matthew wants to prove Jesus fulfilled Jewish law for the Messiah; Mark seeks to show the work of Jesus.

Mark manifests the servant character of the incarnate Son. Jesus emptied Himself of the "form of God" and took on the form of a man to submit to death on the cross. Read Philippians 2:5–11. Summarize the characteristics of Jesus' attitude.

❓What is the instruction to us?

❓How can you apply this to your life?

❓Your ministry?

Jesus, the Servant, is now exalted at the right hand of the Father where He constantly intercedes for us.

1. List several ways Jesus' example as servant has inspired you to serve others.

   How can you put these ideas into practice this week?

2. To what degree does unbelief hinder Christ from exercising His power and control in your life?

3. How can you best exalt Jesus through your life (Mark 16:15,20)?
   (Tell others about Jesus.)

   What are you doing now to implement this?

   How could you increase your efforts in this area?

Conclusion and Application

Imagine yourself as a Roman citizen at the time of Jesus' life. You have little knowledge of the "strange" religion of the Jewish people under Roman rule. You admire a person who can get things done, someone who does not spend long hours debating the fine details of a religious system, but acts decisively. You probably have slaves and servants in your household.

Can you see how Mark's portrait of Christ's life would appeal to the Roman citizen? The picture of a Servant who had all power and who could touch common people must have been irresistible.

In many ways, our culture values many of the qualities the Romans did. As you answer the Life Application questions, be practical about your answers. Just as a servant deals with day-to-day necessities of life, these questions are intended to help you apply the principles that Mark taught to your daily life.

Closing Prayer

Luke

Opening Prayer

Discussion Starter

(Discuss ways to show compassion in the following situations.)

You find out that your neighbor has contracted AIDS, and you know that his lifestyle is a direct cause for the disease. You try to talk to him, but he refuses to acknowledge that anything is wrong in his life.

Months later he cautiously mentions to you that he hasn't been able to work for some time. He's losing his house because of his medical bills, and most of his friends are ignoring him. However, he doesn't actually ask for help.

❓What would you do?

You are involved in a bitter feud with a coworker. The problem began when she took over an area of responsibility in the office that belonged to you. Since your supervisor didn't object, she assumed full control.

One day, your co-worker confides in you. She ran into some personal problems with the supervisor and is now in danger of losing her job. The

Leader's Objective: To help students understand Jesus' role as the Son of Man and encourage them to stand firm in their work for the Lord

Bible Study

Introduction

Read Luke 1:1–4.

1. To whom was this Gospel originally written?
   (Theophilus.)

2. What evidence is there that the recipient of this Gospel had been given some prior instruction in Christianity?
   (Verse 4: "you have been taught.")

3. Why did Luke write this Gospel to Theophilus?
   (So he would know the truth.)

Jesus' Suffering

1. One of Luke's great emphases is that Jesus,

thought strikes you that if she were gone, your chances of advancement would be much better.

❓How would you treat her?

Lesson Development

Ask one of the group members to summarize the paragraphs appearing at the opening of this lesson in the student's book.)

Theophilus was probably a Greek. Luke therefore appeals to the thoughtful, cultured, philosophic Greek mind by relating Jesus' story in an orderly and classical way that has been called "the most beautiful book ever written." Luke depicts the beauty and perfection of the life of Jesus: the ideal man.

Although a physician, Luke was primarily a missionary and in this case an eyewitness with a good understanding of the gospel of Christ (Luke 1:1–4).

❓What way of effective witnessing do you see in Luke's example?

God's best ways to carry out His work often take time and organization.

❓How does this apply to the Gospel that Luke wrote?

Luke is also the author of the Book of Acts. Paul calls him "our dear friend" (Colossians 4:14) and "my fellow worker" (Philemon 24). In Acts, Luke is a frequent companion of Paul. Timothy tells us Luke was with Paul just before Paul's death (2 Timothy 4:11).

The special emphasis of Luke is the humanity of Jesus. Luke shows

though He is the Christ, must nevertheless suffer and die at the hands of sinful men (2:33–35; 9:22–31; 13:31–35; 18:31–35; 24:7,25–27,44–47).

Why do you think Jesus mentioned His death so many times?

(His disciples did not understand what would happen and Jesus wanted to prepare them. Later after Jesus ascended into heaven, they understood and wrote of it in the New Testament.)

2. Read Luke 20–24, the account of the last week leading up to Jesus' death and resurrection.

What are some qualities of Jesus' character that stand out prominently in these chapters?

(Straightforward, truthful, bold, determined, compassionate, perceptive, appreciative, authoritative, earnest, humble, encouraging, submissive, forgiving, understanding.)

What qualities of character in Jesus' enemies stand out in these chapters?

(Accusatory, evasive, crafty, deceitful, cowardly, murderous, cruel, blasphemous, liars, violent, rebellious, unreasonable, stubborn, gamblers, abusive.)

Why, then, did men seek to have Jesus crucified?

(Because He said He was

how Jesus must suffer as a man. Like the other Gospel writers, he also represents Jesus as the Son of God.

❓How does Jesus' suffering show His humanity?

Only a person with a physical body could suffer physically. Jesus exhibited the human characteristics of tiredness, pain, thirst, sorrow, and mental anguish.

❓How does Jesus' suffering show His divine nature?

He forgave in the midst of His pain. He set His mind toward doing what was right. He willingly gave up His life and took it back again. He did not sin during His suffering.

the Son of God. They accused Him of blasphemy; they were fearful of His power and His popularity.)

3. How were the disciples— and thus Theophilus and all the readers of Luke— assured that Jesus' suffering and death occurred according to God's plan, instead of accidentally, simply because of men's evil hearts?
(Jesus foretold it so many times.)

What difference does that make to you?

If Christ's suffering was inflicted on Him without His choice, we would not have understood the depths of God's love. But since Jesus willingly died for us, we can see how much He cares for us.

Jesus' Prayers

1. Read the three parables on prayer in Luke 11:5–13; 18:1–8; and 18:9–14. What qualities of prayer are described?
(Certainty of a complete answer; friendship with God; God treating us like His children; praying without giving up; prayer brings justice and mercy; true prayer requires humility.)

2. Now read about some of Christ's prayers (5:16; 6:12; 9:28,29; 11:1; 22:32,44; 23:46). How did Jesus follow through with these qualities?
(5:16—Jesus' prayers were not for show; 6:12— Jesus spent much time with His Father; 22:32— Jesus kept praying for Peter; 23:46—Jesus prayed

(Regarding the first parable:) Eastern homes usually had one room. Father, mother, and children slept on mats on the floor. Anyone who knocked on the door late at night would disturb the entire household. But a true friend would open the door and extend hospitality to the traveler. That is how God treats us when we pray.

(Regarding the third parable:) Jesus repeatedly taught that attitude was more important than actions. The Pharisee in this parable did not have to fast twice a week; he was exceeding the requirements of the Law. He thought his actions made him righteous. But since his heart was not right, no amount of good deeds would satisfy God. On the other hand, the repentance of the tax collector covered his many sins, making him righteous in God's eyes.

*until He had completed
God's will.)*

3. What elements of Jesus'
   prayers can you apply to
   make your prayers more
   effective?

Jesus' Humanity

1. Since Luke writes about
   the humanity of Jesus,
   list people whom Jesus
   touched and the results
   of His ministry on them.

   6:17–19
   *(Sick and demon pos-
   sessed—Jesus healed
   them.)*

   7:36–50
   *(Sinful woman—She
   loved Him so much she
   kissed His feet and poured
   perfume on them; her sins
   were forgiven.)*

   8:1–3
   *(Demon possessed and
   diseased women whom
   Jesus had delivered—Out
   of gratitude and love, they
   followed Him and sup-
   ported Him financially.)*

   15:1–7
   *(Tax collectors and sin-
   ners—Their sins were forgiven and they were
   accepted.)*

   17:11–19
   *(Ten lepers—They were
   healed, and one praised
   God and thanked Jesus.)*

   23:39–43
   *(Crucified criminal—He
   was in paradise with Jesus
   that day.)*

2. Where do you think Je-
   sus would likely minister

Jesus ministered to people others
shunned. Think of the people closest
to Him—fishermen, a tax collector, the
diseased, demon possessed, people
who had lived morally sinful lives.
That is not a collection of the elite of
society. Yet He took time with religious
leaders, intellectuals, and the rich. The
contrast showed most clearly at His
death. He ministered to the criminal
crucified next to Him and His body
was buried by a rich man who loved
Him.

Our task is to regard people as
Jesus did. Luke 19:10 says, "The Son
of Man came to seek and to save what
was lost." The position, wealth, or ability of a person did not matter to Jesus—
just his or her need of a Savior who
could give new life.

(Encourage your group members
to write their own description of how
Jesus interacted with outcasts.)

today if He were in your area?

Jesus' Resurrection

1. Why do you think the women were the first to discover that Jesus was alive (Luke 23:26,27,48, 49,55,56; 24:1–9)?
   (They were the most faithful at the end—they followed Jesus to the cross; they stayed through His agony and death; they went to the tomb to see where He was buried; they went to the tomb again on the third day to anoint His body.)

2. What does that mean to your faithfulness in service to the Lord?
   (Jesus rewards those who remain faithful through easy times and through crises.)

3. What was the reaction of Jesus' friends after His ascension (Luke 24:50–53)?
   (They worshiped Jesus, felt great joy, and praised God in the temple.)

LIFE APPLICATION

1. Luke presented Christ as the Son of Man. What does that title mean to you?

2. Seeing the types of people Jesus ministered to, how will this affect your mnistry?

   List several practical ways you can show the

Many of the principle actors in the death and resurrection were unlikely participants from a human view. Simon, a Cyrenian who carried Jesus' cross, just happened to pass by. Joseph of Arimathea, the man who provided the burial, was a member of the Sanhedrin who condemned Jesus to death. Joseph was a disciple of Christ and most likely did not participate in the accusations. While the disciples fled when Jesus was arrested, the women stayed near Him.

How like people today! Who can predict the one who will receive Christ's forgiveness and follow Him? New believers come from every walk of life, from all over the globe. Our responsibility is to simply take the initiative to present God's message of love and forgiveness to all who will listen in the power of the Holy Spirit and leave the results to God. And watch the miracle of new birth and spiritual growth take place.

Conclusion and Application

The Gospel of Luke presents Christ as the Perfect Man. As a man, He reacted to every situation as a godly man should. Luke 20:19–26 is an illustration of His conduct under stress.

Luke shows that although Jesus was perfect in every way, He was not aloof and untouchable. Rather, His perfect nature caused Him to love and

kind of compassion Jesus did.

3. How can Jesus' example of righteousness during suffering help you face crises in your life?

4. Read 1 Corinthians 15:58. Considering the actions of the women during the crucifixion, name one way you can stand firm in your work for the Lord.

care for others around Him like no one else could.

Closing Prayer

John

Opening Prayer

Discussion Starter

The first three Gospels are called the Synoptic Gospels. The word *synoptic* implies that the three writers look at the life of Christ from a similar point of view. About half of Matthew's material is found in Mark also. About a third of Luke is found in a similar form in Mark. All but 55 verses of Mark can be found in Matthew or Luke. About a fourth of Matthew's and Luke's Gospels is similar material that is not found in Mark.

Each writer gives a running account of the life and teachings of Christ but with a different slant. Matthew was an eyewitness of many things in his Gospel. Mark, it is believed, wrote with the help of his eyewitness companion, Peter. Luke, a historian, used various first-hand source material.

The fourth Gospel, written by John, is different from the other three. It, too, is the testimony of an eyewitness (John 21:24). But it is not a rapidly moving account of Christ's life and teachings. This had already been pro-

❖

Leader's Objective: To help students see the urgency of bearing fruit and to show how the four Gospels give a complete portrait of Christ

Bible Study

Titles for Jesus

Read John 1:1–18.

1. Why is Jesus called the Word?
   (He expresses, manifests, and shows God to us. Jesus is the visible, physical witness of God.)

   Why is He called the light?
   (Jesus shows us the way to God, out of the darkness of sin.)

   Why is He called the Son?
   (He is the physical form of God the Father.)

2. John also gave other names for Jesus. Write each and a short explanation of what it means.

   6:35
   (Bread of life—He is the spiritual food that gives us eternal life.)

   8:12
   (Light of the world—He is the only way anyone can know God and go from Satan's gloom to God's light.)

   11:25
   (Resurrection and the life—Only through Jesus can we be made alive to live with God for eternity.)

   14:6
   (The way, the truth, and the life—Jesus is the only way to the Father.)

vided in the other three, which were written a number of years before. John's account is more reflective, more philosophical, more subjective, more interpretative.

John brings out new material omitted by the other three writers. He takes a few events and enlarges and amplifies their treatment. The miracles he incorporates are chosen to foster belief in Jesus.

(Ask volunteers to read Matthew 6:33; Mark 10:34; Luke 19:10; and John 20:30,31. Discuss the different pictures and objectives each author gave of Jesus' ministry.)

Lesson Development

(Ask one of the group members to summarize the paragraphs appearing at the opening of this lesson in the student's book.)

The first chapter of John has some similarities with the first chapter of the Bible—Genesis 1.

❷What similarities do you see?

God has no beginning; He is eternal; everything was made by Him.

❷What is different between John 1 and Genesis 1?

God comes in human form in John 1; instead of creation witnessing the power of God, Jesus bears witness of the love of God.

Compare Colossians 1:16,17 and Hebrews 1:2.

❷What further information do you find in these verses?

Jesus made everything and holds everything together. Jesus is the One through whom God speaks to us today.

A spiritual application of these miracles of Jesus include:

Miracles of Christ

1. Why did John take the trouble to relate the various signs, or miracles, found in his Gospel (John 20:30,31)?
   (That we may believe that Jesus is the Christ, the Son of God, and might have life in His name.)

2. Skim through this Gospel and see if you can list the seven miracles of Jesus that John recorded:

   1) *(Turned water into wine—John 2:1–11.)*

   2) *(Healed nobleman's son—4:46–54.)*

   3) *(Healed sick man at pool—5:1–9.)*

   4) *(Fed five thousand men plus women and children—6:1–14.)*

   5) *(Walked on water—6:16–21.)*

   6) *(Healed blind man—9:1–7,25.)*

   7) *(Raised Lazarus from the dead—11:38–44.)*

1) The waterpots picture the thirsty human heart, empty without Christ. The water spoken of in John 3:5 is the Word of God, and it is the means to salvation (1 Peter 1:23).

2) The nobleman heard of Jesus; hearing is not enough for salvation. Seeking Him out isn't adequate. The man *believed* Jesus and his son was healed. This pictures how our salvation is obtained by faith—by believing in God and the promise of His Word.

3) The man was unable to help himself—a picture of man's inability to help himself or do anything to deserve salvation. The Lord chose this man and healed him. Salvation is by grace!

4) No mattter what or how much a person may possess, no one but Jesus Christ can ever supply his real need. Jesus multiplied what the boy had, and it more than met the need of the crowd. Christ broke the loaves to provide physical sustenance; His broken body on the cross provided redemption for the whole human race.

5) When the frightened, helpless disciples saw Jesus unnaturally walking on the sea, they grew even more anxious. But when He spoke to them, they recognized His power

and authority—and gladly received Him into the ship. And they immediately reached their destination and were out of danger. When an unbeliever, alarmed at his own need, recognizes Christ's supernatural ability to meet that need and receives Christ into His heart, he immediately arrives at an eternally safe haven for his soul.

6) Blindness indicates darkness. The unbeliever is in spiritual darkness, unable to perceive God's truth. After receiving Christ, one of the first miracles is that he begins to see spiritual truth, understand the Bible, and take note of the Lord's guidance in his life.

7) Before a person is born into the family of God, he is said to be spiritually dead and without hope. Christ raising Lazarus is a complete likeness of His miraculous work in the human heart when He brings a person out of spiritual death into spiritual life.

❓What miracle did the most to confirm the disciples' faith in Jesus as the Christ?

His resurrection proved that Jesus is God.

Representatives for Christ

Read John 13 and 14.

1. What attitude of the heart must you demonstrate if other people are to realize that you are Christ's representative in the

For many people, the words *love* and *commandment* are opposites. Christ, however, linked them as an inseparable pair. If you do not obey Christ's commands, it shows your lack of love. If you are anxious to obey His commands, you demonstrate your love.

world (13:34,35)?
(Love for one another.)

2. What is God's provision for enabling Christians to be true representatives of Christ in the world (14:16–18)?
(A Helper, the Holy Spirit, who lives in us.)

Christ's Deity

1. John quotes seven witnesses to the deity of Christ. Who are they?

    1:19,34 *(John the Baptist.)*

    1:49 *(Nathanael.)*

    6:68,69 *(Simon Peter.)*

    11:24–27 *(Martha.)*

    20:28 *(Thomas.)*

    20:31 *(John.)*

    10:34–36 *(Christ.)*

2. Why was each person qualified to testify?
(John the Baptist—forerunner and herald of Christ's coming; Nathanael—one of the disciples; Simon Peter—one of Jesus' inner circle of friends; Martha—saw her brother Lazarus raised from the dead; Thomas—the disciple who doubted Jesus at first; John—writer of the Gospel, witness of these things; Christ—testimony of His own claims.)

The Holy Spirit

1. John also teaches us about the Holy Spirit. How does the work of the

❷ How would you describe the relationship between love and obedience?

❷ What conditions must you fulfill to experience this provision fully (14:15,21,23,24)?

We must keep His commandments to experience the full love of the Father.

Since the Book of John was written so we would believe Jesus is the Son of God, John includes the statements of several witnesses. These were people who had known Jesus for many years. Their words reflect their deep commitment to Christ's claim to be God.

Dr. Henrietta Mears says of these verses in her book, *What the Bible Is All About:*

Holy Spirit affect your life and ministry?

3:5
(New birth.)

4:14
(Eternal life.)

7:38,39
(Satisfies spiritual thirst.)

14—16
(Comforts, gives truth, will never leave us, teaches us, testifies of Jesus, convicts of sin, glorifies Jesus.)

2. What is the promise given in John 14:15–31?
(We will receive a Comforter that the world does not have. He will teach us and help us live the Christian life.)

The Vine and the Branches

Read John 15:1–8.

1. Describe the relationship between the vine and branches.
(The branch abides in the vine; the branch brings forth fruit because of the vine; a branch not connected to the vine is cast out.)

2. How can you use this picture to have a more fruitful ministry?
(My ministry is totally dependent on Christ living His life through me.)

◆ *The Incoming Spirit* (3:5): This is the commencement of the Christian life, the new birth by the Spirit. We are born by the Spirit into the family of God.

◆ *The Indwelling Spirit* (4:14): He fills us with His presence and brings us joy.

◆ *The Overflowing Spirit* (7:38,39): Out of his inmost being shall flow rivers of living water—not just little streams of blessing, but rivers—Mississippis and Amazons, if the Holy Spirit dwells within us.

◆ *The Witnessing Spirit* (14—16): He speaks through us. This is the particular task of the Christian through the Holy Spirit—to testify of Christ.

In the spring time, sap rises through the trunk and out to the smallest branches. New life blooms from this life-giving source. Within a few weeks, you will know which branches are connected to the trunk and which are not. The ones that are separate remain bare and lifeless. The fruit we see in our lives is an indication of how we are abiding in Christ.

❓What does it mean to bear fruit?

(Compare these Scriptures:)

◆ Psalm 92:13

We flourish in God's garden.

◆ Galatians 5:22,23

We exhibit the fruit of the Spirit.

◆ Philippians 1:11

We do righteous acts.

LIFE APPLICATION

1. According to John 15:16, 27, what was to be the disciples' function after Jesus left the earth?
   (To testify of Christ and bring others to Him.)

   How are you obeying that command?

   What promises can you claim from these verses that will help you bear fruit?

2. Read John 21. Summarize what these verses mean to your ministry for Jesus.

❖ ❖ ❖

Conclusion and Application

In John, the Lord Jesus continually depended on the Father and absolutely obeyed Him (John 14:10). He was a perfect man walking in the power of the Holy Spirit throughout His life on earth. Through His life, we have eternal life. Knowing this can inspire us to tell others of this marvelous news.

We have seen that the four Gospel writers each presented a different aspect of Christ's life. Some comparisons between the Gospel of Luke and the Gospel of John are:

◆ Different ways of describing the Incarnation: Luke 1:26–38; 2:1–20 and John 1:1–14.

◆ Different treatments of the same miracle (one was a self-evident narrative, the other was used as a background for a sermon): Luke 9:10–17 and John 6:1–14,22–59.

Each Gospel writer had his own way of telling about Jesus' life, death, and resurrection. We are the richer for having four accounts of the most important event in history.

Closing Prayer

❖ ❖ ❖

The Acts of the Apostles

Opening Prayer

Discussion Starter

Describe what you think the early church was like.

❓ How do you think the early church differed from churches of today?

❓ Why?

Lesson Development

(Ask one of the group members to summarize the paragraphs appearing at the opening of this lesson in the student's book.)

Leader's Objective: To help students trace the ministries of Peter and Paul in the early New Testament Church and to motivate students to follow their obedience and faithfulness

LESSON 5

Bible Study

Empowerment of the Holy Spirit

The Book of Acts begins by referring to the material presented in the Gospels as "all that Jesus began to do and to teach" (Acts 1:1). It tells of the works that the resurrected and ascended Christ continued to do through the Holy Spirit poured out on His disciples at Pentecost. Acts 1:8 has often been considered the key verse of this book. Survey the book and answer these questions.

1. What chapters tell of the witness of the disciples at Jerusalem?
   (Chapters 2 through 7.)

   In Samaria?
   (8 through 9.)

   To the ends of the earth?
   (10 through 28.)

Peter

1. The following are some of the major messages that Peter gave as he witnessed for Christ: Acts 2:14–36; 3:11–26; 10:34–43.

   What was the most important point about the life of Christ that Peter was trying to get across?
   (His death for our sin, and His resurrection.)

2. Read chapter 10. What significance does Peter's experience with Corne-

The book of Acts is a record of the early church in action. Acts 1:8 is a prophetic outline of what happens later in the book in the spreading of the gospel. The gospel first spread to the Jews in Samaria (Acts 8:14). The Samaritans were half Jewish and half Gentile. Their reception of the gospel was one step toward Gentile evangelism.

God gave a vision to Peter, then arranged circumstances so that the gospel was taken to the Gentiles (Acts 10, especially verse 45). As the book continues, Gentile acceptance of the truth grows, while Jewish rejection becomes more and more pronounced (Acts 13:46; 18:6; 28:25–28).

In the first part of the book, Peter is the prominent person. Jerusalem is the center of his activities and his ministry is primarily to the Jews. His characteristics include boldness and preparedness.

lius have for the church?
(God's message of love and forgiveness was to be given to the Gentiles.)

Paul

Of all the apostles, Paul stands out most prominently in Acts and other books of the New Testament.

1. What kind of man was Paul before he was converted (8:1–3; 9:2; 22:1–5; 26:4–12)?
   (Strict and zealous for God, persecuting Christians, murderous, hostile.)

   When Jesus appeared to Paul on the road to Damascus, what did He tell Paul he was to do (9:4–6)?
   (Continue to Damascus where he would be given further instructions.)

2. To whom did Paul seek to minister first at Cypress (13:4–12), at Antioch of Pisidia (13:13–52), and at Iconium (14:1–7)?
   (To the Jews in the synagogues.)

   To whom did Paul preach after this first group rejected the gospel?
   (The Gentiles.)

3. In preaching to the Jews, Paul was able to make a point of contact with them by referring to the Old Testament Scriptures. What was the point

Beginning at 7:58, Paul (Saul) becomes more prominent. The keys to his effective ministry were instant obedience (Acts 9:6; 26:19,20) and the filling of the Holy Spirit (Acts 13:4).

(Take time to compare your lives to Paul's ministry in the following areas:)

◆ Paul's motivation (Philippians 3:7–14)

◆ Paul's obligation (Romans 1:14–17)

◆ Paul's message (1 Corinthians 1:18–25)

◆ Paul's attitude (1 Thessalonians 2:3–12; Acts 20:24)

◆ Paul's fruit (1 Thessalonians 1:5–10)

◆ Paul's willingness (Acts 22:10)

◆ Paul's reward (2 Timothy 4:7,8)

❓Where did Paul preach (Acts 13:5)?

❓What significance does this have for us?

We should share Christ in key centers of learning as well as other places. We should go where the people are, not merely bring the people to church.

Paul's strategy of evangelism also included the following:

◆ He concentrated on centers of culture, commerce, and influence. Examples include Antioch, Athens, Corinth, Ephesus, Jerusalem, and Rome.

of contact Paul used in speaking to the pagan Gentiles at Lystra (14:8–18)?

(Their attempt to sacrifice to Paul and Barnabas as gods.)

What did Paul do to establish his converts in the faith (14:21–23)?

(Strengthened them, encouraged them, appointed elders, committed them to God.)

Romans 15:20 tells us one more thing about Paul's evangelism strategy. What is it?

(He went to areas that had not heard the gospel before.)

The Holy Spirit

1. According to these Scriptures, what are some of the ways in which the Holy Spirit empowered the early church?

◆ When he came to a city, he first went to the Jews, if possible. He built on the foundation of the Old Testament, showing Jesus of Nazareth as the Messiah. He then presented the message to the Gentiles.

◆ When he went to Gentiles, he appealed to their innate knowledge of God the creator and sustainer of the world. He told them how they could know the true God through Jesus Christ (Acts 17:22–34).

◆ He built up the converts and established local organized groups of believers (Acts 14:21–23; 16:5).

◆ He trained the believers to be witnesses for Christ (Acts 19:8–10; 1 Thessalonians 1:6–8).

❓What might be a good strategy for evangelism today? (Compare 1 Peter 3:15; 2 Timothy 2:2,15; 1 Thessalonians 5:19.)

❓How can we employ Paul's strategy?

❓Should we wait for people to come to church meetings to tell them about Christ?

❓In the early church, who was responsible for evangelism (Acts 8:1,4)?

It is not the duty of the pastor alone to introduce others to Jesus. He is to build up Christians so they can evangelize as well (Ephesians 4:11–13).

❓Why does the church lack power today?

The early church was given the ability to accomplish supernatural

1:8 *(Gave power in wit-nessing.)*

4:31 *(Gave boldness in witnessing.)*

2:4–8; 10:46; 19:6 *(Gave power to speak in other languages.)*

7:54–60 *(Gave peace and confidence in the face of danger and death.)*

10:19,20; 13:2–4 *(Gave guidance.)*

11:28; 21:10–13 *(Gave power to prophesy.)*

2. How did the Holy Spirit work through Paul as he ministered at the following places:

Cypress (13:4–12)?
(He gave Paul insight into the motive of the magician.)

Iconium (13:52–14:3)?
(He granted Paul and the others the ability to perform signs and wonders.)

LIFE APPLICATION

1. What is the most important thing you now try to tell others about Christ?

   How does that compare with what Peter and Paul preached?

2. What can you learn from Paul to help in your discipling of others?

3. What are some of the ways in which the Holy Spirit is currently empowering you?

tasks through the power of the Holy Spirit (Acts 2:4; 4:8,31; 6:3,5,8; 7:55; 9:17; 11:24; 13:9,52). Today the church needs that message of the filling of the Holy Spirit. We cannot expect to do God's work by our own power, but only by that of the Holy Spirit. We also need to share with others how to be Spirit-filled (John 14:16,17; 16:7–15).

Conclusion and Application

The early church was commissioned by Christ and empowered by the Holy Spirit to take the message of Christ to every creature on earth. The early church brought the message to the known world. The commission has not changed. But only as the church of today works in the power of the Holy Spirit can we reach our community and the world with the message of life.

Closing Prayer

Romans, 1 and 2 Corinthians, Galatians

Opening Prayer

Discussion Starter

(Explain that the word *gospel* means "good news." Ask students to write four reasons they believe that the Christian message is good news. Then invite each person to share his answers.)

Lesson Development

(Ask one of the group members to summarize the paragraphs appearing at the opening of this lesson in the student's book.)

This brief outline of the book of Romans shows what the gospel of Christ includes:

◆ Provisions for forgiveness of sin (chapters 1—5)

◆ Power to live a victorious life (chapters 6—8)

◆ Program for the ages (chapters 9—11)

◆ Principles for Christian living (chapters 12—16)

Leader's Objective: To understand what the gospel is and how it is personally appropriated, and to show the need to share the good news with others

Bible Study

Romans

This epistle was written from the city of Corinth to the believers in Rome shortly after Paul had finished his work in Ephesus. Rome was the center of the civilized world, the great metropolis of a vast empire. The city had already become the home of many Christians.

Paul is telling the Romans the good news concerning the way in which God, in His infinite love, has provided free and full salvation for sinners. Paul's main insistence is that man's justification before God rests not on the Law of Moses, but on the mercy of Christ.

1. Read Romans 1:1–3,16, 17.

   What is the main theme of Romans?
   (The gospel of Christ.)

   What is the gospel of Christ?
   (His death for our sins, His burial, and His resurrection for our justification.)

   What does it reveal?
   (God's grace and His love for mankind.)

2. Read Romans 3:9–18. Man is sinful and lives a life separated from God.

   Write the five characteristics of a sinful man listed in these verses:

Many think the gospel refers only to the fact that a Christian is saved from hell. But as this outline shows us, it is much more inclusive. The gospel guarantees we will go to heaven. Because of our position in Christ (chapter 6) and the Holy Spirit in our hearts (chapter 8), the gospel also guarantees we can live the abundant, fruitful life God wants us to live here on earth.

The gospel also includes the future salvation of the Jewish nation (chapters 12—16). As Paul contemplated the extent of the gospel, he broke into an exclamation of praise:

> Oh, the depth of the riches of the wisdom and knowledge of God! How unsearchable His judgments, and his paths beyond tracing out! (11:33)

The gospel of Jesus Christ is God's answer to every human dilemma. There is no problem it will not solve, no need it cannot satisfy, no question it cannot answer. Paul was not ashamed of it, and he felt obligated to preach it to every creature (1:14–16).

? What is sin?

Sin can be summarized as *the lack of obedience to the revealed will of God, the absence of righteousness, an attitude of opposition or indifference toward God.*

Verse 9
(All are under sin.)

Verse 10
(None are righteous.)

Verse 11
(None understand or seek for God.)

Verse 17
(No one knows the path of peace.)

Verse 18
(No one fears God.)

What righteousness does a man have that he can offer God (Romans 3:10)?
(None.)

3. Read Romans 3:21–28 and 5:1–5.

What has God declared to you (3:25,26)?
(His justice.)

Therefore, how are you justified (1:17; 3:28; 5:1)?
(By faith, apart from the works of the law.)

Man is sinful before a holy God. Sin originated with Satan (Isaiah 14:12–14), entered the world through Adam (Romans 5:12), is universal (Christ alone excepted—Romans 3:23), incurs the penalties of spiritual and physical death (Genesis 2:17; 3:19, Romans 6:23), and has no remedy but the sacrificial, substitutionary death of Christ (Hebrews 9:26; Acts 4:12) which must be accepted by faith (Acts 13:38,39).

❓What has God done for us to bring us into a right relationship with Himself?

He has redeemed us (Romans 3:24; 5:6–8; Galatians 3:13).

To redeem means "to buy back; to deliver by paying a price," especially "to purchase out of a slave market," in this case, the slavery of sin. Only a free man can purchase the slave's freedom.

He has justified us (Romans 3:26; 4:25—5:2; Galatians 2:16).

To justify someone is to declare him righteous. God's justice is a judicial act where He declares a person righteous because he believes in Jesus Christ. Literally, God imputes or credits to our account His righteousness, which is the only righteousness.

That is the gospel! God redeems us, justifies us, and gives us His righteousness. He does it all because of His grace. This is certainly good news!

4. Being justified by faith, what is your spiritual resource (5:5)?
   (The Holy Spirit has been given to us.)

5. Being justified by faith, what is your spiritual worship (12:1)?
   (To present our bodies a living and holy sacrifice, acceptable to God.)

6. List five ways in which this sacrifice will affect your daily walk (12:6–13:10).
   (Possible answers include: Serving God with my talents; loving without hypocrisy; abhorring evil; clinging to good; living at peace; doing good to my enemies; submitting to authority; paying taxes; paying debts; loving my neighbor.)

   Which area do you need to apply most?

God has given us the power to live for Him through His Holy Spirit (Romans 8:11,15; Galatians 5:16). The Holy Spirit gives us the strength to demonstrate God's love in whatever we do.

Many people do not consider their bodies as a resource through which they can worship God. When we present every part of our physical selves to God to use in His service, we are giving Him true worship. (Read James 1:27.) This verse shows us that God considers our physical actions as part of our worship to Him.

I Corinthians

This epistle was written three years after Paul left Corinth. The Corinthian church sent a delegation of its leaders to Ephesus to consult with Paul about some serious problems that had arisen in the church.

1. Read 1 Corinthians 1:17–31. Paul makes it clear that God is wiser than men and chooses the foolish things of the world to confound the mighty.

   How has God ordained that men should hear and

The main theme of 1 Corinthians is Christian conduct (1 Corinthians 10:13,31–33). This includes discussion of the following:

◆ Divisions among Christians (1:10–17)

◆ Morality (6:18–20)

◆ Marriage (7:1–40)

◆ Questionable practices (8:1–13)

Conduct had to be stressed because these Christians were worldly, thus remaining infants in Christ (1 Corinthians 3:1–4).

believe?
(Through the preaching of His Word.)

Whom has He chosen for this task?
(The foolish, the weak, and the lowly.)

What happens, then, if you boast about what you are doing for God?
(You take the credit for what God has done.)

2. Read 1 Corinthians 9:22–24.

   Give in your own words definite proof that Paul had forsaken all that he had to follow Christ (verse 22).

   To what does he liken his task?
   (A race.)

   Why is this so appropriate?
   (A runner eliminates anything that interferes with running the race.)

   What have you given up to help reach someone for Christ?

3. Read 1 Corinthians 13. In verses 4–8, insert your own name in the place of "love" or "charity."

   Which verse does not fit you and what do you think God would have you do about it?

2 Corinthians

Soon after Paul had written 1 Corinthians, he met Titus on his way to Corinth. Titus brought word that Paul's let-

Outline of 1 Corinthians:

◆ Position in grace (1:1–9)

◆ Problem of divisions in the Church (1:10—4:21)

◆ Problem of immorality (chapters 5—7)

◆ Problem of food offered to idols (8:1—11:1)

◆ Problem of public worship (11:2—14:40)

◆ Doctrine of the resurrection (chapter 15)

◆ Practical concerns of Paul (chapter 16)

The main theme of 2 Corinthians is the vindication of Paul's apostleship (2 Corinthians 4:1–7).

ter had accomplished much good but some were still disloyal, and there were problems with people who put the law before the needs of people.

Paul was physically weak, weary, and in pain. His spiritual burdens were great: first, the maintenance of the churches; second, his concern about the legalists; and third, his anguish over the distrust of him by some members of the churches.

1. Read 2 Corinthians 4:1–6. Notice how carefully Paul handles the Word of God.

   Describe how Paul spreads the gospel of Christ (verse 2).
   (By plainly telling the truth.)

   Why did God shine into our hearts (verse 6)?
   (To give us light so we could know the glory of God in Christ.)

2. What is it that Paul fears and of which we all must be well aware (2 Corinthians 11:3)?
   (Being led astray.)

3. Read 2 Corinthians 12:1–10. Paul prayed to be relieved of his "thorn in the flesh" (a physical disability). What was the Lord's answer to his prayer (verse 9)?
   (God's grace is sufficient.)

   What was Paul's attitude toward the final outcome?

Outline of 2 Corinthians:

◆ The characteristics of Paul's ministry (chapters 1—7)

◆ Giving to the Christians at Jerusalem (chapters 8—9)

◆ A defense of Paul's ministry (chapters 10—13)

❓How have you seen God work through your weaknesses?

❓Is it hard for you to delight in your weaknesses? Why or why not?

(He would delight in his weakness b⋅cause he knew the power of Christ would make him strong.)

What lesson can you learn from his experience (12:10)?
(Be content; we have Christ's strength when we are weak.)

Galatians

Some time after Paul left Galatia, certain Jewish teachers began to insist that Gentiles could not be Christian without keeping the Law of Moses. The objective of this epistle is the defense of the gospel of grace that Paul had received by revelation from Jesus.

1. Paul shows that the gospel was not of man, neither did he receive it of man, nor was he taught it of man. What was its true origin (Galatians 1:12)?
   (A revelation of Jesus Christ.)

2. What is Paul's relationship with Christ (Galatians 2:20)?
   (Christ lives within Paul.)

   What effect does this have on his daily life?
   (It is no longer Paul who lives, but Christ lives in him.)

3. Read Galatians 5:16–21. In this passage Paul lists the works of the flesh. How can we as Christians

The main theme of Galatians is that the gospel of God comes by grace and is sustained by grace. Law has nothing to do with it. We can do nothing to receive grace or to keep it. For examples, see Galatians 3:1–3,10,11; 4:9,10; 5:1–6.

❖ What is grace?

Grace is the unmerited love of God shown toward sinful men. Grace means that God has *given* us the gospel as a gift, without any strings attached; we can do nothing to *earn* it. We must simply receive it by faith. Faith is the only channel through which grace can operate. (See Ephesians 2:8–10.)

The Galatians were making the mistake of trying to impose the law of Moses on the gospel. They said it was necessary to do some work, such as submit to circumcision, to be saved.

Though they realize they cannot do anything to be saved but receive God's gift, many Christians today make the mistake of trying to earn their way in the Christian life. In Galatians 3:1–5, Paul speaks against these heresies.

avoid doing the works of the flesh?
(By living in the Spirit.)

1. According to Galatians 5:22,23, what will be the result in your life of walking in the power and control of the Holy Spirit? List the definite characteristics.
(The fruit of the Spirit in my life: love, joy, peace, patience, kindness, goodness, faithfulness, gentleness, self-control.)

2. Which work of your flesh do you most need to surrender to the Holy Spirit's control today?

Take time to do that right now.

3. Which fruit of the Spirit is God trying to strengthen in your life?

How?

4. What one attitude of Paul's do you desire for your life and ministry?

How will you make it your own?

Outline of Galatians, the gospel of grace:

◆ Paul's apostolic authority (chapters 1—2)

◆ Grace contrasted with the Law (chapters 3—4)

◆ Results of practical living (chapters 5—6)

Conclusion and Application

Grace transforms Christian living from moralistic striving in our own efforts to an attitude of rest and faith where we let Christ live in us and through us. Galatians 2:20 and 5:16 are two of the key passages of the book, teaching us that our only responsibility is to trust Jesus Christ to live through us by the Holy Spirit.

Here is the secret to victory: We give up our own struggling and striving—our own efforts to please God—and by faith we trust Him to live His life in and through us.

Closing Prayer

Prison Epistles, Thessalonians, Pastoral Epistles

Opening Prayer

Discussion Starter

A particular church was in need of a pastor. One of the elders was interested in knowing just what kind of a minister the congregation desired. He wrote the following letter as if he had received it from the applicant and read the letter before the pulpit committee.

"Gentlemen: Hearing that your pulpit is vacant, I would like to apply for the position. I have many qualifications that I think you would appreciate. I have been able to preach with power and have had success as a writer. I have been told that I am a good organizer. I have been a leader in most places I've gone.

"Some people, however, have things against me. I am over fifty years of age. I have never preached in one place for over three years at a time. In some places I have left town after my work caused riots and disturbances. I have to admit that I have been in jail three times, but not because of any

Leader's Objective: To give your students a brief survey of the Prison, Thessalonian, and Pastoral Epistles

LESSON 7

Bible Study

Prison Epistles

Ephesians. The purpose of this letter was to show the Gentiles that they were on an equal footing with the Jews in receiving the blessings of salvation (see Ephesians 2:8–22; 3:6).

1. What had been the prospects of Gentiles receiving the blessings of salvation in previous times (2:11,12)?
    (None; they were separate from Christ, excluded from Israel, with no hope and without God.)

2. Through what event were the blessings of salvation made available to all (2:13–18)?
    (Christ destroyed in His flesh the wall of hostility. His death destroyed the barriers, reconciling the two through the cross.)

3. From Paul's prayer in Ephesians 3:14–19, list the blessings of salvation that all Christians now enjoy.
    (A heavenly name, power through the Spirit, Christ dwells in hearts, knowledge of love of Christ, fulness of God.)

4. How can you use this information for encouragement?

wrong doing. My health is not good, though I still get a lot of ministry done. I have had to work at my trade to help pay my way. The churches I have preached in have been small, though several were located in large cities.

"I have not gotten along too well with the religious leaders in different towns where I have preached. In fact, some of them have threatened me, taken me to court, and even attacked me physically. I am not too good at keeping records. I have been known to forget whom I have baptized. If you can use me, however, I shall do my best for you, even if I have to work to help with my support."

❓How do you suppose the committee responded?

(After hearing some replies, continue reading.)

The elder who read this letter to the committee asked for their reply. The committee said the pastoral candidate would never fit into their church. They were not interested in an unhealthy, contentious, troublemaking, absent-minded jail-bird. After inquiring about the name of the applicant, the elder answered, "The apostle Paul."

This illustrates how modern Christians are often more concerned with surface issues in a person's life, but know little of true spirituality. In Paul we have a man who is truly spiritual. This lesson gives us many interesting insights into his life.

Philippians. Paul wrote this letter to the church he had founded (Acts 16) to thank them for the money they sent him for his support while in prison. In writing it, he also sought to overcome the disunity in the church between two women, Euodia and Syntyche (Philippians 4:2). With this disunity overcome, the church could stand firmly together in preaching the gospel without fear to those around them (1:27,28).

1. Read Philippians 1:12–30. What had Paul been doing in Rome that would encourage the Philippians to be bold in proclaiming the gospel (1:13,14)?
   (Witnessing to everyone.)

2. How did Paul's attitude regarding the future help to encourage the Philippians to stand fearlessly for Christ (1:18–26)?
   (He was not afraid of death, rather he desired it as much as life.)

3. What was Paul's chief reason for being happy about the gift the Philippians had sent him (4:10–19)?
   (Because of what will be credited to their accounts.)

Take time to thank God for the gifts (spiritual and material) that Christians have given you this past week.

Lesson Development

(Ask one of the group members to summarize the paragraphs appearing at the opening of this lesson in the student's book.)

Paul gives us interesting pictures of his spiritual life in the epistles. His two recorded prayers in Ephesians are monumental. He doesn't pray for material blessings, or that the saints would receive spiritual blessings, but that they should know the spiritual blessings they already possess. "I pray also that the eyes of your heart may be enlightened in order that you may know the hope to which he has called you, the riches of his glorious inheritance in the saints" (Ephesians 1:18). (Read Ephesians 3:18,19.)

This is in accord with Ephesians 1:3. We already have all we need in Christ; we only need to realize it and appropriate all that is our heritage by faith. It is not wrong to pray for material things, especially when they affect our spiritual well-being. But our main concern should be about our spiritual vitality.

Paul wrote Philippians while he was a prisoner in Rome. Not many prisoners are happy about imprisonment, even when justly punished, but Paul, unjustly punished, rejoiced.

❓Why?

Because his great concern was Christ and His work. For him, "life" was Christ and his misfortunes did not overcome or discourage him. Note circumstances that could have discouraged Paul:

◆ Unjustly imprisoned

◆ Had been there for some time (first jailed in Jerusalem)

◆ Opposed by others who claimed to be Christians

◆ Rejected by his own people

◆ Probably alone and inactive much of the time

◆ In a large, strange city

◆ Uncertain about his future

◆ Had to take charity from others (chapter 4)

These things would throw a lesser Christian into self-pity and keep him from witnessing at all. But Paul considered them an open door for spreading the gospel in a new place. He recognized that his disappointments were really God's appointments. His mind was focused not on time but on eternity.

Colossians. Paul had never visited the church at Colosse, but reports regarding the increase of false teaching there had reached him in Rome. Since he was an apostle to all the Gentiles, he felt it necessary to write and warn that church.

The false teaching stated that instead of Christ being the only mediator between God and man, there were certain angelic beings through whom man must also go in order to know God. Consequently, Paul's main emphasis in this Epis-

In Colossians, Paul emphasizes Christ as the head of the Church. The letter was a message of goodwill to Christians. Paul warns believers and builds them up in Christ and shows them how to live as godly families and co-workers.

tle is the deity and all-sufficiency of Jesus Christ.

1. List at least three things Paul says about Jesus Christ that show it is unnecessary to seek any additional way to reach God (Colossians 1:12–22).
   (By Him all things were created; He is before all things; in Him all things hold together; and others.)

2. Since Christ is all-sufficient, what is the Christian to do (2:6,7)?
   (Live in Him by trusting and obeying.)

3. What practical effect will submission to the Lordship and uniqueness of Christ have upon the Christian's life (3:1–11)?
   (He will not be so concerned with his position or his circumstances on earth.)

4. What evidence of submissiveness do you find in your life?

5. Where do you need to improve in this area?

Philemon. While in prison at Rome, Paul had led Onesimus, a runaway slave, to the Lord. He discovered that this slave's master was Philemon, a personal friend of Paul's living at Colosse. In those days, the penalty for a slave who had run away was either death or brutal punishment. Paul wrote Philemon asking him to forgive Onesimus for what he had

Christ is everything. Some of the Colossians believed that Jesus was just a man. This is the error that many cults teach. Our faith is based on the fact that Jesus was more than a man. Jesus was God in the flesh, wholly God, fully man.

As we go through this study, examine your beliefs in this area. We would never say that Jesus is not God, but do we make Him the Lord of our lives? Giving Him total control of our lives is the only way we can find the abundant life He has promised us.

❷ How does this principle of forgiveness relate to us today?

Compare the story of Onesimus with that of the prodigal son in Luke 15:11–32.

❷ What is similar in the two stories?

Both ran away, then repented and wanted to return.

done and to receive him as a Christian brother.

This Epistle stands as a great example of the profound change for good that Christ makes in all human relations.

1. State in your own words at least three arguments Paul used to persuade Philemon to receive Onesimus in love:
   (Onesimus' conversion; receive him in Paul's place; Philemon is indebted to Paul; and others.)

2. Who do you know that needs this kind of forgiveness?

The Thessalonian Epistles

The first epistles Paul ever wrote were those to the churches he had founded at Thessalonica in Macedonia. These were written from Corinth (Acts 18:1–18) soon after Paul had left Thessalonica.

1 Thessalonians. Paul had had to leave Thessalonica very hastily because of persecution (Acts 17:10). The enemies of the gospel there had tried to disillusion the newly won Christians by charging that Paul was only a fair-weather friend who had left them alone because of difficult circumstances. To answer this charge Paul wrote 1 Thessalonians.

1. What effect had the Thessalonians' conversion had on the Christians of

We are often exhorted to win others to Christ, but sometimes we carry the importance of evangelism so far that we put no emphasis on our own Christian character.

A person who witnesses all the time and has many so-called "results," yet whose life in un-Christlike, dishonors God and harms his converts. He gives them the wrong example to follow, and his spiritual children are unhealthy and spiritually malformed, just like he is.

On the other hand, one can live what appears to be a holy, Spirit-filled life, but if he is not witnessing for Christ, he is disobedient to Christ's command to "follow me and I will make you fishers of men" (Matthew 4:19). He also made it very clear that we glorify God when we "bear much fruit" (John 15:8).

the surrounding area (1:7–10)?
(They became an example of faith.)

2. The lives of those to whom Paul wrote had been changed. How did this prove that those who had preached the gospel to them were godly men (1:5,6)?
(We tend to copy those we follow, and these new Christians were Spirit-filled.)

3. Give two ways in which Paul's ministry at Thessalonica made it impossible for him to be an insincere person (2:1–10).
   1) *(Did not try to please men.)*
   2) *(Worked to support self; endured hardship.)*

4. Think of someone who exemplifies qualities that Paul had. What can you learn from that person's example?

2 Thessalonians. Some questions regarding the circumstances of Christ's second coming had arisen after the Thessalonians received Paul's first epistle. They were troubled because they had to unjustly endure great sufferings and persecutions for Christ (2 Thessalonians 1:3–12). Some also had become slack in doing their

❓How has seeing someone come to know the Lord changed your life and other Christians around you?

There is *no* substitute for Christian character. This is why Paul was successful. Note some of his characteristics in 1 Thessalonians 2:1–10:

◆ Boldness

◆ Sincerity

◆ Ability to please God

◆ Not seeking to please men

◆ Gentleness (not harsh, argumentative, or unkind)

◆ Love for converts

◆ Hardworking

◆ Holiness, righteousness, blamelessness

❓How do you feel about Christ's return to earth?

❓Why?

work because they thought Christ's second coming would occur at any moment.

1. What do you think the Christian's attitude should be toward persecution (2 Thessalonians 1:3–12)?
   (Thank God, rejoice, pray for each other, glorify God.)

2. What is to be his attitude toward work (3:6–15)?
   (Don't be idle, work hard, don't be busybodies, avoid those who won't work.)

3. How can you apply this to your life?

The Pastoral Epistles

These letters were written in the period between Paul's first Roman imprisonment in A.D. 60–62 (Acts 28) and his final martyrdom under the emperor Nero in A.D. 66. He wrote 1 and 2 Timothy to help Timothy in his work with the church at Ephesus. Titus was written to Paul's co-worker on the island of Crete.

1 Timothy. Read 1 Timothy 6.

1. What are the two things that are necessary for contentment in life (1 Timothy 6:6–8)?
   1) *(Food and clothing.)*
   2) *(Godliness.)*

2. What great danger confronts those who seek after riches (verses 9–12)?
   (Falling into temptation and wandering away from the faith.)

❓Do you think we are persecuted in our country?

❓How do your work habits reflect on God?

In the pastoral epistles, Paul writes a lot about material possessions.

❓Why?

Because in his day, as it is now, this was the consuming drive in the lives of many. Perhaps there were many wealthy people in Timothy's church.

Money is like luggage on a trip. It is necessary for the trip—we have to take luggage along—but it is not the main thing. We are concerned about where we are going, what we will see on the way, and what we will do when we get there.

❓Have you ever seen people in airports so loaded down with luggage that they can barely get from place to place? How is this like a materialistic Christian?

One way to tell if money is too important to you is to look through

3. What attitude should Christians who are wealthy have toward money (verses 17–19)?
   (No conceit, fix hope on God, do good, share, take hold of true life.)

4. How does money tempt you?

5. Which verse will help you overcome this wrong desire?

2 Timothy. Paul wrote 2 Timothy just before he was martyred. He writes as though it may be his last word to Timothy.

1. What are the last commands Paul gave him (4:1–5)?
   (Preach the Word; be prepared always; fulfill your ministry; and others.)

2. What two means will help Timothy remain true to his calling after Paul has gone (3:10,11,14–17)?

   1) *(Imitate Paul's example.)*

   2) *(Continue in what he had learned.)*

3. List several ways this Bible study has helped you remain true.

Titus. Paul wrote this Epistle after his first imprisonment in Rome to encourage Titus

your checkbook. Where are you spending your money? How much do you give to God?

A good way to evaluate is to write down your goals. Compare your goals with how you are spending your money. Do your finances reflect your goals? If not, are you realistically trying to achieve your goals?

Then look to see how much compassion there is in your checkbook. Is your debt so high that you can't help a person in need? Where do you spend your extra cash? Only on yourself? Do you regularly give over and above your normal donation to your church?

? Are you preparing someone to take over your work when you are gone?

Whether we move, change ministries or churches or even neighborhoods, we can leave behind someone who will carry on the ministry we have started. Not only will training someone to carry on after us benefit the people for whom we are burdened, but it will also help us as we transfer our joy of ministry to another Christian, and it will benefit the Christian we invest our time with.

Note the concern about "good works" in this book. It is important to understand Titus 3:5,8. Christians do

and strengthen his ability to minister under opposition. Paul instructed Titus to admonish the people to be "sound in the faith" and hold to "sound doctrine."

1. What are some of the things a Christian should be careful to do in the unbelieving world in which he lives (Titus 3:1,2)?
   (Be subject to rulers; be ready for good deeds; slander no one; be considerate of all.)

2. How can you apply verses 1 and 2 to a situation in your life?

3. What reason does Paul give for a Christian living this way (3:3–7)?
   (We were once foolish ourselves, but God saved us and we are renewed.)

LIFE APPLICATION

1. Name two things you have learned from Paul's character in this study.
   1)
   2)

2. From Philippians 3:1 and 4:4, what approach to life do you think Paul would advise for you?

   Is that always possible?

   How?

good works, but *never* to earn God's approval or our salvation. Salvation is a free gift, received by faith alone (Ephesians 2:8,9).

This is contrary to the belief that many of us are good enough to "get by" with God. Good works are the result, not the cause, of becoming a Christian.

Conclusion and Application

Christ is our supreme example (1 John 2:6). But the Scriptures have also given us the example of Paul. He is another proof that Christianity changes lives. Paul, who began as a murderer of Christians and "chief of sinners," went on to become one of the most dynamic witnesses for Christ (1 Timothy 1:15).

Closing Prayer

The General Epistles

Opening Prayer

Discussion Starter

The Bible refers to people who love and obey God as wheat, and those who do not love God as weeds. The writers of the General Epistles view the church as a body in which the wheat and weeds are mingled (Matthew 13:24–30). These writings give warnings to those who merely profess religious faith, but do not commit themselves to Christ as Lord.

Why do you think those warnings are important for us today?

Lesson Development

(Ask one of the group members to summarize the paragraphs appearing at the opening of this lesson in the student's book.)

Leader's Objective: To show students that God gives us everything we need for life and godliness

514

LESSON 8

Bible Study

Hebrews

The early church called this book "Hebrews" because it was originally addressed to Jewish Christians. In the early days following their conversion through the preaching of some of Jesus' original disciples (2:3), they had become exemplary Christians and had helped supply the needs of other Christians (6:10). They had taken cheerfully the loss of their own possessions as they were persecuted for Christ's name (10:32–34).

However, at the time this letter was written their original teachers and leaders had died (13:7). Now they were on the verge of slipping back from a confession of Christ into the Judaism out of which they had been converted (13:13,14). The writer of Hebrews exhorts the readers to remain true to Christ even at the price of having to shed their own blood (12:3,4).

That writer had to have been an outstanding leader in the early Christian church, but his identity is unknown. Many believe it was written by the apostle Paul, but this cannot be confirmed.

1. What four things must a Christian do, according to Hebrews 10:22–25?

The first chapter of Hebrews fulfills the promises given about Jesus in Genesis 1:1 and John 1:1. His deity and everlasting glory are plainly evident and he is described as the only true Son of God. By an eternal act of God, Jesus, once for all, paid the penalty for the sin of the world and provided everlasting salvation for the whole human race.

Major points of doctrine in Hebrews include: Christ's unity with man (chapter 2), God's rest for His people (chapter 4), the New Covenant as superior to the old Law (chapters 8, 10), and great heroes of the Old Testament (chapter 11).

This Epistle shows how many Old Testament doctrines were mere "shadows" of truths to come in the person of Jesus Christ. Some of them are:

The position of faith (Hebrews 10:19–21):

◆ We are placed in Christ, a position of perfection, acceptable to the Father.

◆ This position gives boldness rather than fear when approaching God.

◆ The blood cleanses us and makes forgiveness of sin possible.

1) *(Draw near to God with a sincere heart.)*

2) *(Hold unswervingly to the confession of our hope.)* `·`

3) *(Spur one another to love and good deeds.)*

4) *(Not give up meeting together.)*

2. Summarize in your own words the two lines of argument that the writer uses to support these commands.

10:26–31

10:32–34

3. What attitude did the original readers of this Epistle need to remain true to Christ in the midst of persecution (10:35–39)?
(Confidence and perseverence.)

4. How did the Old Testament believers acquire this necessary quality (11:1–40)?
(By faith.)

5. In view of the way these Old Testament believers lived, what should you do (12:1–3)?
(Put aside sin and "run with perseverence" in holy living.)

The assurance of faith (Hebrews 10:22–25):

◆ Obedience gives us assurance before God.

◆ Our hope is based on God who is faithful.

James

The writer of this Epistle is thought to have been the half-brother of Jesus. Though not counted as one of the twelve apostles, James became a prominent leader

James was surnamed "the just" by his countrymen and chosen a "bishop of Jerusalem" where he was very influential in the church. He endorsed Paul's Gentile work, but was a Jew himself and primarily concerned with

in the early Jerusalem church (Acts 15:13; Galatians 1:19; 2:9). Because the name "James" was so common in those days, it is felt that only this James, who figured so prominently in the early church, would have announced himself to the readers of this Epistle without going into any detail as to who he was (James 1:1).

James wrote this Epistle to remind Christians about the qualities of heart and life that should characterize true Christian devotion in contrast to dead orthodoxy. In so doing, he made it clear how a Christian can find joy in Christ even when suffering for Him.

1. Why should the Christian consider adversity a reason for the greatest happiness (James 1:2–4, 12)?
   (Because God is maturing him, and will give him the crown of life.)

2. In what way does the Christian receive the necessary resources to stand for Christ while suffering greatly (1:5–8)?
   (Ask God in faith for his needs.)

3. What two things should the Christian always remember when he feels tempted to do wrong? 1:13–16
   (Temptation does not come from God.)

Jews. His life's work was to win Jews and aid them in a smooth transition to Christianity.

Major doctrines and subjects of James' Epistle include:

◆ The testing of your faith

◆ Avoiding discrimination

◆ Contrast between faith and works

◆ Controlling your tongue

◆ Worldly-mindedness

◆ Difficulties with wealth

◆ Patience in suffering

The theme of James is outward willing service as true evidence of an inward faith. Certain aspects of Christian conduct are brought out in the following passages:

◆ Partiality (2:1–4)

◆ Conversation and the tongue (3:9–12)

◆ Humility and obedience (4:6–17)

❓According to James 3:13–18, what is the difference between the world's wisdom and God's?

1:17,18
(Every good thing does come from God.)

4. Instead of simply hearing what God has to say in His Word, what should the Christian do (1:21–25)?
(Be a doer of the Word, live what he has learned.)

What should we do instead of simply talk about being Christians (1:26, 27)?
(Control our tongue, and act.)

5. Read chapter 5. List several commands that you will apply this week.

Peter

1 Peter. Peter addresses the various churches scattered throughout Asia Minor (present-day Turkey). But like James, Peter's purpose in writing was to strengthen Christians so they could stand firm against the terrible persecutions by the Roman Empire. He begins by pointing out the wonders of the salvation that his readers possess (1:3–12). Then he gives certain commands that when obeyed will help a person to realize the wonders of this salvation.

1. List the five commands Peter gives in 1:13–2:3:

1:13
(Keep mind and hope on Christ.)

1:14–16
(Be holy as God is holy.)

❓How can a business person apply James 4:13–16?

According to Peter, some of the other differences Christ can make in our lives are:

◆ We are dead to sin and alive to righteousness (2:24).

◆ We are sanctified (set apart) because of Christ within us (3:15).

◆ We are alive in the will of God (4:2).

1:17–21
(Conduct selves in the fear of God.)

1:22–25
(Love one another from the heart.)

2:1–3
(Crave the pure milk of the Word.)

2. When one fulfills these commands, how does his attitude toward Christ differ from that of those who do not believe and obey Him (1 Peter 2:4–10)?
(The Christian will not be disappointed or shamed by Christ.)

3. How, in general, does the Christian witness to those around him by his life (1 Peter 2:11,12)?
(They live in such a way that observers will glorify God.)

How, in relationship to the government, does the Christian demonstrate the praises of Christ (1 Peter 2:13–17)?
(He obeys the laws as a matter of personal choice, not because of force.)

How, in his relationship with an employer, can a Christian demonstrate the praises of Christ (1 Peter 2:18–25)?
(Through respectful obedience.)

How can a Christian wife best testify of Christ to an unbelieving husband (1 Peter 3:1–6)?
(By being submissive to

The persecution of Peter's day was the first world trial for the church. On many occasions, Christians were burned in Nero's gardens, and this example of their emperor encouraged the enemies of Christians to take advantage of his permission to persecute. From Jesus' words in John 21:28, we judge that Peter himself died a martyr's death.

Doctrines in this Epistle include:

◆ The Christian's incorruptible inheritance

◆ Behavior of Christians (attitudes toward the elect, government, family, etc.)

◆ Painful trials and the reward for patience and endurance

❓ How have you seen Peter's advice work for Christians you know who have unbelieving spouses?

*him, gentle, and respect-
ful.)*

How about a Christian
husband (1 Peter 3:7)?
*(He is to be considerate
and respectful of his wife.)*

2 Peter. As 2 Timothy records Paul's last words before martyrdom, so 2 Peter
was Peter's last message before his martyrdom (1:14;
see also John 21:19). This
Epistle is a continuation of
the theme of 1 Peter. The
sufferings that his readers
had just begun to endure
when that Epistle was written have continued un-
abated, and Peter's purpose
in writing this second Epistle is to encourage his readers to endure steadfastly to
the end.

1. From what two sources
   have the readers heard of
   God's grace?

   1:12–18
   *(Peter told of his witness of
   Christ's majesty.)*

   1:19–21
   *(They read the Old Testa-
   ment Scriptures.)*

2. However, there have always been those whose
   teaching would keep
   God's people from the
   truth. Name three ways
   to recognize those who
   are false prophets (2:1–
   22).

   1) *(They have eyes full of
      adultery and sensual-
      ity.)*

The objective of Peter's second
Epistle to the same people was to warn
them of coming apostasy (time of
great unbelief).

Some of the methods of defending
the faith are:

◆ Claiming the promises of God
  (2 Peter 1:4)

◆ Allowing the world to be an eyewitness of the love and truth of God as
  seen through lives lived for Him

◆ Recognizing those who are not true
  to the faith

◆ Paying attention to prophecy
  (2 Peter 1:19)

◆ Being aware of false prophets and
  their teachings (2 Peter 2:1)

◆ Living holy lives (2 Peter 3:11)

The principal doctrines of 2 Peter
include:

◆ The great and precious promise
  for faith

◆ The destruction of false teachers
  and the ungodly

◆ The time of the Lord's coming

2) *(They are experts in greed.)*

3) *(They have left the right way to follow after wickedness.)*

3. What great event should determine the present conduct of Christians (3:10–14)?
(The coming day of the Lord.)

How does Christ's return help you live daily?

John

1 John. During his later years, the apostle John settled at Ephesus among Christians who had found Christ through Paul's ministry.

While he was there, a certain false teaching became popular which declared that God did not become truly incarnate in Jesus Christ and that a life of actual holiness was not essential to the Christian life.

The first Epistle of John was written to counteract this heresy. However, it is more than a mere refutation; it is one of the most beautiful and inspiring documents of the New Testament.

The key verse is 1 John 5:13: "I write these things to you who believe in the name of the Son of God so that you may know that you have eternal life."

1. See if you can find at least five tests of this assurance of eternal life in the

When these Epistles were written, Christianity had been in the world some 60 or 70 years, and in many parts of the Roman Empire it was an important influence. Feeling the impact of the church, false teachers tried to neutralize its power. These epistles were written to correct false doctrine and to describe God's love and the Christian's righteousness.

Major doctrines of 1, 2, and 3 John include:

◆ How to walk in the light of God

◆ True righteousness

◆ Love

◆ False prophets and teachers

◆ The need for recognizing the authority of the apostles and their chosen servants

material leading up to 5:13.

1:7 *(If we walk in the light.)*

2:3 *(If we obey His commands.)*

2:15 *(If we do not love the world.)*

3:6 *(If we do not habitually sin.)*

4:7 *(If we love one another.)*

2 John. It is not clear whether the recipient of this brief Epistle is an individual, or whether the term "elect lady" figuratively denotes a church whose members are her "children" (verse 1).

1. Summarize in your own words the burden of the message John gives to this church.

2. How can you better demonstrate love for those walking in truth?

3 John. The principal characters of this Epistle are Gaius and Diotrephes. As church leaders went from town to town establishing new congregations, they depended on the hospitality of fellow believers. Gaius was one who welcomed them into his home. John wrote this Epistle to thank Gaius for his hospitality and faithfulness and to encourage him in the faith.

1. What example is Gaius to continue to follow in the future (verses 2–8)?

John's first Epistle is intensely personal and recognized as a circular letter from John the apostle to the churches around Ephesus. First John emphasizes the main essentials of the gospel in addition to warning against heresies.

❓What was John's joy in 2 John 4?

List some ways of walking in love (2 John 6).

❓If a person claims he believes in God, but not in Christ, what does the Word say about him (2 John 9)?

❓What was John's joy in 3 John 4?

Hospitality is different than entertaining. Hospitality is concern about the needs of the person at your doorstep. Entertaining is impressing others.

❓How important is hospitality to church life today?

❓What can you do to be more hospitable to other Christians?

(That of hospitality to the brethren.)

2. What is there about Diotrephes that Gaius is to avoid imitating (verses 9–11)?
   (Gossiping; doesn't welcome others; causes dissension.)

3. What do you think an attitude like Diotrephes' can do to church unity?

Jude

Many biblical scholars believe that Jude was another one of Jesus' brothers who was converted after His earthly ministry. He calls himself "the brother of James" (verse 1), and in verse 17 he indicates that he was not himself an official apostle.

1. What was Jude's reason for writing as he does in this Epistle (verses 3,4)?
   (To counteract heresy.)

2. What are two things that Jude wants his readers to remember?

   Verses 5–16
   (How God deals with unbelievers.)

   Verses 17–19
   (The words of warning spoken by apostles.)

3. What is the Christian's responsibility in view of the many false teachers that exist (verses 20–23)?
   (To stand firm for their faith.)

The entire tone of Jude is that every Christian should contend for the faith that has been delivered to the saints (verse 3).

Major doctrines and subjects of this book include:

◆ Warnings connected with the imminent apostasy

◆ Descriptions of false teachers

◆ Fallen angels and their fate

◆ Michael's contention with the devil

◆ The prophecy of Enoch

4. Praise God for His qualities found in verses 24 and 25.

1. Determine one main truth from each book that is particularly helpful to you and list it here.

   Hebrews

   James

   1 Peter

   2 Peter

   1 John

   2 John

   3 John

   Jude

2. Describe how you will apply each to your life.

❖ ❖ ❖

(Take time during the study to praise God for His qualities.)

Conclusion and Application

We can praise God today because in His matchless grace He has given us everything we need for life and godliness. Nothing depends upon what we have been in the past, or what we will become in the future.

On the cross Christ said, "It is finished." This was an eternal sign to us that He had completely accomplished everything needed to make us acceptable before God.

Closing Prayer

❖ ❖ ❖

The Revelation of Jesus Christ

Opening Prayer

Discussion Starter

 Why do you think it is important to be familiar with prophecy?

Lesson Development

(Ask one of the group members to summarize the paragraphs appearing at the opening of this lesson in the student's book.)

This book is "The Revelation of Jesus Christ" to John (Revelation 1:1). It unveils God's future plan for the earth and for His redeemed saints, for both time and eternity.

The figures and symbols in the book, which furnish the basis of its interpretation, are found elsewhere in the Bible. They can be better understood as a coherent and connected study of all other lines of prophecy as they converge upon the book of Revelation.

Revelation assures God's people again and again that we are under God's protection, with an eternity of blessedness ahead.

❖

Leader's Objective: To teach the students some fundamentals of God's prophetic plan and to help them know how to prepare for the coming of Christ

LESSON 9

Bible Study

Jesus Christ

1. Write in your own words your impression of Jesus Christ as John describes Him in Revelation 1:9–20.

2. How is this picture of Jesus different from the one of Him as Savior? *(His appearance is more than human.)*

The Churches

1. Name the seven churches to whom John was commanded to write, and tell the one main message he was to give to each (chapters 2 and 3).

   1) *(Ephesus: Left their first love, remember and repent.)*

   2) *(Smyrna: Encouragement in face of suffering.)*

   3) *(Pergamon: Warning against their evil teachers.)*

   4) *(Thyatira: Warning of judgment upon their sin.)*

   5) *(Sardis: Exhorting dead church to awaken.)*

   6) *(Philadelphia: Encouragement and promise.)*

   7) *(Laodicea: Warnings against compromise and lukewarmness.)*

The book alternates between scenes on earth and in heaven. Revelation also contrasts the joys of the redeemed with the agonies of the lost.

God dictated the book through Christ by an angel to John (Revelation 1:1) around A.D. 96. John wrote it down and sent the completed book to seven representative churches. John, called "the beloved disciple," was the most intimate earthly friend of Jesus (John 21:20,24).

There are several different ways of understanding Revelation, but the best seems to be to follow the outline suggested in Revelation 1:19:

◆ "What you have seen"—including the vision of a glorified Christ—is in the first chapter.

◆ "What is now"—the letters to the seven churches—is in the second and third chapters. These seven churches represent all facets of Christianity, good and bad, during the church age.

◆ "What will take place later"—the unfolding of the prophetic events—is in chapters 4 through 22. These chapters contain descriptions of the great tribulation, the second coming of Christ, and the millennium.

2. What qualities do you see in your church that are like the ones you read about?

Final Events

1. What great events are described in Revelation 19:1–21?
   (Marriage Supper of the Lamb; coming of Christ; doom of beast and false prophet.)

2. What will be the fate of the devil at the beginning of Christ's thousand-year reign (20:1–3)?
   (He will be chained for 1,000 years in the abyss, the bottomless pit.)

3. What will be the devil's final fate at the end of Christ's thousand-year reign (20:7–10)?
   (He will be thrown into the lake of fire and be tormented forever.)

4. What will be the fate of all unbelievers (20:11–15)?
   (They will be judged and thrown into the lake of fire.)

5. List three ways in which the Christian's ultimate destiny will differ from this present existence (21:1–7):

   1) *(They will live in a new Jerusalem.)*

   2) *(Christ will dwell among His people.)*

   3) *(There will be no mourning, crying, or pain.)*

Give these questions to your students to use as a guide for further study of Revelation:

❓What is the tribulation? What are some of the events that happen during this time?

❓What events accompany the second advent of Christ?

❓What is the condition of the world during the millennium?

❓What events happen after the millennium?

❓What is the "eternal state"?

LIFE APPLICATION

1. How can you prepare spiritually for Christ's coming and the events that will be taking place?

2. Below are a few of the commands to the churches. After each, write one way you can obey the command in a specific area of your life.

Ephesus: Keep first love fresh.

Smyrna: Be faithful during trials.

Pergamum: Repent.

Thyatira: Keep My deeds.

Sardis: Keep yourself pure.

Laodicea: Be zealous for God, not lukewarm.

Philadelphia: Keep God's Word.

Conclusion and Application

Jesus Christ will actually return to earth! All the material accomplishments of mankind will be destroyed. Christians will be judged on the basis of what they have done with Jesus Christ and what they have allowed Him to do with and through their lives.

For the faithful, Christ's return will be the highlight of their lives. Are you looking forward to His return? The closer we become to Him, the more excited we will get about our future with Jesus.

(Go over the chart in the student's book.)

Closing Prayer

Recap

Opening Prayer

Discussion Starter

❓What benefit do you think a non-Christian would gain from reading the New Testament?

❓How have the preceding lessons changed your life?

Lesson Development

(Any appropriate material from previous lessons that was not sufficiently covered could be used at this time, and you also may deal with any point that the group members may not understand as well as they could.)

(Then go over the remaining Recap questions and answers. This material will benefit both the students and you by giving you a deeper appreciation of God's Word.)

Leader's Objective: To lead students in a review of New Testament highlights, and to encourage students to make any commitments still necessary for them to prepare for Jesus' second coming

LESSON 10

The following questions will help you review this Step. If necessary, reread the appropriate lesson(s).

1. What is the focus in Matthew regarding the person of Christ?
   (Jesus as the King of kings.)

2. How does Mark differ from Matthew?
   (Mark shows Jesus as the Servant.)

3. How did Luke and John each present Christ?
   (Luke: Perfect Man; John: Jesus as God.)

4. What does it mean to bear fruit? (Compare John 15:1–8; Psalm 92:12–15; Galatians 5:22,23; Phillipians 1:11.)
   (To produce characteristics like love, joy, peace, and righteousness.)

5. What changes took place in Paul's life after he became a Christian?
   (He became outspoken for Christ; he loved others instead of hated them; he gladly suffered abuse for Christ.)

6. What are the three results of justification by faith (Romans 5:1,2)?
   1) *(Peace with God.)*
   2) *(Gained grace.)*
   3) *(Rejoice in hope.)*

7. How can the Christian be an effective witness for Christ in the midst of sufferings (1 Peter 3:8–17)?

(Spend time during this lesson going over any material that confuses your students about Revelation or in discussing questions about the New Testament that your students may have. Rather than trying to give answers, lead your students to begin studying the parts of the New Testament that can help answer their questions.)

Jesus' fulfillment of prophecy, the miracles He performed as proof of His deity, the examples of His life, and the fact of His death and resurrection all attest to His authority to forgive sin.

The gift of the Holy Spirit for power, the establishing of the church, the admonition to live godly in this present world, and to carry His message to those who have not yet heard it are evidences of God's continuing love for man. In light of the things foretold in the Book of Revelation, we realize how vitally important that message is.

(Bless instead of curse; love instead of seeking revenge; seek peace; do good.)

8. On a piece of paper, write the names of the books of the Old Testament, listing them by division.

9. On a piece of paper, identify the divisions of the New Testament, and list the New Testament books by division.

LIFE APPLICATION

1. Select the book of the New Testament that interests you most. Using the "How to Study the Bible" guide on the following pages, study this book over the next few weeks.

   (See pages 76 and 77 of the student's book.)

2. As you study, jot down the points you feel God is leading you to apply to your life.

❖ ❖ ❖

Conclusion and Application

When we invite Christ into our lives, we have just begun our journey with Him. As we walk in the Spirit, God has many exciting things in store for us—including the abundant life He has promised us and the ongoing process of being conformed to His image.

Closing Prayer

❖ ❖ ❖

How to Study the Bible

Dwight L. Moody

Someone has said that four things are necessary in studying the Bible: admit, submit, commit, and transmit. First, admit its truth; second, submit to its teachings; third, commit it to memory; and fourth, transmit it to others. If the Christian life is a good thing for you, share it with someone else.

Use a notebook as you study the Bible. Write out the answers to the following questions as you study a portion of the Bible:

1. What persons have I read about, and what have I learned about them?

2. What places have I read about, and what have I read about them?

   If the place is not mentioned, can I find out where it is?

   Do I know its position on the map?

3. Can I relate from memory what I have just been reading?

4. Are there any parallel passages or texts that throw light on this passage?

5. Have I read anything about God the Father?

   Or about Jesus Christ?

   Or about the Holy Ghost?

The Christian life is a "good thing" to share with someone else.

6. What have I read about myself?
   About man's sinful nature?
   About the spiritual new nature?
7. Is there any duty for me to observe?
   Any example to follow?
   Any promise to claim?
   Any exhortation to guide me?
   Any prayer that I may echo?
8. What is the key verse of the chapter or passage?
   Can I repeat it from memory?

How to Share Christ With Others

A well-known Christian leader, highly gifted as a theologian, shared with me his frustration over his lack of effectiveness and fruitfulness in witnessing for Christ.

I asked him, "What do you say when you seek to introduce a person to Christ?"

He explained his presentation, which was long and complicated. The large number of Bible verses he used would confuse most people and prevent them from making an intelligent decision.

I challenged him to use the *Four Spiritual Laws* presentation daily for the next thirty days and report his progress to me at the end of that time.

When I saw him two weeks later, he was overflowing with joy and excitement. "By simply reading the booklet to others," he said, "I have seen more people come to Christ during the last two weeks than I had previously seen in many months. It's hard to believe!"

The *Four Spiritual Laws* booklet, reproduced on the following pages, presents a clear and simple explanation of the gospel of our Lord Jesus Christ.

The *Four Spiritual Laws* presents a clear and simple explanation of the gospel.

This booklet, available in all major languages of the world, has been developed as a result of more than forty years of experience in counseling with thousands of college students on campuses in almost every country on every continent in the world, as well as with a comparable number of laymen, pastors, and high school students. It represents one way to share your faith effectively.

Benefits of *Four Laws*

Using a tool such as the *Four Spiritual Laws* offers many benefits. Let me list some of them:

◆ It enables you to open your conversation easily and naturally.

◆ It begins with a positive statement: "God loves you and has a wonderful plan for your life."

◆ It presents the gospel and the claims of Christ clearly and simply.

◆ It gives you confidence because you know what you are going to say and how you are going to say it.

◆ It enables you to be prepared at all times and to stick to the subject without getting off on tangents.

◆ It makes it possible for you to be brief and to the point.

◆ It enables you to lead others to a personal decision through a suggested prayer.

◆ It offers suggestions for growth, including the importance of involvement in the church.

◆ Of special importance, it is a "transferable tool" to give those whom you introduce to Christ so they can be encouraged and trained to lead others to Christ also. Paul exhorted Timothy, his young son in the faith:

> The things you have heard me say in the presence of many witnesses entrust to reliable men who will also be qualified to teach others (2 Timothy 2:2).

The *Four Spiritual Laws* enables those who receive Christ to go immediately to friends and loved ones and tell them of their new-found faith in Christ. It also enables them to show their friends and loved ones how they, too, can make a commitment to Christ.

Various Approaches

You can introduce the *Four Spiritual Laws* to a non-believer. After a cordial, friendly greeting, you can use one of the following approaches:

◆ "I'm reading a little booklet that really makes sense to a lot of people. I'd like to share it with you. Have you heard of the *Four Spiritual Laws?*"

◆ "Do you ever think about spiritual things?" (Pause for an answer.) "Have you ever heard of the *Four Spiritual Laws?*"

◆ "A friend of mine recently gave me this little booklet that really makes sense to me. I would like to share it with you. Have you ever heard of the *Four Spiritual Laws?*"

◆ "The content of this booklet has been used to change the lives of millions of people. It contains truths that I believe will be of great interest to you. Would you read it and give me your impression?"

◆ "It is believed that this little booklet is the most widely printed piece of literature in the world apart from the Bible.[1] Would you be interested in reading it?"

Here is a direct approach that you can use when you have only a few moments with an individual:

> "If you died today, do you know for sure that you will go to heaven?"

If the answer is yes, ask:

> "On what do you base that knowledge? This little booklet, the *Four Spiritual Laws*, will help you know for sure that you will go to heaven when you die."

If the answer is no, say:

> "You *can* be sure you are going to heaven. This little booklet, the *Four Spiritual Laws*, tells how to know."

God will show you other ways to introduce this material. The important thing is to keep your introduction brief and to the point.

---

[1] It is estimated that over one-and-a-half billion *Four Spiritual Laws* booklets have been printed and distributed in all major languages of the world.

How to Present the Four Spiritual Laws

1. Be sensitive to an individual's interest and the leading of the Holy Spirit. The simplest way to explain the *Four Spiritual Laws* is to read the booklet aloud to a non-believer. But be careful not to allow the presentation to become mechanical. Remember, you are not just sharing principles, you are introducing the person to Christ. The *Four Spiritual Laws* is simply a tool to help you effectively communicate the gospel. Pray for God's love to be expressed through you.

2. If there is any objection to the term "laws," use the term "Four Spiritual Principles" instead.[2]

3. When questions arise that would change the subject, explain that most questions are answered as you go through the *Four Spiritual Laws*. Or say, "That's a good question. Let's talk about it after we have completed reading the booklet."

4. Be sensitive to the individual. If he doesn't seem to respond, stop and ask, "Is this making sense?"

❖

Millions have received Christ through reading the *Four Spiritual Laws*.

---

[2] You may want to use an adaptation of the *Four Spiritual Laws* entitled *Would You Like to Know God Personally?* It is available through your local Christian bookstore, mail-order catalog distributor, or NewLife Publications.

5. Hold the booklet so the individual can see it clearly. Use a pen to point to key areas. This will help hold his attention.

6. In a group, give each person a *Four Spiritual Laws* booklet. Pray with those who are interested in receiving Christ. If only one is interested, be sensitive and in most cases talk with that person privately. Make sure each one understands that Christ comes into his life by faith. If he prays the prayer without believing Christ will answer, nothing will result.

   Also be sensitive about whether he wants to pray his own prayer or use the prayer from the booklet. Some will request silent prayer.

7. If someone has already heard of the *Four Spiritual Laws*, ask him what he thought of them, and if he has any questions. If he is interested and the gospel is not clear to him, go over the booklet again.

8. When a person does not receive Christ when you first share the *Four Spiritual Laws* with him, make another appointment if he is interested. Give him the booklet *A Great Adventure* to take with him. (The booklet is available at your Christian bookstore or can be ordered through NewLife Publications.)

9. Pray for the person. Occasionally ask him if he has thought further about your discussion or if he has any questions.

10. Leave the *Four Spiritual Laws* or *A Great Adventure* with the person you have witnessed to whether or not he received Christ. Millions have received Christ through reading these booklets.

Have You Heard
of the
Four Spiritual Laws?

Just as there are physical laws that govern the physical universe, so are there spiritual laws that govern your relationship with God.

LAW ONE

GOD **LOVES** YOU AND HAS A WONDERFUL **PLAN** FOR YOUR LIFE.

God's Love

God so loved the world that He gave His only begotten Son, that whoever believes in Him should not perish, but have eternal life (John 3:16).

God's Plan

[Christ speaking] "I came that they might have life, and might have it abundantly" [that it might be full and meaningful] (John 10:10).

Why is it that most people are not experiencing the abundant life?

Because...

LAW TWO

MAN IS **SINFUL** AND **SEPARATED** FROM GOD. THUS HE CANNOT KNOW AND EXPERIENCE GOD'S LOVE AND PLAN FOR HIS LIFE.

Man Is Sinful

All have sinned and fall short of the glory of God (Romans 3:23).

Man was created to have fellowship with God; but, because of his own stubborn self-will, he chose to go his own independent way and fellowship with God was broken. This self-will, characterized by an attitude of active rebellion or passive indifference, is an evidence of what the Bible calls sin.

Man Is Separated

The wages of sin is death [spiritual separation from God] (Romans 6:23).

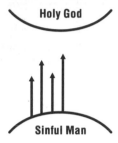

This diagram illustrates that God is holy and man is sinful. A great chasm separates the two. The arrows illustrate that man is continually trying to reach God and the abundant life through his own efforts: good life, ethics, philosophy, and more.

The Third Law gives us the only answer to this dilemma...

LAW THREE

JESUS CHRIST IS GOD'S **ONLY** PROVISION FOR MAN'S SIN. THROUGH HIM YOU CAN KNOW AND EXPERIENCE GOD'S LOVE AND PLAN FOR YOUR LIFE.

He Died In Our Place

God demonstrates His own love toward us, in that while we were yet sinners, Christ died for us (Romans 5:8).

He Rose from the Dead

Christ died for our sins... He was buried... He was raised on the third day, according to the Scriptures... He appeared to Peter, then to the twelve. After that He appeared to more than five hundred... (1 Corinthians 15:3–6).

He Is the Only Way to God

> Jesus said to him, "I am the way, and the truth, and the life; no one comes to the Father but through Me" (John 14:6).

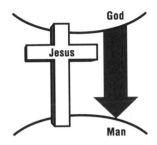

This diagram illustrates that God has bridged the chasm that separates us from Him by sending His Son, Jesus Christ, to die on the cross in our place to pay the penalty for our sins.

It is not enough to know these three laws...

LAW FOUR

WE MUST INDIVIDUALLY **RECEIVE** JESUS CHRIST AS SAVIOR AND LORD; THEN WE CAN KNOW AND EXPERIENCE GOD'S LOVE AND PLAN FOR OUR LIVES.

We Must Receive Christ

> As many as received Him, to them He gave the right to become children of God, even to those who believe in His name (John 1:12).

We Receive Christ Through Faith

> By grace you have been saved through faith; and that not of yourselves, it is the gift of God; not as a result of works that no one should boast (Ephesians 2:8,9).

When We Receive Christ, We Experience a New Birth

(Read John 3:1–8.)

We Receive Christ Through Personal Invitation

> [Christ speaking] "Behold, I stand at the door and knock; if any one hears My voice and opens the door, I will come in to him" (Revelation 3:20).

Receiving Christ involves turning to God from self (repentance) and trusting Christ to come into our lives to forgive our sins and to make us what He wants us to be. Just to agree intellectually that Jesus Christ is the Son of God and that He died on the cross for our sins is not enough. Nor is it enough to have an emotional experience. We receive Jesus Christ by faith, as an act of the will.

These two circles represent two kinds of lives:

Self-Directed Life
S – Self is on the throne
† – Christ is outside the life
● – Interests are directed by self, often resulting in discord and frustration

Christ-Directed Life
† – Christ is in the life and on the throne
S – Self is yielding to Christ
● – Interests are directed by Christ, resulting in harmony with God's plan

Which circle best represents your life?

Which circle would you like to have represent your life?

The following explains how you can receive Christ:

You Can Receive Christ Right Now by Faith Through Prayer

(Prayer is talking with God)

God knows your heart and is not so concerned with your words as He is with the attitude of your heart. The following is a suggested prayer:

> *Lord Jesus, I need You. Thank You for dying on the cross for my sins. I open the door of my life and receive You as my Savior and Lord. Thank You for forgiving my sins and giving me eternal life. Take control of the throne of my life. Make me the kind of person You want me to be.*

Does this prayer express the desire of your heart?

If it does, pray this prayer right now, and Christ will come into your life, as He promised.

How to Know That Christ Is in Your Life

Did you receive Christ into your life? According to His promise in Revelation 3:20, where is Christ right now in relation to you?

Christ said that He would come into your life. Would He mislead you? On what authority do you know that God has answered your prayer? (The trustworthiness of God Himself and His Word.)

The Bible Promises Eternal Life to All Who Receive Christ

The witness is this, that God has given us eternal life, and this life is in His Son. He who has the Son has the life; he who does not have the Son of God does not have the life. These things I have written to you who believe in the name of the Son of God, in order that you may know that you have eternal life (1 John 5:11–13).

Thank God often that Christ is in your life and that He will never leave you (Hebrews 13:5). You can know on the basis of His promise that the living Christ indwells you and that you have eternal life from the very moment you invite Him in. He will not deceive you.

An important reminder...

Do Not Depend on Feelings

The promise of God's Word, the Bible—not our feelings—is our authority. The Christian lives by faith (trust) in the trustworthiness of God Himself and His Word. This train diagram illustrates the relationship between **fact** (God and His Word), **faith** (our trust in God and His Word), and **feeling** (the result of our faith and obedience). (Read John 14:21.)

The train will run with or without the caboose. However, it would be useless to attempt to pull the train by the caboose. In the same way, as Christians we do not depend on feelings or emotions, but we place our faith (trust) in the trustworthiness of God and the promises of His Word.

Now That You Have Received Christ

The moment you received Christ by faith, as an act of the will, many things happened, including the following:

◆ Christ came into your life (Revelation 3:20; Colossians 1:27).

◆ Your sins were forgiven (Colossians 1:14).

◆ You became a child of God (John 1:12).

◆ You received eternal life (John 5:24).

◆ You began the great adventure for which God created you (John 10:10; 2 Corinthians 5:17; 1 Thessalonians 5:18).

Can you think of anything more wonderful that could happen to you than receiving Christ? Would you like to thank God in prayer right now for what He has done for you? By thanking God, you demonstrate your faith.

To enjoy your new life to the fullest...

Suggestions for Christian Growth

Spiritual growth results from trusting Jesus Christ. "The righteous man shall live by faith" (Galatians 3:11). A life of faith will enable you to trust God increasingly with every detail of your life, and to practice the following:

G Go to God in prayer daily (John 15:7).

R Read God's Word daily (Acts 17:11); begin with the Gospel of John.

O Obey God moment by moment (John 14:21).

W Witness for Christ by your life and words (Matthew 4:19; John 15:8).

T Trust God for every detail of your life (1 Peter 5:7).

H Holy Spirit—allow Him to control and empower your daily life and witness (Galatians 5:16,17; Acts 1:8).

Fellowship in a Good Church

God's Word admonishes us not to forsake "the assembling of ourselves together" (Hebrews 10:25). Several logs burn brightly together, but put one aside on the cold hearth and the fire goes out. So it is with your relationship with other Christians.

If you do not belong to a church, do not wait to be invited. Take the initiative; call the pastor of a nearby church where Christ is honored and His Word is preached. Start this week, and make plans to attend regularly.

Resources to Help You Witness

A Man Without Equal. A fresh look at the unique birth, teachings, death, and resurrection of Jesus and how He continues to change the way we live and think. Good as an evangelistic tool.

Life Without Equal. A presentation of the length and breadth of the Christian's freedom in Jesus Christ and how believer's can release Christ's resurrection power for life and ministry.

Witnessing Without Fear. A step-by-step guide to sharing your faith with confidence. Ideal for both individual and group study; a Gold Medallion winner.

Four Spiritual Laws. One of the most effective evangelistic tools ever developed. An easy-to-use way of sharing your faith with others.

Would You Like to Know God Personally? An adaptation of the *Four Spiritual Laws* presented as four principles for establishing a personal relationship with God through faith in Jesus Christ.

Spirit-Filled Life booklet. Discover the reality of the Spirit-filled life and how to live in moment-by-moment dependence on Him.

Transferable Concepts. Exciting tools to help you experience and share the abundant Christian life:

How You Can Be a Fruitful Witness

How You Can Introduce Others to Christ

How You Can Help Fulfill the Great Commission

Ten Basic Steps. A comprehensive curriculum for the Christian who wants to master the basics of Christian growth. Used by hundreds of thousands worldwide. (See page 550 for details.)

The Ten Basic Steps Leader's Guide. Contains Bible study outlines for teaching the complete series.

Reaching Your World Through Witnessing Without Fear.
This powerful six-session video series can equip your church or small group to successfully share the gospel in a natural way through everyday relationships.

Practical, proven witnessing techniques are illustrated through exciting drama and in-depth training by Bill Bright.

Handy Facilitator's Guide enables lay-people to effectively lead training sessions.

Available through your local Christian bookstore, mail-order catalog distributor, or NewLife Publications.

About the Author

BILL BRIGHT is founder and president of Campus Crusade for Christ International. Serving in 152 major countries representing 98 percent of the world's population, he and his dedicated associates of nearly 50,000 full-time staff, associate staff, and trained volunteers have introduced tens of millions of people to Jesus Christ, discipling millions to live Spirit-filled, fruitful lives of purpose and power for the glory of God.

Dr. Bright did graduate study at Princeton and Fuller Theological seminaries from 1946 to 1951. The recipient of many national and international awards, including five honorary doctorates, he is the author of numerous books and publications committed to helping fulfill the Great Commission. His special focus is *NewLife2000*, an international effort to help reach more than six billion people with the gospel of our Lord Jesus Christ and help fulfill the Great Commission by the year 2000.

Ten Basic Steps Toward Christian Maturity

*Eleven easy-to-use individual guides to help you understand
the basics of the Christian faith*

INTRODUCTION: The Uniqueness of Jesus

Explains who Jesus Christ is. Reveals the secret of His power to turn you into a victorious, fruitful Christian.

STEP 1: The Christian Adventure

Shows you how to enjoy a full, abundant, purposeful, and fruitful life in Christ.

STEP 2: The Christian and the Abundant Life

Explores the Christian way of life—what it is and how it works practically.

STEP 3: The Christian and the Holy Spirit

Teaches who the Holy Spirit is, how to be filled with the Spirit, and how to make the Spirit-filled life a moment-by-moment reality in your life.

STEP 4: The Christian and Prayer

Reveals the true purpose of prayer and shows how the Father, Son, and Holy Spirit work together to answer your prayers.

STEP 5: The Christian and the Bible

Talks about the Bible—how we got it, its authority, and its power to help the believer. Offers methods for studying the Bible more effectively.

STEP 6: The Christian and Obedience

Learn why it is so important to obey God and how to live daily in His grace. Discover the secret to personal purity and power as a Christian and why you need not fear what others think of you.

STEP 7: The Christian and Witnessing

Shows you how to witness effectively. Includes reproduction of the *Four Spiritual Laws* and explains how to share them.

STEP 8: The Christian and Giving

Discover God's plan for your financial life, how to stop worrying about money, and how to trust God for your finances.

STEP 9: Exploring the Old Testament

Features a brief survey of the Old Testament. Shows what God did to prepare the way for Jesus Christ and the redemption of all who receive Him as Savior and Lord.

STEP 10: Exploring the New Testament

Surveys each of the New Testament books. Shows the essence of the gospel and highlights the exciting beginning of the Christian church.

Leader's Guide

The ultimate resource for even the most inexperienced, timid, and fearful person asked to lead a group study in the basics of the Christian life. Contains questions and answers from the *Ten Basic Steps* Study Guides.

A Handbook for Christian Maturity

Combines the eleven-booklet series into one practical, easy-to-follow volume. Excellent for personal or group study.

*Available through your local Christian bookstore,
mail-order catalog distributor, or NewLife Publications.*

Notes

Notes